Assisting Development in a Changing World

The Harvard Institute for International Development, 1980–1995

Harvard Studies in International Development

Other volumes in the series include:

Reforming Economic Systems in Developing Countries
edited by Dwight H. Perkins and Michael Roemer, 1991

The Challenge of Reform in Indochina
edited by Börje Ljunggren, 1993

Macroeconomic Policy and Adjustment in Korea, 1970–1990
by Stephan Haggard, Richard N. Cooper, Susan Collins, Choongsoo Kim, and Sung–Tae Ro, 1994

Framing Questions, Constructing Answers: Linking Research with Education Policy for Developing Countries
by Noel F. McGinn and Allison M. Borden, 1995

Industrialization and the State: The Korean Heavy and Chemical Industry Drive
by Joseph J. Stern, Ji–hong Kim, Dwight H. Perkins, and Jung–ho Yoo, 1995

Moving to Market: Restructuring Transport in the Former Soviet Union
by John S. Strong and John R. Meyer, with Clell G. Harral and Graham Smith, 1996

Economic Recovery in The Gambia: Insights for Adjustment in Sub-Saharan Africa
edited by Malcolm F. McPherson and Steven C. Radelet, 1996

The Strains of Economic Growth: Labor Unrest and Social Dissatisfaction in Korea
by David Lindauer, Jong-Gie Kim, Joung-Woo Lee, Hy-Sop Lim, Jae-Young Son, and Ezra F. Vogel 1997

Between a Swamp and a Hard Place: Developmental Challenges in Remote Rural Africa
by David C. Cole and Richard Huntington, with Francis Mading Deng, 1997

Getting Good Government: Capacity Building in the Public Sectors of Developing Countries
edited by Merilee S. Grindle, 1997

Environment and Development in a Resource-Rich Economy: Malaysia under the New Economic Policy
Jeffrey R. Vincent, Rozali Mohamed Ali, and Associates, 1997

Volumes published jointly with the International Center for Economic Growth:

Markets in Developing Countries: Parallel, Fragmented, and Black
edited by Michael Roemer and Christine Jones, 1991

Progress with Profits: The Development of Rural Banking in Indonesia
by Richard Patten and Jay K. Rosengard, 1991

Green Markets: The Economics of Sustainable Development
by Theodore Panayotou, 1993

Building Private Pension Systems: a Handbook
by Yves Guérard and Glenn Jenkins, 1993

Asia and Africa: Legacies and Opportunities in Development
edited by David L. Lindauer and Michael Roemer, 1994

Green Taxes and Incentive Policies: An International Perspective
by Glenn Jenkins and Ranjit Lamech, 1994

Industrialization and the Small Firm: Patterns and Policies
by Donald R. Snodgrass and Tyler Biggs, 1996

Harvard Studies in International Development

Assisting Development in a Changing World

The Harvard Institute for International Development, 1980–1995

Edited by Dwight H. Perkins,
Richard Pagett, Michael Roemer,
Donald R. Snodgrass, and Joseph J. Stern

Harvard Institute for International Development

Distributed by Harvard University Press

Published by Harvard Institute for International Development, 1997

Distributed by Harvard University Press

Editorial Management: Don Lippincott
Editorial Assistance: Jolanta Davis
Design and production: Desktop Publishing & Design Co., Boston, MA

Front cover photo credit: Betty Press/Panos Pictures
Back cover photo credits, left to right: Fernando Reimers, Richard Goldman, Gretchen O'Connor, and Louis Wells

Library of Congress Cataloging-in-Publication Data

Assisting development in a changing world : the Harvard Institute for International Development, 1980-1995 / edited by Dwight H. Perkins, Richard Pagett et al.
p. cm.
Essays designed to give an overview of HIID projects and their accomplishments from 1980 to 1995.
Includes biliographical references (p. 465) and index.
ISBN 0-674-04996-9 (cloth). -- ISBN 0-674-04997-7 (paper)
1. Harvard Institute for International Development--History. 2. Economic assistance--Developing countries--History. 3. Economic development projects--Developing countries--History. I. Perkins, Dwight Heald. II. Harvard Institute for International Development.
HC60.A838 1997 97-21936
338.9'009172'4--DC21 CIP

This history of HIID
is dedicated to our late friend and colleague

MICHAEL ROEMER

The accomplishments described here could not have
occurred without his guidance and wisdom

Table of Contents

About the Editors

Dwight H. Perkins served as director of the Harvard Institute for International Development from 1980 to 1995, and has been a faculty fellow of HIID since 1974. He is the H.H. Burbank Professor of Political Economy at Harvard University, and former chairman of the economics department. He received his A.M. and Ph.D. at Harvard University after receiving his B.A. from Cornell University. He is a leading scholar on the Chinese and Korean economies, and has field experience in China, Korea, Malaysia, Vietnam, and Japan.

Richard Pagett was executive director of the Harvard Institute for International Development from 1989 to 1994. He is currently director of research administration for Harvard University. He received his A.M. from Harvard University after receiving his B.S. from Brigham Young University. He has lived and worked in Ghana, Kenya, India, Nigeria, Sierra Leone, and Indonesia.

Michael Roemer was an institute fellow of the Harvard Institute for International Development and twice served as HIID's executive director. He was also a senior lecturer in the economics department at Harvard University. He served as resident advisor to the governments of Ghana, Kenya, Tanzania, and Indonesia, and did fieldwork in Peru, Venezuela, Korea, Taiwan, Malaysia, and the Gambia. He earned his B.S. and M.S. from Stanford University and his Ph.D. from Massachusetts Institute of Technology. His unexpected death in December of 1996 was a great loss to HIID.

Donald R. Snodgrass is an institute fellow of the Harvard Institute for International Development, coordinator of the education group, and research coordinator. During the transition between HIID directors, he served as coordinator of the transition committee. He has taught in the economics department and the Graduate School of Education at Harvard University. His B.A. is from Miami University in Ohio, and his M.A. and Ph.D. are from Yale University. He has lived and worked in Sri Lanka, Malaysia, and Indonesia, and has consulted in Korea, Namibia, the Philippines, Thailand, and other countries.

Joseph J. Stern is an institute fellow and former executive director of the Harvard Institute for International Development and is a lecturer in economics at Harvard University. He has been resident advisor in Pakistan, Ghana, Malaysia, and Indonesia, and has served as a consultant in numerous countries including Sri Lanka, Thailand, Bangladesh, and Tajikistan. He received his M.A. and Ph.D. from Harvard University and his B.A. from Queens College, New York.

About the chapter authors. A large number of HIID development professionals prepared brief essays describing the individual projects in which they participated. These essays laid the groundwork for the chapters in this volume. The authors of these history chapters are all long-term HIID personnel, who themselves participated in one or more of the projects described.

Preface

The Harvard Institute for International Development has been working with developing countries for forty years. A history of the early years of HIID and the Harvard Development Advisory Service was written by Edward Mason, covering the experience of the institute up to 1980. This volume carries the story forward from 1980 through 1995.

HIID's involvement with developing countries is constantly evolving, just as the problems that these countries face are themselves evolving. The work of the institute in the 1980s and 1990s consequently has some similarities with what went before, but also has many differences. In a similar fashion, the institute in the late 1990s and beyond will change in many ways, some of which can be anticipated and others which cannot.

Every decade or so, an institution such as HIID needs to pause and look back on where it has been. In part, this is a learning experience for the institute itself, but it can also be of use to others who have struggled with the complex problems of working with countries around the world to reform their economic and social systems and to rise out of poverty.

This history is by no means a definitive appraisal of the experience of HIID. Rather, it is a guide to the kinds of issues that have occupied the institute over the past decade and a half, and the problems that have been encountered along the way. I hope that it will inspire those interested in these issues to delve further into the HIID experience by using the institute's archives or by working directly with the many HIID staff who have been involved.

The editors of this volume were the director and senior managers of HIID during the period covered. They and I wish to thank all of the many individuals who prepared the background papers for this volume as well as those who wrote the summary chapters. We particularly want to thank Gretchen O'Connor, who managed the production of this volume from its inception through the editorial process; Jeanne Anderer, our very able editor, who brought order out of the diverse styles and experience of our many authors; Don Lippincott and Jolanta Davis of HIID's publications office, who managed the book production and design processes; Ruth Rautenberg, who indexed the book; and Katherine Yost, Deborah McCarthy, and Carolyn Sabin, who helped with proofreading and related tasks.

Jeffrey D. Sachs
Director, HIID

Introduction

Dwight H. Perkins, Richard Pagett, Michael Roemer,
Donald R. Snodgrass, and Joseph J. Stern

The Harvard Institute for International Development (HIID) is a unique institution in both the North American and the broader international context. It is, in part, a research institute like thousands of others scattered across university landscapes; it is also a service-oriented organization that works directly with developing countries aiming to reform their economic and social systems. University-research institutes elsewhere in the world occasionally provide advisory services, and consulting firms occasionally do research. At HIID, the two functions are inextricably linked: research has been based largely on the advisory experience, and advice has been based largely on the research.

It is this combination of closely-linked research and advisory work that gives HIID its special strength, but it can also be a source of weakness. Research that is informed through direct work with policy makers in Asia, Africa, and Latin America produces publications that speak to issues of real concern to these policy makers. Advice that is based on this research is likely to be more useful to the policy world than pure academic research motivated by other kinds of concerns. But research based on concrete policy issues can have limitations. Some policy issues in particular countries cannot be written about because of possible political repercussions. More important, sometimes a researcher needs to step back from current policy concerns and pose questions that policy makers have not thought to ask. HIID, by being part of Harvard University, has been able largely to avoid the blinders created by being tied up completely with day-to-day concerns.

The Evolution of HIID

HIID's unique role has evolved historically. Broadly, the institute has gone through several phases, and will undoubtedly go through others. The first phase began in the early 1960s with the establishment of the Harvard advisory groups to the planning commissions of Pakistan and Iran. The Pakistan effort was the basis for the founding, in 1962, of the Harvard Development Advisory Service (DAS). With funding largely from the Ford Foundation, DAS worked with governments primarily to introduce good economic analysis into economic policy decisions. The institutional vehicle for accomplishing that goal was the buildup of a strong economic analytical capacity within an economic planning unit that usually reported directly to a prime minister or a president. Efforts of this sort were mounted in many countries, including Colombia, Ethiopia, Malaysia, and Indonesia. With the formation of DAS, Harvard had created an institution that was designed explicitly to provide economic advisory services on a sustained basis. This initiative required changes in the university's rules, including the establishment of a separate career track for senior economists who were prepared to devote their professional lives to this special combination of research and advisory work with long periods of residence overseas.

This work with economic planning commissions continued as the main focus of DAS until the early 1970s. At that time, changes were occurring that would have an immediate impact on DAS. The then President of Harvard, observing the benefits of these international activities for the university's economists, wanted to make similar opportunities available to others in the university who also had something to offer the developing world. Thus, in 1974, the institute's name was changed to the Harvard Institute for International Development and its mandate was expanded. The institute was taken out of the Faculty of Arts and Sciences and put directly under the President and a committee of deans, made up initially of the Deans of Arts and Sciences, Public Health, Education, and Design. In the early 1980s the committee was expanded to include the Deans of the John F. Kennedy School of Government, the Harvard Business School, and the Harvard Law School. The HIID staff was enlarged to include professionals in health, education, public management, and other arts and sciences disciplines, including political science, biology, sociology, and anthropology.

The creation of HIID coincided with the Ford Foundation's decision to phase out support for economic advisory services and the buildup of planning commissions in developing countries. HIID, which depended mainly on external funding, thus faced the formidable challenge of finding new sources of support and, simultaneously, of expanding the kinds of services offered. In retrospect, the late 1970s was a period of transition from the old role of DAS to what was to become the new mandate of HIID. In addition to hiring people from various disciplines, the institute began experimenting with new kinds of projects, most of which were essentially multidisciplinary. The major new projects were in rural development and health, mainly in Africa. However, a few economic policy projects continued in some countries, such as Malaysia and Indonesia, usually on a more modest scale than in the past.

HIID learned much from these new projects, both positively and negatively. The Mali maternal and child health project, for example, provided considerable knowledge of health issues in the African context, including the difficulties associated with reaching rural women and children at a cost that a country such as Mali could afford. The rural development projects in Kenya, for all of their early teething problems, were the start of a relationship with that country that has continued to this day. The one integrated rural development project, undertaken in a remote area of Southern Sudan, revealed, among other things, that a Cambridge-based institute was not properly structured or located to manage a project with complex logistic requirements associated with such a remote area.

The history of DAS and HIID up through 1980 is covered in a book by Edward S. Mason, the founder of DAS.[1] The Pakistan project of the 1960s is dealt with at length in a book by George Rosen,[2] and HIID staff have produced books on several other projects, including those in Mali, Sudan, and Argentina. Scholars and advisors associated with HIID projects have written hundreds, probably thousands, of articles about the work. Many of the development economists in North America and Europe worked on a DAS or an HIID project, at one time or another, and many of the economists from Asia, Africa, and Latin America who were part of these efforts for planning commission development went on to become major figures both in their own countries and in international institutions such as the World Bank.

HIID from 1980 to 1995

Fittingly, this volume of essays takes up the story of HIID from 1980 through 1995. For HIID, this was a period of expansion of staff, funding, and areas of policy advisory and research work. More important, HIID defined and developed a group of research/advisory areas and skills, which were needed by the developing world and could be provided effectively by a university-based organization. This group of areas and skills built, in part, on the experience of previous years, at least where such experience was available. A criterion for selecting projects, among several, was whether Harvard had worked enough in the area to provide effective quality control.

The focus of HIID programs in the 1980s and early 1990s can be broadly categorized. One cluster of projects involved working across a wide range of issues with countries making the transition from a highly interventionist system to a more market-oriented system. In countries such as Indonesia, Kenya, and The Gambia, HIID worked on issues ranging from macrostabilization to tax and financial reform, from public budgeting to food policy. The common theme of these efforts was to help these countries change their policies, rewrite their laws and regulations, and train their personnel to achieve policy goals through the effective use of market forces, rather than, as in the past, through the suppression of these forces. In the 1980s, most of these broad-based efforts were directed at mixed economies where market forces already existed, at least in some sectors. In the early 1990s, HIID began working on such issues in the former command economies of Vietnam and Russia, where market forces had barely existed prior to the beginning of reform.

Not all of HIID's efforts to aid in the transition to a market economy were broad based and long term. In many countries, the institute was asked to help in a particular area of the transition process. For example, in many countries HIID was involved in tax reform; in other cases, the focus was on helping to open up the international trading regime, while in another project, the institute helped a government to reform its price setting policies.

The second broad category of HIID's program, closely related to the first, was the work on the environment. Involvement with environmental issues began slowly in the mid-1980s, and then rose to play a leading role in the institute in the early 1990s. HIID recognized that environmental issues could be approached in several ways. As a policy-oriented institute, HIID was interested in policy changes that could better protect the environment. As an organization helping countries to make the transition to market-oriented economic systems, HIID regarded market-based incentives as powerful tools for achieving environmental goals. Laws and regulations were considered necessary as well, but wherever possible these laws and regulations should rely on market incentives to encourage compliance, rather than on police powers and the courts. For developing countries, and particularly for countries making the transition from a command system, reliance on police powers and administrative intervention alone is not likely to advance environmental goals.

Work on social sector reform, mainly in health and education, comprised the third broad category of HIID's programs. The goal of most social sector reform in developing countries has been to reach all of the population with at least some basic level of health and education services. This emphasis on reaching the whole population, including the poorest members, has led most developing countries to rely on government to provide these services. Often, the responsible government ministries have little capacity to carry out their mandate. Much of HIID's work in health and education, therefore, was devoted to helping these ministries, at first, to develop information systems that would enable their officials to know what was actually happening in their countries. As reliable information became available to these officials, HIID worked with the ministries to make the changes necessary for expanding and improving the services. Basic Research in Developing Educational Systems (BRIDGES)—the largest and longest-running HIID project in education—involved extensive research and dissemination to ensure that the recommended education policy changes would be informed by worldwide state-of-the-art knowledge.

HIID's work on health issues went beyond assistance to national health ministries for developing information systems. The institute also worked directly with local officials on the design and implementation of maternal and child health services in rural areas, and on the effective delivering of more health services at lower costs to AIDS patients. Applied Diarrheal Disease Research (ADDR)—the largest and longest-running HIID project in health—involved working with health researchers in developing countries to strengthen their capacity for research on diarrheal and other childhood diseases. HIID believes that applied research, rooted in the real problems of countries, can lead to practical solutions to those problems, and that first-rate local researchers are in a better position to persuade local policy makers than are distant, foreign experts.

While the above broad categories cover most of the larger projects, HIID addressed several related themes that can be found within these projects and in separate research and advisory work designed explicitly to look at these themes. For example, all of the projects were concerned with reducing poverty, but some of the work was targeted to helping the poorest and most vulnerable members of society. The institute's ongoing research on the problems of rural women and widows would fall into this grouping. In developing countries, the nutrition level of the poorest members of society is an important concern in the setting of food prices. The institute shares the view of many others that decisions made close to those most affected by them, rather than in some distant capital, are most likely to meet the needs of particular localities. Decentralization of decision-making, therefore, was an underlying theme of some of HIID's efforts over this fifteen-year period.

Much of HIID's work has involved working directly with government ministries. Training and institution building, not just good policy work, are goals that HIID shared with many of those funding its work. For several projects, however, the training was the main purpose—and not just a component—of the policy reform assistance. All of the major training efforts were aimed at building local capacity to better manage the kinds of policy reform efforts in which HIID was involved. The training program on economics and management for officials of Indonesia's finance and planning ministries, which was held mainly at the graduate level in the United States, represents HIID's largest and longest-running effort of this kind. In Singapore and Bolivia, HIID also worked with local universities to develop graduate programs in public policy, which became an integral and permanent part of those universities. In Cambridge, HIID's summer workshops have expanded in number and size to where, by the mid-1990s, there are six workshops annually, with a combined enrollment of more than 300 participants from developing countries. The workshops offer rigorous training in subjects ranging from project appraisal and public budgeting, to macropolicy, education planning, environmental economics, and public enterprise reform and privatization. Moreover, HIID professional staff teach over eighty regular-term courses offered annually to students within the various faculties of Harvard.

The Intent of the Essays

The essays that follow are designed to give the reader an overview of HIID projects and their accomplishments from 1980 to 1995. The volume is in no sense definitive of the reforms efforts in which HIID was involved or even of its role within those efforts. For one thing, the range of issues and the number of countries involved are simply too large to be captured in a single volume. More important, these essays were written by many of the participants in the process. Each author was urged to discuss problems and failures, as well as successes, but it is unlikely that any of the essay writers can be a completely objective observer. Most of the writers have devoted a substantial part of their lives to promoting the success of these projects. Thus, a truly objective view of the work will have to wait until outside researchers have looked at these efforts in whole or in part, and from other points of view. For similar reasons, the names of advisors and consultants to the projects are excluded from the essay narrative. Others, less directly involved in the process will have to sort out those responsible for specific actions and advice.

This volume is mainly a historical overview of what HIID has attempted over these fifteen years, from 1980 to 1995. It is designed partly to give HIID personnel a clearer idea of how the many different pieces fit together. With a full-time staff now of roughly two hundred and several hundred additional part-time consultants associated annually with HIID, few people have been completely informed about what others were doing over this period. This has been the case, despite—or perhaps because of—the many seminars and meetings held about the institute's work. The volume is also a rich source of information for those at Harvard interested in learning more about HIID's work, as well as other interested parties in the development community outside of Harvard. Finally, these essays are a valuable guide to the contents of the Harvard archives for those wishing to delve further into one or more of the projects in which HIID was involved.

Notes

1 Mason (1986).

2 Rosen (1985).

Part I

Overview

Technical assistance and research with developing countries in the university context

1 Technical Assistance in the University Context

Dwight H. Perkins

Universities, particularly research universities, are staffed with many individuals who provide policy advice, but few universities have tried to organize themselves to meet the demand for such services or to turn the experience into something of value for the university. Individual professors may commute on weekends, say, from Cambridge to Washington D.C. after teaching during the week. All may gain policy experience, and a few may gain fame, but the university community is highly ambivalent about the process. Are these academics exploiting their university position for personal gain, or do they bring back valuable experience unattainable by other means? However one answers these questions, few perceive a need to consciously organize these weekly commutes or the occasional one- or two-year absences when academics take the opportunity to play operational policy roles. Government officials in Washington D.C. are a product of the university system; in many cases, they maintain close ties with the system, and the exchange between government and the university is continuous. Generally, universities limit their involvement to the establishment of fellowships for government officials on leave and, increasingly, to the provision of short-term executive courses.

The relationship between university-based policy advising and the developing world has features in common with the Cambridge–Washington D.C. connection, and some differences. Universities, particularly internationally-oriented universities such as Harvard, have large numbers of students from developing countries and even larger numbers of U.S. students whose lives ultimately will be intimately involved with the developing world. But for these studies there is no weekend commute to Dakar or to Kuala Lumpur. The distances are too great, for one thing. More to the point, U.S. university professors usually are not citizens of Senegal or of Malaysia, nor, with the occasional exception, do they have a natural or a built-in basis for continuous relations with these countries. However much officials in a developing country may feel the need for outside technical assistance—usually they are ambivalent about it—seldom do they have either the contacts or the funds to directly manage the use of U.S. academic consultants. Typically, international and bilateral aid agencies fill this gap, often contracting out such technical assistance to consulting firms or individuals.

Policy advising in developing countries by foreign experts is further complicated, because neither the developing countries nor the aid agencies want such technical assistance to become a permanent activity. Technical assistance, therefore, is usually combined with institution building. The job of the advisor is not just to give good policy advice, but also to help build local capacity that ultimately will eliminate the need for policy advice from foreigners. The buildup of a planning department in a developing country ministry is more difficult than advising a minister on exchange rate policy. Institution building cannot be the activity of a lone consultant; the consultant must be backed up by an organization capable of providing diverse training opportunities and of providing them over a long period, often many years.

For many reasons, universities are poorly structured to meet the needs of developing countries for policy advising and institution building. When U.S. academics become involved in these efforts, usually it is as consultants to private firms, to the World Bank or to the United States Agency for International Development (USAID). Universities only occasionally become directly immersed in institution building in developing countries, and typically do not reward faculty members for their involvement. Whether this attitude serves the university well is an issue that is explored later in this chapter. First, it is important to understand what is involved in policy advising and institution building in developing countries. Only then can one decide whether a university is well suited to the task, should it choose to organize itself appropriately. The analysis here draws mainly on HIID's experience—experience described at length in the individual project histories that follow this introductory essay.

Policy Advising in Developing Countries

Policy advising, and the supporting research, differ fundamentally from the kind of research that is most appreciated and rewarded in an academic setting. Academic research, as exemplified by most faculties of arts and sciences, is oriented to the requirements of an academic discipline. Highest praise goes to those who contribute to the basic theory underlying the discipline, and even applied research remains largely within disciplinary boundaries. What passes for policy-oriented research in this context often involves little more than a paragraph or two at the end of a discipline-based essay. Normally that paragraph will say something to the effect that the policy maker should take the results of this research into account when making policy and that failure to do so will lead to results very different from those intended. The negative consequences of existing policies may be analyzed at length, but it is far less common to spell out what should be performed. The latter depends on too many conditions over which the academic researcher has little control.

Policy advising, and the supporting research, start from a radically different point than academic research. The departure point is the policy maker, and his or her needs and interests. The advisor must begin by trying to understand those needs and interests. The need can be general, "where do we find enough revenue to close a large budget deficit?," or highly specific, "should we finance the deficit with bonds denominated in yen or in dollars?" The policy maker, not the advisor, sets the agenda. If the policy maker has a vague or a poorly articulated agenda, the advisor can help articulate the agenda. Still, it is the policy maker's agenda.

What if there is no policy maker with an agenda with whom the advisor can work? There are numerous examples of this in the developing world, partly because aid agencies frequently design programs that no one in the country involved wants. A decade ago HIID considered bidding on a project in Egypt to create an economic policy unit in the government, a task for which HIID was ideally suited. During a short visit to the country, an HIID team discovered that no one in the Egyptian government was interested in what, it was learned, was a USAID-designed proposal. HIID, therefore, chose not to bid on that proposal. On another occasion, HIID was involved in a project in Kenya designed to promote the decentralization of development decision-making to the district level. However, the then president of Kenya, Kenyatta, had little interest in any kind of decentralization away from Nairobi. In this case, the project was rescued from irrelevance when Kenyatta's successor, President Moi, with a different political base from Kenyatta, made "district focus" a centerpiece of his government. One cannot count on such luck. Government warehouses are full of reports that go largely unread and unused, because policy makers commissioned them only formalistically.

Policy makers typically are busy, high-level officials. Individuals deep in the bureaucracy seldom play a role in policymaking, even indirectly. Often the policy maker's agenda is cluttered with hundreds of issues requiring decision. A policy maker may not focus on an issue until Monday, when the decision must be made by Thursday. The advisor first learns of the issue Monday night, and then is expected to have advice ready, preferably in writing, by Wednesday morning so that the ministers can discuss the issue before deciding.

The issue is usually presented as a problem requiring a solution. Ministers usually do not ask for an analysis of the underlying economic causes of inflation; they want to know the steps needed now to reduce excessive inflation levels. Or, they may want to determine whether a program to lower infant mortality in a poor district deserves additional funding in the budget about to be submitted. Will there be enough money and will it be well spent? They have little time for an in-depth analysis of alternative oral rehydration techniques.

What are the implications of this kind of decisionmaking for the role of advisors and for policy research? In such cases, the immediate need is for a short memorandum—of two or three pages—spelling out the options available. In this context, an advisor must be on the spot when the issue arises, and must be aware of the options. An eminent scholar flown in three weeks later during the university spring break will be of little help in tackling this issue. Nor does the advisor have several weeks to study the problem before reaching a conclusion. Effective policy advisors of this sort, therefore, usually reside in the developing country, have worked on the issue addressed for some time, and have worked with the decision-makers on a close and ongoing basis so that they know what the decision-makers want and the form they want it in. In the course of a three-year span in Indonesia, for example, advisors on the fiscal reform project produced nearly one thousand memoranda of this sort. HIID individuals in Cambridge are known to have played this kind of role in Washington, which is just a one-hour airplane commute. Recently HIID scholars have even commuted to Moscow to play this role, usually when on leave or at considerable cost to their academic duties.

What stands behind a resident advisor's short policy-option memoranda? A three-page memorandum, after forty-eight hours of thought, is not likely to be a sufficient basis for making a correct decision. And being correct in the policy advising business matters. Academic researchers often contribute by creatively helping individuals to see a problem in a new light. Their prognosis may be terribly wrong, but their analysis furthers understanding of the problem. There are few rewards for the policy advisor who is original, creative, and wrong. How does one provide correct advice without first doing careful research?

Some kinds of policy analysis and advice travel well across borders and cultures. Lessons learned in other contexts can be readily applied in a new country. HIID, for example, has been involved in reforming the tax systems of at least eight countries. No country requires exactly the same system, but the differences are predictable and can be readily diagnosed—whether the country has a strong or a weak control of the goods flowing across its borders, for example. Taxpayer identification numbers and a computerized system with numerous cross-checks greatly aid enforcement, whether in Zambia or in Nepal. Moreover, much time is needed for designing such a system and for making it operational. For an experienced tax reformer, broadly outlining a new system does not require years of prior study in the country contemplating reform.

In other developing country situations, the direction of the change required is so obvious to the experienced advisor that new research is largely unwarranted. For example, in the early 1980s Bangladesh and Indonesia had trade regimes based on high and uneven tariffs, numerous quotas, and other trade barriers. Only a diehard dependency theorist would have argued that such a level of protection was optimal. For most economists, the issue was one of eliminating as many quotas, and of reducing as many tariffs, as possible. Given the political context of Bangladesh and Indonesia at that time, there was little danger of overshooting the mark and of leaving infant industries at the mercy of the market. Under these conditions, the goal was not to produce highly refined estimates of effective rates of protection, although these were made, but to estimate the cost to various groups of the then current high rates of protection. The advocates of liberalization needed the political ammunition about how these protection rates hurt constituencies; they did not need estimates to the third decimal point of the general loss in economic efficiency.

Not all policy advice and analysis travel well across borders. And, the direction of change required is frequently not as obvious as it is in countries emerging from decades of excessive intervention in the economy. The design of a school reform to increase access for young girls to education in Pakistan cannot be drawn directly from the experience of Sweden or even of Sri Lanka, for example. The influence of gender on the efficacy of interventions in education, health, and agricultural production is different in sub-Saharan Africa from what it is in East Asia. Politics, everywhere, is deeply rooted in culture, and the political context ultimately shapes the possibilities in all areas of reform. Advisors who do not understand the specific bureaucratic and national political context in which they operate are a major risk to the programs of which they are a part. HIID learned this lesson the hard way some twenty years ago in Ghana, where its advice about devaluation, impeccable on technical economic grounds, contributed to a coup that brought down the government.

The principal solution to the problem of acquiring the requisite knowledge for reliable short-term advice is to have policy analysts with a long-term, not necessarily an exclusive, commitment to the country in which they have been asked to work. It is no accident that HIID's single, most productive relationship over the past dozen years has been with Indonesia. HIID advisors/researchers spent sufficient time in Indonesia to have developed an in-depth understanding of the Indonesian sectors in which they worked, and key Indonesian ministers, in turn, learned what HIID could and could not do well. Among the countries where HIID has spent only two or three years, there are scattered small successes, and only a few footprints remain in the sand. The shortness of time was only one element in what was often a superficial relationship with the host country; time and superficiality of understanding are closely related.

Another HIID approach to acquiring knowledge for reliable short-term advice has been to work with developing countries to build their own effective research capacity which they can draw upon. This is pursued by letting local officials do the short-term advising, while foreign technical assistance provides the long-term research underpinnings. HIID has played this role in a number of countries, beginning in the 1970s with the Korea Development Institute (KDI) and continuing to the present with the Thai Development Research Institute (TDRI) in Bangkok, the Center for Policy and Implementation Studies (CPIS) in Jakarta, and the Unidad de Analisis de Politicas Economicas (UDAPE) and the Unidad de Analisis de Politicas Sociales (UDAPSO), both in La Paz, Bolivia. This same basic principal has underscored HIID's work with health research institutes around the world, through the Applied Diarrheal Disease Project. With the exception of the CPIS project, all work was funded by USAID.

Revolutionary situations are an exception to the principle of long-term involvement and research as prerequisites for effective short-term advice. Such situations create new problems that cannot await solutions from long-term research. For the past several years, for example, HIID has been intimately involved with the Russian privatization effort. Privatization advice to Russia was rooted in property rights theory, but the process was also shaped fundamentally by Russia's chaotic political scene. The result falls far short of an efficient private market system, but it is far superior to what would have happened if nothing had been done. There was little international experience to draw upon, and no time for much research. Bright individuals, Russian and foreign advisors alike, improvised.

An analogous situation existed in Vietnam where, since 1989, HIID has worked on food policy, industrial policy, macro stabilization, and other issues. When past training had been geared entirely to the needs of a centralized command system and that system is suddenly jettisoned in favor of a market system, those who understood the workings of a market system were able to contribute, even if they did not have much knowledge about Vietnam.

Are some disciplines more useful than others for policy work? HIID's experience is not definitive here, among other reasons, because HIID has not worked much in areas that draw on the natural sciences, except in public health and forestry. One conclusion has a wide degree of generality. As stated earlier, policy work begins with a problem requiring a solution, and few problems fit neatly within disciplinary boundaries. The scholar determined to remain within those boundaries will not be of much help to the policy maker. The disciplines required are not necessarily those that one thinks of when social scientists talk about multidisciplinary analysis.

Much of HIID's work over the past fifteen years, for example, has involved the drafting of law, for taxes, for reformed financial systems, and for commercial relations of all kinds. Lawyers may have little training relevant to deciding whether a value-added tax is good for a country, but they are the only individuals with knowledge of how to draft effective laws, once the broad objectives of the laws have been determined. Economists, in contrast, know when a particular tax system is appropriate, but generally have no drafting skill. The design of a health care system capable of providing health care to poor women and children in a rural area far from the capital city requires individuals who understand the required medicines and therapies. For the design, it is also necessary to have individuals, such as anthropologists, who understand the channels through which these women and children can be brought into the process, and economists who can help to design a financially viable system.

Much of HIID's work has required knowledge only vaguely related to the standard arts and sciences disciplines. Two of the senior educational planners, though trained as social psychologists, have focused their work on the many dimensions needed for an effective school system, work that only occasionally has drawn on social psychology. HIID has been heavily involved in the reform of public budgeting systems, in the decentralization of authority to the local level, and in the reform of rural banks. The institute's leaders in these fields have degrees in political science, public administration, management, or anthropology. Disciplinary training at the Ph.D. level provided these advisors with general research and analytic skills, but it is their accumulated experience working on similar problems around the world that makes them so valuable in the field.

Implementation and Institution Building

Policy makers want more from an advisor than the advisor's view on, say, the value of a new banking law or of the enrollment of more girls in the public school system. The policy maker, wishing to make a change, wants assurance that it will work in practice. When HIID's predecessor, the Harvard Development Advisory Service (DAS), was helping to build effective planning units around the world, the issue of whether to become directly involved in policy implementation arose infrequently. Planning commissions mainly had an advisory role. The operating ministries actually had to make the recommended change work. The job of DAS was to perform the economic analysis (or to train local individuals to do the analysis) that would establish whether a project, or an overall development plan, was sound in principle.

In the early 1980s, HIID increasingly was asked to become involved in activities that included more than advice about basic objectives. During the Indonesian tax reform, HIID faced the issue of whether to withdraw once the draft laws had been discussed, written, and approved by the Indonesian authorities, or whether to help the Indonesians make the new laws work in practice. The immediate issue was whether to help with the computerization of the system; yet more than computers were involved in the implementation of an effective tax system. Ultimately, HIID decided to work on the computerized system, and has been heavily involved in tax implementation ever since. This learning process has benefited Harvard's International Tax Program, which HIID has helped to run.

The issue of whether to become involved in implementation became explicit in the tax reform case, but it had arisen in a variety of contexts. One could talk easily about the importance of maternal and child health and preventive health care in rural areas; but could one design and set up a program that would work in practice and at a sustainable cost? HIID tried in Mali, failed, and then tried again with better, although not necessarily sustainable, results. The institute did much better in Cameroon, some years later. No one would argue with the desirability of an effective health care information system for guiding preventive and curative health activities. But can such a system be introduced in a society where health institutions are weak and fragmented? HIID worked on these issues with some sustainable success in the difficult setting of Chad, and later in Pakistan.

As HIID probed more deeply into the issue of making a program work in practice, like much of the development community it came to recognize that implementation issues were at the heart of what differentiated successful programs from unsuccessful programs. Deciding what needed to be done was easy. Creating local institutions that could actually do it was another matter.

Not all policies, to be sure, are difficult to implement. Devaluing a currency may have serious political consequences, but developing country governments usually have the power to simply order the central bank to start selling foreign exchange at a new rate. If the state has a food procurement agency which guarantees a minimum purchase price to farmers, it is not a difficult technical problem to change that price by government fiat, although again, as with the exchange rate, there will be political consequences. There is nothing simple about getting farmers to use integrated pest management in place of pesticides, or about creating a rural credit and savings system that works without continuous subsidies. Nor is there a simple way of getting a ministry of finance bureaucracy to change how officials handle budgetary procedures. A budgetary system designed decades earlier to meet simpler colonial needs chugs along at enormous cost in wasted development funds. Creating a new system requires restructuring the way large parts of the government operate against the resistance of many who have wide ranging reasons for opposing change.

The issue of reform implementation, as this brief discussion indicates, often involves the building of new institutions in the sometimes infertile ground of developing country societies. Implementation has much in common, therefore, with another nearly universal goal of most aid agencies and internationally-oriented foundations—institution building to make foreign advisors obsolete.

Most technical assistance projects in developing countries include a component that calls for expatriate advisors to give way, over time, to local individuals with comparable skills. To help these local individuals to acquire the required skills, short courses are run and a number of candidates are selected for graduate level or even Ph.D. training abroad. When these trained personnel return from abroad, they work with the expatriate advisors to learn the practical side of policy work, and then take over the work when the expatriate advisor goes home. With the investment of a few million dollars over five or ten years, the developing country acquires a high powered, locally staffed policy unit issuing advice that saves the country hundreds of times what the project cost—a benefit-cost ratio of monumental proportions.

Why is it that the reality of institution-building projects seldom lives up to this idealistic goal? HIID has had projects that come close, and many that have not. One explanation, popular in the developing countries and heard in frustrated development assistance agencies as well, is that expatriate advisors and the organizations providing them have vested interest in failure, because it keeps the expatriates in demand. Certainly, some agencies act as if their primary goal is to find lucrative employment for their staff. But the countries that have achieved sustained development have had little trouble replacing expatriates with local individuals, even without the assistance of institution-building projects. How many expatriate advisors are there today in Korea, or in Chile, or in Thailand? Once there were legions of expatriate advisors in these countries, particularly in Korea, but now they are all gone. Is the problem in Africa, where the charge is most often heard, that expatriates love living there so much that it is impossible to push them out? Nothing in the author's experience suggests that this is the case. The HIID personnel who are committed to a long-term career in Africa are a precious few.

Institution building in the early stages of development is difficult because expectations in that context are often wildly optimistic and unrealistic. To begin with, creating an island of excellence in a sea of mediocrity, or worse, is almost impossible; yet that is what most institution-building efforts try to do. Why is it nearly impossible? HIID's experience with the Development Planning Division in Kenya's Ministry of Agriculture illustrates the problem unambiguously. Over a decade, HIID trained over thirty economists abroad to a master's degree level in economics, but the only two economists in the division when the institute closed the project were on the payroll at expatriate salaries. All others had been hired away by the private sector, and by the very aid agencies that talked so much about the importance of institution building. When HIID ended its participation, the division was largely devoid of expatriates where once there had been ten such individuals, twenty if one goes back to the 1970s. This story is not one of expatriates squeezing out local staff.

The Kenyan Government could have done more to make this institution-building effort successful, but the task was formidable. There were ample employment opportunities in the private sector and with the international agencies that dotted the Nairobi landscape, usually at salaries several times those paid by the government. The government made an effort to raise the salary of economists in the civil service, but the effort came to naught seemingly because those who managed the civil service could see no reason for giving economists special privileges. An alternative was to promote a few individuals rapidly. But how can a true merit promotion be introduced into a system where discretionary promotion easily ends up favoring particular individuals on grounds having nothing to do with merit? A general government wage increase was impossible, because that would have created macroeconomic problems. Thus the aid agencies, in selected cases, increased salaries—a practice that worked until the patience, or the priorities, of the aid agency changed. Institution building of all kinds is not impossible in the early stages of development. Rather, the problem is this kind of institution building. What kinds of institution building are successful?

Even the least developed societies and their governments function according to rules and procedures. Many of these rules and procedures were designed decades earlier to meet colonial needs, and made use of the technology available at the time. These rules and procedures can be changed and new technologies can be introduced. Local officials seldom have much difficulty learning the new procedures, or the new technologies, once in place, provided the procedures and technologies take local conditions into account.

Local officials are seldom in a position, however, to redesign the rules and procedures, or to know what is an appropriate new technology. These skills rest with small groups of individuals who have acquired extensive experience with alternative systems around the world, through participation in earlier redesign efforts, through research, and through teaching about such systems. HIID has developed cadres of individuals with these kinds of skills in tax reform, redesign of public budgeting systems, financial reform, design of educational information systems, and in other areas. The individuals come from countries in Latin America, southern Asia, and all over the world. It is both unnecessary and unrealistic to expect a developing country to develop such a cadre on its own, unless the country happens to have an international consulting firm specializing in the area being reformed. Few developing countries possess that kind of firm, at least in the areas in which HIID works. The skilled expatriate firm can, with full local cooperation, develop a system and make it operational within a few years. The expatriates can then go home or, if the country prefers, work on further refinements in the system. At no time do the expatriates need to play anything that plausibly can be described as an operational role better handled by local staff.

Another approach to institution building is to attempt to raise the level of the system as a whole, rather than to pick selected institutional targets. The Indonesian Government, with the help of HIID and many others, has sent thousands of individuals abroad for advanced training in key areas. Hundreds in the finance ministry have been trained to the master's degree level in economics or business administration, and the ministry has more individuals with Ph.D.'s in economics than many developing countries. The Indonesian Government also has made more effort to retain good individuals than have many other governments. By training so many people, the government has raised the level of the system as a whole. Outside temptations are, therefore, less than what they might have been had no effort been made.

The alternative to sending thousands of people abroad each year is to develop appropriate training programs within the country. However, first-class graduate training programs require even more highly trained faculty, the scarcest resource of all in most early-stage developing countries. For many developing countries, this means relying on expatriate teachers for some time and at great expense. For other countries, the higher salaries and good working conditions of a genuinely independent and quality program are enough to attract back trained nationals who have gone abroad in search of better opportunities. Building independent, quality institutions, even ones in the private sector out of direct reach of government bureaucracy, is a formidable task, especially when most local educational institutions are not high quality, and the financial resources required are well beyond what most aid agencies are willing to fund. The islands of educational excellence built up earlier in Asia and Latin America were mostly funded by groups such as the Ford Foundation, the Aga Khan Foundation, and the Catholic Church.

In the absence of large-scale training efforts, small targeted training serves a purpose, even if that purpose is only indirectly related to what the effort was intended to help. The more targeted training programs there are, the more the general level of human resources will rise. If trained individuals work for a time in a well-run organization, even if that organization disappears or reverts to mediocrity when the expatriates leave, those trained individuals will remember the requirements of a well-run organization.

Several years ago a major figure in development spoke at HIID. He had been a key individual in one of the institute's efforts to build an effective planning commission in his home country. That planning commission, after a decade and more of good work, had fallen on bad times, and he had gone abroad with many of his colleagues to work in an international agency. At the time of his speech in Cambridge, he had returned to his country to serve as a senior minister. One of his themes was what he had learned in those earlier years. He had not realized it earlier that the lessons learned from working closely with first-class policy analysts on the job had stayed with him thereafter and underlay his approach to his current tasks. While this is only one incident, the phenomenon has appeared in other countries. Perhaps one of the most extreme examples is a group of Chinese, who had been trained at missionary schools in China and abroad before 1949, whose institutions were destroyed and themselves persecuted, only to reappear after 1979 to help China open up to the outside world. These individuals were able to accomplish this task because they understood the benefits of opening their society to the outside world and how China could gain access to these benefits.

When the effort for institution building is genuine, even a failure can have some merit. Indeed, if the task were an easy one, there would be no need for technical assistance in the first place.

The Evolving Role of Technical Assistance

The demand for technical assistance has changed over time for reasons that are both positive and negative. The negative reasons have largely to do with the changing fads of the various aid agencies, fads that often reflect the changing domestic politics in the aid-giving country or the bureaucratic shifts within the international agencies themselves. "Basic needs" and "privatization" have been favorite code words, after which "income redistribution to alleviate poverty" was rediscovered. On the positive side of these shifts, there are many aid givers and many different ways of operating. A good program dropped by one agency can often be picked up by another. For the technical assistance organization tied to a single aid provider, however, the shifts can be dizzying. When the emphasis shifts to privatization, an organization built to work on integrated rural development projects suddenly finds itself with a large staff trained to do something the aid agency no longer wants to support

Fortunately, HIID has been able to find support from a wide variety of agencies and foundations. In the 1960s, DAS was largely dependent on the Ford Foundation, a dependence that had near catastrophic consequences when Ford withdrew support for the kind of assistance DAS was then giving. Over the 1980s and early 1990s, HIID received major financing directly from the governments with whom it worked, in particular from Indonesia; from USAID, which has ranged from as low as 3 to 4 percent to nearly 50 percent of the institute's total budget; from the World Bank; from the United Nations Development Programme (UNDP); from the Christopher Reynolds Foundation; and from various Scandinavian bilateral aid agencies. From 1980 to 1995, HIID's two largest sources of funding each amounted to about one-quarter of the budget. No other single source averaged as much as 10 percent over the whole period. Shifting aid agency priorities has been a problem for some projects, but not for HIID as a whole. Even individual projects cut off in midstream often have managed to continue with alternative sources of funding.

The positive side of shifting technical assistance priorities is that, for countries achieving sustained development, capacity building does take place, and technical assistance from outside the country is no longer needed in many areas. In the 1960s, Harvard's primary role was to provide good general and sectoral economists to both staff and train planning commissions in developing countries. Today, these planning commissions, or their equivalent, exist worldwide staffed by local people, and HIID has not had such a team overseas since the early 1970s.

HIID has provided high-level specialized knowledge in economic areas, such as macroeconomic policy, trade policy, and food policy. Much of this recent work has been in Africa, where local capacity building in economics lags behind other regions of the world. The institute has also provided economic advisors of this sort in Indonesia, and in some of the former Soviet-style command economies converting to a market system. Indonesia is a special case, where an unusually able group of senior economics ministers has wanted to be able to check their staff's judgment against the best international advice available. The Russian and the Vietnamese situations reflect a lack of experience with market economies among local economists, a situation that is changing rapidly as highly trained individuals learn how a market economy works. When HIID withdraws its last economic policy advisor from Indonesia—which is envisaged for some time in the not very distant future—the institute will have no resident economic policy advisors of this kind anywhere in Asia, Latin America, and probably in Russia.

Nevertheless, Africa will continue to need high quality economic advisors of this type for another ten or twenty years, with some countries able to graduate more quickly than others. Whether that need will be recognized either by the countries themselves or by international aid agencies remains to be seen. A current view among several international aid agencies, based on evidence known only to them, is that most African governments are in a position to graduate from this kind of assistance now.

If general resident advisors in economics and public management are gradually fading from the world of technical assistance, there is no comparable decline in the need for teams of specialists with extensive international experience in the design and reform of economic and public management systems. The tax and financial systems of most developing countries are in a rudimentary state. Budgeting often follows principles that have not been state-of-the-art since the 1920s. Modern computer-based information systems in fields ranging from education to health and to the management of food distribution have only begun to be introduced. Pension and health insurance schemes are increasingly important in countries well into the industrialization process.

Industrialized countries often need reforms in these systems as well. One reason for countries, like the United States, to have so many specialists able to help developing countries with system reform is that these specialists first struggled at home with the issues. Ironically, sometimes it is easier to design and introduce a first-rate system in a developing country than it is in an industrialized society. Often, an industrialized country will have thousands of well-educated, highly articulate special interest groups with access to the political decision makers. In the United States, for example, the tax reform efforts resulted in a new tax law riddled with similar, if slightly different, distortions from those in the old tax law. In developing countries, expatriate design teams typically work with a handful of senior government officials. The business community works through the political process to protect special interests. Low-level bureaucrats resist change, when reform threatens to eliminate their sources of "informal" income, as is often the case. But these forces, if they failed to completely derail the reform process, usually do not become as intimately involved in the details of the reform design as is the case in industrialized societies. While the developing country may not yet have the staff required to implement the new system with a high degree of efficiency, the system will be well designed. And a well-designed system in a developing country, among other things, is one that puts the smallest possible implementation burden on the relevant agencies.

Some fields are relatively new in both industrialized and developing countries. Although environmental issues have been around since the beginning of time, only in recent decades have they become a major focus of national policy. Mostly the high-income countries have begun to spend real resources on the many dimensions of environmental problems. Eastern Europe and the republics of the former Soviet Union are monuments to the cost of totally ignoring the environment while pushing economic development. Developing countries, particularly those with high population densities, are finding that air and water pollution reach unacceptable levels earlier in the development process than was the case in land-rich countries, such as the United States. Globally, the developing countries have most of what remains of the tropical rain forest. Are there international arrangements that can save those forests, or will Indonesia and Brazil copy the path of destruction laid down by the industrial world?

Only a handful of economists worldwide have seriously studied the relationship of economic development, economic policy, and the environment, and most of them are in a few industrialized countries. Given that the problems caused by these relationships exist as much in the developing countries as in the industrialized world, there should be a role in the developing world for specialists from industrialized countries. As the aid agencies have begun to recognize the need, the funding to support such activities has become available.

The environment is not the only issue of this sort. Most new technology is developed at first in high-income countries, and that applies to economic and social policy software as much as it does to engineering hardware. The computer-based information systems in health and education mentioned earlier are one of many examples. As specialists learn to use these systems in developing country contexts, they are likely to learn much of value for their use in high-income countries as well. An organization set up to provide technical assistance in these areas must be familiar with the cutting-edge technologies involved. It follows, more or less automatically, that an organization of this sort must be involved in cutting-edge research. Simply applying a widely known "best practice" is a declining industry in the technical assistance field.

Policy-based research is an area where high-income countries are likely to have a comparative advantage vis-à-vis developing countries for some time to come. The research universities and think tanks that nurture such research are highly concentrated in the industrial world. The developing world produces first-rate researchers, many of whom stay in the industrialized countries where they were trained. Those who return home often are promoted rapidly into high positions in government and the private sector, and have no time for research. The few who remain in research frequently feel isolated and not rewarded for their efforts. Even in Confucian cultures where teachers traditionally are awarded a high status, economic development in its initial decades typically provides policy researchers with only low salaries and poor working conditions.

Clearly there is a role for research organizations from industrialized countries to work with new policy research institutes in the developing world. The policy researchers from the industrialized world have several functions in this context. They can fill critical research gaps in the developing country, gaps that exist because the country does not have enough research personnel to fill them. Senior researchers can be mentors and guides to developing country researchers, many of whom are recent graduates with limited policy research experience. Primarily, researchers from industrialized countries can help build and maintain networks in which policy-oriented scholars from industrialized and developing countries can share work and insights. When the local environment provides little support for these scholars, an international environment in which their work is respected can be a partial substitute.

Since the mid-1980s, HIID has worked increasingly with developing country researchers and research institutes in Latin America, Africa, and especially in Asia. Often funding has been a problem, because most research funds have been given exclusively to either industrialized country researchers to work on their own projects, or to developing country researchers. Far less money has been available for supporting research collaboration involving both industrialized and developing country researchers. HIID has received significant funds from USAID for this purpose, but much of this funding has come from sources in the developing world.

The Role of the University in Providing Technical Assistance

A research university in an industrialized country has advantages in providing the kinds of technical assistance required by the developing world. A research university also has several significant shortcomings that inhibit or outright prevent the university from playing a constructive role in the provision of technical assistance. The university's advantages are largely in the intellectual realm: universities are the repositories of the advanced knowledge the developing world is seeking. The disadvantages are in the way universities are organized. Universities, and their component schools and departments, evolve in accordance with their own internal logic, and respond only intermittently to the demands of the society around them. When they do respond, typically it is after long delays and in a partial manner. The societal pressures that matter most are those in their own country; developing country concerns play almost no role.

That research universities, in the United States and Europe at least, are the main repositories of cutting-edge technologies in the policy sciences and in the natural sciences requires only brief comment. They are not the only such repositories, however. There are numerous first-rate think tanks that stand alone. Yet there are far more research universities, and these universities are more open to involvement with the developing world than are most independent think tanks.

If the future of technical assistance in the developing world rests mainly in the areas of systems reform and policy research, research universities are well positioned intellectually to help. Most research, in the United States at least, is carried out in universities, and research on developing countries is almost exclusively a product of universities, although the World Bank and a few others are also important contributors. Many, perhaps most, of the ideas for reforming economic systems, education systems, or health systems come from the universities. The U.S. system, where academics move from teaching and research into government and back again to academia, is well suited to producing informed new ideas about how the institutions of society could be improved.

The research university, with its cutting-edge ideas, does not readily produce the ideas that reformers in developing countries require. Rewards within the university context strongly emphasize the originality or creativity of an intellectual contribution. Academic status, particularly in arts and sciences departments, goes first to those who contribute to basic theory, rather than to those who try to apply theory to solve society's problems. Universities should reward creativity and contributions to basic theory. If they do not do so, who will? Original ideas are also important to the university's core teaching function of stimulating young minds to view their surroundings through more than just the prism of tradition.

Developing countries, however, can ill-afford creative ideas that turn out to be wrong when applied to their particular situation. Political support for reform is seldom strong enough to sustain itself through a series of experiments that fail until someone finally succeeds. Foreign technical assistance must be right, or the whole process, and the foreigners in particular, will be discredited. In this context, experience in putting in place workable reforms counts for more than originality. Also, those advising on reform should understand the bureaucratic and the broader political and social context in which they are working. The brilliant scholar who gets off the plane, gives a lecture, and then leaves, may stimulate useful debate, but no country wants its economic system redesigned by such a scholar. The ideal reform advisor has extensive experience with similar reforms elsewhere and the willingness to make a sustained commitment to working with local individuals in the new environment.

HIID has performed well when it identified first-class minds who were willing to make such a sustained commitment and, in the process, had accumulated the necessary experience. The institute's earlier work with planning commissions around the world fits this pattern. In the 1980s, HIID's work with tax reform exemplified this tradition. Experienced tax reformers spent years working with a country and then brought that experience back to the teaching program, where these same reformers could improve upon what they had learned and then go overseas to a new country. The institute's work in education system reform also fits this pattern. The integration of ongoing practical system design efforts with research, summer workshops, and regular classroom teaching has been the primary formula for success.

Sometimes direct practical experience is not available to draw upon. Economic reform in Russia, at first, faced many problems for which there was no clear solution, given the unusual nature of the Russian political context and the magnitude of the transition problems to be tackled. In that situation, the best one can do is to draw on bright academics with mostly theoretical knowledge who will work with local reformers, remaining with them long enough to gain the level of understanding required. Most of HIID's economic reform efforts have been able to draw on directly relevant experience. The work in Zambia, in the early 1990s, drew directly on the work in Kenya and in The Gambia over the latter half of the 1980s. Even the institute's work with Vietnam on the transition from a command economy to a market economy drew heavily on its experience with similar efforts in Indonesia and China.

Whatever advantages universities have, in principle, in providing technical assistance in the developing world, in practice they will have little success unless they organize themselves to provide such assistance appropriately. HIID is virtually unique in the U.S. university setting, not because Harvard has special advantages over other universities in working with the developing world. Rather, in the 1960s Harvard created an organizational structure appropriate for a university that wanted to see whether ideas developed in the classroom could work in practice. Several land-grant universities in the United States have created similar capacities within their agricultural schools, but no other U.S. university has tried to do so as broadly as Harvard.

Several key elements must be in place for an organization, like HIID, to function in a university context:

- There must be a career ladder that rewards academics for technical assistance work.
- There must be a system for developing the relationships that eventually lead to funded projects.
- There must be administrative staff capable of both supporting large numbers of advisors in the field and of meeting the financial and legal requirements of myriad aid agencies with complex and differing rules.

The organization must be an integrated component of the university, contributing directly to the teaching and research mission of that university.

Universities reward those who contribute to their primary functions of research and teaching. Outside consulting is allowed, and in some schools even encouraged, because it provides experience critical to the credibility of teachers in certain applied fields, such as business. The rewards for consulting are the fees earned on the outside. Rarely does the university itself reward its faculty for such activities. If a faculty member chooses to work in a developing country, that work must be done during vacations or while on sabbatical. Long leaves of absence abroad, unless they produce reams of published research, usually result in termination of the teaching contract.

But the essence of HIID's technical assistance work involves long absences from the university that must be geared to the needs of the developing country, not the rigid timing of vacations in the academic calendar. While the time abroad usually produces material for research that is often unique, the period abroad leaves little time for reflection and writing. Reforming an economic system is a full-time, often exhausting job. Writing up the lessons from the experience comes after the advisor has returned to the university.

For a university to have an institute capable of providing technical assistance of this kind, there must be a separate career track for those whose primary job is to make this assistance effective. The core teaching faculty can, and should, be used when leaves and vacations coincide with project needs, but project leadership and much of its long-term staffing must come from those whose primary role it is. If the technical assistance function is to attract individuals who can also perform as researchers and teachers in the academic context, the career structure must mimic that of the university of which it is a part.

Universities receive funding from tuition and endowment, sources that are both steady and predictable, at least at places like Harvard. Technical assistance is usually contract funded, which is neither a steady nor a predictable condition. The university career ladder, typically, has three to four steps ending in tenure, with half or more of the faculties being tenured. Consulting firms providing technical assistance, or contract-based research, usually do not give tenure, even to the firm's principals. To do otherwise would be to risk bankruptcy at the first downturn in business. HIID's career structure is a compromise between the two kinds of institutions. HIID awards tenure to a small number of scholar-advisors who it sees as playing a long-term leadership role both in the university and abroad. HIID also makes long-term appointments of three to five years, some with expectation of ready renewal. But of HIID's one hundred-plus development professionals and total staff of two hundred, fewer than fifteen percent of the development professionals have tenure. Whether fifteen percent is too large or too small depends on the quality of the individuals chosen. There are not many individuals with the skills, the desire, and the flexibility to be consistent leaders in the world of technical assistance over a thirty-year period, the typical length of a tenured appointment. But not to make tenured appointments is to deny the institute access to precisely the kind of scholar-advisors that cutting-edge technical assistance requires.

Contracts for technical assistance are not easily obtained. Many individuals, including some at HIID, believe that Harvard's name is all that it takes to win a contract. During the fifteen years when the author was HIID's director, seemingly only one or two contracts were awarded because of Harvard's name. Formally, contracts are awarded either through a bidding process or as sole-source awards to an organization the decision-makers feel is best suited to do the job. In the 1960s, most contracts awarded to DAS were of the sole-source variety, and were funded by the Ford Foundation on a cost-plus basis. Those relaxed days came to an end in the early 1970s. HIID was left with a reputation for good work in certain areas, but with little knowledge of how to get the work funded in this new environment. The learning process that followed was not easy.

The essence of winning contracts in the technical assistance world, and no doubt elsewhere, is establishing trust and confidence in those making the award that you can do the job. Usually this trust and confidence are achieved by working at first with senior government officials in developing countries on a short-term basis, or with aid officials in a similar manner. Occasionally, mid-career developing country officials spend a year at Harvard and become acquainted with HIID through courses taught by its professionals. HIID's work in Kenya began this latter way; its subsequent work grew out of the confidence various Kenyan officials had in the skills of particular advisors. The institute's work in Indonesia in the 1980s built on the reputation of several advisors provided in the early 1970s, and on the skills of one advisor in the early 1980s who worked with key ministers to define an appropriate role for outsiders in meeting the ministers' desire to reform the Indonesian tax system. Providing help with one reform effort led to requests for assistance with other subsequent efforts.

Much of HIID's success in finding work in developing countries, like that in Kenya and Indonesia, has been built on establishing its competence and loyalty to reform-minded ministers, permanent secretaries, and other local officials. In the 1980s, HIID also began to learn how to work with the various aid agencies and to bid successfully on competitively awarded contracts. When the institute first became involved in the bidding process, it believed it could win by fielding the best team of advisors or the best consortium of universities—best at least on paper. After a half dozen or more failed bids, HIID realized that winning a bid involved, first, establishing trust and confidence among those deciding on the bids that the institute could do the job well. For every aid official who thought Harvard was full of competent individuals, there were at least as many who felt that Harvard academics had little idea of how to function usefully in the field.

A decade of research and advising on educational reform was a product of the confidence of one or two individuals at USAID in HIID's senior education specialist, and there are many other examples. The work in the field of environmental economics, now one of HIID's largest programs, grew mainly out of years of small consulting assignments and one small overseas project in Thailand carried out by the individual who now leads the larger program. The work on privatization and legal reform in Russia grew out of the ad hoc consulting assignments of a faculty member of Harvard's Economics Department and of a recent graduate of the Harvard Law School who was resident in Moscow.

A number of HIID's overseas projects have come from initiatives taken by individuals who did not have long-term contracts with the institute. Tenure can be a disincentive for academic entrepreneurs. If one is to rely on entrepreneurial efforts of those without long-term ties to the university, it is critical that senior management ensure that such efforts contribute to the broader non-financial goals of the institute. A university will never be comfortable with an organization run primarily in accordance with the profit-maximizing principles of most private consulting firms.

After a contract is awarded, there is more to providing effective technical assistance than fielding the brightest and best informed advisors. Advisors must establish trust with local officials that they are there to work in the country's interests, not for their own selfish goals or for the agenda of the aid agency funding the project. Aid agencies often have the best of intentions, but they have their own agendas. Advisors with their own agenda or that of an outside agency will not be fully trusted. Indonesia has dealt with this issue by financing HIID work with its own funds, but politics usually preclude such arrangements. In most developing countries, it is easier for the government to explain to the public that the expensive outside advisor is provided "free" by the aid agency. Otherwise, the government could become embroiled in a politically damaging argument over why the foreigner is being paid ten or twenty times as much as a local official. If the foreigner does not contribute benefits that are several multiples of his or her expatriate salary, then there is no justification for having a resident expatriate. But advice on reforming an economic system, if done well, can generate benefits in the billions of dollars in a large country at a cost of a few million dollars for the technical assistance required.

An advisor in the field, to be effective, requires a strong support system at home. An important part of this support system is purely administrative. All aid agencies have elaborate reporting requirements and other complex administrative rules. These things often give the impression that it does not matter whether the money is used to accomplish something, as long as it is not stolen. Some aid agencies award contracts and monitor them at a distance; others try to "micro-manage" the contractor. Whatever the case, the field advisor should not be responsible for financial reporting, for getting the permissions required for sending short-term consultants to the country involved, or for negotiating the contract with that consultant. HIID's Cambridge office has more than twenty individuals whose primary function is the management of finances, contracting, personnel, recruitment, and the proposal preparation work connected with the roughly US$40 million a year in overseas and Cambridge-based projects.

In addition to general administrative support, a field project requires specialized home office staff geared to the particular needs of that project. A good Cambridge backstopper is intimately involved with the project, particularly when it comes to finding the right short-term consultants or finding the answer to questions a senior official poses to an advisor. Advisors cannot be expected to know the answer to everything they are asked, but they can be expected to know how to get the answer. Many advisors are in locations where the right computer parts are unavailable and must therefore be purchased in the United States and shipped overseas. When the advisor's paycheck is incorrectly routed or someone has forgotten to pay the warehouse storing household goods, the advisor in N'Djamena or Almaty cannot be expected to solve the problem alone. HIID's administrative support in Cambridge is there for that purpose.

Field operations are highly decentralized, with much autonomy. The person in the field must decide what advice is appropriate in the local context. HIID senior management can choose the advisor and can monitor performance, but only at a distance. Ultimately there must be trust that the advisor and the senior HIID management have common goals and are doing their best to meet them. When trust breaks down, the breakdown of the whole project often follows.

Too many things can go wrong on an overseas project to attempt to catalogue the reasons. However, two common problems deserve mention. Many (if not most) advisors overseas, even those with long previous residence in Cambridge and tenure with the institute, have periods when they feel the Cambridge home office does not care about the project even though the project checks keep coming. At HIID, this feeling is referred to as "field paranoia," and is "cured" through frequent communication between the home office and the field. Saving on overseas phone calls is a false economy. The backstopper and senior management should visit the field as often as possible; the advisor should travel to the home office periodically.

A related problem is when advisors begin to see the project as belonging to them, and the country as being theirs. Long-term resident advisors abroad are more valuable than short-term advisors, but only if the former avoid this trap. The country may pay for the project and it belongs to the country; the advisor is there on the sufferance of the country. Even the most inside advisor ultimately is an outsider. When an advisor forgets his or her role, this can lead to conflict in the developing country. It can also cause friction between the field and the home office, particularly when the advisor combines this attitude with field paranoia. From the advisor's perspective, the home office is an alien force interfering with the true needs of the country as defined by the advisor.

For these reasons and for many more, a university entering into this kind of work must build a strong support system designed explicitly to meet the needs of overseas aid-funded projects. To rely only on the existing university administrative apparatus is to invite disaster, since this has been set up to meet very different needs and to operate on different principles. Ultimately, the administrative rules and procedures of the university must be reconciled with those of its overseas technical assistance arm. Reconciliation requires a set of specialists within the technical assistance area and in the core administration of the university. HIID's contracts must meet the requirements set down for all Harvard contracts, including the stipulation that no contract have clauses restricting publication and that the contract also meet the needs of the developing country.

What does the university gain from all of this special effort? For those who believe that the university's exclusive role is to develop and teach basic theory, taught by social and humanistic scholars involved only in pure scholarship, the answer is "not very much." But U.S. universities in general, and Harvard in particular, long ago rejected this definition of the role of the university. The students who come to Harvard's professional schools, and many of those in arts and sciences as well, expect to learn skills and to gain insights of value when they enter or return to these professions. They want to have their vision of the world around them widened, and they want to learn what works and what does not work.

Business school faculty, therefore, consult actively with the U.S. corporate community and with firms outside the United States. Many faculty of Harvard's John F. Kennedy School of Government commute to Washington D.C. for short- and long-service periods. Medical and public health faculty work in local clinics or study the epidemiology of Massachusetts towns. All of this experience feeds back into the classroom and applied research.

All research universities have faculty who have lived outside of the United States, and have studied foreign cultures and learned their languages. Most have a few faculty who have worked on applied problems in these countries as well, but the emphasis is on the word "few." Many departments and faculties have no one who has had experience working in a developing country on the redesign of its financial systems or on helping to set up an information system in a developing country's ministry of education or health.

The students coming to these research universities increasingly are individuals who will go back home or will join international agencies and nongovernmental institutions to work on precisely such issues. International development is one of the largest interests of the U.S. students of the Kennedy School, not to mention the fifty plus mid-career students from developing countries. Over half of the economics Ph.D. candidates at Harvard are from outside the United States, many from Latin America and Asia, and roughly half of the graduates of the program will end up outside of academia, mainly in policy-related jobs. The world's greatest public health challenges are in Africa and South Asia, yet the students come to the United States in large numbers to learn about how to deal with these issues. Specialists on cancer epidemiology in Massachusetts will have much essential knowledge to give these individuals, but direct developing country experience is essential in a balanced program.

Institutions such as HIID, the international wings of the land-grant agricultural colleges, and the international activities of universities like Johns Hopkins, add greatly to both the quantity and the quality of the developing country experience that enters the university classroom. If this activity were confined to the international and bilateral aid agencies and to independent consulting firms, much of this experience would be lost to U.S. universities. The universities would be the poorer, as would be the world of international development that would at least partially be cut off from what the research universities potentially have to offer them.

2 Research and Publication: Lessons of Experience

Michael Roemer

The institute embraces a rare, if not unique, trio of activities: technical assistance provided to developing countries, often in competition with commercial consulting firms; academic research and publication on development, generally flowing from overseas projects; and teaching development courses and workshops at Harvard University, as well as guiding Harvard students interested in development. The opening essay to this volume discusses the complementarities and tensions among these activities. This chapter explores the nature of HIID's research and publications, discusses its relation to overseas advisory projects and, by identifying the major concentrations of output, points to the literature where HIID's contributions can be found. It covers the twenty-one years since the institute was founded in 1974, but concentrates on the years since 1980.

The Nature of Research at HIID

HIID was created as a multidisciplinary provider of technical assistance, with the dual role of bringing university expertise to field work and of bringing field experience to the university. Research and teaching at Harvard were to be an inherent part of this dual role, but the basic mission has remained that of providing technical services. Appointments and promotion have come to depend increasingly upon research capacity and accomplishment. Nevertheless, promotions also require successful service abroad and the screening process has tended to exclude even talented researchers who were unwilling to serve abroad. Funding was expected to come principally from executing overseas development projects. Hence the culture of the organization, and its claim to uniqueness, centered around active service in developing countries. Research and publication have been highly regarded, a great deal more so than in commercial consulting firms, but the generation and operation of overseas projects have always had a strong competing claim on the institute's energies.

The institute has taken steps to promote research and publication within its overseas project-focused culture. One class of appointment—Faculty Fellow—has brought to HIID five Harvard professors whose principal appointments are not at HIID but whose research has been done substantially through the institute. Promotion to Institute Fellow, the core tenure appointment at HIID, has always depended on research accomplishment as well as on overseas service, and now promotion to the nontenured but long-term position of Fellow also requires some research and publication. Moreover, the criteria for both positions were broadened in the early 1990s to make it possible, if still exceptional, to base an appointment principally on research accomplishment; one such appointment to Fellow was made (although the appointee has since become a professor and thus a Faculty Fellow at HIID). Since the mid-1980s, when the institute's growing project funding generated some discretionary resources, these have been used liberally if informally to support research; in recent years the institute has offered formal research awards to its staff, totaling US$75,000 a year, to complete work on research and publications arising from HIID projects.

Starting in 1990, the institute has taken steps to have its work published and to publicize its research output. HIID publishes its own book series, *Harvard Studies in International Development*, which is distributed by the Harvard University Press; to date there are twelve titles in the series and a few other books currently in press. All manuscripts are refereed by readers outside HIID before publication. In the past six years, seven more volumes have been published jointly with the International Center for Economic Growth, which has a large distribution network of research institutes in Africa, Asia, and Latin America. A quarterly newsletter, the *HIID Research Review*, carries one-page synopses of books and articles published by HIID staff. The *HIID Research Review* has been published since 1987 and is widely distributed to the academic and professional community.

HIID's research, formed as it is within a culture of overseas advisory work, has been motivated almost exclusively by concerns about development strategy and policy: its formulation, its analysis, its management, and its outcomes. The institute's work covers the entire range of academic research, including the creation and application of theory, studies employing analytical techniques of the social sciences, empirical studies that gather and analyze new data, and case histories that are used as research tools and as teaching devices. Whatever the approach, research design focuses on variables related to public policy and management. The ultimate test of HIID's research is its impact on thinking about development policy and management.

Research and Overseas Projects

Because HIID's claim to uniqueness as a university organization is its combination of academic and development advisory work, it is natural to ask how research fits into the overseas project culture that dominates the institute. Four reasonably tight linkages can be identified, as described below.

First, some field projects are designed as research projects; these are generally either empirical studies, covering several professional disciplines, or country economic histories. In the late 1970s, a multidisciplinary team from HIID inaugurated a five-year study of four rural sites in Indonesia that led to a follow-on project to create the Center for Policy and Implementation Studies (CPIS). CPIS, which continued into the early 1990s, conducted applied, long-term research on the development of small-scale rural banking, smallholder tree crops,[1] the design and use of fertilizer packages, the economics of the informal sector in Jakarta,[2] integrated pest management, and malaria control.

The defining features of the Indonesia CPIS project were its dual aims of producing good quality research on policy issues and of developing the capacity of a local institute to conduct such research. HIID has had at least three other involvements with these dual aims. In the 1970s, HIID worked with the Korea Development Institute (KDI) to develop KDI's policy research capacity and to produce a definitive history of Korean development.[3] During the 1980s, HIID began a series of projects in Bolivia, continuing to the present, that have enhanced the capacity of two institutes to conduct economic and social policy analysis. Also during the 1980s, HIID worked with the Thailand Development Research Institute (TDRI) on issues of resource management[4] and social policy, especially the financing of health services.[5]

Under the Applied Diarrheal Disease Research (ADDR) project, HIID has used a policy agenda to develop overseas capacity in research on health and nutrition. In this case, the research was conducted entirely by host country professionals with the aim of improving policy and practice in their own countries.[6]

Another set of overseas research projects was intended principally to formulate policy recommendations. Since 1985, for example, HIID has been engaged in a program of research to define the major factors that contribute to school effectiveness, defined as the production of student learning and measured as achievement on curriculum-based examinations. Studies have been carried out, in collaboration with local professionals, in Colombia,[7] Egypt, Honduras,[8] Jordan, Pakistan,[9] Sri Lanka,[10] and Thailand.[11] Since the late 1980s, HIID has conducted socioeconomic surveys and ethnographic studies of rural households in Malawi, to assess the impact of economic stabilization and structural adjustment policies on rural incomes and welfare.[12] During the 1990s, HIID has established several research sites in tropical rainforests in Southeast Asia and Central America to gather data that will help to design improved approaches to forest management. A final example of policy-based empirical work is the study, conducted from 1979 to 1984, of the financing of recurrent costs of development projects in the Sahel, which documented that the waste of resources as donor-funded projects could not be maintained because their recurrent costs could not be funded.[13]

The following country historical studies had no immediate policy role, though they dealt with policy issues, but did involve one or more HIID residents and periodic visits by Cambridge-based researchers: (1) two studies on Korea with the Korea Development Institute, in the mid-1970s and in the late 1980s;[14] (2) the volumes on Malaysia with the Institute of Strategic International Studies (ISIS), which will be completed in 1997; and (3) the current research on Taiwan at the Chung-Hua Institute for Economic Research (CHER).

Second, HIID's field projects can be a rich source of case histories documenting the results of policy and management reforms and their implementation. At the institute, some case histories are seen as finished products, providing lessons from HIID's work for other professionals. The conference volume, *Reforming Economic Systems in Developing Countries*, contains case studies of trade reforms in Indonesia and Bangladesh, financial market reforms and rural credit in Indonesia, food price stabilization and smallholder export production in Indonesia, and the politics of health reform in Chad.[15] A book was recently published on stabilization and structural adjustment in The Gambia, based on an HIID field project.[16] A volume on rural health care management in Mali, a project implemented from 1979 to 1984, appeared in 1990.[17] Papers have been presented on the property tax reforms in Indonesia.[18]

Other case studies, however, are employed as inputs for broader research projects. A prize-winning book on the political economy of policy reform emerged from a series of case histories collected by the authors from participants in the reforms, including several in which HIID was involved.[19] Extending that approach, a recent manuscript employs four case studies, designed for the purpose, to draw conclusions about building governmental capacity in developing countries. Each of two manuscripts, suggesting prescriptions for the reform of monetary and exchange rate management in Africa, was inspired by HIID experience in Africa and are based on case studies of four countries, though HIID has not worked in all of them.[20]

Third, and perhaps the most important linkage at HIID—overseas advisory work—inspires concepts and hypotheses for research. Sometimes the urgency of policy analysis prevents advisors from fully exploring the problems they must analyze, leaving interesting work to be done when the heat is off, or the advisor is back in Cambridge. Alternatively, a consultant's experience in the field may plant the seed of a research idea that matures over time. In other cases, similar policy issues in different countries suggest the need for cross-country comparisons that may not be appropriate material for work in the client country. (Increasingly, HIID has been asked to provide precisely that—cross-country comparisons that provide guidance to decision-makers in the host country.)

A large body of HIID research and publication has sprung from this well. The importance of rural public works in Pakistan during the late 1960s pointed the way to a worldwide research project, one of the first undertaken after HIID was formed.[21] HIID's pioneering advisory work on rural, small-scale banking has already inspired an influential monograph, with a book-length manuscript in process.[22] Advisory work in Indonesia in the early 1970s helped to create a major body of work on food policy analysis projects.[23] Projects in Kenya that dealt with district-level planning and budget management resulted in numerous articles and longer works on decentralization, capacity building, and the introduction of management information systems.[24] Rural public health projects in Africa focused attention on the financing of health care systems.[25]

Tax reforms, at first in Bolivia, then in Indonesia, and eventually in several countries, have led to books and articles that draw broadly applicable guidelines for tax policy in developing countries.[26] Articles on resource-based industrialization emerged from industrial planning work in Tanzania in the 1970s and an article on the inflationary impact of counterpart funds was the finishing touch to work in Kenya in the 1980s.[27] Experience with development strategy and economic reforms in a number of project countries gave impetus to an integrative, cross-country volume drawing lessons from Asian development for African countries.[28] It could be argued that, because much of the HIID's understanding about development has derived from field projects, most of the research has been heavily influenced by the institute's collective experience overseas.

Fourth, there is a reverse influence. Perhaps the best reason to conduct research at HIID is that research improves the formulation of public policy and the implementation of public management reforms, not only in the institute's projects but for development practitioners everywhere. All of the research projects mentioned above were intended to influence the practice of development, and many have done so. The nature and extent of this influence is discussed in a later section. Moreover, when professionals write for publication, they need to keep up with the literature. By establishing publication as a criterion for promotion, HIID ensures that its permanent staff understands developments in their field and is thus better equipped to provide technical assistance.[29]

Although overseas advisory projects have inspired and produced research for HIID, such projects have at times inhibited some kinds of writing. First, analysis or advocacy of strategies and policies under continuing consideration are sometimes too sensitive for public discussion by an advisor. Second, an insider's discussion of the forces behind recent policy decisions could jeopardize the positions of some decision-makers, although from a perspective of several years such material becomes less sensitive.

Such restraints have sometimes redirected HIID's research output. The institute has published a considerable body of work on countries like Indonesia and Kenya, where its involvements have been long and intimate. It has been possible to write about analytical questions and even to relate the histories of economic reforms without conflict. At a minimum, these projects provide examples for reference in cross-country research. Although some of these articles have dealt with controversial issues, HIID participants are capable of writing still more definitive and critical histories of development in these and other countries. The promise has always been that such histories will be written once HIID's involvement has ended and its principal clients have left their positions. In Indonesia, continued involvement—a sign of effectiveness—has put off this work. This has been less of an issue in Kenya. The institute, to fulfill its role as a research center, must provide mechanisms and funding for its staff to reflect and write on their experience in developing countries when the projects themselves have ended.

Multidisciplinary Research

The most important difference between HIID and its predecessor, the Development Advisory Service (DAS), was the expansion to include more disciplines than economics. The institute now embraces economists, political scientists, anthropologists, sociologists, education experts, physicians and public health experts, management experts, and others. The promise was that interdisciplinary activities, including research, would enhance understanding of development in ways that single disciplines cannot.

Much of HIID's research has involved more than one discipline. This work should be called multidisciplinary in the sense of incorporating the analysis of more than one discipline. The institute has not achieved the elusive target of interdisciplinary research in the sense that different disciplines merge to find a new way of analyzing problems. Some prominent examples of multidisciplinary research include:

- the rural policy studies in Indonesia, in which economists, anthropologists, sociologists, and others collaborated to study rice intensification programs, education, family planning[30] and other rural development activities;
- the Center for Policy and Implementation Studies (CPIS), where multidisciplinary teams worked on rural saving and credit[31] and commercial activities in the informal sector of Jakarta;[32]
- projects on tax reform and mineral contracts that involved, in addition to fiscal economists, lawyers, tax administration experts, and mining engineers;[33]

- work on public health costs and financing[34] and on AIDS research,[35] in which physicians and public health specialists were joined by economists;
- studies of drug-prescribing practices in Mexico, Peru, Indonesia, and Nigeria involving clinicians, anthropologists and epidemiologists;[36]
- rural household research in Malawi by a team including an anthropologist, a public health and nutrition specialist, and an economist;
- collaborative efforts on tropical forest management involving a plant ecologist, economists, zoologists and an anthropologist;[37]
- a book on El Salvador's educational policy featuring contributions from educators, economists, and a political scientist;[38]
- a study of competition policy in Zimbabwe involving economists, management specialists, a political scientist, and an antitrust lawyer; and
- a computer database on nongovernmental organizations, compiled and analyzed by a team of economists, a political scientist, and an anthropologist.[39]

Several of these studies span another divide: that between macroeconomic and sectoral policies and micro-impacts. The CPIS studies on the informal sector relate urban policies to microenterprise performance. The Malawi surveys measure the impact of macroeconomic stabilization on rural households. Forestry research in Southeast Asia and Central America concerns natural resource policies and the livelihoods of forest dwellers. Educational specialists at HIID have documented the impact of economic stabilization and the debt crisis, especially in Latin America and Africa, on provisions for education.[40]

These are all studies that could not have been done, or could not have been done as effectively, without contributions from different disciplines. Indeed, policy research generally invites multidisciplinary participation, because policy and public management issues are often complex and because legislating and implementing change require a range of skills. The institute has not erected any special mechanisms to encourage these interactions. The ingredients for collaboration have been the existence of HIID itself, which puts different disciplines under the same roof; a generally collegial atmosphere that has been characteristic of the institute; and an incentive structure that makes a direct connection between individual activity and institutional prosperity. In generating multidisciplinary research, HIID has at least partly fulfilled the expectations of its founders.

Nevertheless, the large majority of research at HIID is still conducted within a single discipline. This is not surprising, as single-disciplinary research remains the norm in most academic work. Within HIID, however, even traditional research generates some cross-fertilization of ideas as colleagues read and discuss each other's work. Proximity has helped HIID's political economists to reflect on economic policy and public management, for example, and has kept economists and managers abreast of developments in political science. These kinds of interactions can be multiplied across fields.

The Quantity of HIID Publications

There are a number of approaches to measuring the impact of HIID's research and publications. A crude start is to measure the quantity of output. Although quantity is a poor measure of research impact, it does give some measure of the extent to which the staff writes for publication. Over the years 1980 to 1993, HIID averaged close to fifty professional staff,[41] who produced an average 6.8 books or monographs each year over the thirteen-year period; if the output is restricted to books published by commercial and university presses, the average was 4 books per year. In addition, the same staff published on average 43 articles per year, not including working papers and reports. These averages have varied over those years with a dip during the mid-1980s but no discernible trend. During the last two academic years for which there are data, 1991–1993, there were seventy-three professional staff in HIID who published a total of twenty-one books (eleven by commercial or university presses) and one hundred and thirty-eight articles.

These averages must be seen in context. A Cambridge-based HIID professional who is actively engaged in the institute's work would spend close to 75 percent of his or her time engaged in funded project work, teaching, and unfunded administrative duties, leaving up to three months of the year for research. One comparison would be with a faculty member who teaches two or three courses a year, which may account for four to six months of time, and may be able to free four to six months for research, sponsored or otherwise. On the basis of numbers, the quantity of HIID's research output seems reasonable given the other duties of its staff.

Contributions to Scholarship, Teaching, and Practice[42]

HIID has three distinct audiences for its research output. First, as an academic organization, the institute attempts to reach scholars and to influence thinking on development. More than most academic departments, HIID tries especially to reach scholars in developing countries, to acquaint them with HIID work and to promote collaborative research and independent work by them. Second, the institute aims to contribute to the teaching of development in universities, foreign aid agencies, and private institutes by publishing textbooks and case studies. Third, in common with professional graduate schools, HIID writers try to reach practitioners of development, and thus to influence strategy and policy decisions and implementation.[43]

One indicator of the impact of HIID research on scholarship is the frequency of published citations by other authors. The names of thirty-three long-term HIID staff members with substantial published output were checked against the Social Science Research Index. Among the thirty-three, over the period beginning in 1980, the index lists 2,531 citations, an average 77 citations per person. Two of these writers had more than 300 citations over the fifteen years; two more had more than 200; and another four had over 100.[44]

These contributions are not associated with any single, focused set of concerns as, for example, Williams College was known for its research on import substitution during the 1960s, the University of Wisconsin's Land Tenure Center has been associated with its eponymous research, or the Institute for International Economics is known for its books on exchange rate management and trade. HIID has, instead, made identifiable contributions to the literature in a number fields, spanning several disciplines. This section discusses these contributions without attempting to assess HIID's impact.

HIID's impact on the teaching of development can be measured roughly by the sales of its texts and other books suited for classroom use and these will be noted where appropriate below.

It is especially difficult to gauge the impact on HIID's third audience, development practitioners, who do not generally write for publication. It can be said that the practice of economic development has undergone dramatic change over the past two decades. Propositions that had to be vociferously argued during the 1970s have become orthodox in the 1990s. Today's consensus among development economists, favoring market-based strategies, open economies and supporting economic reforms, was embraced by DAS economists in projects dating to the 1960s and has been at the core of HIID practice and research from the beginning. Thus HIID has been in the vanguard of changing development practice. However, much larger organizations, notably the World Bank and the International Monetary Fund, and a host of smaller ones have promoted similar approaches to development. HIID professionals have played a unique role as advisors and writers. They have taken positions, based on the chastening realities of experience, that differ, in ways noted below, from the orthodox neoclassical view. Nevertheless, HIID's writing on development has been like a few voices in a large chorus: although the institute's role has been distinctive, it may not even be sensible to ask how great its influence has been.

HIID has, perhaps, had a more distinctive voice in such development fields as education, public health, fiscal and public management, and political economy. In these areas the chorus is not so large and HIID's contributions have been more focused.

Instead of trying to evaluate HIID's impact on its three audiences, this section identifies the major clusters of HIID resource output and suggests the kinds of contributions made by each. This should at least suggest where to look for HIID's impact. The following classification of research and publications, though necessarily arbitrary and overlapping, is as convenient for the purpose here as any: (1) development strategy; (2) economic reform (including financial markets, small-scale credit, small-scale industry and food policy); (3) environmental and natural resource management; (4) educational effectiveness; (5) public health; (6) fiscal management (tax reform, budget management, project appraisal, management information systems, and decentralization); (7) other public management (integrated rural development, public enterprise management and privatization, capacity building and implementation); (8) political economy; and (9) gender and development.

Development Strategy

Development strategy is one of two organizing themes for much of HIID's research, the other being the closely related topic of economic reform. An impressive body of work has been published on development strategy. The book, *Economics of Development*,[45] now going into its fourth edition, has sold almost 60,000 copies since it first appeared in 1982, making this one of two leading undergraduate texts in the field. The institute has undertaken multi-volume studies of development in Korea, Taiwan, and Malaysia, of which the first (a ten-volume Korea study[46]) and the second Korea series (three volumes) have been published.[47] HIID has also published books and numerous articles on development in China,[48] Indochina,[49] and a recent volume applying the lessons of East and especially Southeast Asian development strategies to Africa.[50]

This work is written within the neoclassical paradigm that supports market-based, outward-looking development strategies. But HIID's adherence to neoclassical orthodoxy is not slavish. Authors have explored non-orthodox strategies, such as an emphasis on resource-based industrialization.[51] HIID writers were among the first to identify the extra-market elements that propelled Korean development in the 1960s and 1970s[52] and subsequent work on Asia continued to acknowledge the importance of government interventions in East and Southeast Asia. Analysis of foodgrain strategies in Asia started with the border price paradigm for rice pricing, but emphasized the need for stabilization that requires periodic deviations from world prices.[53] Adherence to market principles is only partly based on theoretical considerations and much more a consequence of pragmatism. To a considerable extent, HIID's exposure to policymaking and implementation in the field has convinced its economists that elaborate, disciplined government interventions are unlikely to work for long in most developing countries outside East Asia.

Economic Reform

Economic reform is the second major organizing theme for HIID research. HIID was advising on stabilization and structural adjustment a decade before those terms came into use and economic reform continues to be a mainstay of overseas work. Of all fields, economic reform represents both the strengths and the weaknesses of tying research to policy advising. Except for work on tax reform discussed below under fiscal management, HIID was slow to bring its experience into publication. *Reforming Economic Systems in Developing Countries*,[54] a collection of conference papers published in 1991, was the first systematic attempt to reflect HIID's experience in advising on structural adjustment. Other potentially important contributions have been written and some have been published, including a volume on stabilization and reform in The Gambia during the 1980s[55] and two more prescriptive books on monetary and exchange rate management in Africa.[56] Of course, several of the books on strategy noted above also deal extensively with economic reform.

HIID has participated in the reform of money and financial markets in both Asia and Africa. A number of case histories have been published on monetary and financial reforms in Indonesia,[57] Korea,[58] Asia in general,[59] and The Gambia,[60] while a volume on monetary reform in Africa is being revised for publication. In Indonesia, HIID has worked on legislation and regulations that would enable private pension systems to become factors in modern financial markets.[61]

HIID's distinctive contribution to both the practice and the literature in financial market development has been its pioneering work in rural, small-scale credit and savings institutions. HIID was instrumental in the development of the small-scale credit and savings facility in the Bank Rakyat Indonesia (BRI), now the largest facility of its kind in the world. A book and several articles have already appeared documenting this experience, with another book in preparation.[62] These publications have had a strong influence on the rural credit literature and are beginning to influence the design of small-scale lending schemes in several countries. The BRI program is distinguished from most rural and small-scale credit schemes in that it charges interest rates that fully cover costs and earn a profit for the bank, and is self-financed by attracting saving deposits in small amounts at market rates of interest. Work on rural financial markets has been extended to Africa as well.[63]

In the 1980s, HIID conducted a comprehensive research project on small-scale industry. In a recent publication, institute economists see no special virtues in arguments that justify the conventional approach to protecting and promoting small-scale firms.[64] In any case, that approach has not been demonstrably effective in promoting small-scale industrialization. Deregulation of markets is likely to have a more beneficial impact on small firms. Under the CPIS project during the 1980s, HIID carried out a multi-year study of the informal sector in Jakarta. Its major finding was that scavengers, pedicab drivers, and curbside vendors performed services that were in demand among the poor and were thus able to earn incomes well above subsistence levels.[65] A related body of work, contained in two conference volumes, explored the ways in which parallel markets soften the effectiveness of market and price controls, although at a cost in reduced market efficiency, and thus weaken the impact of subsequent market reforms.[66]

In food policy, HIID research has emphasized the critical role played by market forces in stimulating farmer investments to increase production and permitting consumer access to food. At the same time, the research has emphasized that "getting prices right" is not a simple matter of letting domestic prices equal border prices. Instead, governments must be actively involved in markets to stabilize basic food prices and correct the historic undervaluation in world markets and in development plans of agriculture's contributions to economic development. Countries that have managed these interventions effectively have grown much faster than those that have not.[67] HIID research has also been concerned about the impact of food policy and agricultural market reforms on the welfare of rural households.[68]

HIID's approach in these works is of a piece with its work on development strategy: orthodox but with a difference. The practical reasons for market-based reforms are emphasized, especially the impact of rent-seeking, the limited administrative capacities of many governments, the sometimes inchoate or hostile institutional base, and the need to concentrate efforts on a few essential and unavoidable interventions. Although prescriptions are consistent with neoclassical views, HIID writers recognize the difficulties of jumping from one regime to another when capacity is limited. Thus, for example, African central banks need to move slowly towards market-based monetary management, given that the markets for government paper are rudimentary and dominated by a few investors, mostly large banks. And protective tariffs need to be reduced, not only because economic efficiency demands it, but because tariffs required complex interventions to counter their impact on export industries.

Environmental and Natural Resource Management

Environmental and natural resource management has been a long-term focus for HIID, one that has intensified in recent years. During the 1970s and early 1980s, HIID consulted extensively on mining contracts, forest management, and the fiscal treatment of natural resource rents. Several articles, a book, and case studies reflect this experience.[69] The genesis of its current environmental program was a research project on natural resource management in Thailand, under the Thailand Development Research Institute, which identified policy problems affecting rainforests and fisheries.[70] During the 1990s, the institute developed a major program of research and advising on environmental management and is conducting long-term, on-site research on rainforest management in Southeast Asia and on indigenous people's use of the rainforest in Latin America.

Green Markets,[71] which has sold more than 5,000 copies since it was published in 1993, is one of a growing body of related publications that have been influential with environmental scientists and others.[72] These publications argue that the use of market forces—and prices that reflect opportunity costs—are more effective and efficient than direct controls as means of reducing environmental degradation and resource depletion. HIID is applying this prescription in advising several governments in Central and Eastern Europe on environmental policy.

Education

Educational (school) effectiveness in developing countries has been the focal point for research and advisory work by the institute's education group for the past decade. Field work, much of it done under the BRIDGES project, was carried out in Colombia,[73] Egypt, Honduras,[74] Jordan, Pakistan,[75] Sri Lanka,[76] and Thailand.[77] HIID's research strategy was a departure from the previously accepted approach: instead of using uniform research designs for all countries, the institute's investigators adapted their study designs to fit the needs of each country, based on extensive, preliminary field interviews.

Several strong results have emerged from this body of work. Physical facilities seem to bear no relationship to levels of student achievement. Nor are the personal attributes of teachers systematically associated with student learning, but higher levels of formal academic training of teachers do apparently improve student achievement. Active engagement of students in the learning process also contributes to achievement. Learning is enhanced by more hours of instruction in a year and greater concentration on a few subjects. These and other results have been widely disseminated, and have begun to influence education research and practice, through fourteen issues of the BRIDGES project's refereed journal, *Research Report*, eight articles in other professional journals and two books, [78] and a self-directed guide to education policy, *Framing Questions*,[79] published by HIID.

HIID research on educational effectiveness has also focused on the processes by which policy makers convert research-based information into policies that are then implemented. Studies carried out in Egypt, El Salvador, Honduras, Jamaica, Jordan, Pakistan,[80] and Paraguay have traced the generation, flow, and employment of information in the routine management processes of ministries of education; participated in the design and execution of comprehensive diagnoses of the education sector; and carried out research with high levels of participation by policy makers and functionaries in design and analysis. In each case the objective has been to understand how to use the research process to generate consensus about the issues and the best ways to address them. The results of this work have been published as books and monographs in four of the host countries and a cross-country analysis is contained in a book now in press.

Public Health

Public health research has centered on three topics: control of diarrheal and respiratory diseases, health systems reform, and the economics of disease and health care. HIID has sponsored an impressive body of research on the improved case management of diarrheal and respiratory diseases. Most of the work has been done by researchers in developing countries supported by the ADDR project staff. One hundred-and-twenty-two research studies have been completed and have produced 100 articles in the international literature.[81] Many more articles have been published locally. Project support has also generated seven doctoral theses. As part of the ADDR project, HIID staff have tracked the research capacity-strengthening aspects of the ten-year effort. The lessons learned from this experience were published in a special issue of *Social Science and Medicine.*[82]

Health system reform projects have generated another body of HIID research. In Cameroon, the primary health care system was drastically reformed, with the goals of improving quality and increasing utilization. User fees and a revolving drug fund were instituted to defray recurrent costs and improve availability of essential drugs. Published studies conclude that the introduction of multiple fees did not decrease utilization even among the poorest members of the society, because patients responded to a perception of improved quality of service, particularly in the availability of drugs.[83]

The economics of disease and health care became a central concern in the Mali rural health project, when it became apparent that health care delivery costs per patient needed to be an order of magnitude smaller than had been originally planned.[84] Since then, HIID researchers have published studies on improving the cost effectiveness of AIDS care in Puerto Rico,[85] the economic impact of AIDS and malaria in Africa,[86] the cost of illness among rural households in Burkina Faso,[87] and health care finance in Thailand.[88]

Although HIID's health program has not encompassed family planning, one member of its staff has been active over two decades in issues of the implementation and ethics of population control programs.[89]

Fiscal Management

Fiscal management, incorporating a cluster of activities at HIID, has generated some of the institute's most distinctive contributions to development. Of all economic reforms, HIID is probably most closely associated with tax reform. HIID (and DAS) have been the principal advisors and, in some cases, the implementers of major tax reforms in Bolivia, the Dominican Republic, The Gambia, Indonesia, Kenya, Lesotho, Malawi, Nepal, and Zambia. Descriptions of the work in Bolivia[90] and especially in Indonesia[91] have been a part of the tax reform literature for over a decade. Recent articles on property tax reform in Indonesia have added to these contributions.[92]

This body of work typifies most HIID writing on economic reform. The traditional approach—neoclassically based prescriptions for tax policy and structure—provides the background. But HIID goes beyond this perspective in two ways. First, in tax reform success is in the details and HIID's analysis delves beyond general rules to prescribe the crucial, detailed applications of principles. Second, HIID reformers recognized early on that good tax policy depended on good tax administration and focused their efforts on improving administrative practices. In recent years this has included the installation of computer-based systems. Thus HIID has been an innovator in tax reform in developing countries, has written extensively about its experience, and has influenced practice.[93]

The institute has also made contributions to the management of public expenditures. From 1970 to 1985, HIID and the University of Montreal undertook a study of the financing of recurrent costs of development projects, especially in the Sahelian region of West Africa but also in Kenya and other African countries. Researchers found that donors burdened host governments with ambitious projects whose subsequent operating costs could not be covered, wasting much public investment and other development expenditures. In the project report and related meetings with host countries and donors, HIID economists documented the need for stabilization and structural adjustment to restore fiscal soundness in the Sahelian region.[94]

Project appraisal has been a staple of HIID (and DAS) teaching and advising for almost three decades. The institute produced one of the early primers for developing countries, *The Appraisal of Development Projects*,[95] an Indonesian language text that has been widely used since it first appeared in 1985,[96] a still unpublished manual incorporating the developments in cost-benefit analysis for the past twenty years,[97] and a study of the parameters for project analysis in Asian countries.[98] Arising out of the fiscal work in the Sahel, the institute conceived and propagated the notion of an accounting price for uncommitted government funds absorbed or generated by development projects in conditions of fiscal austerity.[99] Through its texts, classroom teaching, and a long-standing summer workshop, the institute has played a major role in spreading the understanding and use of appraisal techniques.

In all of these fiscal reform activities, the introduction of computer-based information systems has been essential. HIID experts have advised on or managed the introduction of computer systems for most of its tax projects and for financial management in Kenya. Perhaps the single most important factor determining whether a computer-based reform succeeds is whether there is strong and continuous management commitment at all levels. The task is especially daunting because reforms must be implemented while the old system continues to operate. A second requirement is to build an appropriate information system in modules, rather than all at once. Modular change creates an iterative learning environment, fits a government's limited managerial capabilities, and begins to deliver results without long delays. A third need is organizational change. A computer-based information system is no substitute for the reforms needed to overcome organizational ineffectiveness and inefficiency; indeed, the computer system is likely to exacerbate these weaknesses.[100]

Public Management

Public management research at HIID has included work on rural development, decentralization, public enterprise management, privatization and capacity building in government. An early concern at HIID was rural development, with field projects in Sudan and Kenya and additional research interests in Botswana and Ethiopia. Institute advisors participated in and commented on the trend towards integrated rural development schemes of the 1970s, documenting the stresses placed on African bureaucracies and on local societies from the intricately designed, centrally directed schemes and arguing for a more decentralized, participatory approach.[101] HIID anthropologists in particular studied the interaction between local institutions in Africa and development policies, from land reform in Kenya,[102] to stabilization and structural adjustment in Malawi.[103]

Decentralization of government activities featured in two of HIID's longest-standing involvements. In Kenya, HIID worked to help strengthen district level planning systems and to implement a decentralized district focus strategy that transferred more responsibility to district personnel and emphasized the promotion of rural trade and production centers. Over the fifteen years of this project, institute advisors produced a number of publications.[104] In Indonesia, HIID helped to redesign the property tax system as a means of providing local governments with resources to finance local infrastructure and other services. Documentation of this experience[105] has led to work in other countries on fiscal decentralization.

Concerns about public enterprise management and privatization have, at different times in HIID's history, been high on the agenda. The Public Enterprise Workshop generated considerable teaching material, occasional overseas consultancies, and stimulated a number of publications.[106] From its work in developing countries, HIID has concluded that the performance of public service companies does not depend so much on the ownership of the enterprise as on the introduction of more market-oriented pricing policies, harder budget constraints, and the generation of competition.[107]

Privatization has been the focus of two HIID advisory projects in Russia, one advising on the massive privatization of state firms by issuing vouchers to the public in 1993 and 1994, and the second providing a legal framework for private enterprise. The lessons from the first of these are contained in a recently published book, *Privatizing Russia*, which argues that successful reformers must recognize privatization as a process of depoliticizing firms in the face of massive opposition, making the firm responsive to market rather than political influences.[108] In transition economies, privatization has also raised the issue of the pension schemes that were offered to workers but not funded by state corporations.[109]

HIID has frequently been directly involved in building capacity as part of its advisory projects. Research growing out of this involvement has focused on better understanding the range of advisory strategies and their relationship to capacity building, the design of human resource training programs, the constraints on effective utilization and retention of trained personnel in targeted government units, and the factors affecting the strengthening of overall institutional capacity of governments.[110] An HIID team recently completed a cross-country, comparative study of governmental capacity with the collaboration of local researchers. A companion volume to this one explores in depth the institute's experience in capacity building.[111]

Political Economy

Political economy spans HIID's involvement in all these areas of policy reform and implementation, from education and health to decentralization and public management, from macroeconomics to privatization. A prize-winning volume, *Public Choices and Policy Change*,[112] presents an analytic framework to integrate political and bureaucratic analysis into policy analysis. The framework is based on three questions: How do policy agendas get set? Why are some options chosen and others rejected? What kinds of political and bureaucratic reactions determine how policy is implemented? This research, contrary to most writing on political economy, emphasizes the possibility for change rather than the forces preventing reform. Case histories of some HIID projects were used in formulating the hypotheses discussed in this book.

This line of research has been extended in a book, *Challenging the State*, based on case studies of Mexico and Kenya that explore the capacity of states to deal with the economic and political crises of the 1980s and 1990s.[113] The studies show that, although governments have been undermined by the years of crisis, they have also revealed a capacity for innovation in their thinking, policies, political coalitions, and public institutions.

Gender and Development

Gender and development research at HIID has focused on rural societies in Africa and South Asia. Institute researchers have contributed to a new approach that considers gender—roles of both females and males—as a factor in research, policy analysis, and project implementation, rather than the traditional focus principally on women in development. Work has included critiques of the unitary household model, research on intra-household processes such as the earning and expenditure of income, development of bargaining models to capture these processes, and discussion of the form and significance of female-headed households.

Research has also been conducted on the impact on low-income women of development policies and programs as they interact with traditional kinship and marriage systems. Research in India and Bangladesh has dealt with the formation of different kinds of households, differences among households, family-based social security systems, and household strategies for coping with seasonality and drought.[114] Continuing fieldwork in Malawi has investigated the effects of economic reforms and agricultural commercialization on gender roles, family organization and women's rights to land.[115] And policies to promote women's work, especially micro-credit and micro-enterprise schemes, have been a focus of research in South Asia.[116]

Conclusion

This review of research at HIID suggests active involvement in research, a substantial publications record, and considerable impact across several fields of development. It is difficult to judge whether the institute has produced as much research, or made the impact, of which it is capable. The talent exists within HIID to engage in more research for publication if funding and the incentive structure were shifted in that direction. Similarly, there is a considerable well of knowledge, data, and ideas that could lead to published output, with funding and incentives. And the institute could be restructured to encompass more appointments based principally on research capacity.

The question is how to move in this direction while retaining HIID's structure as an academic institution devoted to practice, teaching, and research. It is this combination that makes HIID a unique resource at Harvard and produces research and publications that advance the understanding of development practice and theory.

Notes

The author is grateful to Faith Paul of HIID for gathering much of the material used in this chapter; and to many HIID colleagues who responded to my requests for help in completing references and synopses of their work.

1 Tomich (1991).

2 Robinson et al. (1993b).

3 Cole et al. (1980).

4 Panayotou (1991).

5 Myers (1988).

6 Trostle (1992).

7 Loera and McGinn (1992).

8 McGinn et al. (1992a).

9 Warwick and Jatoi (1994).

10 Cummings et al. (1992).

11 Raudenbusch et al. (1991).

12 Peters (1992).

13 Gray and Martens (1981).

14 Cole et al. (1980); Haggard et al. (1994); Stern et al. (1995).

15 Perkins and Roemer (1991).

16 McPherson and Radelet (1995).

17 Gray et al. (1990).

18 Kelly (1992).

19 Grindle and Thomas (1991).

20 Duesenberry and McPherson (1991); Duesenberry et al. (1994).

21 Thomas et al. (1976).

22 Patten and Rosengard (1991); Robinson (1992, 1994b).

23 Timmer et al. (1983); Timmer (1986c).

24 See, for example, Cohen and Hook (1986); Evans (1992); Lewis (1991); Smoke (1994).

25 Sauerborn et al. (1995b).

26 Gillis (1989); Jenkins (1991).

27 Roemer (1979, 1989).

28 Lindauer and Roemer (1994).

29 I am grateful to Louis Wells of Harvard University for this point.

30 Warwick (1986).

31 Snodgrass and Patten (1991); Robinson (1994b).

32 Robinson et al. (1993).

33 Gillis (1978); Gillis and Beals (1980); Jenkins (1991).

34 Gray et al. (1990); Myers (1988); Sauerborn et al. (1995b).

35 Henn and Myers (1988); Kouri et al. (1992).

36 See, for example, Paredes et al. (1995).

37 Panayotou and Ashton (1992).

38 Reimers (1995).

39 Grindle et al. (1989).

40 Reimers (1991).

41 Defined as Institute Fellows, Faculty Fellows, and other Fellows as well as Institute Associates, Research Associates, and Faculty Associates, but omitting Project Associates whose work does not generally involve writing for publication. The average number was 51.5; the number grew from 29 in 1980–1982 to 73 in 1991–1993.

42 This section is selective and illustrative only; it is not a complete review of the work published by HIID staff. The section is necessarily brief: the forbearance of HIID colleagues in accepting these terse summaries of their work is much appreciated.

43 At the Harvard University Business School, the criteria for promotion to tenure explicitly incorporate these three audiences and require a substantial impact on any two of them. (Communication from Louis Wells of Harvard University.)

44 The figures for individuals are substantially understated because the index only counts the first listed author and many HIID works have multiple authors.

45 Gillis et al. (1983, 1992).

46 Cole et al. (1980).

47 Haggard et al. (1994); Stern et al. (1995); Lindauer et al. (1997).

48 Perkins (1986); Perkins and Yusuf (1984).

49 Ljunggren (1993).

50 Lindauer and Roemer (1994).

51 Roemer (1979).

52 Jones and Sakong (1980).

53 Timmer (1991c).

54 Perkins and Roemer (1991).

55 McPherson and Radelet (1995).

56 Duesenberry and McPherson (1991); Duesenberry et al. (1994).

57 Cole and Slade (1992a).

58 Cole and Park (1982).

59 Cole et al. (1995).

60 Duesenberry and McPherson (1995).

61 Guerard and Jenkins (1993).

62 Patten and Rosengard (1991); Robinson (1994b); Snodgrass and Patten (1991).

63 Shipton (1992a).

64 Snodgrass and Biggs (1996).

65 Robinson et al. (1993b).

66 Jones and Roemer (1989); Roemer and Jones (1991).

67 Timmer (1986c, 1991c); Timmer et al. (1983); Tomich et al. (1995); Jenkins and Lai (1989).

68 Peters (1992).

69 Gillis (1978); Gillis and Beals (1980); Panayotou and Ashton (1989); Godoy (1990b, 1992).

70 Panayotou (1991).

71 Panayotou (1993).

72 Jenkins and Lamech (1992); Markandya (1993); Vincent (1992).

73 Loera and McGinn (1992).

74 McGinn et al. (1992a).

75 McGinn et al. (1992b); Warwick and Reimers (1996).

76 Cummings et al. (1992).

77 Raudenbusch et al. (1991).

78 See, for example, Warwick and Reimers (1995).

79 McGinn and Borden (1995).

80 Reimers (1993b).

81 See, for example, Henry (1994).

82 Trostle (1992).

83 Sauerborn et al. (1995a).

84 Gray et al. (1991); Gray (1986).

85 Kouri et al. (1991).

86 Henn and Myers (1988); Shepard (1991).

87 Sauerborn et al. (1995b).

88 Myers (1988).

89 Warwick (1982, 1994).

90 Gillis (1978).

91 Gillis (1989).

92 Kelly (1992, 1995).

93 Jenkins (1991).

94 Gray and Martens (1981).

95 Roemer and Stern (1975).

96 Gray et al. (1985).

97 Harberger and Jenkins (1991).

98 Jenkins and El-Hifnawi (1994).

99 Gray (1989).

100 Leonard et al. (1987); Peterson (1990a, 1991); Peterson et al. (1997b).

101 Cohen and Hook (1986); Cohen (1987); Cole and Huntington (1994).

102 Shipton (1988).

103 Peters (1992).

104 See, for example, Cohen and Hook (1986); Lewis (1991); Evans (1992); Gaile (1992); Smoke (1994).

105 Kelly (1992).

106 Mallon (1981, 1982).

107 Mallon (1984).

108 Boycko et al. (1995).

109 Jenkins (1992).

110 Cohen (1992, 1995).

111 Grindle (1997).

112 Grindle and Thomas (1991).

113 Grindle (1995).

114 Chen (1990, 1991).

115 Peters (1992, 1996).

116 Chen (1992, 1995c).

Part II

Structural Adjustment

In a number of countries, HIID has been involved in broad-based reform efforts designed to create a market-friendly environment. In these countries, success in one area of reform has led to efforts in other areas ranging from the design of financial systems, budget systems, and trade liberalization to legal reform and privitization.

3 Indonesia: Economic Policy Reform

Michael Roemer and Joseph J. Stern [1]

Harvard's involvement in economic policy reform in Indonesia is probably unique in the world. Work began in 1963 under the Development Advisory Service (DAS), the predecessor to HIID, and, with two major interruptions in the 1960s and 1970s, has continued until this day. During the peak of involvement in the late 1980s, Harvard managed as many as seven projects and had twenty resident advisors in Jakarta. HIID projects were broad in scope, dealing with major reforms of taxes, trade, and financial markets; rural small-scale banking; the economy of the informal sector; urban development; integrated pest management for rice farming; export agriculture; macroeconomic management; and overseas training of officials in the Ministry of Finance and state banks—to name only the most prominent issues addressed.

No single essay could do justice to the variety and depth of these advisory activities, yet a partial view would miss the rich matrix of relationships into which each project fell. To orient the reader, Figure 3-1 shows the Harvard projects undertaken in Jakarta from 1978—the genesis of the continuing involvement there—until 1995. The lines present, roughly, the genealogy of these projects.

This chapter covers those projects shown in the shaded areas of Figure 3-1: Fiscal Reform, Financial Policy Studies and Training, Customs and Economic Management, and Economic Analysis. The unifying feature of these projects is their concern with the major economic reforms carried out within the Ministry of Finance and the Office of the Coordinating Ministry for the Economy. The large-scale project of training in the Ministry of Finance and the State Bank Training project are treated in Chapter 18; the Center for Policy and Imple-

FIGURE 3-1
Harvard Projects in Indonesia, 1978–1995

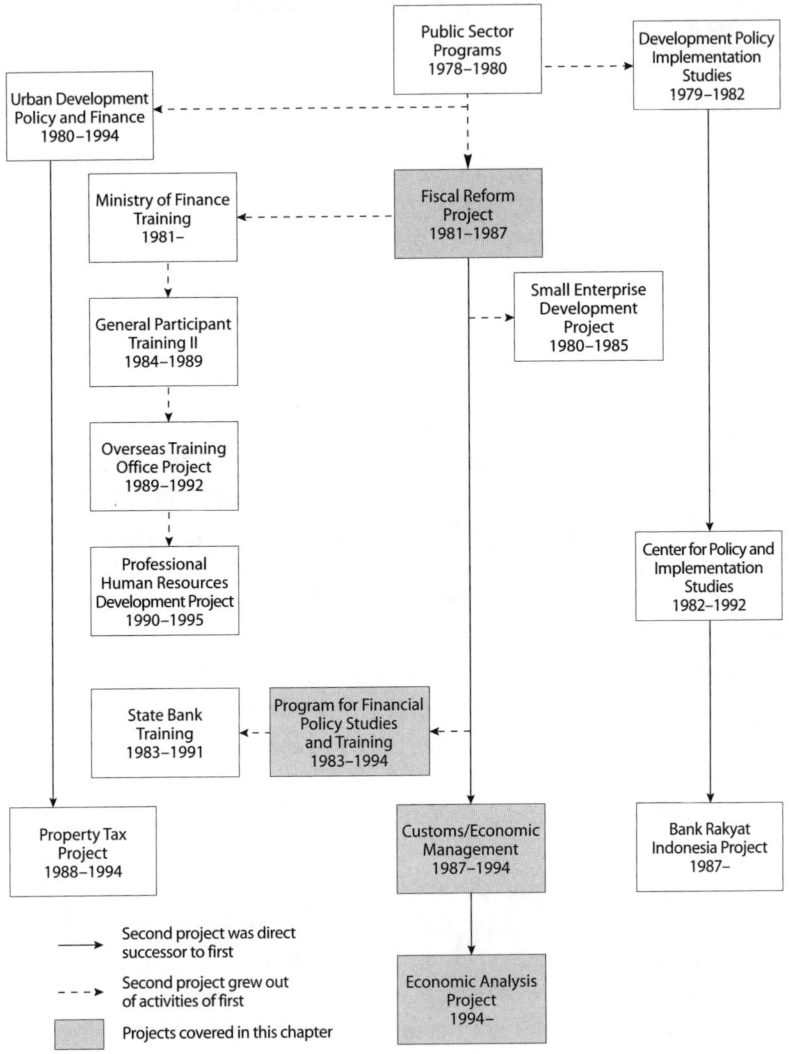

mentation Studies (CPIS) and its predecessor the Development Policy Implementation Studies (DPIS) are discussed in Chapter 17; the Small Enterprise Development Project and the Bank Rakyat Indonesia project are discussed in Chapters 11 and 12, respectively; and the Property Tax project and, to some extent, the Fiscal Reform Project are discussed in Chapter 7.

Origins

The DAS began its first project in Indonesia in 1963. This work stopped when President Soekarno ended relations with U.S. donors, including the Ford Foundation, which had supported the DAS team. In 1966, after the "new order government" had been established under President Soeharto, an experienced DAS advisor returned to Jakarta to work with senior government officials in drafting an economic stabilization program. In 1968, a full-scale advisory project began in the Ministry of Planning. HIID withdrew voluntarily in 1975, when the ministry reduced the presence of foreign advisors.[2]

Three years later HIID returned to Indonesia with a team of short-term consultants, under the leadership of an HIID Fellow, to analyze policy issues during the summers of 1978 and 1979. This scholar had been a resident in the Ministry of Planning project in the early 1970s, and had maintained a close relationship with senior Indonesian economic policy makers. The usefulness of these short-term studies paved the way for a more ambitious project—the DPIS. Begun in the summer of 1979, the DPIS project led, in turn, to the CPIS and the Bank Rakyat Indonesia project.

For the purpose of this essay, the Fiscal Reform Project (FRP) was the most important offspring of the summer studies of the late 1970s. The FRP began in 1981, after the Minister of Finance became convinced that oil prices had peaked and would decline in real terms, creating potentially significant fiscal and foreign payment deficits for Indonesia which, in the 1980s, received three-quarters of its tax and export revenues from oil. Focusing at first on tax reform, the work of the FRP later shifted to trade and industrial policy and macroeconomic management. These activities continued under the Customs and Economic Management (CEM) project, and since 1994 have been carried out under the Economic Analysis Project (EAP). While the scope of these activities and the project names have changed over time, these three projects essentially constitute a single activity for analyzing a variety of economic issues.

Harvard's presence in Indonesia under the FRP opened the possibility for other advisory relationships. One of the most productive was with an expert on financial markets, who had been with the DAS since the 1960s and had been a resident in the Ministry of Planning project. His continued involvement with financial policy issues in Indonesia led, in 1983, to the establishment of the State Bank Training project and the Center for Financial Policy Studies and Training, later renamed the Program for Financial Policy Studies and Training (PFPST).

In a more complex way, HIID's multifaceted presence in Indonesia made it possible to bring in a plant biologist, whose work led to the Integrated Pest Management (IPM) program. Located at first in the CPIS as a one-person advisory project, the IPM program was later transferred to the CEM project.

The economic development of Indonesia has intrinsic interest for a development center like HIID. Indonesia is the fourth most populous country in the world and is rich in natural resources. Yet the economy performed poorly throughout the 1960s and early 1970s. It seemed clear that better policies could improve the economic status of many poor people and establish a model to guide other countries. Starting in the late 1960s Indonesia's chances for economic improvement—and the desirability of working on policy reform in Indonesia—were enhanced by two developments.

First, a group of U.S. trained economists—the so-called "Berkeley Mafia"—had been given senior cabinet and government positions in the new order government.[3] These policy makers – also called the "technocrats" – were willing to implement new policy measures, and had a strong grasp of what would be politically acceptable and administratively feasible. The two leading figures in this group, who were also the most closely associated with the Harvard team over a span of twenty-seven years, were Professor Widjojo Nitisastro, who was Minister for National Development Planning, Coordinating Minister for Economic, Financial and Industrial Affairs, and eventually Senior Economic Advisor to the Government of Indonesia; and Professor Ali Wardhana, who was Minister of Finance, then Coordinating Minister for Economic, Financial and Industrial Affairs, and then Senior Advisor to the Government of Indonesia. For an economic policy advisor, it would be difficult to conceive of a more receptive working environment.

Second, the rise in oil prices, beginning in 1973, gave Indonesia an unprecedented inflow of resources for development. The mettle of the technocrats was tested early during the oil boom, when they had to deal with the threatened insolvency of Pertamina, the state-owned oil company. Having resolved that crisis, the technocrats gained the credibility that enabled them to convert Indonesia's oil wealth into sustainable development in a way that no other oil exporter was able to match over the next two decades.

Methods of Operation

HIID's economic reform projects in Indonesia were unusual for several reasons. First, the projects were financed entirely by the Government of Indonesia. This condition provided considerable flexibility for project management, eliminating many of the bureaucratic constraints often imposed by bilateral or multilateral donors. For example, the projects could—and did—recruit staff internationally, and the projects enjoyed considerable line-item flexibility, which made it possible to shift resources to activities as required. Then too, the government funding clearly indicated the value the technocrats attached to HIID's contribution. The government had the option of terminating HIID's economic reform projects, but it never did so.

Second, the scope of the work was extremely flexible. While a specific set agenda drove the FRP, the PFPST, and the IPM program for several years, even these projects—and especially the EAP and the CEM project—worked within broad terms of reference that left considerable scope for shaping the work program and for suggesting new issues of analysis. This allowed the projects to change direction and to recruit staff as priorities changed and as recommendations were either implemented or proved to be impractical or inappropriate.

Third, the projects enjoyed substantial direct contact with senior government policy officials. Such contacts were crucial in obtaining hearings for policy recommendations. Yet for some projects—the FRP, the CEM, and the EAP, but not the PFPST—these contacts also made it difficult to maintain close relationships with middle-level ministry staff (as discussed later in the section on staff development and institution building).

Fiscal Reforms

In early January 1981 the Minister of Finance requested HIID assistance in designing a thoroughgoing tax reform. He was convinced that the oil price, having reached a historic high in the late 1970s, would fall over the next few years. The tax reforms were meant to diversify the revenue base, remove a number of anomalies in the tax code, increase fiscal equity, and bring the Indonesian tax structure in line with modern international practices. Although the reforms stressed changes in the legal structure of taxation, the minister recognized that successful reforms would also require basic changes in taxation procedures, administrative machinery, and the tax information system. The reforms introduced a value-added tax and a taxpayer identification system that were the basis for the revised income tax. These approaches, in turn, called for improvements in the computer-based information system available to the Ministry of Finance—a system HIID helped to design and develop. To support the reforms, the ministry agreed to invest heavily in an overseas training program for tax officials, which was managed by HIID.

The FRP began in late January 1981. Over the next three years, and under the direction of an experienced HIID fiscal economist, a multinational team of twenty-five experts—economists, accountants, data processing experts, and lawyers—worked directly with ten Indonesian officials. All of the work was coordinated in Cambridge until January 1982, when a recent graduate of the Harvard Law School and the John F. Kennedy School of Government was placed in Jakarta. Her role, aside from professional input, was to facilitate the work of the short-term consultants and to maintain regular contact with the HIID coordinator in Cambridge.

By mid-1983, the group had presented a full complement of reform proposals to the government. The centerpiece of these proposals was the introduction of a low-rate, simplified value-added tax and the reform of the personal and corporate income tax codes. The government studied the package intensively, from April to October, and then presented it to the Parliament late in 1983, when it was enacted.[4]

The tax reforms had a dramatic impact on the Indonesian economy. Coupled with improvements in tax collection, the new system raised non-oil taxes, in relation to non-oil gross domestic product (GDP), from under 6 percent in 1982–1983 to an estimated 10 percent in 1993–1994.[5] The tax reforms helped to reestablish fiscal stability, which had been lost in 1986 when oil prices declined precipitously. The improvement in the efficiency and equity of the tax system contributed to the subsequent revival of the economy. The widespread use of taxpayer identification numbers increased the possibility that those above the minimum income level would be taxed, and the relatively high income-tax exemption ensured that the lowest income groups would not be taxed. There is relatively little doubt that HIID's work on tax reform in Indonesia was a cost-effective technical assistance project, with high returns to the government and society.[6]

Financial Market Reforms

The fiscal reforms of the early 1980s were part of a broader program—now known as the gradualist structural adjustment program—that included the reform of both international trade and domestic financial markets. The first step in financial reform took place in 1983, with the deregulation of the state-owned banking system; this was followed five years later by changes in money and capital markets and in insurance and private pension systems. As background to these reforms, Indonesia revised its approach to monetary and exchange rate policies.

Shortly before the 1983 reforms were introduced, HIID was asked to undertake two projects for the Ministry of Finance. The PFPST at first assisted policy makers in the development of policies, laws, and regulations for the financial system as a whole, and also provided a forum for research and policy analysis. Later, the focus shifted to reforming insurance and pension systems and to providing training and technical assistance for capacity building. The second project, State Bank Training, supported financial reform by enhancing the capacity of the country's largest banks to manage their portfolios in the increasingly competitive market.

HIID managed the PFPST with one-to-four resident advisors in Jakarta. But it also built up a roster of consultants, many of them eminent authorities in fields such as capital markets, insurance and pension system regulation, actuarial sciences, monetary policy, management information systems, investment funds, and custodial operations. These consultants regularly visited Jakarta, and established productive relationships with Indonesian officials. Both the resident advisors and the consultants worked with Indonesian counterparts at many levels.

Between 1983 and 1988 the government took bold steps toward reforming financial markets. These reforms reduced bureaucratic controls over financial activity more than any controls thus far implemented in Asia.[7] The major thrust of the PFPST was to help the government to reduce its direct controls over the financial system and to replace these controls with market-driven forces, coupled with prudential regulations for stabilizing the system and protecting the public.[8] The government understood that competition could improve productivity but could also destabilize financial markets. Balancing these concerns was important if the financial markets were to attract funds and to allocate these funds efficiently to the industries made newly profitable through other economic reforms.

Although the implementation of prudential regulations moved in tandem with deregulation, it became clear early on that the implementation of regulations would lag behind. The regulation of capital markets became controversial, and the legislation and regulation of pension and insurance systems took several years to implement. Nevertheless, by the end of 1994 these instruments were substantially in place and staff was well trained to manage them. A recent World Bank study states that the Indonesian law on pensions schemes may become a standard for developing countries.[9]

To date, these reforms have not caused any major financial crises, although there have been failures of individual banks and securities companies. The state-owned banks, not yet fully prepared for the newly competitive environment, have seen their share of total banking assets fall from 77 percent in 1983 to 41 percent in 1993, while their non-performing loans were reportedly 15 percent of the total loans outstanding. But these adjustments have not led to runs on the banking system as a whole or to capital flight from Indonesia

These reforms successfully expanded and diversified financial intermediation, as Table 3-1 shows. The ratio of financial assets to GDP doubled from 1969 to 1982—a period just before the introduction of the reforms—and then almost tripled to 128 percent over the next eleven years, partly because of these reforms. By 1993, equity and debt securities—which were negligible as late as 1987—had risen to 23 percent of GDP, and insurance and pension assets had doubled to 7 percent of GDP.

TABLE 3-1
Total Financial Assets and Ratios to GDP (in trillions of rupiah)

Institution	1969	1982	1987	1993
Banking system	0.6	26	74	278
Non-bank financial institutions		1	4	12
Insurance and pension systems		1	5	23
Equities and bonds				72
Total	0.6	28	83	385
Percent of GDP	23	45	67	128

Source: Biro Pusat Statistik, Jakarta, Indonesia.

The distinctiveness of the Indonesian experience has added to HIID's understanding of financial reforms in general. Indonesian policy makers did not insist on advanced planning for all aspects of reform. Rather, they consistently pursued an opportunistic approach, at first reducing controls and then implementing prudential regulations as fast as possible, to respond to the obvious pressures of newly competitive markets. HIID monitored the deregulation process and pressed for prudential measures as needed.

Indonesia, by making its currency convertible in 1970 and by liberalizing its capital account in the late 1980s, has demonstrated that the conventional wisdom on sequencing—that the capital account should be deregulated last—may not be necessary or even effective. Indonesia appears to have benefited from convertibility used as a tool for making credible the government's macroeconomic policies and for attracting foreign capital.[10] But in another respect the lesson from Indonesia is conventional: because financial liberalization preceded the deregulation of some monopolized sectors of the economy, it has probably contributed to a misallocation of finances and a concentration of wealth in Indonesia.

Trade Reforms

After the tax reforms had been implemented in 1983, the FRP turned to trade issues, especially the impact of protection on efficiency in agriculture and industry. This quickly led to the realization that reforms were also needed in the day-to-day administration of the Directorate-General of Customs and Excise. These activities would constitute the bulk of the work of the FRP and the CEM project until the early 1990s.

In the mid-1980s Indonesia provided considerable protection to domestic producers through high tariffs, import licenses, and other restrictions that raised domestic costs and destroyed export potential. Compounding these difficulties were a series of bureaucratic bottlenecks, focused on investment licensing and the clearing of cargo. The "high-cost economy," a phrase coined at that time, conveyed the widespread perception that Indonesia's emerging comparative advantage in manufacturing was being suppressed.

Initial efforts to deal with the high-cost economy relied on the usual broad studies, some done by HIID, of industry-wide effective rates of protection that attempted to measure economic efficiency.

But broad indicators had little force in convincing skeptics that the trade regime should be reformed. Recognizing the need to provide much more specific information, the project developed a research style that produced either firm-level or subsector case studies through interviews and data collection. These studies offered detailed and well-documented information—sometimes referred to as "horror stories"—on the rents earned by those protected through tariffs and import restrictions. The studies provided the evidence the economic technocrats needed to persuade their colleagues, and eventually the president, that protection in Indonesia was excessive and that it would continue to stifle industrial exports and growth.

Pressures for trade reform were building as oil prices fell and Indonesia's neighbors—Malaysia, Singapore, and Thailand—showed that outward-looking policies could power rapid growth in manufactured exports. Aid donors to Indonesia, too, were delivering an insistent message that deregulation and tariff reform were essential to move Indonesia into its post-oil-boom phase of development.

Impelled by these pressures, the government announced a series of deregulation packages that lowered tariffs, reduced reliance on import licenses and quotas, and generally reduced effective protection. The resulting improvements in the tariff structure are illustrated in Table 3-2.[11]

The FRP (and later the CEM project) also dealt with customs reform. Although it was generally acknowledged that clearing goods through customs was difficult and time-consuming, the project provided considerable evidence of the costs of such delays to importers and potential exporters. Customs procedures were antiquated, from the lack of computers to the legal basis for assessing duties and levying penalties for malfeasance.

In 1985 the government began a two-pronged approach to customs reform. First, it contracted with a private surveying company to take over the most basic customs function—the assessment of duty values. Second, the government committed itself to the reform of the entire customs machinery.

The FRP (and after 1987 the CEM project) provided a number of resident advisors and numerous consultants (many of whom had previously worked for Canadian customs) to assist in the design of new customs legislation and procedures. Harvard also placed a number of Indonesian customs officials in overseas training programs. Recognizing the government's long-term objective of restoring the

TABLE 3-2

Changes in Tariff Schedule and Protection Rates (percentage)[a]

	Pre-1985	1985	1988	1990	1992
Average tariff rate					
Unweighted	37	27	24	22	20
Weighted by:					
(i) import value	22	13	15	11	9
(ii) production	29	19	18	17	13
Average effective tariff[b]	n.a.	4.9	5.1	6.2	4.8
Effective rate of protection					
(i) total	n.a.	n.a.	16[c]	14	13
(ii) manufacturing	n.a.	n.a.	68[c]	59	52

[a] Including surcharges.

[b] Revenues from import duties in relation to non-oil imports, fiscal years.

[c] For 1987.

Source: World Bank, *Indonesia: Sustaining Development.* 25 May 1993: 66 and 70.

Directorate-General of Customs and Excise to full control over imports, the advisors and consultants worked to strengthen the administrative capacity of the customs agency. The Customs Fast Release System (CFRS) was developed to provide speedy customs clearance, using computerized valuation techniques. With the adoption of the CFRS, the Directorate-General of Customs and Excise began to reclaim some of the valuation work from Société Générale de Surveilliance S.A. (SGS). Modern customs legislation was prepared, as were new regulations.

These HIID projects also worked with BAPEKSTA, the Indonesian agency created to provide duty drawbacks and exemptions to exporters. Project staff helped to establish procedures that gave the agency the primary role of promoting exports, instead of monitoring claims for duty rebates. BAPEKSTA quickly became a major export promotion tool and one that earned a deserved reputation for efficiency.

The evaluation and analysis of trade policies were institutionalized through the creation of *Tim Tarif* (Team Tariff), an interdepartmental group that recommended, assessed, and monitored tariff reforms. The CEM project worked closely with *Tim Tarif.* Initially much of the data on tariffs and non-tariff barriers were maintained in the

CEM project office. As trained staff returned to the Ministry of Finance, it became possible to turn the database over to *Tim Tarif*, which eventually functioned independently of the CEM project.

No serious observer of Indonesia's economic history could doubt that the trade reforms of the 1980s were critical in generating the rapid growth of manufactured exports, which began in 1986 and continues to date (see Table 3-3). What was HIID's role in these reforms? It is difficult to be certain how influential the Harvard's advisors were; it is probably safe to say that the FRP and the CEM project provided much of the evidence needed to persuade the government to make changes in the trade regime.

Over time some reform measures became entangled in bureaucratic infighting. As a result, as of 1995 the reform agenda is incomplete and some of the reforms have been eroded. In recent years, the Directorate-General of Customs and Excise has increased its role in clearing goods, even though there is considerable evidence that its management capacity has not been sufficiently strengthened or improved. Recognizing that further customs reforms were becoming increasingly difficult, HIID suggested, and the Ministry of Finance agreed, that no further assistance in this area would be provided after 1994.

BAPEKSTA's duty drawback system also came under attack, motivated by a concern that the agency's monitoring was growing lax and that too many unjustified rebates were being granted. Eventually the government followed advice, some from HIID consultants, to tighten rebate procedures. However, the adjustments implemented by BAPEKSTA tended to tip the balance from an export support agency towards a revenue-monitoring agency. When exporters com-

TABLE 3-3
Share of Industrial Exports in Total Exports, Indonesia: Selected Years (in millions of US$ and percentage)

Year	Industrial Exports (US$ millions)	Total Exports (US$ millions)	Share of Industrial Exports in Total Exports (%)
1987	6,696	17,136	39
1990	11,879	25,675	46
1993	22,944	36,823	62
1995	29,328	45,418	65

Source: Biro Pusat Statistik, *Statistik Perdagangan Luar Negeri Indonesia* (various years), Jakarta, Indonesia.

plained about the change and its impact on their operations, the government created new mechanisms that allowed exporters access to duty-free imports, including duty-free zones, manufacturing in bond, and a new customs clearance facility. HIID did not play a role in these constructive initiatives. Despite these efforts, concerns remain that Indonesia's competitive position may have been eroded and that further administrative reforms are needed.[12]

Economic Management

When the Fiscal Reform Project ended in 1987, its functions were taken over by the Customs and Economic Management project, which continued to work on trade reform issues. Like its predecessor, the CEM project had from four to six resident advisors, with the capacity to draw upon consultants for specific tasks. As its name implied, the CEM project began to concentrate more on issues of macroeconomic management. The project developed Indonesia's first debt database and model, providing a first overview of Indonesia's total debt by source and terms and constructing a software program that could project future repayment obligations. The debt model was effectively employed to analyze the benefits of using some of Indonesia's own financial resources to repay some high interest debt, and to assess the cost of additional foreign borrowing. Eventually this work was supplanted by efforts at Bank Indonesia which, with BAPPENAS, the planning agency, were the primary information sources on debt.

CEM project staff continued to assist in the extension of the deregulation process for both trade and investment. Advisors prepared preliminary analyses of proposed trade reform packages and conducted retrospective analyses of their impacts. A number of consultants studied the investment approval process and recommended steps to simplify it. The ensuing reforms contributed to the marked increase in foreign direct investment that proved essential to the development of Indonesia's manufactured export base.

CEM project advisors developed and revised over time an energy pricing model that linked domestic prices to world prices, providing estimates of the implicit subsidies or taxes in the official fuel prices. This model was useful in projecting the budgetary impact of various energy price scenarios. The project also provided analyses to the technocrats that helped them to manage the reforms that, by 1994, had converted subsidies on many fuels into taxes compensating the state budget for environmental and other costs associated with road transport.

In 1989 Harvard received a request for short-term assistance in public enterprise management. The CEM project was able to bring out a consultant who eventually was asked to stay on as resident advisor to work with the Directorate-General for State Owned Enterprises. This work led to the development of criteria by which enterprise performance could be monitored and management rewards could be set. In addition, efforts were made to develop a database on public enterprise sector performance, tracking both costs and profits or losses of the numerous state-owned enterprises. Consultants worked with some state enterprises, prominently including the national airline, Garuda, to assess their investment programs and revenue structure.

CEM was one of the most flexible projects ever executed by HIID, permitting the government to employ advisors whose mandates strayed far from HIID's original terms of reference. One of its most important contributions, integrated pest management, is described in the next section. Other consultants covered topics from higher education reform to industrial policy, resource management, and pension policy. At times, the resources available under the CEM project were used, with the concurrence of the senior officers of the Ministry of Finance, to support work at other government institutions, such as the CPIS.

Integrated Pest Management

From 1987 through 1994, the CEM project was the base of operations for a plant biologist who was the leading advocate of, and the government's senior advisor on, integrated pest management (IPM). The IPM program developed in Indonesia, which included the training of 350,000 rice farmers in new methods of ecology-based pest control, won international acclaim and became a model for environmentally responsible pest management programs in seven other Asian countries.

The story of HIID's involvement in pest management began in 1983 with a study, under the DPIS project, of the BIMAS (rice intensification) program. During this study, HIID consultants made contact with an Austrian plant biologist, living in Java, who was concerned that the genetic uniformity of the rice varieties being introduced under BIMAS made the national crop particularly vulnerable to attack by pests, notably the brown planthopper. The growing practice of using chemical pesticides to control infestations—encouraged by government subsidies—made the problem worse, because the pesticides killed both planthoppers and their predators and permitted the genetically less complex planthoppers to evolve more rapidly and to develop immunity to the pesticides. The continuing use of pesticides would put the entire rice crop at risk.

There was a solution to the problem: encouraging farmers to use natural methods to control planthoppers, and establishing conditions under which the pest's insect predators could thrive and reestablish a natural balance. This meant ending the use of fertilizer and quickly creating a national program of integrated pest management, which had never been done before in any rice-growing country. However, policy makers first had to be convinced of the magnitude of the problem and the soundness of the solution. Early in 1985, the plant biologist became a consultant to the newly established Center for Policy and Implementation Studies, where he worked with other international and Indonesian consultants to alert the technocrats to the danger. Armed with further studies from CPIS, the government became committed to the new approach. In November 1986 President Soeharto made a dramatic announcement, issuing a new decree that banned the use of pesticides and adopted integrated pest management for Indonesia.

Moving to the CEM project in 1987, the IPM advisor worked with the Indonesian Government (spearheaded by BAPPENAS) and with advisors from the Food and Agriculture Organization (FAO) to further develop IPM methods and, crucially, to establish training programs, at first for trainers and then for farmers. A highly unorthodox, fifteen-month trainers' course was initiated, in which trainees did all the farm work while learning rice ecology, IPM, and adult education methods. Trainers then entered university for a semester and emerged with diplomas in IPM. Training of about 100,000 farmers began in late 1989. In 1991 the new IPM program received a stern test with an outbreak of white-rice stemborers in West Java. Over 350,000 farmers and 80,000 school children were mobilized, and the outbreak was controlled without pesticides, only a few months after the first farmers in that area had been trained.

By 1994 IPM had become well-established in Indonesia, and HIID's resident advisor left the country. His unique contribution over a decade owed much to HIID's long-term and broad-scope involvement in Indonesia. Harvard advisors provided access to policy makers and lent support that got the pesticide problem on the government's agenda before greater damage was done to the rice crop. The broad scope and flexibility of HIID's presence made it easy to keep the IPM advisor involved in developing the program over a decade, something that might have been difficult under a more traditional, aid-funded technical assistance project.

Transition: A Reduced Presence in Indonesia

The CEM project was scheduled to end in 1992 but was extended (within the original budget) to carry the project through to the installation of the new cabinet in March 1993; the PFPST was extended through 1994. Between the presidential and the parliamentary elections and the installation of the new cabinet, the work of HIID became a matter of public debate. In February 1993, an opposition party member of Parliament suggested that the government's monetary policy was masterminded by foreign consultants, charging that "the Ministry of Finance is unable to free itself from foreign influence." The Minister of Finance denied the allegation, noted that the Harvard group was broadly international, and added that the Ministry of Finance was assisted by numerous advisors, including many Indonesians.[13] Despite this strong public support, the attacks continued and gained strength through the next two months. Essentially the attacks focused on three issues. First, the HIID advisors, unfamiliar with local customs and traditions, were unduly influencing government policy. Second, the work done by the HIID advisors could be equally well-performed, and at lower cost, by local consultants. And third, the reform policies had worsened Indonesia's income distribution.

To suggest that the advisors influenced policy was to confuse the role of analyst with that of decision maker. The advisors certainly provided analysis of various policy issues, but decisions on what policies to implement and when were entirely in the hands of the government. Moreover, Harvard's voice was not the only one decision makers heard. Undoubtedly, the pool of younger, well-trained, Indonesian economists had grown over the years, and many of them were already engaged in policy analysis. The larger question, whether Harvard's role in Indonesia had advanced or retarded the development of Indonesian analytic capacity, is addressed in a later section.

The third charge was misguided. The evidence available, which is on expenditure rather than on income, shows that since 1987 expenditure shares have increased for both the richest and the poorest 20 percent of Indonesia's population. Though some wealthy people have undoubtedly become richer, many of them have done so in sectors untouched by the reforms. Economic growth since 1986 has contributed to job creation and to an increase in real wages for middle- and low-income groups. Most important, growth has led to a substantial reduction in the incidence of poverty, from 40 percent in 1976, to 17 percent in 1987, to 14 percent in 1993, and to 11 percent in 1996.[14]

As the public debate about HIID's role continued, Harvard's resident project coordinator sought guidance from all the economic ministers and the senior Indonesian advisors. He informed them if at any time it appeared that HIID's presence was detrimental to effective policy formulation, the institute would withdraw without question. The consensus was that the press attacks reflected a number of internal Indonesian issues, none of which would be resolved by ending HIID's presence. Consequently it was decided to remain, although continuing attacks in the popular press and weekly magazines made it difficult for the advisors to work effectively.

In March 1993 a new cabinet was installed and the attacks ceased, nearly immediately. After a few weeks, the government decided to continue the association with HIID but that henceforth the CEM project would be responsible to both the State Coordinating Minister of Economic, Financial, and Development Supervision and the Minister of Finance, rather than the Minister of Finance alone, while the PFPST would remain in the Ministry of Finance. In May 1994 the EAP began under a contract that ends in June 1998. With the exception of a small remaining presence in Bank Rakyat Indonesia, the EAP is the only remaining Harvard project in Jakarta. The PFPST closed its doors in December 1994, as its advisors and officials of the Ministry of Finance agreed that Indonesian staff were now capable of carrying on the financial market reforms—particularly in pensions and insurance systems—without a continuing Harvard presence.

The EAP continues many of the activities of the CEM project, and can cover any residual activities in financial market reforms. The EAP has also begun to focus on new concerns, such as the persistence of Indonesia's inflation rate, even in the face of budgetary and monetary restraints, and the appropriate means of managing an open-capital account in an era of increased international capital flows. As in the past, the ability of the project to respond to new issues remains one of its strengths and continues to make work in Indonesia so attractive to HIID and the staff of the EAP

STAFF DEVELOPMENT AND INSTITUTION BUILDING

The FRP, the PFPST, the CEM project (including the IPM program), and the EAP have provided influential analyses that supported numerous economic reforms in Indonesia. To what extent have the projects also served to train and strengthen the Ministry of Finance and the State Coordinating Minister's office?

Institution building and staff development can be carried out in a number of ways. One approach is for foreign advisors and consultants to work directly with counterpart staff. Alternatively, or additionally, training programs can be used to develop and strengthen staff. And having designed and implemented new analytic methods or management systems, the project staff can then transfer these tools to ministry staff. An evaluation of HIID's staff development efforts within the Ministry of Finance is complex and differs by project. The FRP, the CEM project, and the EAP have worked without counterparts, reporting directly to the senior economic policy makers; direct on-the-job training of counterpart staff has not played an important role. The PFPST not only worked closely with Indonesian staff, but also had capacity building at the top of its agenda. All projects promoted formal training, and both the fiscal and the financial reform projects were closely associated with massive overseas training for ministry and bank officials.

When the FRP was established in 1981, it was agreed that a massive overseas training effort would be needed to prepare tax and other ministry officials to manage the new system and to provide the core senior staff of the finance ministry over the next two decades. The resulting Ministry of Finance Training project was a bold, innovative program that prepared Indonesian staff—at first in Jakarta and then at the Economics Institute in Boulder, Colorado—in both economics and English, and then placed and monitored them in graduate programs, mostly in the United States. At first, HIID was reluctant to become involved in large, dedicated training programs. But it soon became evident that overseas training would become an essential support for continuing economic reforms and a major activity for both the Ministry of Finance and HIID. Similar thinking guided the establishment of the State Bank Training project as an adjunct of the PFPST. The fundamental contribution of capacity building made by these projects is discussed in Chapter 18 of this volume.

Both the fiscal and the financial reform projects also conducted training seminars in Indonesia, designed to provide background in policy analysis to specific directorates of the ministry, especially in the fields of trade policy, public enterprise management, and insurance system regulation. From 1979 (before the FRP project began) to 1982, HIID conducted fifteen intensive seminars on monetary economics, mining and mineral taxation, urban development, foreign investment, and international trade. During the 1980s, the PFPST mounted eleven monetary and financial policy courses and ten training courses in insurance and pension system reform, all in Indonesia, some taught in both Indonesian and English, plus two pension scheme training courses in Canada. The PFPST and the CEM project also conducted continuous informal training sessions in the Ministry of Finance.

The PFPST devised a number of imaginative overseas training experiences, including ten on-the-job, month-long field examination programs at regulatory commissions in four countries; five observation tours at regulatory commissions in Australia and Canada; two data-gathering tours on property appraisal and capital market operations in Asia; two high-level finance courses in New York; two pension scheme training courses in Canada; ten English courses; and three long-term overseas training programs, including internships for the trainees in private companies.

These training activities have done much to strengthen the capacity of the Ministry of Finance. In the early 1980s, the ministry was superbly staffed at the most senior levels, but had little analytic capacity at the intermediate and junior levels. The current situation is vastly different. There are numerous younger staff members capable of managing new regulatory systems and of providing the ministry with data and analysis relevant to economic policy. The growing institutional capacity of the ministry is one reason that HIID advisors currently are called upon less and less to work on day-to-day tasks.

HIID's economic reform projects have pioneered the use of junior expatriate staff to assist the project team. Such project assistants have been Harvard graduates who have completed an MPP or a two-year MPA program at the John F. Kennedy School of Government, or graduate students in Harvard's Economics Department who have completed all Ph.D. requirements except the dissertation. Project assistants, who receive modest salaries and few benefits, have been extremely cost-effective in supporting the work of the projects' resident advisors. They have also worked effectively with the junior staff of the Ministry of Finance, and have effectively run some of the informal training seminars. A number of project assistants have worked as counterparts to the junior ministry staff.[15]

Aside from training, the economic reform projects have enhanced Indonesian capacity in economic analysis through the transfer of analytic tools, developed by HIID, to ministry and other staff. The most prominent examples are the trade databases, especially the import duty and licensing database, the customs fast release system, the debt service model, and the IPM system, all of which were discussed above. During the 1990s, the focus of financial reforms was to establish modern regulatory systems in pensions and insurance within the ministry's Directorate-General of Monetary Affairs.

Thus it is not correct, as some Indonesian and many outside observers have alleged, that HIID's economic reform projects made no effort to train counterpart staff and have done nothing to transfer knowledge or technology. Massive training has taken place and considerable transfer of technology has occurred through programs developed by the FRP, the PFPST, and the CEM project.

This mistaken impression may be traced to the lack of direct Indonesian counterpart involvement in the FRP, the CEM project, and the EAP. This came about partly because it was judged that the work on tax reform could not be widely shared, except by the senior staff from various ministries and departments who were fully involved in the tax reform work. After the tax reforms had been implemented, it would have been possible for the EAP and the CEM project to move toward a more traditional technical assistance style, working with counterparts and under the direction of various Director-Generals, rather than reporting directly to the most senior members of the ministry. At various times senior officials considered this option. But the response was generally that the existing arrangement served the ministry well, that the work needed to be done quickly, and that this would be best served by having the advisors concentrate on analysis rather than on staff development issues.[16] While it was never suggested that relations with junior staff should not be encouraged, it was clear that reporting responsibility should be directly to the senior staff.

The PFPST followed a more traditional pattern. Although its advisors maintained ready access to senior officials in the ministry and elsewhere, the project worked under the Director-General of Monetary Affairs and involved Indonesian staff in many of their activities. Indeed, in pensions and insurance system reform this arrangement was essential for establishing the new regulatory procedures. The PFPST engaged more than thirty young Indonesian professionals for varying lengths of time to work alongside resident advisors and consultants as researchers, computer specialists, and trainees.

Assessment

HIID's economic reform projects in Indonesia essentially have served as an economic "think tank" for the Ministry of Finance. They have been successful for several reasons. First, HIID has been able to supply an exceptionally able and experienced group of advisors, many of them long-term members of the institute, and to draw on a large pool of talented consultants. For this, the impressive resources of Harvard have been important. Second, these advisors and consultants have owed allegiance strictly to the Indonesian Government. Because Indonesia funded the work, no foreign assistance agencies played a role in the selection or guidance of the Harvard teams. Third, the Harvard teams have brought an international perspective, and access to worldwide information and analysis, that was not readily available to the government from within Indonesia. This perspective has defined HIID's role in tax reform, financial reform, debt analysis, trade issues, investment deregulation, prudential regulations for pensions and insurance systems, and a host of other topics.

The limitations of Harvard's role and contribution must also be acknowledged. The four economic reform projects were strictly advisory. Even though this function included both policy design and implementation, HIID did not supply managers, and its advisors did not make the decisions. Moreover, in many cases the government sought advice from other expatriate and Indonesian experts on the same topics. These included the international donor agencies as well as resident advisory teams from other organizations. HIID has been an important and influential contributor to economic reform in Indonesia, but by no means a dominant force. The institute has worked for some of the most senior, successful, and respected policy makers in the developing world. It has been their wisdom and political acumen that has determined the course of Indonesian development. HIID has been fortunate to be one of several supporting players.

Notes

1 Based in part on conference papers by David C. Cole and Betty F. Slade; by Wolfgang Linser; and by Joseph J. Stern and Michael Roemer.

2 This early history is covered in Mason (1986).

3 The term "Berkeley Mafia" is used loosely here to identify a group of senior economic officials, not all of whom attended the University of California but who all shared common views about economic management. Most of the others were educated in graduate schools in the United States.

4 The property tax legislation was not enacted until January 1986. HIID assisted Indonesia's Directorate-General for Taxation, under a separate project that began in April 1988.

5 *Statistical Yearbook of Indonesia,* various issues. Biro Pusat Statistik, Jakarta, Indonesia.

6 Gillis (1984).

7 White (forthcoming).

8 These reforms are spelled out by Cole and Slade (1991).

9 World Bank (1994b).

10 Cole and Slade (1992b).

11 The early trade reforms are discussed by Barichello and Flatters (1991).

12 In early 1995, HIID completed a study of export potential for Indonesia's Ministry of Industry (now the Ministry of Industry and Trade) which covered a number of sectors and made recommendations on additional policy measures to support the export drive.

13 *Jakarta Post,* Friday, 18 February 1993.

14 Calculated from *National Socio-Economic Survey* (SUSENAS), various issues. Biro Pusat Statistik, Jakarta, Indonesia.

15 The various economic projects have also served as "clients" for students of Harvard's John F. Kennedy School of Government writing their Policy Analysis Exercise. Some of these exercises have proved extremely valuable and have been passed on to the senior officials of Indonesia's Ministry of Finance.

16 In 1991, the HIID advisor on customs reform moved part-time into Indonesia's Directorate-General of Customs and Excise, though remaining formally in the Ministry of Finance. The new arrangement proved difficult when the inevitable differences of view emerged between the ministry and the director-general, placing the advisor in an untenable position.

4 Kenya: Advice and Training

John M. Cohen and Stephen B. Peterson[1]

Technical Assistance will be needed in Sub-Sahara Africa for many years to come in virtually all sectors of the economy, if Africa is to reach anticipated development goals in a timely fashion.[2]

Africa...has perhaps received more bad advice per capita than any other continent.[3]

Between 1976 and 1995, the Government of Kenya was a major focus of HIID's technical assistance. During that period HIID implemented four large-scale projects. These were multi-year projects that used resident advisors contracted by the government and funded by aid agencies. The projects provided advisory services and training on economic policy and planning, revenue and budgetary policy, agricultural policy, information technology, and financial management, among others. The history of these projects is instructive for the objectives pursued and the insights provided on the current debate on how aid agencies can build capacity in the public sector in Africa.

As discussed at length later in this chapter, HIID carried out four major projects in Kenya:

- The Technical Assistance Pool (TAP) project was carried out from 1977 to 1992, within various ministries, including the Ministries of Agriculture, Livestock Development, Supplies and Marketing, Planning and National Development, and Finance. The TAP project ended in late 1992, but was in effect extended by a follow-on project known as the budget component of the second Agricultural Sector Adjustment Operation (ASAO II) program, which ended in May 1994.

- The Budget and Economic Management Project (BEMP) was implemented from 1990 to 1995, within the Ministry of Finance.
- The Tax Modernization Project (TMP) began in 1990 and in 1994 was extended to 1997; it is based in the Ministry of Finance.
- The Rural Planning Project (RP) was carried out from 1976 to 1985; it was succeeded by the Resource Management for Rural Development (RMRD) project, which completed its activities in 1992. Both projects were based in the Ministry of Planning and National Development.

History, Design, and Objectives of the Projects

The invitation to HIID to assist the Government of Kenya came from Harris Mule, who in 1976 was Deputy Permanent Secretary in charge of statistics and planning in the Ministry of Finance. The initiative was supported by another Ministry of Finance officer, Francis Masakhalia, an economist who, like Mule, was a graduate of Harvard's Mason Fellows Program. In 1970, Mule became Permanent Secretary of the Ministry of Finance. Masakhalia subsequently became the Permanent Secretary of the Ministry of Planning and National Development. Both men held these positions until they retired from public service, Masakhalia in 1983 and Mule in 1986.

The importance of having Harvard-associated godfathers, such as Mule and Masakhalia, guiding HIID projects over this long period cannot be over-emphasized. Mule, who for much of the time Harvard was involved in Kenya, was one of the most influential economic policy makers in the government and a strong advocate of using qualified and experienced expatriate advisors in the public sector. In the words of biographer David K. Leonard:

> He [Mule] had a major influence on the way Kenya has shaped its rural development efforts, and he shares the credit for the economic policies that make Kenya one of the most prosperous African states today.[4]

Mule conceived both the TAP and the RP projects. After HIID bid for and won these projects in 1976–1977, Mule and Masakhalia assisted in their implementation and in ensuring funding. Because HIID advisors had close and productive relationships with these and other senior government officials, HIID was able to work in the key public sectors of finance, planning, and agriculture.

All projects were fully financed by aid agencies through so-called "host-country" contracts.[5] The proposal to use this type of funding and contracting modality in Kenya came from Mule, who wanted to ensure that the advisors working on the proposed projects would be loyal to the government and not beholden to the aid agencies providing funding. As conceived, the contract for each project would be between the government and the supporting aid agencies. A second contract would be entered into by the government and the organization selected to execute the project. While the aid agencies resisted this double-contract approach, eventually Mule's proposal was accepted.

The host-country contract approach worked satisfactorily. After Kenyan officials and aid agency personnel agreed on the project design, a contract was executed. The government was responsible for tendering and awarding implementation contracts; aid agencies would participate in the review and award process. Usually the government's decision prevailed. Under this approach, the government contracted directly with HIID. The host-country contract approach ensured effective oversight, evaluation, and payment. More important, insulated by the double-contract mechanism, HIID advisors had more potential to be trusted and committed to the government's objectives than would have been possible with the typical contract between the aid agency and the contractor. As a result, the host-country contract approach was used for the subsequent extensions of the TAP and the RP projects, as well as for the BEMP and TMP contracts.

These projects assigned high priority and substantial resources to building the capacity of the government's economists, planners, statisticians, and financial managers. The projects differed in the tasks carried out, the systems developed, the equipment provided, and areas of training. The RP and the RMRD projects concentrated on strengthening district and sectoral planning in the Ministry of Planning and National Development. TAP's advisors worked on strategy formulation, project design, and management systems in the Ministries of Agriculture and of Livestock Development, whereas BEMP's advisors concentrated on strengthening financial management systems in the Ministry of Finance. And TMP's advisors focused on reforms in tax policy and administration in the Ministry of Finance.

These projects pursued a wide range of training and capacity-building strategies. Substantial resources were allocated to training, which varied by project but often included long-term master's level training, short-term specialized training overseas, regional diploma training, local-level workshops, seminars, and in-house training. Collectively, the projects trained more than one hundred government officers to the master's level in economics and planning; several hundred government officers took part in short-term overseas programs, and thousands of government officers and staff attended local workshops and courses on such topics as tax implementation regulations and budget preparation, district planning techniques, and microcomputer and software use.[6] For example, by May 1994, the RMRD project had trained over 3,000 Kenyans in microcomputer use at the Kenya Institute of Administration through a program established, staffed, and equipped with project funds.

Project efforts to build professional and technical capacity in the ministries served had similar outcomes. Briefly, both HIID and the aid agencies supporting the projects were concerned about the government's inability to retain in the targeted ministries those individuals trained at the master's level. Low salaries, inadequate benefits, poor senior manager leadership, poor prospects for career advancement, and ample employment opportunities in the higher paying private sector were, as in most African countries, the major causes of low retention.[7] But, as discussed later in this chapter, the short-term and local training strengthened the capacity of the targeted ministries ultimately to do the work for which the HIID advisors were initially responsible.

The projects were generally successful in carrying out their advisory tasks. Evaluations by the government and aid agencies document the projects' major contributions to helping senior decision makers formulate and adopt economic strategies, sectoral policies, planning systems, management systems, and other activities. However, implementation of these strategies and policies was frequently inadequate, a problem that will be discussed later in this chapter.

HIID's advisory work in Kenya resulted in a substantial number of publications that have contributed to the development literature. These studies were of high quality because they were done by professionals focused on concrete problems, solutions, and lessons.

Description and Evaluation of the Projects

The Technical Assistance Pool Project and the Budget Component of the Second Agricultural Sector Adjustment Operation Program

The Technical Assistance Pool Project

The TAP project, implemented in several phases from 1977 through 1992, provided policy and management advisory services and training to the agriculture ministry, which in 1980 was split into two ministries—the Ministry of Agriculture and the Ministry of Livestock Development. The project received funding from a shifting consortia of aid agencies comprised of the World Bank, the United Nations Development Programme (UNDP), and bilateral aid agencies including Canada, Germany, the Netherlands, Sweden, and the United States. The use of multiple aid agencies diversified the funding sources and lessened the influence of a particular donor on the project. Throughout its lifetime, the project emphasized advisory support and training for economists of the Development Planning Department, which was located within the Ministry of Agriculture.

To understand the constraints the TAP project faced in building capacity for policy analysis in the agriculture sector, it is useful to consider the origins of the Development Planning Department. The proposal for this department originated in the late 1970s with Mule, then in the Ministry of Finance but slated to become the Permanent Secretary of the Ministry of Agriculture. Mule wanted to ensure that the Ministry of Agriculture would have an effective policy-making unit. Because the initiative for the department did not come from the Ministry of Agriculture, the department was located outside this ministry, with its head reporting directly to the Permanent Secretary. The department's head and staff were employed under a poorly administered scheme of service for economists, directed by the Ministry of Finance (and later by the Ministry of Planning and National Development). Issues of staff promotion, for example, were the responsibility of the Ministry of Finance. These arrangements limited the department's institutional strength and increased the vulnerability of its staff.

From the beginning, TAP's numerous economic advisors were, as planned, involved in agricultural strategy formulation, price policy system development, and project design and implementation. However, during the first few years of the project the two management and budgeting advisors met stiff internal resistance. This situation changed in the early 1980s when microcomputers were successfully introduced in the budgeting area of the Ministries of Agriculture and of Livestock Development, resulting in increased management advisory work. As a result of the adequate progress in planning and budgeting, TAP was extended in 1986 for a second phase. This phase, and subsequent phases, involved a smaller number of advisors, who focused largely on management, budgeting, and price and marketing policy.

The TAP project formally ended in December 1992 and, in January 1993, its management and budget component was converted into a new HIID project for which HIID had successfully bid: the budget component of the ASAO II program. This program focused on financial management, budgeting, and accounting. Computerization accompanied the procedural reform and integration of budgets and accounts. This phase ended in May 1994.

The importance of the TAP project to the agriculture and livestock sectors was magnified, because these sectors were a focal point of aid agency-supported policy and management reforms, many of which were tied to structural adjustment reforms and involved major changes in agricultural policy and management practice. The TAP project, which included both policy and management assistance, was one of the principal resources the government used to formulate these reforms.

HIID advisors and their Kenyan counterparts contributed to the agricultural and livestock sectors component of several five-year national development plans and to strategic policy papers. The sessional papers on national food policy (1981) and on economic growth (1986) provide examples of good policy work that received different government responses.

The 1981 food policy sessional paper addressed the country's food production and marketing problems. This paper set forth an officially approved strategy to maintain self-sufficiency in the main foodstuffs, so that Kenya could feed its citizens without using scarce foreign exchange for food imports, achieve a calculated degree of security of food supply for all areas of the country, and ensure that the distribution of foodstuffs would provide all people with a nutritionally adequate diet.[8] HIID advisors were not involved in implementing the paper's strategy, largely because the government never seriously intended to give it financial or manpower support.

The 1986 sessional paper on economic growth provided a long-term framework for economic policy, which became the blueprint for Kenya's development strategy throughout the late 1980s and early 1990s.[9] A senior HIID macroeconomist was a principal architect of the work. The paper outlined an economic strategy for coping with the kinds of external economic shocks that occurred in the late 1970s and for promoting growth and employment for Kenya's burgeoning population. Specifically, it proposed: (1) a stronger budgetary policy to increase the productivity of government investments and services in the face of severe fiscal constraints; (2) a strategy to promote a balance between rural and urban sector development; (3) the increased role of the "informal sector" in employment creation and income growth; (4) strategies to achieve food security, income growth, employment creation, and export expansion within the agriculture sector; and (5) measures to open up the economy and intensify Kenya's structural adjustment in modern industry and trade.

The TAP project also helped to establish a more timely and systematic annual price review of commodities whose prices, by legislation, were set by the government. Although political objectives still influence price setting, beginning in the early 1980s a consistent and economically sound framework has underscored the analysis and recommendations of prices by the targeted ministries. Border price standards were established for tradable commodities. Although unforeseen exchange rate adjustments complicated the exercise, throughout much of the decade the government-adopted prices provided economic incentives for farmers.

The annual price review exercise was a useful learning-by-doing environment for the younger Kenyan economists. In addition, more senior officials learned to use economic analysis for proposing price levels. The exercise, nevertheless, contained shortcomings. For example, the exercise could not predict the budget costs of policies for maize price stabilization, and covered only producer prices. Although the exercise called attention to the consumer price implications of its recommendations, the government often ignored these lessons. Consumer prices were set through another process, outside both the Ministry of Agriculture and the Ministry of Livestock Development.

Throughout the duration of the TAP project, HIID advisors and their counterparts addressed numerous commodity and marketing policy issues, resulting in policy papers on cereals marketing, cotton processing, pyrethrum policy reform, and payment arrears to several small-holder coffee farmers, among others.

In the late 1980s the government adopted market liberalizing policies, which reduced the need for price setting. The experience gained under the TAP project in evaluating the structure and performance of these publicly administered markets provided input to the liberalization process, and helped public managers to anticipate problems that would occur during the transition from public to private marketing arrangements.

Project preparation and evaluation was another TAP project activity. HIID advisors and their Kenyan colleagues worked together on the government's preparation of the World Bank funded Training and Visitation Extension Project. Further, they assisted the government in evaluating irrigation projects, cutting back over-designed schemes, developing investment programs to improve milk marketing and processing, and contributing critical input for decisions to modify the agriculture ministry's most expensive and problem-plagued investment, the Bura irrigation project. TAP advisors also helped to formulate and strengthen the design of the government's Arid and Semi-Arid Lands Program. They worked with the National Cereals and Produce Board to introduce information technology and computers for the management of food stocks. However, these large-scale investments were not successful, partly because of the politicization and rents connected with the management of that parastatal.

TAP advisors had difficulty in getting the target ministries to consider their proposed management reforms and systems. This was largely because of the frequent transfers to other ministries of the senior officers with whom they worked, a practice used extensively by the head of the administrative cadre, a Permanent Secretary in the Office of the President. The officers heading up the budgetary and account departments in the target ministries were risk-averse and poorly trained, and resisted budgetary reform proposals that did not come directly from the Ministry of Finance. As a result, between 1977 to 1981 the recommendations of TAP's three management advisors were either largely ignored, or weakly tested and then withdrawn.

The situation greatly improved in 1982, when TAP advisors, recognizing the benefits to the government of microcomputers, introduced these methods into the budgetary departments of the target ministries.[10] The introduction of microcomputers coincided with the beginning of a protracted period of macroeconomic adjustment in Kenya. Prior to the 1981–1982 financial year, budget allocations from the Ministry of Finance were regularly exceeded by the large ministries, such as agriculture and livestock development. Beginning in 1981–1982, it became difficult to fund these expenses through "supplemental" budgets, because of Kenya's macroeconomic problems and its agreements with the International Monetary Fund (IMF). Kenyan senior managers in the target ministries began to rely more on the TAP project and its growing management information systems for preparing and modifying budgets and monitoring expenditures. TAP advisors also helped to introduce development objectives and a more problem-solving approach to rationalizing project commitments within annual and forward budgets. The reforms in financial management introduced in the agriculture sector under the project were extended to the Ministry of Finance through the seconding of TAP's budget advisor to that ministry.

The Budget Component of the Second Agricultural Sector Adjustment Operation Program

The budget component of the ASAO II program, implemented from 1993 to mid-1994, completed many of the management initiatives launched by the TAP project and introduced management information systems. For Kenya's public sector, budgets and accounts were now linked procedurally with computers, providing finance staff with an up-to-date view of the financial position of the Ministries of Agriculture and Livestock Development.[11] After nearly three and one-half years of effort, personnel management records were now computerized,[12] giving these ministries an accurate list of all staff.[13]

Considerable work was also done on improving financial management in the agriculture sector. As the target of a structural adjustment operation, the sector was selected to receive improved levels of recurrent cost financing and emphasis was given to improving the position of the ministry in that area.[14] The project also contributed to the work of HIID's Public Investment Program based in the Ministry of Finance.[15]

The budget component of the ASAO II program continued TAP's commitment to training in the agriculture sector. The project initiated an innovative day-release program for accountants to gain professional certification through local training institutes; over sixty staff participated in this program. To ensure that its field staff understood the financial regulations and principles of financial management, the Ministry of Agriculture conducted eight one-week-long regional training sessions throughout the country. Collectively, the project trained over five hundred staff of the Ministries of Agriculture and of Livestock Development and established an important dialogue between field staff and headquarters staff. The participation of representatives of the Office of the President and the Ministry of Finance strengthened the training program, providing those institutions with an understanding of both the financial constraints faced by field staff and the appropriateness of financial policies and procedures.

When the budget component of the ASAO II program ended in May 1994, HIID's Kenyan contract staff were retained under personal services contracts with the government, financed by the World Bank under the ASAO II program. They are responsible for maintaining existing information systems, completing systems under development, and designing new systems. As of June 1995, the contract staff were still working in the Ministry of Agriculture, thereby sustaining and even expanding the initiatives of the budget component of the ASAO II program.

The Budget and Economic Management Project

The Budget and Economic Management (BEMP) project emerged in 1990, mainly from the work of a TAP management advisor, who during the mid-1980s assisted the finance and budget officers in the Ministries of Agriculture and Livestock Development and was later seconded to the Ministry of Finance to help the Budgetary Supply Department strengthen the management of the national budget. The BEMP was carried out until 1995. [16]

The financial reforms initiated in the Ministry of Finance, at first by TAP's management advisor and then by four BEMP advisors, were complemented by the work of the RP and RMRD projects. For example, the use of microcomputers for budgeting, done under the RP, provided the Ministry of Finance with a computerized budget for improved financial management.[17] The BEMP project provided advisory assistance and training in budgeting, macroeconomic forecasting, public investment planning, and aid management.

BEMP's budget advisor helped the Ministry of Finance to implement its budget rationalization program. Launched by the government in 1986, this program sought to change trends in the composition of public expenditures and to bring about a more efficient use of financial resources. Specifically, this program aimed to: (1) improve resource productivity in the recurrent and the development budgets through resource allocation in accordance with well-defined priorities; (2) strengthen the planning and budgetary processes in the Ministry of Finance and in line ministries and districts, so as to institutionalize the productivity improvements and implement these through the normal budgetary processes; (3) increase the contribution of user fees and other non-tax revenues; and (4) obtain donor contributions for increasing aid on soft terms and for structuring external assistance. To achieve these objectives, the budget advisor assisted the ministry's staff in containing the deficit and improving budget procedures.

To improve macroeconomic policy and strengthen the reliability of the budget process, a BEMP advisor, specializing in quantitative modeling techniques, helped economists in the planning ministry to restructure the computerized Kenyan macroeconomic policy model. The advisor also periodically reported on the balance of payments, advised the central bank on treasury auctions, and assisted the central statistics bureau on the annual economic survey.

The project's third major activity was the design and implementation of the public investment program, which supported the work of the budget rationalization program. In addition to BEMP advisors, the work on the investment program involved HIID advisors from the RMRD project and the TAP/ASAO II projects.[18] At the time the investment program was introduced, Kenya had many government and externally funded development activities under way, and a weak project planning system. Since 1990, the public investment program has strengthened linkages among government financial and planning institutions, improved collection and processing procedures for obtaining information on projects and their funding, supported decision-making on public budgetary issues, reduced the number of development projects, and helped to launch the project cycle system in the planning ministry. In 1994, the public investment program was transferred from the finance ministry to the planning ministry, because it was basically a planning exercise. Despite extensive training efforts, this program has not yet been fully embedded in the government's project cycle system. (A former BEMP advisor is working to achieve this under funding from the United Kingdom's Overseas Development Agency.)

The fourth major initiative of the BEMP project was the work on improving the management of external aid and government loans. A management advisor assisted the External Resource Department of the Ministry of Finance to better manage external aid contracts and to coordinate and implement aid-agency agreements. Working with Kenyan managers and economists in the department, BEMP's external resource advisor reviewed the department's management information needs and outlined an action plan for developing computerized information systems, covering hardware and software requirements, training, and equipment. During the final year of the BEMP project, the advisor worked with the head of the External Resource Department to implement the recommended action plan, and the department's staff were trained in accounting, computer management, and records management.

The BEMP project also involved the provision of training for government officials. The work included master's-level training at overseas institutions, short-term training locally and abroad, and local seminars on financial management.

The Tax Modernization Project

From 1985 to 1989 Cambridge-based HIID professionals carried out two short-term studies of Kenya's tax system, funded by the World Bank. The first study reviewed existing and alternative tax and administrative policies in the Ministry of Finance's departments for income tax, sales tax, and customs and excise, and considered a strategy for computerizing the work of these departments. The second study reviewed alternative strategies for income and sales tax policy and administration, and provided advice on sales tax enforcement procedures. The group also assisted the government in developing tax policy options and possible administrative improvements in its tax system, which were proposed in the 1988–1989 budget speech to Parliament by the Finance Minister and Vice President.

The Tax Modernization Project (TMP), which emerged out of this work, was contractually two projects: a tax policy reform project, funded by the World Bank, UNDP, and the United States Agency for International Development (USAID); and a customs system reform project funded by the African Development Bank. HIID carried out its TMP activities under a subcontract with the firm of Peat Marwick.

These tax system reform projects have provided advice and assistance to the government on tax policy, the development of a tax policy unit, the development of tax databases and models, training in tax analytic methods, and overall coordination of the tasks. Support for this work has involved administrative reform and computerization of the income tax, the value-added tax (VAT), and the custom and excise systems. The TMP project advisors have worked with the Department of Customs and Excise to improve its ability to facilitate trade and enhance revenue collection, strengthen investigation and audit capabilities, implement administrative procedures for export promotion, and manage the computerization of its work.

HIID advisors and their Kenyan counterparts have made progress in tax policy reform, including the reform of trade policy and export development, with significant rationalization of tariff rate structures. For both the income and the VAT, the tax base has been significantly expanded and rates have been reduced and standardized.[19] A tax policy unit has been established in the Ministry of Finance, charged with supplying reports, analyzing tax policy issues, and developing and coordinating the overall tax revenue system.

Considerable progress has also been made in the enhancement and automation of management information systems. These accomplishments include procedures for revenue estimation and tax assessment, legislation allowing for taxpayer identification numbers, a self-assessment system, and procedures for examining taxpayer books and records. A proposal was approved to establish a revenue authority, which would provide flexibility to overcome the constraints to modernizing the tax administration.

HIID has also assisted the Customs and Excise Department to promote revenue protection and enhancement and to facilitate trade liberalization and export development programs. Progress has been made on rapid release clearance procedures and selective examination of goods. New procedures have been developed for transit and warehouse control, investigations, valuations, and communications. The improved processing and control measures have helped the government to exceed current revenue targets.

Training has been a major activity of the TMP. Kenyan customs officials are being trained in policy and planning, valuation, investigation, intelligence, and computerization. On-the-job training has been provided through the continuous interaction of HIID advisors and the tax department staff engaged in policy formulation, budget preparation, and computer database development. Local workshops aimed at transferring tax management skills central to the sustainability of project gains have been held on such topics as VAT structures, export promotion through duty/VAT exemption, tax policy analysis and revenue estimation, pension design, administration and taxation, import duty and VAT database production and use, income tax policy, LAN operation and management, and insurance taxation. Officers in the Ministry of Finance and in the three revenue departments have been trained in such areas as tax policy and legislation, computerization, administration, management, and training of trainers. Collectively, several thousand Kenyan officials have been involved in these skill enhancement activities. In addition, the TMP has helped the training school of the Department of Income Tax to revise and strengthen its curriculum and operations; training for the head of the school was arranged to strengthen these reforms.

The Rural Planning Project and the Resource Management for Rural Development Project

The Rural Planning Project

The RP project (and its successor the RMRD project) shared the overall objective of assisting the planning ministry to strengthen decentralized provincial- and district-level planning. Carried out from 1976 to 1985, the RP project sought to improve rural planning especially at the district level, to develop and assist in implementing the rural trade and production center growth strategy, and to consolidate and extend the microcomputer initiatives. The project's first phase focused on understanding the problems facing the widely differing rural areas of Kenya, preparing strategies to address the problems identified, identifying and designing investment projects to meet the standards of central financing agencies (including aid agencies), drawing the strands together in the form of multi-year development plans for providing input for the national five-year plans, and undertaking continuous review of the progress of the plan and its implementation. These efforts were supported by training courses for district-level government personnel, along with staff development for the Rural Planning Division, which was the central unit of the planning ministry administering the RP project.

HIID assistance helped to develop the division from its embryonic form in 1976, to a well-established body by 1981. Subsequently, during the second phase of the RP project and the two phases of the RMRD project, the division continued to gain strength and to offer sound technical support to both its home ministry and its field officers. When HIID assistance to the planning ministry ended in mid-1992, the Rural Planning Division had been raised to the status of a department and comprised several divisions.

Within the task of improving rural planning, the RP project assisted the government in five areas: famine relief, the Rural Development Fund, the Arid and Semi-Arid Lands program, the production of district plans, and the District Focus Strategy.

To help the government avoid famine among the population as a result of the 1983 drought, HIID advisors worked with senior government officers to formulate a crisis program. Working with the TAP project advisors on tracking production and shortfall and identifying options for obtaining overseas food grains, the RP project advisors developed a microcomputer system to track the import and distribution of food grains throughout the country. Kenya experienced virtually no famine as a result of these government efforts to manage the crisis.[20] This was a major achievement, considering that Kenya's shortfall relative to demand was far higher than that faced, for example, by Ethiopia during its disastrous 1983–1984 famine.

A second activity of the RP project was strengthening the operation of the Rural Development Fund, which ran from 1974 through 1992. When launched, the fund represented the only source of discretionary funding then available to districts. As such, it was a major vehicle for the districts in their efforts to direct rural development initiatives. Specifically, the fund sought to broaden the base of rural development efforts, to include the mobilization of local initiatives in project identification and implementation, and to enhance district-level responsibility for development planning, project implementation, management of development resources, and local procurement of goods and services. Although the implementation of the fund rested with a team of advisors (mostly field engineers) funded by a consortium of Scandinavian aid agencies, HIID advisors played a contributive role in improving these activities.

A third activity of the RP project was the formulation, in 1979, of the Arid and Semi-Arid Lands program and the design and implementation of the district-specific integrated rural development projects it generated. This program was a major government-led initiative to induce development in the drier and more marginal areas of the country. Beyond extensive assistance to the planning ministry in its efforts to conceptualize the program initiative and the policy paper, RP project advisors helped in the design and implementation of initial work under the program.

The fourth, most visible, activity of the RP project was the production of forty development plans, one for each district, that complemented Kenya's Fourth Development Plan. Advisors and their colleagues in the Rural Planning Division formulated comprehensive guidelines on the form and content of the development plans, to give the plans comparative utility and strength. Extensive effort was also given to improving and reissuing a district planning handbook, first issued by the project in 1983. The 1994–1998 development plans, carried out under the guidelines and systems set up for the 1989–1993 development plans, were successfully produced on time without expatriate assistance.

The fifth major activity of the RP project was assistance to the government in formulating and implementing the District Focus Strategy launched in 1983. This exercise in administrative de-concentration was aimed at promoting more effective and efficient use of domestic resources through efforts to strengthen the planning capacity at the district level, improve horizontal integration among operating ministry field agents, and expand authority to district heads of operating ministries for managing financial and procurement aspects of local project implementation. The intent of the strategy was the realization of the statement in the National Plan that districts are the operational centers for rural development planning and implementation.

Advisors with the RP and the RMRD projects undertook a number of activities in support of the District Focus Strategy.[21] First, they helped the government to craft a national training strategy for implementing the initiative. Second, they organized national and district level seminars to disseminate the policy, carried out annual training workshops for district planning officers, and stepped up overseas training for economists and planners working on the strategy and on rural planning projects, particularly through the Cornell University program. HIID advisors and their Kenyan colleagues also helped to create district information and documentation centers for providing information to district planning officers.

In addition to the above planning initiatives, the RMRD project assisted the planning ministry in designing and implementing the ambitious Rural Trade and Production Centre program.[22] This program, largely funded by USAID, financed packages of productive investments and services to promote economic growth through the strengthening of linkages between small urban centers and their rural hinterlands. A small team of RMRD project advisors and ministry economists worked closely to develop both the criteria for selecting urban centers and the guidelines for implementing investments. These developments did much to ensure that the centers were selected on the basis of their potential for contributing to a policy of rural-urban balance, rather than on the basis of politics. The RMRD project advisor concentrating on this activity, as well as the Kenyan economists he worked with, selected investment packages, designed and approved package components, contracted and tendered, supervised construction, and handed over completed components. Despite these efforts, the implementation of the first round of eight such rural centers faced many delays and was not completed when the RMRD project ended. The RMRD project assisted in the selection of towns to be covered by a second round of centers, but the government has had considerable difficulty obtaining funding for implementing this round.

The final initiative to support planning was the introduction of microcomputers into the planning and other critical systems. Beginning with the computerization of the 1984–1988 district plans, the RP management advisor recommended and jointly managed the introduction of microcomputers in the budget process.[23] These initiatives were continued under the RMRD project until the activity became too large and complex to fit within the project's terms of reference; at that time, the Ministry of Finance established a separate project with other USAID funding.

Three principal computer activities were carried out under the RMRD project: building information systems, developing a microcomputer training facility, and providing policy and strategic management advice on the application of information technology. The first and largest activity was the design and implementation of microcomputer-based transaction and decision information systems. The most important system was the import licensing system, which linked the Ministry of Commerce and the Central Bank and managed the allocation of import licenses and foreign exchange releases. Other systems developed included: the export compensation system, the district infrastructure inventory system, the Rural Development Fund expenditure and monitoring system, and the project monitoring system.[24]

Second, the RMRD project created a training program to promote the use of computers. In 1987, the project's management advisor, in collaboration with the research department of the Kenyan Institute of Administration, established a microcomputer training facility[25] and provided hardware, two resident trainers, full maintenance support, and full instructional recurrent cost support. The RMRD advisor worked extensively with the head of the research department to develop the curriculum and build the program. In May 1995 when the last HIID project (the budget component of the ASAO II program) supporting the program ended, over 3,000 government staff had been trained and the facility had become the government's primary computer training unit.

Third, the RMRD project created a policy framework. As early as 1987, HIID advisors assisted government staff in preparing a government-wide draft policy paper to guide the rapid spread of microcomputers. The effort has yet to bear fruit, largely because of disagreements among the leading computer agencies, such as the Central Statistics Bureau, over who should have overall responsibility for the government's computer activities. However, a more restricted policy definition was accepted within the planning ministry, which has guided computer operations within that ministry.

Assessment of the Advisory and Training Experience in Kenya

Throughout the history of HIID's involvement in Kenya, the government, with advisor assistance, formulated good policies. But the government generally failed to implement or sustain these policies. Other studies[26] have explored the reasons most African governments have formally adopted policies recommended by aid agencies but have yet to implement these policies. Here, it is noted that HIID advisors on all four projects made major contributions to the formulation of promising policy positions, some of which have not been taken seriously or fully implemented. This situation makes it difficult to evaluate the impact of HIID's advisory work in Kenya.

Nevertheless, the government adopted many of the systems HIID advisors helped to advance, such as the computerization of the budgeting process, the preparation of district level data systems, and the district plan preparation system.

The failure of the government to seriously support the widely publicized policy recommendations of external advisors was a major reason why aid agencies decided in 1991 to drastically reduce development assistance to Kenya. By this action, the aid agencies intended to put pressure on the government to implement these policies. As of mid-1995, there was only limited government response to the 1991 signal.

Human Resource Capacity Building

The conventional wisdom among those associated with HIID's projects in Kenya—be they advisors, aid agency personnel, or Cambridge-based staff—is that the institute was not successful in building the human resource capacity in the ministries targeted. This conclusion rests largely on the perception that those trained to the master's level under the various HIID projects have not been retained in the positions and units they were intended to serve after their training.

The data give some validity to this conclusion. As of mid-1995, 43 (39.8 percent) of the 108 Kenyan officers who completed project-funded master's-level courses are still working in the units and ministries the projects were serving before training.[27] An additional 18 officers (16.7 percent) are still serving as economists and planners in other government ministries, agencies, and parastatals. Of the remaining officers, 37 (34.3 percent) are working for the private sector, aid agencies, nongovernmental organizations, or universities, and 10 (9.2 percent) are retired or deceased. Still, most of those trained under the TAP project have remained in Kenya, contributing to the public sector, if not directly, then as consultants.

The conventional wisdom as to why the government and HIID encountered difficulties in moving these officers beyond training to retention is largely accurate. In Kenya, as in many late developing countries, the major factors leading many of those trained to leave their targeted units and ministries are low salaries, demoralizing working conditions, limited prospects for advancement, inadequate benefits, poor senior manager leadership, and ample employment opportunities in the higher paying private sector.[28]

Aside from the master's level training, all four projects invested in short-term training, which critics frequently overlooked when considering only retention rates for those receiving graduate-level training. Collectively, the projects trained hundreds of government staff in short-term specialized overseas courses and thousands of officers and staff were trained in local workshops and courses. The short-term external courses ranged from budget management and cost-benefit analysis to microcomputer applications and regional planning.

Managing the short-term training of professionals and technicians in the target ministries was a demanding task. The time demands for carrying out this process in Kenya were such that at least one advisor on each project focused substantially on identifying training needs and potential trainees, matching needs and trainees with the wide range of courses offered in the region and in Europe and North America, and getting such officers organized to attend courses. The management task involved not only ensuring that those selected had the qualifications and motivation to benefit from such training, but also negotiating diplomatically to ensure there were no tribal biases in the selection procedures or the candidates chosen.

Considerable support for such training came from HIID's Cambridge-based Training Office. Once the project advisor got the short-term trainee on an airplane, the Training Office assumed responsibilities that included meeting the needs for financial support, housing, training, and dealing with diverse and unexpected academic and personal problems trainees often encountered during overseas courses.

The Kenyan projects, at various times, made efforts to strengthen the training capacities of Kenyan training institutes. These included: the TAP project work on strengthening teaching at national universities of agricultural policy analysis and project design skills; the RP project efforts to help the Kenya Polytechnic to launch training for Kenyans in computer programming, management, and maintenance for the many computers that HIID and others were rapidly introducing into government; and the RMRD project's substantial investment in building the capacity of the Kenyan Institute of Administration to train middle- and senior-level staff in microcomputer management and use.

An integral part of the training was the daily counterparting with Kenyan staff. Most advisors made sincere efforts to undertake assignments jointly with Kenyan economists and managers in the units they assisted. This was done in a variety of ways. These included insisting that junior officers be assigned to work with them when receiving assignments, ensuring that junior officers were invited to the meetings where papers they had worked on were discussed, and working side-by-side on the computer, as was common practice in the RMRD project during the formulation of the district plans.

HIID projects in Kenya led to the establishment of two capacity-building summer workshops in Cambridge, which provided short-term training for economists and managers from a wide range of late developing countries, including Kenya. The two workshops are: Budgeting in the Public Sector, which grew out of the management work done under the TAP and the BEMP projects; and the Macroeconomic Policy and Management Workshop, which grew out of the policy work of the TAP project.

Contribution to Knowledge Building

A major strength of HIID as a university institute is that its staff can draw upon their project experience to publish in the academic and professional literature, thereby enhancing understanding of development issues and strategies, generally and specific to the country in which they worked. Writing on the practice, rather than on the theory of development, has benefits. Perhaps the most important is that little is written from a practitioner's standpoint. Development practitioners are busy working, and have little time for reflection, much less for authoring the lessons. As a result, many development practitioners work with limited understanding (often their own personal experience) of the options for improving policy and administration. Another benefit of publishing on advisory work is that it keeps the advisors relatively current in their specialties, which is important given that they are often seconded for long periods of time in the field.

Despite the benefits, publishing is difficult and, in some situations, discouraged by government officials. The task is also arduous because advisors are fully occupied with implementing their terms of reference, and reflecting and publishing therefore have to be done on their personal time. Further, the task is difficult because advisors hold positions of trust with government officials and publishing can erode that trust. Still, HIID's advisors in Kenya have published on a wide variety of topics while maintaining the trust of their government counterparts.

Project advisors have published on six areas: macroeconomic policy, agricultural policy, rural planning, financial management, information technology, and tax policy. Many of these publications began as part of the HIID's Development Discussion Papers series and were then published in books and articles for wider distribution. Only some of these publications are cited in this chapter.

Lessons on Delivering Technical Assistance and Training

HIID's four Kenya projects worked on diverse tasks and at different levels of the public sector. Some advisors worked at the elbow of a minister, while others assisted clerks in the use of information technology. Despite their differences, the projects had common features in terms of their impact on making these interventions effective. The lessons of the institute's projects also provide a voice to the current debate on the relevance of long-term expatriate technical assistance to Africa.[29]

As noted earlier, Kenya is not an easy environment in which to effectively implement a public sector project. While policy reform is often articulated and well-received by senior government staff, implementation by ministers and senior civil servants falls far short of expectations.

In Kenya implementation is policy and systems. What lessons can be gleaned from these projects about how to cope with the difficult development environment which characterizes not only East Africa, but the continent in general? Six factors have promoted effectiveness in Kenya: (1) insulated contracts, (2) long time frames, (3) flexibility in defining the terms of reference, (4) loose management of project advisors, (5) extensive experience of field staff, and (6) the role of godfathers. These are discussed briefly below.

Insulated Contracts

The host country contract arrangement promoted counterparting between government staff and technical assistance advisors and gave advisors a necessary independence from aid agencies, which promoted objective advisory services. The recent trend by aid agencies to rely on personal service contracts with individuals, rather than on arms-length contracts with institutions, principally because of cost, is short-sighted. This trend also may lead to advice that is not objective, and compromise the trust advisors need to work effectively in government.

Long Time Frames

Projects that seek to significantly reform either policy or administration, as well as to build financial, planning, and management systems, take a long time to become effective. It takes time to establish the trust of government staff, especially at the senior level, and this trust is essential to receiving the senior staff's commitment to the reform. While policy reform may move quickly if there is a progressive window of opportunity, it often takes a long time to establish the trust to gain access to senior decision-makers. Similarly, administrative reforms take time because the structure of organizations and the behavior of individuals are difficult to change. The time frame of most technical assistance projects is often far shorter than the time needed to implement policy and administrative reform. Indeed, a considerable amount of time is taken in managing the contract process and ensuring the continuity of effort. The Kenya projects overcame these constraints because of their relatively long duration.

Flexibility in Defining the Terms of Reference

The leadership of a technical assistance project knows when to redefine the terms of reference. Perhaps the principal reason for the effectiveness of the Kenya projects in assisting the government to formulate policy and design systems was that they were flexible and creative in defining their work.[30] Development projects are often overly programmed. Project documents especially for multi-year, multi-staff, and multimillion-dollar initiatives, often have a myriad of objectives that are to be implemented in an unreasonable time frame. The experience of the HIID's four Kenya projects suggests that many of the key breakthroughs were not in the terms of reference; there were windows of opportunity that were pursued creatively. For example, the initiatives to apply computer technology to the production of the national budget and the creation of a computer training facility were not in the terms of reference and are examples of adaptive responses to the government's needs unforeseen in the original project designs. Transferring budget staff from the agriculture ministry to the finance ministry is another example of project flexibility. Because it takes time to understand the environment and to establish trust with counterparts, and because advisors are naturally pulled into "fire-fighting" or daily administration, over-programming an advisory project is counterproductive. While recognizing the demands of the procurement process to pre-program and over-program a project to justify the initiative, projects are more effective if they can redefine their priorities and select only the most essential.

Loose Management of Project Advisors

Flexible contractor and host national management of advisors are necessary to promote a flexible and adaptive response to the demands placed on public bureaucracies in Africa. As a university institute, the

HIID culture is to allow considerable latitude to professional staff, be they in headquarters or the field. While this approach places a premium on recruitment, it is appropriate for the delivery of technical assistance because of the difficulties of micro-managing overseas projects and the contingent nature of development assistance. Because many of the tasks of the four projects required extensive analysis, staff were often recruited with advanced degrees and academic backgrounds. The HIID culture and the professional background of its staff stressed a technical assistance style of individualism and flexibility.

Extensive Experience of Field Staff

One striking feature of the staff of these four projects was the extent of their experience in development generally and in Kenya specifically. Some advisors had several years of experience in Kenya and years of experience on the continent prior to joining the projects. This is important, because one policy advisor on the TAP project commented that it took four years for him to understand the marketing systems in Kenya and only then was he able to begin to feel confident in recommending reforms. It takes time to understand complex markets and organizational systems. No matter how experienced the consultant, to be effective one must "pay his or her dues" and learn the environment. In his essay on types of management in Africa, David Leonard notes that the problem with technical assistance in Africa is not that it is provided by expatriates, but that turnover is excessive and advisors are not in place long enough to be effective.[31] The argument being made by some aid agencies currently—that technical assistance should be done in part through brief consulting work by expatriates—flies not only in the face of the experience of these four projects, but technical assistance historically and in other regions.

The Role of Godfathers

The design and effective implementation of these four projects was in no small measure the result of one or two senior government officials who took the effort and the risk to promote reform. Technical assistance interventions, whether staffed by expatriate or local staff, need committed government staff to shoulder the risk and change the policies, procedures, organizations and behaviors needed for a reform. Technical assistance personnel can guide and assist, but they cannot institute change. A critical question in designing technical assistance projects is what do to if there are no godfathers to shepherd the projects. The current rhetoric about the irrelevancy of expatriate technical assistance to Africa overlooks the important role that expatriate assistance (at an appropriate level) provides for strong political supporters who want to initiate policy and system reforms.[32]

Notes

1 This chapter benefits from the comments of Subramaniam Ramakrishnan, Graham Glenday, John R. Wheeler, and Richard C. Goldman.

2 Lamb (1982, pp. 295–296).

3 Mahbub ul Huq (1994, p. 20).

4 Leonard (1991, p. 10).

5 No research has been done on the extent to which this form of aid agency–government–contractor arrangement is used in Kenya or other late developing countries for the provision of technical assistance. It is the authors' assumption that this creative form of contracting is infrequently used and should be considered more frequently as a contracting mechanism.

6 Peterson (1990b).

7 Cohen (1992).

8 For an analysis of the Session Paper No. of 1981 on national food policy, see Cohen (1984).

9 Republic of Kenya (1986).

10 Leonard, Cohen, and Pinckney (1987).

11 Peterson (1994a); Peterson et al. (1997a); and Peterson (1996, p. 177–194).

12 Peterson et al. (1997b).

13 Currently the World Bank is interested in the Ministry of Agriculture's personnel management information system because staff complement control is not well done in Kenya and is a precondition to effect Civil Service reform.

14 Peterson and Kiragu (1990) and Peterson (1997b).

15 The Ministries of Agriculture and Livestock Development were selected by the Ministry of Finance to be the first line ministries to implement a Public Investment Program (PIP). HIID's project under the ASAO II be-

gan implementation of the PIP in 1993. For more information on this subject, see Peterson (1997a).

16 For 1995–1997, the principal HIID budget advisor has continued to work within the Ministry of Finance under funding by the Government of Kenya.

17 Wescott (1987, pp. 67–93).

18 Cohen and Wheeler (1994).

19 Glenday (1991, pp. 2–6).

20 Cohen and Lewis (1987, pp. 269–296).

21 Cohen and Hook (1986).

22 Evans (1992); Gaile (1992); Smoke (1992b).

23 Wescott (1987).

24 These computer initiatives are described in Peterson (1990a).

25 Peterson (1990b).

26 Hyden (1983) and Sandbrook (1987). A case study directly focused on Kenya's assistance to what most development professionals negotiating with the Government consider good policy advice is found in Harden (1990, pp. 217–270).

27 Cohen and Wheeler (1997).

28 These are problems common to African public sectors. See, for example, Chew (1990) and Cohen (1992).

29 Wai and Rice (1991); Berg (1993); Pfaff (1995).

30 Korten (1980) argues that effective rural development is best achieved through projects that use a flexible process approach rather than an inflexible blueprint approach.

31 Leonard (1987, p. 905).

32 Peterson refers to these government reformers as saints; see Peterson (1994b).

5 The Gambia and Zambia: A Common Path to Macroeconomic Stability

Malcolm F. McPherson

Introduction

This chapter discusses the Economic and Financial Policy Analyses project (EFPA) in The Gambia, and the Macroeconomic Technical Assistance Project (METAP) in Zambia. The first section sketches the development context in Africa which led The Gambia and Zambia to adopt reform programs. Subsequent sections discuss the origins and objectives of both projects and the assistance provided, review the projects' accomplishments and the lessons learned, and provide concluding comments.

The EFPA project began in June 1985, was reviewed by USAID in 1987, extended in 1988, and came to an end in August 1992.[1] The METAP began in January 1991, was reviewed by the funding agencies in February 1993, and in June 1994 was extended to June 1997. Each project was based in the respective Ministry of Finance[2] and each was donor-funded.[3]

These projects had common objectives: (1) to assist the country concerned to implement its economic recovery program, and (2) to improve the capacity of government officials to undertake macroeconomic policies that would achieve sustained growth and development.

The Development Context in Africa

A concerted effort was made to accelerate economic growth and to spread its benefits more broadly. Most African leaders were convinced that governments should (and could) take the initiative. They believed that the public sector could stimulate sustained and equitable progress by raising the rate of investment, managing the necessary industrial and service enterprises, building the growth-enhancing infrastructure, and broadening and deepening the supply of social and human capital. Few governments would accept that the private sector could be the engine of growth. Markets in Africa were believed to be too thin, human capacity too limited, resources too scarce, and entrepreneurship too undeveloped. It was presumed that the public sector, through appropriate development planning, could (and would) effectively overcome the constraints holding back the private sector.[4]

What was not fully appreciated by African leaders was that the market failures, which were seen as blocking growth, were far less potent than the bureaucratic failures associated with broad-based public-sector intervention.[5] They were also convinced that world trade was "rigged" against their countries.[6] As a result, "bootstrap" strategies which focused on self-reliance and self-sufficiency gained favor. African leaders found it convenient to craft their own development ideologies.[7]

Whether these ideologies could have produced growth and development—if only economic management had been more prudent—is a matter of debate. With few exceptions, political concerns dominated economic considerations.[8] National plans (of which many were written) became blueprints for excess.[9] Moreover, even with exceedingly high levels of per capita foreign assistance, most African countries failed to grow and develop.[10]

By the early 1980s, most African economies were in deep trouble. Some of the problems resulted from adverse movements in world commodity and financial markets; most of the trouble, however, derived from economic policies which reduced the scope for growth and development. Foreign reserves were depleted, external debts were unserviceable, public sectors were overextended, inflation was high (and rising), real output was declining, and many aspects of development (infant mortality, food availability, primary school enrollment) were regressing.[11]

This economic tragedy has been widely studied.[12] Many solutions have been proposed.[13] African governments, the international donor community, academics, and others have formulated many strategies for resolving Africa's economic problems. Missing, however, has been the determination of most African governments to impose the type of broad-based economic discipline which has transformed the countries of Asia.[14]

African governments have adopted many adjustment programs. In general, however, these programs have not been sustained. For example, between 1977 and 1991, Zambia had no fewer than seven donor-supported adjustment programs. Each was abandoned. Successful, sustained reform has been rare.[15] Ghana and Uganda are exceptions.

Most African governments remain ambivalent or hostile to reform. Experience, however, provides few options. Countries can continue to collapse (which Zaire, and others, have been doing). Or, they can fundamentally change direction so as to enhance their prospects for growth and development. The Gambia did that; so has Zambia.

Designing reform programs for countries which are seriously imbalanced is not difficult. Countries which have large budget deficits, rising inflation (due to excess money creation), unserviceable external debt, capital flight, low savings, declining investment, and falling per capita real incomes, have to bring expenditure into line with income, and keep it that way. The only issue is whether the process will be systematic (via a formal adjustment program), or ad hoc (through official neglect).[16] To date, Africa has too few examples of the former, and, too many of the latter.

The EFPA Project and METAP

The EFPA project and METAP had common objectives and approaches primarily because The Gambia and Zambia had similar economic

TABLE 5-1
Selected Economic Data on The Gambia and Zambia Prior to Adjustment Programs (percentages and millions of US dollars)

	The Gambia (1975–1985)	Zambia (1982–1992)
Consumer prices (%)	205	19,092
Exchange rate (relative US$, %)	–54	–99.4
Real GDP (whole period, %)	–7.5	0
Per capita real GDP (%)	–35.0	–42
Money supply (%)	436	3,916
Exports/GDP (average, %)	22.5	27.4
Imports/GDP (average, %)	51.8	29.0
Savings/GDP (average, %)	0	14.4
Budget deficit/GDP (%)	14.6	9.2
Increase in external debt (US$ millions)	222	3,277

Sources: *International Financial Yearbook 1995* (1995:382-5; 806-9); GDATA computer file, The Gambia, and *Macroeconomic Indicators*, Zambia.

and institutional problems.[17] The data in Table 5-1 are indicative. They relate to the decade prior to the commencement of each country's adjustment program: 1975–1985 for The Gambia; and 1982–1992 for Zambia.

For both countries during these periods inflation was high, the exchange rate depreciated rapidly, and per capita real income fell. Budget deficits were large and the growth of money supply and the dollar value of foreign debt were high, and domestic savings rates had collapsed.[18]

The key data are the budget deficits. Both countries had large deficits in the context of declining real output per capita. This pattern of mismanagement was exaggerated by the diminishing capacity of both governments to gather and use economic information. As a result, economic "policy" degenerated into a series of ad hoc and (often) ill-advised reactions to events. Crisis management became the norm, and even that lacked direction.[19]

Origins of the Projects

The EFPA Project in The Gambia

HIID's support for macroeconomic reform in The Gambia began in March 1983. The resident representative of the United States Agency for International Development (USAID) requested the institute to provide short-term assistance for the Minister of Finance, who was seeking to improve the ministry's operations and the capacity of its staff to undertake economic reform. The HIID advisor concluded that the staff lacked the training necessary to cope with the ministry's normal work, let alone the tasks associated with adjustment.[20] Suggestions were made to enhance the performance of the ministry through reorganization and staff training; USAID based its proposals for the EFPA project on these suggestions.

Other advisory services followed. In June 1985, an HIID staff member was part of the team which designed The Gambia's Economic Recovery Program (ERP). This comprehensive adjustment program provided a framework for moving government policy beyond crisis management. By happenstance, the EFPA project formally commenced at the same time. Thus, from its inception, the project had a clear focus: it would assist the Government of The Gambia to turn the economy around and to create the local capacity to support economic development.

The METAP in Zambia

HIID first learned of the METAP in February 1990 when it received a letter from Zambia's Minister of Finance. (The same letter was also sent to other development institutions.) Attached were terms of reference for a five-person technical assistance team. HIID was asked whether it was interested in providing the team.

Reactions at HIID varied. Some staff were skeptical, since Zambia's reputation as a chronic non-reformer was well-known. Yet since the economy had sunk so low, some staff felt that eventually the government would take reform seriously. (The METAP provided an entry point.) HIID's response to the minister was positive, but cautious.

In August 1990, HIID learned, in a roundabout manner, of its selection. Inquiries at the World Bank led to a contact in the Swedish Embassy in Lusaka who had assembled donor support for the METAP. A visit by HIID to Lusaka was hastily arranged, and this produced an agreement for HIID to undertake the project. Nonetheless, HIID remained doubtful about the project for several reasons. First, there was little enthusiasm among Zambian staff for the project. Second, the expectations of the Zambian government officials and the donor community regarding METAP diverged. The Zambian officials saw the METAP as providing access to resources (automobiles, fuel, computers, training, and travel abroad) which were in short supply in the country. The relevant donors saw the METAP as a means of improving macroeconomic policy.[21] Third, the United Nations Development Programme (UNDP), which helped to design the project, had withdrawn from the donor consortium. Fourth, the amount budgeted by the donors was too small to support the services required (namely, five advisors and large amounts of training). And, fifth, Zambian officials were so reticent to discuss the economy's troubles that HIID found it difficult to complete even the final project design.[22]

HIID and the others concerned signed the METAP contract in January 1991. Staff were identified and, by mid-1991, the project was fully operational.

The Role of the HIID Advisors

In The Gambia and Zambia, HIID provided: (1) resident advisors who understood the main macroeconomic issues (including similar developments in other countries); (2) consultants who could advise on special topics; and (3) training, both locally and abroad. The major difference between the two countries was the time profile of reform. The Gambia completed its stabilization program before Zambia's effort began.[23]

The Gambia

The presence of HIID advisors in The Gambia from mid-1982 to the second half of 1992 significantly influenced the policy debate. The advisors gained a reputation for reliable performance, and sound, consistent views. Their advice was taken seriously, even if it was not always accepted.[24]

Some advice was instrumental. One example deserves mention. An advisor for the EFPA project was in The Gambia as the government was deciding to float its national currency (the dalisi). In discussions with the Minister of Finance, the advisor emphasized that with a floating currency all macroeconomic shocks would show up in the exchange rate. For the float to succeed, the government would have to take the necessary steps (related to the budget, money supply, interest rates, and wages) to minimize the shocks. This advice became a guiding principle for subsequent macroeconomic policy.

HIID's staff were heavily involved in training. Many Gambians were sent abroad for special courses and some degree training. Large numbers were also trained locally. As a result of this capacity building, EFPA project staff began to selectively disengage from line-ministry work. Local officials took over much of the work that used to be done by the advisors—data collection, debt management, monitoring of programs of the International Monetary Fund (IMF) and the World Bank, and revenue projections.

This progression of tasks became more pronounced as the economic crisis eased and The Gambia began to meet regularly the IMF performance criteria. The policy horizon began to lengthen noticeably.[25]

Zambia

In Zambia, the relationship of the METAP team members to the government changed substantively after the elections in October 1991. In the final months of the Kaunda regime, the METAP advisors had been sidelined. They used their time to work on the key issues that would confront the new government. By November 1991, the team had prepared papers on topics such as the budget, inflation, monetary policy, debt management, tax reform, exchange rate management, and wage policy. The debt management advisor and the macro data advisor also began to update the relevant databases.

This work was highly relevant when the government changed. The Movement for Multiparty Democracy, which formed the new government, had emphasized the need for fundamental economic and social reform. Its *Manifesto* was a blueprint for the transformation of the Zambian economy. The new Minister of Finance welcomed the METAP contributions and drew the team into the mainstream of the ministry.

METAP's capacity-building effort began slowly. Initially, the advisors were so deeply engaged in crisis management that only limited attention was given to local and on-the-job training.[26] Most of the training offered consisted of short- and long-term courses abroad. Beginning in mid-1993, the training effort was expanded and its direction changed. As the economic crisis moderated, the staff organized more seminars and workshops. In addition, the METAP began providing support to local institutions to design and conduct special courses for large groups within the ministry. The first such program was a series of two-week workshops for sixty registry clerks. This was followed by a management and supervision course for one hundred and five senior accountants.

Such courses have been repeated for other groups. The responses of their participants and supervisors, and follow-up surveys, show that they have been successful. This approach has several benefits. It is cost-effective (relative to sending officials abroad); the courses and their material are closely monitored; and the approach helps to engage everyone—supervisors, trainers, participants—in the learning process. A further benefit is that it helps to improve the performance of broad groups of staff throughout the ministry, thereby raising overall productivity. This approach directly strengthens the capacity of local institutions to further enhance other local capacity.[27] Finally, it is an effective way to create broadly-based capacity in a setting where the attrition rate is high due to AIDS.

Modalities of EFPA and METAP Assistance

The original design of the EFPA project had one resident advisor, local support staff, and consultants who would assist with special assignments and training. The workload began to overwhelm the advisor, so that a project assistant and an administrator/training officer were added in 1986. The original scope of work for the METAP included five advisors, some consulting assistance, and large amounts of training. But to fit the project to the budget, only four advisors were included, and consultant time and training were cut.[28]

The advisors on both projects worked directly with the respective ministers and permanent secretaries. In The Gambia, the advisor was attached to the Office of the Minister. In Zambia, the advisors were originally intended to have Zambian counterparts one level down from the permanent secretary. Under these arrangements, contacts with the minister and permanent secretary were meant to be limited. In practice, the advisors have operated at all levels.[29]

Concerns and Accomplishments of the Projects

The basic concerns of the EFPA project and the METAP derived from the long history of economic mismanagement in The Gambia and Zambia. Both governments had repeatedly shown that they had no capacity to address their economies' substantive problems.

Concerns

The EFPA project and the METAP were designed when the economies of The Gambia and Zambia were in sharp decline, important institutions had become dysfunctional, and attitudes of key economic actors had changed significantly. In principle, economic decline can be readily reversed if the basic institutions remain intact and attitudes (and thus behavior) do not change in socially perverse ways. Problems can arise when institutions regress and attitudes become counterproductive. When these occur, as happened in The Gambia and Zambia, reformers face the task of simultaneously attempting to reshape economic policy, rebuild key institutions, and reverse generally adverse consumer and business views about the economy's future.

This was the general setting in The Gambia and Zambia. There was an absence of consumer and business confidence, the general public was highly skeptical about the ability of government to manage the economy, and economic fundamentals were seriously out of balance. The institutions needed to reform the economy (the budget office, central bank, and revenue departments) were in disarray, and the basic data needed to monitor the economy were out of date.

Accomplishments

Besides technical support and training, the EFPA and METAP teams provided a core group of professionals whose work gave impetus to the reform programs in The Gambia and Zambia. This support greatly enhanced the ability of both governments to deal with the main economic issues.

General Contributions

The EFPA project had five main accomplishments. The project:

- helped the Government of The Gambia to deal with key issues needed to promote economic recovery;
- assisted the Ministry of Finance and central bank officials to update the relevant macroeconomic data;
- assisted with the development of a program to restructure the Ministry of Finance and other economic institutions;
- provided training for a large number of Gambian officials on financial and economic issues; and
- set a standard of performance for local technical staff to emulate.

With the METAP still being implemented, any assessment of its achievements remains tentative. To date, METAP staff have:

- worked with Zambian Government officials to help shape the economic policy agenda and analyze key economic issues;
- assembled the basic data needed to manage the economy and devised systems to keep these data current;
- trained a large number of staff; and
- assisted in reorganizing and reforming the basic economic institutions.

Macroeconomic Accomplishments

The EFPA project and the METAP were central to attempts by the Governments of The Gambia and Zambia to stabilize their respective economies.

Economic Stabilization in The Gambia

An important turning point in The Gambia was the failure of the currency devaluation of February 1984 to have the positive effects which the central bank had predicted. The economy did not stabilize and capital flight did not cease.

The devaluation had not been supported by measures to control absorption. The situation continued to deteriorate. It was made worse by the drought in 1984 which created a serious food shortage. The government, which was responsible for rice imports (through The Gambia Produce Marketing Board), could not raise the resources needed to purchase food. The government also had difficulty importing fuel. Emergency shipments were requested from the donor community.

Further difficulties arose with the failure of a donor conference, which had been organized by the Ministry of Economic Planning and Industrial Development in November 1984. The government had sought donor contributions amounting to 25 percent of GDP per year for four years to revive the economy. The donor community saw this request as being completely unrealistic.

These failures by the central bank and the planning ministry, both of which were opposed to economic reform, together with the government's demonstrated incapacity to provide staple commodities, cleared the path for action by the finance ministry. Such action became increasingly urgent when the IMF Board resolved to sanction The Gambia for its arrears.

The Minister of Finance responded by appointing a task force to formulate the Economic Recovery Program (ERP). The ERP had all of the important components—exchange rate adjustment, civil service reform, parastatal restructuring, financial liberalization, normalization of external debt, and budget and monetary policy reform—that were needed to stabilize the economy and lay the foundation for sustained economic growth.

Implementation of the ERP, which was announced in the June 1985 budget speech, began immediately. Within twelve months, the economy had stabilized. This occurred primarily because the government was able to bring the budget under control. Stabilization was reinforced by the shift to market-determined interest rates through the regular tender of treasury bills. With the government not printing money and asset holders encouraged through high positive real rates of interest to keep their financial assets "on-shore," the relative demand for foreign exchange and commodities declined. This took the pressure off the exchange rate and the price level.

Further support for stabilization came from the civil service wage freeze and the reduction (by 20 percent) in the number of public sector employees. The wage freeze was maintained from 1986 to 1988, making the public sector wage bill the "nominal anchor" for the system.

Other events also helped. The government crack-down on customs fraud produced a significant increase in revenue. The reduction in oil and rice prices in world markets improved the terms of trade. And, finally, the improvement in agricultural harvests added to the local food supply and helped to improve the balance of payments and the budget. Stabilization, which had seemed so elusive during 1985, became a reality in 1986.[30]

Economic Stabilization in Zambia

In Zambia, 1991 and 1992 were transitional years. In 1991, Zambians had become completely dissatisfied with the government of President Kaunda and the United National Independence Party (UNIP) and voted it out at the general election. Yet even with the change of government, little seemed to change. Zambia's grain harvest failed in 1992 due to drought. With no foreign exchange, foreign arrears of roughly US$3.5 billion, and food reserves running out, the government turned to the donor community. The response was some one million tonnes of food aid.[31]

The new government compounded its difficulties by acceding to demands by civil servants for extraordinary wage increases and by providing large subsidies to Zambia Airways. These unbudgeted expenditures contrasted sharply with the cuts in maize meal subsidies which, the public had been told, were needed to help balance the budget. These actions raised questions about the government's professed commitment to fairness and equity.

Moreover, the macroeconomic situation continued to deteriorate. Inflation, which had been 111 percent in 1991, increased to 191 percent in 1992. The exchange rate rose sharply as well. Again, the contrast was stark. In the 1992 budget, the government had promised to stabilize the economy and reduce inflation.

Finally, the new government had promised the donor community that it would devote more resources to the social sectors. With inflation so high and so much being spent on wages and subsidies, real social sector spending had declined in 1992. Thus, barely a year old, the new government was in deep trouble.

The rise in inflation was due, almost entirely, to a lack of budget discipline. In a speech to donor representatives, Zambia's president stated that "inflation was the cruelest tax on the poor" and made a commitment to bring inflation under control. This revived interest in a "cash budget," which had been suggested by the METAP team in their earlier briefing notes.

The main drawback to the implementation of a cash budget was the lack of data. A Data Monitoring Committee was established between the Ministry of Finance and the Bank of Zambia, with the brief to meet daily until the relevant numbers were brought up to date. The work of this committee, which continues, has been instrumental in enabling the government to remain abreast of fiscal and monetary developments.

Due to continued central bank lending to parastatals in early 1993, it was some months until reserve money stopped increasing. When that happened in late April 1993, inflation began to fall. It was 15 percent in May, 11.6 percent in June, and 2.7 percent in July. The inflation rate has remained in single digits ever since. Reflecting the decline in inflation rates, nominal interest rates began to fall towards the end of 1993 and the exchange rate stabilized as well.

WHAT WAS LEARNED ABOUT SUBSTANCE OR PROCESS?

The EFPA project and the METAP have provided several useful points on economic adjustment and capacity building. Economic reform is an important learning experience, particularly for those at the top. They must remain steadfast and optimistic in the face of harsh and often unrelenting criticism. One lesson from The Gambia and Zambia is that individuals do make a difference.[32]

Other lessons deserve mention. These are listed below and explained briefly in subsequent subsections.

- Budget control is essential for economic stability.
- A pre-condition for effective economic management is timely, relevant data.
- Reform has to be supported by emphasizing the costs of *not* adjusting.

- Optimal sequencing of reforms is overblown.
- The Gambia and Zambia—and the donor community—would benefit from a structured program to reduce aid dependence.
- Experiences in The Gambia and Zambia do not support the view that African countries have adequate local talent to promote and sustain economic reform.
- With suitable modifications, local capacity-building efforts can respond to the disruptions associated with AIDS.

Budget Control and Economic Stability

The first signs of sustained recovery in The Gambia and Zambia emerged only after both governments decisively reduced the budget deficits. Strict control over the budget was not a change in policy since both governments had already made that commitment. The change occurred with structural reform of the budget process. In The Gambia, tax compliance improved. In Zambia, the cash budget, for the first time in the country's history, forced the government to match its expenditure to its revenue. That is, stabilization was preceded by (some) structural reform. The literature asserts that the reverse order generally holds.[33]

Accurate, Timely Data

The Gambian economy was brought on track (and kept that way) only when there was reliable, relevant, and timely information. The same situation has applied in Zambia. From the start, EFPA and METAP staff emphasized the need for timely data so that the government could take a proactive policy stance. Timely information may not offer new options when an economy is collapsing. However, it does help to minimize further economic damage. Relevant data serve a strategic purpose as well. Leaders will often modify a counterproductive policy when they see regular evidence of its adverse effects.[34]

The Costs of Not Adjusting

Critics of economic reform have had a relatively easy time convincing leaders and the general public that the "costs of adjustment" are onerous and inequitable. The Gambia and Zambia (and many other countries in Africa) are case studies in the costs of not adjusting, the effects of which have been devastating to the poor.

Adjustment is never easy, especially for those who experience disruption. But, deepening poverty (because of the lack of adjustment) has been demonstrably worse. Leaders in The Gambia and Zambia only began to make headway against their critics when they focused on the latter point.

Sequencing of Reforms

The issue of optimal sequencing of reforms has been widely discussed in the literature. Much concern has been expressed about whether current accounts should be opened before capital accounts, trade reform should come before financial reform, and so on. Three points seem to be missed. First, in Africa, the primary task has been to return a collapsing economy to a stable, sustainable growth path. To do that, countries often require broad-based action to jump-start the stabilization process. Second, sequencing arguments have implications for planning and control that are counter-productive in most African countries. Reforming governments often have so little credibility that the suggestion of further intervention, even to promote reform, is seen with utmost skepticism. And third, since the object of structural reform is to fundamentally alter the way an economy operates, any so-called "optimal" sequence will change as adjustment proceeds in ways that are not predictable in advance.[35] Sequencing may make sense when there is a choice between adjustment and financing and if the government has the capacity to implement a gradualist approach. These options had long since passed in The Gambia and Zambia.

Overcoming Donor Dependency

The Gambia and Zambia have become highly dependent on foreign aid. Neither country has a strategy for reducing that dependence. In many areas, such as resource mobilization, education, health, and infrastructure, external aid has become a substitute for local effort. Both countries would benefit from a sober assessment of the negative and positive effects of foreign aid, including its compliance and dead-weight costs. Moreover, both countries would benefit from a clearly defined program for reorganizing their economies in ways that reduce their long-term dependence on aid. Years of extraordinarily large donor support have not produced systems which can move forward without further aid. Breaking this pattern will require a special effort by the two countries and by the donor community.

Capacity Building

The experience in The Gambia and Zambia contradicts a proposition which guides the operations of the Africa Capacity Building Foundation (ACBF). This proposition, argued most prominently by the former World Bank Vice President for Africa, is that African countries have available the local talent to reform their economies. The ACBF has numerous activities, including one in Zambia, which have been attempting to identify and appropriately reward these people.

The Gambia specifically requested external technical assistance because the staff of the Ministry of Finance could not handle the task of reforming the economy. There was no pool of local talent to resolve the types of economic problems that the country faced. Zambia was in a similar situation.

Training and AIDS

What is an efficient and effective approach to capacity building when AIDS is widespread? In Zambia, AIDS has already claimed a significant number of those trained under METAP. To help ameliorate the effects of this attrition, the METAP shifted its emphasis to a system of broad-based, targeted capacity building. The resultant courses, most of which were designed and taught by local institutions, have met the Ministry of Finance's immediate need of enhancing its operational capacity. Moreover, since the program covers a large number of people, it ensures that losses due to AIDS do not markedly disrupt the ministry's work.

Concluding Comments

A number of criteria (including external reviews) show that the EFPA project and the METAP have been successful. These projects have provided the type of assistance which helped The Gambia and Zambia to achieve stability and lay the foundations for sustained growth and development.

This assessment has not changed by the coup in The Gambia in July 1994. Critics will argue, correctly, that "economic reform is not enough." The coup, however, was totally unrelated to the outcome of economic reform.[36] The debacle simply reinforces the point that economic reform needs to be accompanied by action to improve all other aspects of society.

Zambia's experience has been somewhat different. The elections of October 1991 restored democracy and led to the adoption of far-reaching political and economic reforms. The expectation has been that these will continue.

In broad terms, The Gambia and Zambia are examples of the advantage of open, democratic government. The Gambia was a democracy that successfully underwent economic reform. Military intervention reversed that. Zambia did not (and could not) reform while it remained a one-party state. Democratic governance encouraged economic reform.

HIID helped The Gambia and Zambia in several ways: advice, training, and technical assistance. The contribution was modest, the returns to both countries considerable, and the institutional experience was highly positive. Much of what HIID was requested to do in both countries was accomplished. More important, EFPA and METAP staff helped to develop systems and procedures which are allowing others to continue their work.

Notes

1 See Mann (1992) and USAID (1993).

2 The EFPA project was located in the Ministry of Finance and Trade, which later became the Ministry of Finance and Economic Affairs. The METAP started in the Ministry of Finance and National Commission for Development Planning (NCDP). Following the 1991 elections, the NCDP was split off from the Ministry of Finance; in September 1996, they were recombined. For simplicity, each entity is treated as the Ministry of Finance.

3 The EFPA project was financed by USAID. The METAP was funded by the governments of Germany, the Netherlands, Norway, and Sweden.

4 The general demise of "planned development" over the last decade makes it easy to forget the emphasis which was once attached to planning. Early literature shows that planning was widely promoted (cf. Lange, 1961; Lewis, 1966; Blitzer et al., 1975; Meier, 1976, Part 12; Gillis et al., 1983, Chapters 5 and 6).

5 Wolf (1979, 1988).

6 The "rigging" was alleged to occur in several ways. The long-term terms-of-trade were systematically declining for primary producing countries (Prebisch, 1950). "Neo-colonialism" continued through international financial arrangements and the operation of world commodity markets

(Nkrumah, 1965). Being small made the African economies "dependent" on the structure of consumption and production elsewhere (Frank, 1969). And, through its control of world trade and commerce, the "center" manipulated the "periphery" in which African countries were trapped because of historical patterns of exploitation (Amin, 1974). All of these views made a deep impression on African leaders.

7 Various "personalized" approaches to post-independence development emerged (Young, 1982; Sandbrook 1987). President Kaunda in Zambia, for example, promoted a brand of socialism which was dubbed "Zambian humanism" (Kaunda, 1969).

8 In Africa, as distinct from East Asia, prudent economic management has held few political rewards, whereas irresponsible economic management has been generally politically benign.

9 As Killick (1976) noted, government intervention and planning are not the same thing. Unfortunately, they were often confused.

10 Two points are relevant. First, the counterfactual (what Africa would have been like without aid) is not available. Second, much of the aid to African countries prior to the fall of the Berlin Wall was provided irrespective of the aid-recipient's economic performance.

11 The World Bank's annual *World Development Report* and the United Nations' *Human Development Report* provide details on the decline in key social indicators throughout Africa.

12 OAU (1979); World Bank (1981, 1984, 1986, 1989); ODI (1982); Hyden (1983); UNECA/OAU 1989; United Nations 1986; Rimmer 1991.

13 OAU (1980); World Bank (1981, 1989, 1994a); Ward (1989); UNECA/OAU (1989).

14 Brent (1990); Lindauer and Roemer (1994).

15 Only Mauritius and Botswana have avoided serious economic difficulties. The former adopted an export-oriented growth strategy in the late 1970s. The latter has prudently managed the development of its natural resources.

16 Lewis and McPherson (1994).

17 For The Gambia, see World Bank (1985); GOTG (1985); and McPherson and Radelet (1991, 1995). For Zambia, see GRZ (1984, 1989); Gulhati (1989); World Bank (1993, 1995); and Lewis and McPherson (1994).

18 Although Zambia's savings rate was positive during this period (due mainly to the accumulation by parastatal organizations), it was significantly less

than half the rate which prevailed from the end of the Second World War to the mid-1970s.

19 Much has been made of the idea of "muddling through." But, as Lindblom (1959) pointed out, this strategy is not chaotic. There is a sense of direction, even if the response patterns are non-optimal. In The Gambia and Zambia, both economies were adrift and both governments lacked any coherent strategy for dealing with the problems.

20 The Permanent Secretary, for example, was trained as a historian and had risen through the ministry's ranks starting at price control. No more than six people had graduate degrees in economics, the best of which was from the University of Wisconsin. The Minister of Finance had a master's degree in economics.

21 The METAP was seen by the donors as a "last-ditch" effort to provide the Kaunda regime with credible macroeconomic advice. The intention was to prevent the Kaunda government from arguing that the economy could not be reformed due to the lack of such advice.

22 One senior official, however, answered many of HIID's questions on what was expected. He summarized Zambia's situation as: "we do not know where we are!" The project was subsequently redesigned by dropping the trade advisor and adding the macroeconomic data advisor.

23 Indeed, The Gambia had already "graduated" from the IMF's Enhanced Structural Adjustment Facility (ESAF) well before Zambia began its Rights Accumulation Program (RAP).

24 On several occasions the minister wisely rejected what the advisors believed was good advice. An example was the mechanics of floating the dalasi. There were three options: a pre-announced devaluation (as in Ghana), an auction (as in Zambia), or a float (rarely tried in developing countries). The advisor recommended the auction. The Minister rejected it. He did not believe that the central bank could handle an auction effectively and transparently. He was also worried that an auction provided the opportunity for The Gambia's CFA-zone neighbors to exert undue influence if they were so inclined. Subsequent events confirmed his judgment.

25 This point was most evident in the Mid-Term Review of the ERP (GOTG, 1987). The Minister of Finance had two objectives. The first was to inform the Cabinet and the country that the basic goals of the ERP were being achieved. The second was to provide guidance on the direction forward. These were important to the minister who, in mid-1987, learned that he was terminally ill. He wished to leave a clear statement of what had been done to overcome The Gambia's difficulties and what was needed to ensure that the progress would be sustained. Many of his ideas were

carried over to the Program for Sustained Development (PSD) which succeeded the ERP (GOTG, 1990).

26 Some local workshops were held on debt and budget issues, and the fiscal advisor had been tutoring his colleagues on the tax policy reform task force.

27 The METAP made allowance in funding these agencies for a "needs-assessment analysis" and staff support for "course preparation." Both activities are Zambian efforts which bring together the trainers and the senior officials who have identified the need for training.

28 The UNDP funded the fifth advisor, the External Assistance Coordinator (EAC), for one year. When that funding ended, the four METAP donors agreed to share the cost. Notwithstanding this separate arrangement, the EAC has always been an integral part of the METAP. His specific contribution to the METAP and Zambia's economic reform has been critical.

29 The advisors were generally able to work without attracting public attention. However, at times the advisors were severely criticized in the press and by Parliament, particularly when the economic adjustment measures were "biting." There were also physical threats against the advisors. These were handled by intervention by donor ambassadors with the respective State Houses.

30 McPherson and Radelet (1995, Chapter 2).

31 Zambia's annual production of maize (its staple food) averages about 1.3 million tonnes in a normal year.

32 The author's personal experience is that it does take special qualities for ministers of finance to stick to a course of action when all of the economic indicators (inflation, interest rates, exchange rates, industrial production, and so on) suggest that the economy is coming apart. From June 1985 to May 1986, there was hardly any good economic news in The Gambia. During that period, the Minister of Finance was severely criticized. In the public's mind, it was *his* economic recovery program that was creating hardship; *he* floated the currency; and *he* insisted that wages could not rise. To The Gambia's benefit, the minister did not waver. The economy improved. A similar situation existed in Zambia in 1993. The newly-appointed Minister of Finance inherited an explosive monetary situation (created by central bank lending to parastatals). Inflation was 15 percent a month. Nominal interest rates on twenty-eight day treasury bills reached 550 percent (on an annual basis) in July 1993. The minister assured his colleagues that the situation would stabilize. He made this point in the budget speech in January 1994. Most Zambians were highly skeptical. But, from mid-1994 the signs of economic recovery were unmistakable.

33 Roemer and Radelet (1991, pp 65–71) deal with this point. An obvious example where there has been major structural reform before stabilization is Russia (*Economist,* 1995).

34 Zambia provides an example. In December 1992, there was agitation among workers who had been laid off from government service. Their representatives were highly vocal and their regular sit-ins embarrassed the government. The President ordered that these workers be paid immediately. Ministry of Finance staff who had been tracking Zambia's performance relative to the IMF benchmarks indicated that making such a large payment would breach a key program benchmark. When informed of this, the President agreed that the payment could be delayed.

35 This is a variation of the Lucas critique of optimal economic policy (Lucas, 1976).

36 The British military in 1987 had made a special effort to warn President Jawara that his plans to expand the military could create trouble. The warning was ignored.

6 Introducing Market Forces into Former Command Economies

Dwight H. Perkins[1]

Overview

Efforts to introduce market forces into Soviet-style command economies began as early as the 1960s and 1970s in countries such as Hungary. Political changes in the leadership of the Communist Party led to market-oriented reforms in China beginning in late 1978 and in Vietnam beginning in 1986. Then the fall of the Berlin Wall in 1989 was followed by radical political and economic changes in Eastern Europe and in what soon became the independent republics of the former Soviet Union.

HIID's involvement with this transition from the command system and toward the market in these economies developed out of the activities of individuals connected with HIID or other parts of Harvard University. As the scope of these activities expanded, they were brought formally under the HIID umbrella. HIID's earliest efforts with transition economies began in Asia, with a small project in China in the early 1980s, and then with a more comprehensive involvement in Vietnam beginning in early 1989. Work on Russian privatization and macroeconomic policy moved from individual consulting to formal HIID project status in 1992 and 1993. HIID work in Central and Eastern Europe has been in the area of environmental policies associated with the economic transition; this topic is discussed in detail in Chapter 13 of this volume.

China

The small China project in the early 1980s came to HIID through a formal process under which HIID bid on and won a contract from the United Nations Development Programme (UNDP) to work with what was then China's Foreign Investment Control Commission (later part of the Ministry of Foreign Economic Relations and Trade). The project involved help in designing an institute for international economic management to train Chinese officials who would deal with foreign traders and investors as China opened its economy. Courses were taught on practical issues of international economics, law, and management, and a team of HIID consultants helped to draft a suggested curriculum for the new institute.

The project came to an end in 1983, largely because of difficulties the Chinese counterparts had in finding a formal institutional home for the new institute, a problem that was not solved until several years later when the program was integrated into the ministry's University of International Business. Individuals in HIID worked with the Chinese throughout the 1980s and after, but China has consistently opposed having high-level foreign resident advisors, even when outside institutions such as the World Bank have been willing to pay for them.

Vietnam

Resident advisors were an equally sensitive issue for the Government of Vietnam, partly because of the history of United States–Vietnamese relations, but mostly because of the government's reluctance to have foreigners closely involved in the policy-making process. In January 1989 an HIID team visited Vietnam to give lectures and to begin discussions of future collaboration between HIID and the government. That initial visit built on earlier visits by the individual who led HIID's Indochina program and by the program officer of the Christopher Reynolds Foundation. The Christopher Reynolds Foundation funded this team visit and much of HIID's work in Vietnam for the next six years.

The Vietnam project that evolved from this initial visit had several interacting components. Arguably most important, particularly in the early stages, were the visiting scholars and students brought from Vietnam to Harvard. At one point in the early 1990s, nearly half of Vietnam's scholars and university-level students were at Harvard or in programs closely tied to the Harvard effort, such as Tufts University's Fletcher School of Law and Diplomacy. This effort, in 1992, formed the basis for the reopening of the Fulbright Program in Vietnam managed by the American Council of Learned Societies, together with HIID.

The second component of the Vietnam project was a series of study tours and workshops that HIID organized in the early 1990s for Vietnamese economic leaders, including the then Head of the State Planning Commission and later ranking Politburo member dealing with the economy (Pham Van Kai); the then Chairman of the Pricing Commission (Pham Van Tiem); and a team led by the then Deputy Prime Minister (Nguyen Khanh). Through these tours and workshops, Vietnam's economic leadership came together with the leaders in Indonesia, Korea, Taiwan, and Thailand who, together with HIID assistance, had designed earlier economic transitions away from regimes of tight government economic control and hyperinflation.

Lectures and visits by HIID personnel in Vietnam evolved into activities within the country that in some ways substituted for the roles played by resident advisors elsewhere. Initially these activities involved mainly short-term consulting, but in 1993 a formula was worked out with the State Planing Commission whereby a team of HIID researchers would carry out research on a range of economic policy topics that were of interest both to Vietnamese policy-makers and to the Harvard researchers. Access to information about the economy for these researchers was similar to what normally would be granted for resident advisors. This research produced a book on the Vietnamese economy that was widely circulated in Vietnam (in Vietnamese) and then published there in 1994 well ahead of publication of the English language version. Earlier HIID had produced another book on the Vietnamese economy that drew on papers presented at a Harvard seminar organized by a visiting scholar from a Swedish aid agency who later became Sweden's ambassador to Vietnam.[2]

Russia

HIID's work in Russia began in 1992, growing out of earlier efforts by two members of Harvard's Department of Economics. In 1989, one of these individuals, together with a small team of associates, began to advise the leadership of Poland's Solidarity, which eventually contributed to the implementation of Poland's radical economic reforms on 1 January 1990. The Polish reforms attracted the interest of several Russian economists, and in early 1990 a Russian economist (Grigory Yavlinsky) led a team of Soviet economists to Poland. Shortly thereafter, at the behest of the Soviet and the then Russian-federated leadership, Yavlinsky was asked to prepare a program of radical economic reform for Russia, which was done in part with the help of individuals at Harvard. The program became known as the "400-Day Plan" and then the "500-Day Plan."

During numerous trips by Harvard faculty to Moscow, an intensive study group was organized with a small number of young Russian economists. In 1991, these economists assumed leadership positions within the Russian Government. Subsequently Harvard, together with the Stockholm School of Economics, set up a team of foreign experts to advise the Russian Government. In late 1991, the interest in privatization by the then Russian Minister in Charge of State Assets (Anatoly Chubais) led to the introduction of the second Harvard economics professor into this effort.

HIID became involved in these activities when one of these professors returned from two years of leave and joined the institute on a half-time basis, together with three of his Cambridge-based associates who had worked extensively in Russia and elsewhere. The work on privatization, including the advisory team that was being formed in Russia by the second Harvard faculty member referred to above, was brought into HIID when major funding for this effort was provided by the United States Agency for International Development (USAID). With such support, by 1993 and 1994 this privatization work involved as many as twenty resident advisors, initially within the ministry in charge of the privatization process and subsequently in the Russian Privatization Center. HIID's work on the reform of Russian economic laws was a direct outgrowth of the work in privatization, when the resident head of HIID's privatization team, a lawyer by training, was asked to lead the legal reform advisory effort. In early 1994, HIID's work in macroeconomics moved out of the government to the new Institute of Economic Analysis, an independent research institute reconstituted from the Macroeconomic and Finance Unit of the Ministry of Finance.

Mongolia

HIID's involvement in Mongolia began as a result of Mongolian interest in the early reform efforts in Russia and Eastern Europe, which led to a small team, made up mainly of Harvard Ph.D. candidates in economics, to take up residence for several months in Ulan Bataar. HIID provided a number of senior consultants to the Mongolian Government to help in the development of the knowledge and systems required to articulate the country's assistance requirements to the various international and bilateral aid agencies that were becoming involved in Mongolia. In 1992, USAID provided funds to the UNDP, which contracted with HIID to place a team of three resident advisors in Ulan Bataar. The leader of the team had been part of the earlier informal group of resident economists from Harvard. This project came to an end in December 1994, although the HIID team leader stayed in Mongolia as an advisor to the government hired directly by the UNDP.

Price Reform

One of the first issues a transition economy must face is the creation of real markets for goods and services. Goods must be made available on markets, rather than through state administrative channels, and prices must be freed up so that these goods can go to their most efficient uses. The price of foreign exchange, the exchange rate, must also reflect market influences if economic liberalization is to lead to a dynamic foreign trade sector.

Individuals from Harvard and HIID played a role in the debates on price liberalization in the 1980s in Eastern Europe, China, and Vietnam, but most price liberalization preceded formal HIID involvement with these countries. One exception was Russia, where HIID advisors were actively involved in the debates that led to the freeing up of markets and prices in 1992.

Another exception was exchange rate policy, particularly in Russia and Vietnam. In Vietnam, for example, HIID economists participated in numerous discussions with officials on the implications of government efforts to influence the exchange rate for Vietnamese exports and imports. Exchange rate policy was also critical to stabilization efforts.

Macroeconomic Policy Issues

Inflation is one of the primary issues tackled early on by most of the HIID advisory teams on transition economies. The exception was China, where inflation did not become a serious problem until 1988 and 1989, the end of the first decade of reform.

There are several reasons why inflation has been such a large problem during the first phases of the transition away from a command economy. Price reform, for example, typically leads to a situation where large numbers of state enterprises start running losses. Rather than force these enterprises into bankruptcy, the government orders the banking system to lend money to these enterprises to cover their losses. Since few of these enterprises are in a position to ever repay these loans, the result is a steady flow of new credits that forces the central bank to increase the supply of money into the system. Tax revenues also tend to fall sharply during reform, because taxes under the command system are based on enterprise revenues generated by high state-set prices. The freeing of prices from state control leads to the elimination of these monopoly profits and a reduction in state revenue.

Prior to the economic transition, government officials and academics in these command economies had little or no familiarity with how macro stabilization was achieved in a market economy. Early efforts by foreign visiting economists, therefore, involved lectures and short crash courses in the basics of macroeconomics in a market economy. Macroeconomic stabilization was a major theme of a four-day workshop HIID organized for a dozen high Vietnamese officials held in Bali in November 1991, for example. The presenters in this instance, in addition to a number of HIID economists, were the Indonesian ministers who had managed Indonesia's transition from hyperinflation in the 1960s.

Stabilization was a constant theme in the work of HIID advisors in Moscow in 1992, and of the Macroeconomic and Finance Unit of the Russian Ministry of Finance that was established in March 1993. This Russian unit prepared many memoranda, detailed reports and draft decrees on monetary policy, exchange rate policy, central bank credit policy, tax and expenditure reform, and recommendations on the conduct of negotiations with the International Monetary Fund and the World Bank. Proposals were supported through the development of quantitative macroeconomic models of the Russian economy (including tax revenue projections, fiscal-federal relations, and linkages of credit policy and inflation). A detailed tax and expenditure model was developed that provided quick, quantitative assessments of the budgetary effects of numerous tax and spending proposals and integrated these effects into a model of inflation dynamics. A thorough review of Russia's system of expenditure and tax allocations between the central government and the regions led to a comprehensive proposal on fiscal federalism, much of which was incorporated into the 1994 budget. The Macroeconomic and Finance Unit also played a leading role in monitoring and analyzing developments in the ruble zone and, more importantly, in the design of policies to establish separate national currencies for the countries of the former Soviet Union.[3] Macroeconomic issues continued to be a major focus of the unit after January 1994, when it was reconstituted as the Institute of Economic Analysis. Through other channels in 1994 and 1995 HIID's international tax experts continued to work directly with the Russian Government on tax reform issues.

Work in Mongolia in the National Development Board (NDB, reconstituted from the State Planning Commission) had many elements similar to the macroeconomic work in Russia and Vietnam. The macroeconomic policy unit of the NDB was restructured and worked with the HIID advisor on budget issues, inflation, interest rates, balance of payments, and gross domestic product (GDP) reporting and forecasting. Reports were also prepared on foreign debt management, including issues regarding Russian claims on Mongolia for repayment of large pre-1991 ruble debts to the then Soviet Union.

China had neither an inflation problem nor an international debt problem when it began reforms in late 1978. By the late 1980s and the early 1990s, however, high growth was increasingly accompanied by bouts of accelerating inflation. Individuals from HIID on visits to China regularly found themselves in discussions with Chinese officials and nongovernment economists on the nature of Chinese inflationary pressures and how inflation could be controlled. Stabilization of the price level was also a major theme of the HIID workshop held in March 1993 at Cambridge, together with China's Development Research Center. At that workshop specialists on macroeconomic issues with experience from Eastern Europe and Russia, as well as China, were brought together to compare stabilization experiences with some of China's best macroeconomists.

Enterprise Reform and Privatization

A fundamental theme of all of HIID's work with transition economies was that real reform involving the creation of an efficient market economy could not take place unless something was done about the behavior of state enterprises. Stabilization of the price level, for example, was not possible as long as these enterprises required large infusions of bank credit or other government subsidies to cover chronic losses. The growth of manufactured exports and a strong balance of payments position would also be hampered if these enterprises could not compete internationally.

The problems of state enterprises were a continuing theme in HIID's work with the Government of Vietnam. They were also the focus of much of the discussion with the Chinese economists attending the 1993 workshop at Cambridge mentioned above. The Governments of Vietnam and China rejected outright privatization of state enterprises as a goal. In these countries, as a result, the focus of HIID analysis and discussion was on ways of cutting the umbilical cord that attached these enterprises to the government ministries. Hardening the soft budget constraint of state enterprises was a regular topic of these discussions, one that was easy to understand but far more difficult to implement. The Russian officials were the least receptive to cutting credits to such enterprises, and the Chinese officials blew hot and cold on the subject. Only the Government of Vietnam cut off money-losing state enterprises from bank credits by 1993. In fact, all Vietnamese state enterprises, including profitable ones, had difficulty obtaining credit, but the money supply and inflation were brought under control. It was no coincidence that the degree to which the budget was hardened varied inversely with the size of the state enterprise sector in the total economy. In Russia, the state enterprise sector accounted for most of the GDP. In Vietnam, the sector constituted less than 10 percent of GDP.

HIID personnel also participated actively in the debate over the corporatization of state enterprises as an alternative to outright privatization. Corporatization involves the sale of enterprise shares to other state enterprises, state pension funds, and to some degree to the general public. If the shareholders are given the authority to select an enterprise's board of directors, and the directors can hire the managers, then the connection between government ministries and the enterprises is broken. But the Government of China has never let shareholders have this kind of authority, and Vietnamese experiments with corporatization were confined to a handful of enterprises.

The alternative to corporatization is outright privatization—the sale of shares in state enterprises to private individuals. HIID has been involved in privatization efforts in Mongolia and Russia, among the various transition economies. Privatization was the centerpiece of the first period of Mongolia's economic reforms, under the first post-Communist government. An ambitious mass voucher privatization program was implemented at that time, which put Mongolia in the forefront of privatization in transition countries. After the 1992 elections, the new government expressed concern about errors in the privatization process, and a marked slowdown in new privatization took place. This slowdown should not be completely attributed to the change in leadership; most of the early privatization had been of smaller or non-strategic enterprises in which the issues were simpler. When the new leadership came to power, the most urgent remaining issues were considerably more complex, relating to commercial banks, public utilities, housing, and a few large state enterprises which were major sources of revenue for the central budget.

The mass voucher phase of privatization was nearly complete, resulting in a widely scattered share ownership structure with little impact on enterprise management. It was understood that the next steps would be to shift to cash privatization, possibly including foreign capital, and to open a secondary equities market to facilitate the concentration of ownership and improve corporate governance. Although the first phase of privatization had been, by design, relatively painless, unavoidably these next steps would create losers, as well as winners, and would require a very strong commitment from the government.

In the face of these difficulties, without a clear mandate from the national leadership to push ahead, HIID's Mongolia project found that there was an understandable tendency on the part of the Privatization Commission to temporize, to request studies, to organize visits to other countries to see what had been done there, and other actions designed to avoid difficult decisions. The areas in which HIID assistance was focused were commercial bank restructuring, regulation of public utilities, and overall competition policy. Because of the importance and range of these issues, all three HIID team members were involved at different times with the Privatization Commission's work, and provided the government with memoranda and reports on these issues. Two short-term consultants were also enlisted. The project report on commercial bank restructuring, prepared by the advisor to the Market Research Institute, identified issues in bank capitalization and focused on the links between the banking sector and the real sector which needed to be resolved as a condition for healthy financial sector development. In the area of utility regulation, a long background report on regulatory issues was submitted, along with more specific studies on key sectors. Several team-written memoranda on competition policy were part of a sustained dialogue about these issues involving the HIID team, the Privatization Commission, and other government officials. These discussions focused on the need to place more emphasis on increasing competitive pressures on enterprises by facilitating entry and exit, rather than the prevalent emphasis on identifying and regulating dominant enterprises in various sectors. As of 1995, it was difficult to point to concrete results in any of these areas, although a groundwork was laid that made it possible for future policy choices to proceed on an informed foundation.

In late 1991, a group of Russian reformers led by the Russian Minister in Charge of State Assets (Anatoly Chubais) made a decision to attempt a far-reaching program to privatize Russia's state enterprises. In November of that year, an informal group of Russian and U.S. advisors was put together, organized under the guidance and protection of the Deputy Minister of State Assets (Dmitry Vasiliev). The work of this informal group evolved into the formal USAID-funded HIID project mentioned earlier. [4]

The Russian privatization effort rested on the reformers' belief that the Russian people were "economic men" who would respond rationally to economic incentives, but that the role of politics in Russian economic life led to massive distortions in these incentives. If the Russian economy were to become efficient, the role of political influence would have to be sharply curtailed. But the Russian Government did not have unchallenged ownership rights over the state enterprises. There were numerous other claimants or stakeholders, including the managers and employees of the enterprise, as well as local governments.

The privatization law was passed in July 1991. It contained one key element that governed the privatization process throughout: privatization was to be carried out by, in effect, giving the enterprises to the Russian people, rather than by selling these enterprises for cash, as was the practice in most West European privatization. The first step taken was to determine which enterprises were to be privatized, or more precisely, which enterprises were not to be privatized. The enterprises to be privatized were corporatized and registered as joint stock companies with all of the stock owned initially by the government. Corporatization nevertheless created a board of directors and that board, not the central ministries, governed the enterprises. A second feature of the effort was that workers and managers were given a far larger share of ownership than would have been the case if shares had been distributed equally to the whole population. These shares went to these workers and managers as individuals, who could elect to sell the shares, and a substantial portion of shares was held for the public at large. Outright worker management was avoided, but managers and workers had been given a substantial incentive to go ahead with privatization. In practice, most privatization was voluntary. If formal privatization had not been carried out, these same managers and workers would have had powerful incentives to carry out a "spontaneous" or uncontrolled sale of state assets for private gain, a practice that was already well underway. Formal privatization gave managers and workers a stake in maintaining the economic integrity of their enterprises.

The remaining shares were then distributed to the public at large. To distribute these shares, Russia chose to introduce a voucher scheme similar to that used in the Czech Republic. Each of Russia's 147 million citizens was given a voucher which could be used to buy shares in any of the privatizing companies. Vouchers could also be sold for cash or turned over to an investment fund which, in turn, bought enterprise shares. The actual sale of enterprises for vouchers was carried out through a series of local auctions rather than a centralized auction as in the case of the Czech Republic. These auctions had to be simple and transparent if small investors were to be fairly treated and their political support retained.

This privatization program was carried out by the State Committee on the Management of State Property (known by the Russian acronym GKI) between October 1992 and June 1994. Some 144 of the 147 million eligible Russians picked up their vouchers. When the process was completed, some 14,000 enterprises were privatized and these enterprises employed 18 million people, or two-thirds of the labor force in Russian manufacturing. Share ownership, according to one sample survey, was 65 percent in the hands of managers and workers, 21.5 percent in the hands of the public, and the remainder of 13 percent still owned by government.

Under the direction of the leadership of Russians in the GKI, HIID personnel, along with others, were actively involved in the design of this system. HIID advisors were also involved in running some of the voucher auctions and in overseeing the many other foreigners that were brought in to help in the implementation of the system.

Of course, privatization did not instantaneously solve all or even most of the problems facing Russian enterprises. Many continued to run losses and to turn to the state for subsidies. The nature of the process left numerous managers in place who were no more effective running their enterprises in a market economy after privatization than they were before privatization. Restructuring of these enterprises, critical to their ultimate success, remained a task for the future. To help in that restructuring, the Russian Privatization Center (RPC) was established under the leadership of Maxim Boycko who, together with the senior resident HIID advisor, had overseen the large numbers of foreign consultants involved in implementing the privatization. HIID, with USAID funding, provided assistance to the RPC while it was being set up and continued to provide consultants on enterprise restructuring issues into 1995.

Privatization and the Environment

HIID's involvement in environmental policy reform, from an environmental perspective, is discussed in detail in Chapter 13. Environmental issues did not play a significant role in the design of the initial phase of Russia's privatization, or in the early privatization efforts of Poland or the Czech Republic. However, environmental issues have played an increasingly important role in the design of privatizing legislation elsewhere in Eastern and Central Europe.

One issue central to potential foreign private investors, and also to local enterprises contemplating the purchase of additional enterprises, is environmental liability. Growth by Soviet-style economic planning ignored environmental issues, with the result that many enterprises in the region are responsible for vast amounts of toxic waste, some of it known and much only guessed at. In industries ranging from chemicals to steel, the potential investor in an existing enterprise faces large potential liabilities involving hundreds of millions of dollars. In the absence of laws defining and limiting these liabilities, investment in such sectors would be foolhardy. HIID advisors in countries ranging from Romania to Latvia have been working with drafters of privatization laws to outline the options available for dealing with these issues.

Other Transition Issues

While stabilization, state enterprise reform, privatization, and environmental reform have been the focus of much of HIID's work with the transition economies, other issues have also received attention. Much of this involvement with other issues has been in Vietnam, where HIID has been asked to provide information on a wide range of issues connected with the introduction of a market economy to Vietnam.

Some of HIID's earliest work in Vietnam, for example, involved the introduction of the techniques of food price policy. A senior agricultural specialist spent several months at HIID in 1989 and a book on food policy, co-authored by an individual at HIID, was soon thereafter translated into Vietnamese. HIID's first book on Vietnam and a general development text co-authored by HIID personnel were also translated by the Vietnamese shortly thereafter.

The principal HIID economist working on Vietnam devoted considerable time to the analysis of a number of major public investments in that country, as a vehicle for introducing the concepts of project appraisal. Under Soviet-style central planning little emphasis is placed on efficiency in the public investment program, with results that often lead to great waste, waste that a country as poor as Vietnam can ill afford.

HIID has also provided consultants to Vietnam on tax reform, on trade policy, and on energy issues. Prior to the ending of the U.S. embargo, and the reestablishment of broad-based institutional support from organizations such as the World Bank, Vietnam had relatively few sources of reliable external advice on transition economy issues, and HIID tried to help in areas where it had relevant knowledge. Fortunately private foundation funds, principally from the Christopher Reynolds Foundation and also from the Ford Foundation and the Henry Luce Foundation, were available to make this kind of HIID assistance possible.

With the end of the U.S. embargo, other kinds of support for HIID work in Vietnam became possible, including support from the U.S. Government through the Fulbright Program. Fulbright funding was made available to Vietnam by Congress in the form of a contract from the United States Information Agency to the American Council of Learned Societies (ACLS), with HIID as a subcontractor to handle program recruitment. In October 1992, an HIID staff member made the first official Fulbright recruitment trip to Vietnam. The closed nature of the Vietnamese system made it difficult to elicit an enthusiastic response from relevant institutions for student exchange in the United States. After many meetings and building on HIID's existing and expanding network of contacts, a pool of sixty applicants was identified. In December 1992, twenty-five grantees were selected by a U.S. committee to come to the United States for graduate study in economics, business, law, and public policy.

In 1993 there was a much larger response to HIID's recruitment efforts and a pool of 200 applicants was interviewed in Vietnam by ACLS and HIID staff, yielding thirty grantees. In 1994 over 400 potential applicants were interviewed. As of 1994 this Vietnam program was the largest Fulbright Program in Asia.

In early 1995 a new phase of the Vietnam Fulbright Program began with the establishment of an in-country training program in Ho Chi Minh City. In February 1995 HIID's two-month Program on Investment Appraisal and Management was taught to a group of Vietnamese officials in Ho Chi Minh City. This short course was followed later in 1995 by a one-year program in public policy with a curriculum modeled after that of Harvard's John F. Kennedy School of Government. HIID had principal responsibility for managing and recruiting faculty for the initial phases of this in-country program. Formally part of Ho Chi Minh City's Economics University, the program, over time, is to be fully integrated with and under the management of that university.

Outside of the case of Vietnam, HIID personnel, as individuals rather than as a part of HIID projects, have participated in other activities in the transition economies. One HIID staff member cochaired a committee that, for a decade, helped to conduct a one-year graduate program in modern economics at People's University and Fudan University in China. Another participated with a team of specialists working jointly with Chinese counterparts on environmental issues. In 1993 an HIID fellow worked together with officials of Romania's Ministry of Labor and Social Protection on the country's 1994 White Paper on Social Insurance Reform. HIID personnel worked with the Kennedy School's Project on Economic Reform in the Ukraine to find funding for the expansion of the program's activities in Kiev, although their efforts were largely (but not completely) unsuccessful.

In 1990–1991 HIID hosted three visiting scholars (two economists and a lawyer) from Uzbekistan. These three individuals spent time at Harvard learning about modern micro and macroeconomics and law before returning home to take up key positions in and out of government. (For example, one of these individuals was briefly the

Foreign Minister of Uzbekistan.) Later an HIID fellow spent two months in Tashkent teaching a course in modern economics. A small HIID delegation visited Bulgaria to explore whether the institute could help by working on reform issues. In 1995, HIID placed an advisor in Bulgaria under the auspices of the environmental project, but with a somewhat broader mandate. Also in 1995, the role of HIID's Kazakhstan environmental advisor was expanded to involve other Central Asian Republics of the former Soviet Union, mainly with respect to environmental issues.

Other HIID personnel participated in World Bank missions to these transition economies, helped to run workshops for donor agencies, and provided other individual consulting services too numerous to list here.

Conclusion

There is no rigorous way of measuring the economic and social impact of HIID activities carried out in the some half a dozen countries that were in the midst of such fundamental transformations between 1980 and 1995. HIID played no role in starting these revolutionary changes and, as in all countries in which HIID has worked, the decisions to implement reform efforts were made by local people in accordance with their own political imperatives.

That said, HIID was heavily involved in these transitions, particularly in Russia and Vietnam, and there is little doubt that the influence of the institute's involvement was substantial. That influence occurred through four channels: (1) through workshops and individual discussions designed to convey knowledge about how the transition to a market economy could be achieved; (2) through formal training programs at Harvard, elsewhere in the United States, and in-country, to develop skills relevant to the emerging market economy; (3) through specific consultancies with the governments involved on policy issues; and (4) through assistance in the design of new laws and regulations.

The influence of informal exchanges of ideas and of more formal educational efforts depends on the quality of the ideas and on the timing of their conveyance. All that can be said here is that HIID personnel and others who were or became connected with the institute were involved in debates on the transition process from the beginning. In some cases, such as in Eastern Europe, there were many other voices being heard. In other cases, such as in Vietnam prior to the end of the U.S. embargo, there were very few other informed and impartial voices. In some of these transition economy efforts, critical to whatever success was achieved is the fact that HIID's funding sources were more flexible and able to move more quickly than is usually the case with official sources of aid. In the case of Russia, USAID waived many of its own rules to ensure timely assistance.

HIID's work on short-term policy issues had some impact on how particular policies evolved, but probably not as much as would have been the case if the institute had more resident advisors working with key decision-makers on a close and sustained basis over several years. Given that such policy advice is confidential, it is not possible here to present examples where HIID advice was consistent with the policy implemented and others where advice was clearly not accepted, at least in the short run. Even advice that is rejected because the political leadership has become too committed to a particular course of action can influence future decisions. Policy advice in that context is a kind of educational tool.

That HIID played an active and important role in the design of certain new laws and regulations, principally in Russia, cannot seriously be questioned. HIID advisors were also involved in the Russian privatization effort from its beginning to the completion of the voucher privatization and beyond, and hence must bear part of the responsibility for both the strengths and the limitations of that program. In the final analysis, however, Russians made the key decisions and the Russian political, economic, and social context shaped the outcome. In Vietnam and the other transition economies in which HIID was involved, it is more difficult to draw a connection between HIID efforts and specific changes in policies or institutions. That HIID involvement had an influence, particularly in Vietnam, is not questioned.

Notes

1 Based in part on conference papers by William G. Bikales; by David O. Dapice and Thomas J. Vallely; and by Jeffrey D. Sachs.

2 Ljunggren (1993).

3 Lipton and Sachs (1992); Sachs and Lipton (1992); Sachs (1994a, 1994b).

4 This discussion of Russian privatization is based largely on Boycko et al. (1995).

Part III

Targeted Economic Reforms

HIID developed expertise in specific areas, including tax reform, food policy, trade reform, pricing policy, and public enterprise reform. This section also includes HIID's extensive work with the design of rural credit and savings systems and with employment and small-scale enterprises. Individual projects dealt with one or another of these areas in many different countries. Unlike the projects described in Part II, these efforts generally focused on one specific kind of economic reform in each country rather than across-the-board efforts.

7 Tax Reform

Glenn P. Jenkins, Robert Conrad,
Graham Glenday, and Roy B. Kelly

Overview

HIID has been active in the area of tax reform for the past twenty years. This work began in 1975, with a study of mineral taxation in Bolivia and has continued through projects in a wide range of countries including: Indonesia (mining taxation, 1976–1977, comprehensive tax reform, 1981–1986, and property taxation, 1988–1994); Kenya (tax modernization, 1986 to present); Malawi (tax reform, 1988–1995); Dominican Republic (tax reform, 1989 to present); Nepal (tax reform, 1993–1994); and Zambia (tax reform, 1992 to present). HIID also has conducted short-term missions dealing with taxation issues in: Bolivia (1977, 1981, 1991, 1993, 1994); Peru (1992); Sri Lanka (1992–1994); Lesotho (1992–1995); Costa Rica (1994); the Palestine National Authority (1994–1995); and The Gambia (1993–1995).

Many of the people involved in HIID's work on the natural resource sector in Bolivia and Indonesia were previously involved in the tax reform commissions undertaken in the 1960s in Chile, Colombia, and Canada. The commodity boom in the early 1970s made the taxation and ownership of the natural resource sector the critical public finance issue of the day. By the early 1980s, concern over the distribution of the resource rents declined with the fall in the real price of commodities. Attention then shifted to other forms of domestic taxation. This shift in emphasis also occurred because of the tremendous instability of prices of natural resources in the 1970s. Governments began to realize the need for a broader base of taxation in order to maintain fiscal balance while undertaking substantial public sector expenditures.

The institute's work in general tax reform in the 1980s and 1990s largely involved the implementation of a package of indirect taxes, including the value-added tax (VAT), excise tax, and trade tax, along with simplified income taxation. The property tax, while always part of the discussion and political debate, was on the agenda for implementation in only a few cases. The emphasis of the work also evolved, from the evaluation of the economic and legal structure to administrative and compliance reforms. Much is now known about the nature of the economic and legal structure of a good tax system, defined as stable, elastic in revenue generation, and tolerably neutral in terms of economic efficiency. In contrast, little is known about how to implement and administer such a tax system. As a consequence, the focus of research and experimentation has dramatically shifted from the design of innovative tax systems found in the tax reform proposals of the 1950s, 1960s, and 1970s. These reform proposals, which were seldom implemented, often emphasized targeted investment incentives and income redistribution schemes. For the past decade, concerns of fairness and technical exactitude have settled for rough justice, while much effort has been made to find creative ways to implement and administer taxes.[1]

A distinct characteristic of the HIID-assisted tax reforms since 1985 has been the inclusion of trade tax reform and customs administration reform as part of an integrated package of fiscal reform for a country. Historically, tax reform was generally thought of as dealing with the domestic part of the economy, to be restricted to income taxes and domestic indirect taxes. Trade taxes and the taxation of natural resources were usually left out of the package, even though these areas are often the dominant sources of revenue in developing countries. Even in recent years, many advisory organizations have not included trade taxes and customs administration as a necessary component of a comprehensive tax reform. In all countries in which HIID has worked over the past fifteen years, the tax reform process has dealt with the restructuring of the import and export duties, quantitative impediments to international trade, and customs administration. The reform of domestic taxes and their administration, without the reform of trade taxes and customs administration (which administers a large part of the VAT), generally results in a temporary change in policy and administration, rather than a permanent modernization of a fiscal system.

In HIID's early work on tax reform, the bulk of time was spent on the economic aspects of taxes, with a much smaller amount on the legal design of the tax, and an even smaller amount on the analysis needed for administrative reform and implementation. As of 1995, of the total time advisors spent on tax reform typically the economic and structural analysis of the tax system and the design and negotiation of the legal structure and laws applicable to the recommended system each accounted for at most 25 percent, while the implementation and administration of the tax reforms accounted for more than 50 percent.

From the beginning HIID's work on tax reform has been interdisciplinary. Tax reform advisory teams have included economists, sector specialists (geologists and mining engineers), business specialists, and lawyers. Since the mid-1980s, the work has become even more interdisciplinary, as economists, lawyers, sector specialists, administrators, and information technology experts work together and closely communicate to develop recommendations on both the tax structure and the implementation strategy for tax reforms.

Natural Resource Taxation Reform

Bolivia

In 1975, the World Bank asked HIID to undertake a major study of mineral taxation in Bolivia. An interdisciplinary team of HIID staff and professors and graduate students primarily from Harvard University undertook this effort. The research began in the summer of 1975 with a series of extended missions by team members to Bolivia. The analysis was done in considerable detail, which is noteworthy considering the basic state of the Bolivian economy at that time. The final report of this project was prepared and published as a book.[2] This volume on the taxation of the mining sector was welcomed for its content and timeliness, as a great deal of work was being done on natural resources in Latin America and elsewhere. Even today, the book is viewed as a classic in the area and is widely referenced.

The main policy theme of that study was the transition to profit taxation of the natural resource sector and away from fixed output royalties which were previously common in the mining sector. In the previous Bolivian taxation system, such royalties were not adjusted for changes in domestic costs; hence, when the currency became overvalued (as was frequently the case), the royalty became an increasingly larger share of the profits of the mining sector. Usually before a devaluation occurred, domestic costs plus the royalty would have driven profits to negative values. As a consequence, the mining sector was financially strangled repeatedly during the 1960s and 1970s.

The Bolivian study concluded that the ideal tax would be a combination of a small royalty and a well-administered income tax. Because of ease in administration, the use of a presumptive income tax was considered an appropriate transition measure. Few of the recommendations were implemented as such, but this study had a major impact on economic thinking in Bolivia and altered how policy makers adjusted the royalty in subsequent years to maintain a balance among taxes, cost recovery, and net profits. This study had extensive participation by Bolivian counterparts, generally high level officials and members of the mining sector who participated daily in the discussions on the sectoral analysis.

Indonesia

When in 1976 the Indonesian Minister of Finance learned of HIID's work in mineral taxation in Bolivia, he recognized an opportunity to bring back to Indonesia some key members of a previous HIID advisory team, and to have them work with him on the analysis of the country's taxation of minerals and other important economic issues. During 1976, many of the HIID staff who had worked in Bolivia were brought to Indonesia to work on mineral taxation. The oil and gas sector was not included in the terms of reference of this study. Because the mining sector in Indonesia was dominated by state-owned enterprises and foreign multinationals, the focus of this work included the fiscal arrangements with state-owned enterprises and natural resource extraction contracts with foreign investors. Both topics were relatively new to the public finance profession at the time and were not a prime focus of the Bolivian tax reform work.

HIID's work began shortly after the 1975 financial collapse of the state oil company, a critical time in Indonesia's economic recovery. There was great demand for good ideas on how to finance, control, and tax the state-owned resource enterprises. Unlike the tax reform study in Bolivia, where few of the recommendations were actually implemented, many of the recommendations emerging from the Indonesian analysis were implemented through the creation of the third-generation model mining contracts which were designed as part of the study.

One output of this work on the taxation and finance of state-owned enterprises in the natural resource sector was a book describing the various studies undertaken during 1976–1978.[3] A more important outcome was that the leadership in Indonesia realized the benefit of conducting research on important topics before such topics became critical policy decisions. By the time the mining and state-owned enterprise study was completed, the Indonesian leadership requested that, under the sponsorship of the Ministry of Finance, similar work be carried out on approximately twenty topics leading up to the next five-year plan. This policy analysis project was the genesis of one of the primary activities HIID has carried out in Indonesia for the past twenty years. Following the completion of the preparation for the third five-year plan, the economic leadership in Indonesia turned to HIID for assistance in the analysis leading to the comprehensive tax reform. Once the tax reform was introduced, the next topic of policy analysis was the steps to be taken in the liberalization of both trade and industrial policy in Indonesia. To carry this out, HIID created the Customs and Economic Management project which later evolved into the Economic Analysis Project. (See Chapter 3 for a discussion of these projects.)

Fiscal System Reforms

Indonesia

Income Taxes, Value-Added Taxes, and Excise Taxes

By 1981, concerns began to develop within the Indonesian Government as to the state of the public finances if oil prices were to drop or the volume of oil sold were to decline over time. The ministers recognized that it would take some time for the government to develop a modern system of domestic taxation strong enough to adequately finance public sector expenditures. Although there were no immediate revenue difficulties, the government asked HIID to assemble a team of fiscal experts to design a modern tax system which could be implemented under Indonesian conditions. This began a process of tax reform, which at that time was unique.

From 1981 to 1984, several dozen leading and prospective public finance experts from around the world came to Indonesia to work on specific topics. Each expert was expected to write one or more short reports, which were carefully reviewed by other team members before being submitted to the Indonesian counterparts for further discussion and adjustment. The HIID project leader also prepared summary memoranda based on the work of the researchers. He tried to screen out any recommendations which were impractical for implementation under Indonesian conditions. There was constant interaction between the senior Indonesian policy makers and the researchers and advisors preparing the recommendations for the design of the new tax system. In all, the HIID team prepared over 200 memoranda, which were reviewed by a team of about a dozen ministers and senior government officials who gave extensive feedback and suggestions for change.

This style of operation differed completely from that of the previous tax reform commissions in the 1960s and 1970s, such as the Carter Tax Commission in Canada, the Musgrave Commission in Colombia, and the work of Kaldor for Sri Lanka.[4] All of these previous efforts tried to be creative in getting the economic analysis correct, and gave relatively little attention to implementation questions. These commissions consistently over-estimated the implementation ability of the tax administrations of the countries for which the tax proposals were being designed. This was not the case for HIID's tax reform work in Indonesia.

The HIID leadership of the tax reform project and the Indonesian policy makers were acutely aware of the extreme weakness of the tax administration apparatus. As a consequence, simplicity and transparency were absolute requirements imposed on all recommendations for the Indonesian tax reform. This practice stimulated hostility from some members of the tax administration in Indonesia who had benefited from the complexity and the lack of transparency of the previous system.

Given the determination of the Indonesian policy makers to break this cycle and the HIID senior advisor's clear understanding of the problem, a design for the tax structure in Indonesia was produced which has become the model for subsequent tax reforms in both developing and developed countries. Reformers in countries as diverse as New Zealand and Kenya discovered that the requirements of simplicity and transparency imposed on the design of the tax reform in Indonesia were much closer to the reality of their countries than the administrative framework often assumed by the more academic tax reform studies undertaken earlier.

The basic recommendations for the Indonesian tax reform were to implement a single-rate VAT to be applied, with few exceptions, to manufacturing, imports, and selective services. In addition, a simplified income tax was proposed, along with a small number of excise taxes. The reform of the property tax was postponed, because of the anticipated heavy political burden of getting the other measures through Parliament and because the property tax reform was expected to be highly controversial while not yielding much revenue immediately.

The legislation for the VAT, the excise tax, and the income tax was passed by Parliament in late 1984. Subsequently, many adjustments were made through regulation to fine-tune the systems for full implementation. HIID advisors and others have written extensively on the Indonesian tax reform.[5]

A major restructuring of the administrative practices of the tax department was considered necessary, but it was felt that HIID was not the appropriate institution to assist in that restructuring given the strong resentment of the career bureaucrats in the tax department toward HIID and the tax reform. However, HIID project advisors did undertake studies of various aspects of the tax administration during the preparation of the tax reform, which provided the basis for the terms of reference of other international advisors. The institute also carried out short-term consulting work on the introduction of computer-based systems in the tax administration. Still, the government decided to bring in a team of advisors from the United States Internal Revenue Service and an advisory team from Germany to assist the tax administration in modernizing its methods of operation.

Despite the resistance of the tax administration to the modernization of its methods of operation, the new VAT and income taxes in Indonesia have been a success. Before 1984, oil and gas revenues represented about 65 percent of total public sector revenues in Indonesia, with other revenues representing the remaining 35 percent of total revenues. Of the non-oil and gas revenues, a large proportion came from import duties and excises. By 1989, the ratio of non-oil and gas revenues to total public sector revenues had risen to 59 percent, and by 1994 non-oil and gas revenues had risen to 76 percent of these total revenues. By 1994, the VAT was contributing 46 percent of total non-oil and gas revenues.[6]

The income tax and the VAT have performed reasonably well because of the particular design of the taxes, and not because of an enthusiastic administration. Indeed, the design of the taxes concentrated tax collections in areas where there is little room for discretion. For example, over 70 percent of the potential total VAT revenues could be collected on imports, sales of state-owned enterprises, and domestic sales of petroleum products. As for the income tax, there is widespread withholding, which means that the government receives its revenues before the tax returns are filed.

Land and Building Tax

In October 1985, the economic leadership of Indonesia again turned its attention to tax reform, focusing on the taxation of real property. It was decided early on to restrict the property tax to land and buildings. HIID advisors were involved in the legislative design in 1986 through the full implementation of such reforms by the middle of 1994. The design of the property tax followed the pattern of research-discussion-modification, which the HIID advisors and the Indonesian counterparts had developed in the early 1980s. From July 1985 to January 1986, the HIID team produced several dozen research memoranda dealing with virtually all aspects of the design, implementation, and revenue implications of the land and building tax.

The resulting property tax legislation is one of the simplest in the world. The tax covers the value of land and buildings, not including equipment. There is one rate per unit value on all land and buildings for the entire country, with a fixed amount of exemption for low value buildings. Following the passage of the law in Parliament, HIID was asked to provide an advisory team to assist in the implementation of this tax. This project, which was initially financed by the World Bank, began in September 1988; this implementation project was an extension of HIID's urban policy project which had operated for the previous six years in the Ministry of Finance.

From September 1988 to April 1994, HIID maintained a resident advisor in Jakarta to assist in developing the systems for the implementation and administration of the property tax. In addition, this project received intensive backstopping from Cambridge, and a steady stream of consultants were sent to Indonesia to assist on specialized topics. This project also benefited from the extensive experience HIID had gained from the implementation of large administrative systems in the rural areas of Indonesia. HIID project staff and others have written extensively about the property tax reform and implementation in Indonesia.[7]

The implementation of the land and building tax contained innovations which have altered how tax professionals approach the implementation of property tax reform around the world. The major reason for the success of the Indonesia land and building tax project was the adoption of a collection-led implementation strategy that emphasized improvements in the tax collection system, while giving lower priority to property tax information and property valuation. Unless collection and enforcement were strengthened, taxpayers could continue to refuse payment, thereby aborting hypothetical revenue or equity gains from more refined property valuation. The collection-led strategy mobilized and focused the attention of tax administration officials on activities which they recognized as essential for the implementation of the land and building tax. This approach created the dynamics for a sustainable property tax reform in Indonesia.

The initiation of the collection-led implementation strategy was immediately followed by the introduction of a new collection system, the payment point collection system (SISTEP). Under this system, the payment of the property tax is made to a specific regional branch of a bank, which is responsible for receiving and recording payments. This system was designed to simplify the collection function, reduce compliance and administration costs, and provide a delinquency list for enforcement purposes.

Implementation of property taxation through pilot projects was also an innovation of this reform. Each component of the administrative reform was tested through pilot projects and then replicated throughout Indonesia. Another innovation was the gradual, but extensive, use of a computerized data administration system that included property registration, valuation of land and buildings, preparation of tax bills, issuance of receipts, and printing of overdue notices. Given the approximately seventy-two million properties throughout Indonesia, this represents a major accomplishment.

In conclusion, the combination of policy and administrative reform enabled the Indonesian Government to substantially improve both the short-term property tax revenue yield and the long-term property tax revenue potential for generating regional government revenues. Presently, no other developing country, and few developed countries, have as extensive and modern a system of property tax (in both theory and practice) as does Indonesia.

Trade Taxes and Customs

In 1983, the Indonesian Minister of Finance asked HIID to provide assistance in trade policy reform. By late 1983, the first two resident advisors were placed in the ministry at a time when trade policies were running counter to the domestic tax reforms. The poor state of affairs in the administration of customs was also jeopardizing the success of the VAT, since more than 40 percent of the total VAT was expected to be collected by customs on imported goods.

To promote understanding of the problems and a consensus for the direction of policy, HIID advisors undertook a series of case studies that pinpointed the effects of the existing trade policies on the functioning of the economy. The results of this work were summarized in a report entitled *The Unintended Effects of Protection in Indonesia.* In addition, a systematic analysis was conducted to identify the economic impact of reallocating new investment from the protected import-substitute sectors to the non-traditional export sectors. The conclusion from the case studies was that, on average, four times as much employment would be generated and four times as much net foreign exchange would be brought into the country if the same amount of investment was made in the export sectors as in the import substitute sectors.

Another feature of the HIID analysis was the establishment of a database of all quantitative restrictions on both imports and exports. All told, 1,150 quantitative restrictions on imports and about 350 quantitative restrictions on exports were found to be present in Indonesia in 1985.

The government's economic management team was surprised to find the extent to which official quantitative restrictions had grown to strangle the operation of markets and international trade. After this information was made available, policies were formulated to reduce the number of quantitative restrictions and, where necessary, to bring these quantitative restrictions into the tariff system. A key strategic innovation in the reform of the international trading system in Indonesia was the decision to not initially reduce tariffs. Instead, the decision was to do everything possible to reduce quantitative restrictions and other market impediments which hindered the exportation of goods and services.

The reform of the international trade taxes and policies began in April 1985 with a series of changes. The first such change was the most dramatic: it liberated exporters from import restrictions, revolutionized customs procedures, and liberalized international shipping practices. During 1986–1987, the major thrust of the work was to free imports from the quantitative restrictions so that exporters could get their inputs at competitive international prices. In addition, a significant tariff reform was introduced in late 1986. In 1988, the work shifted slightly from promoting manufactured exports to focusing on the problems that traditional exporters had been facing in selling their products abroad. This led to a careful analysis of the quantitative restrictions on the export of these products, and also to the problems of inter-island shipping. In mid-1988, a major reform was undertaken of inter-island shipping and, at the same time, several quantitative restrictions on traditional exports were removed. To complement these policies, there was a concerted policy to reduce and maintain the real exchange rate over time so that the traded goods sectors would be profitable relative to domestic activities.

Since 1984 the work of the HIID group has focused on the international trading system both at the macro level and the micro level. The reforms in Indonesia have been designed and implemented, literally, one sector at a time. The Harvard group has comprised a broad interdisciplinary team of economists, customs administration specialists, lawyers, and graduate students, each contributing his or her expertise to the policy analyses.

From January 1985 to June 1989, more than 1,500 policy memoranda were prepared on various policy issues including 1,000 on trade policy and administration reform issues, 124 on pension reform, 24 on privatization issues, 100 on general tax-related issues, 100 on resource-related and environment issues, and 160 on macroeconomic issues. These policy memoranda were brought to a final stage of analysis and were submitted to the Indonesian counterparts. Additionally, many background papers and interview reports were produced. During this phase of the project, the HIID advisors worked closely with five economic ministers and eight individuals at the director and the director-general levels. Most of the policy-related memoranda were distributed simultaneously to these thirteen counterparts, with other memoranda distributed selectively depending on the circumstances and the wishes of the ministers.

The trade policy changes have had an obvious impact on Indonesia. For example, between 1985 and 1989, the average annual growth rate of manufacturing exports was some 35 percent, with the ratio of manufacturing exports to oil and gas exports moving from 0.6 to over 1.5.

The Indonesian tax reform is widely recognized as successful. This reform process has continued for a decade, with the major tax systems now reflecting those of a modern, rapidly developing country. Unlike prior tax reforms, the reform in Indonesia was comprehensive, covering income tax, indirect tax on both domestic and internationally traded goods, and property tax.

Kenya: The Tax Modernization Project

HIID's involvement in Kenyan tax reform began in early 1985, when the institute undertook a review of Kenya's economic policy that led to a sessional paper entitled *Economic Management for Renewed Growth* (see Chapter 4). Among other things, the review indicated that the tax structure and revenue performance were inadequate to support the desired economic growth strategies. In late 1985, HIID undertook an initial review of the Kenyan tax system. The review indicated that Kenya needed to undertake a major tax reform effort. At that time, the government was willing to start work in that direction, but at a slower pace than was recommended.

During 1986–1989, HIID provided assistance under a series of short-term projects to the Ministry of Finance. In 1986, the institute extensively reviewed the tax structures and administrations of the ministry's income tax, sales tax, and customs and excise departments, identifying a range of desirable changes in the tax structures and strategies to strengthen the administrations, including computerization. Assistance was provided in drawing up a major tax reform project proposal, which eventually led to the start of the Tax Modernization Project (TMP) in January 1990. In the meantime, technical advice was provided during 1987–1989 to assist in the development of a number of tax structure changes, including income and sales taxes and the customs tariff policy. The major tax reform initiative was the design and drafting of the VAT legislation to replace the sales tax. The new VAT Act was passed by the Kenyan Parliament in 1989 and commenced operating on January 1990. During 1986–1989, aside from the administrative preparations for the VAT and some initial work in computerization, little emphasis was placed on administrative reform or training.

Since its start in 1990, the TMP has been involved in reforming the tax structure and administration (including computerization), as well as all of the major taxes on income, consumption, and international trade. HIID has responsibility for the overall coordination of the TMP, and for providing assistance and advice to the government on tax policy, the development of a tax policy-making capacity, and the strengthening of customs administration. A selection of other institutions have provided assistance in income tax and VAT administration and computerization. HIID has had a senior resident advisor in the Fiscal and Monetary Affairs Department of the Ministry of Finance since January 1990, to act as a tax policy advisor and coordinator of the TMP. In addition, a resident team of one or two advisors has been working in the Customs and Excise Department since March 1991.

Under the TMP major shifts in the tax structure generally were achieved. Tax rates were lowered, rate structures were rationalized, and tax bases were broadened by legislated changes in the tax bases and by improved tax administration techniques and capacity that broadened the tax net. In addition, tax structures were reformed to support trade liberalization, lower effective protection, export promotion, capital market development, and a greater reliance on consumption rather than income tax bases. In January 1990, the old manufacturing-level sales tax was replaced by a VAT at the manufacturing level and on selected business services. The VAT tax base experienced significant expansions while the rate structure was markedly rationalized; for example, in 1995, over 76 percent of goods are taxable at the standard rate compared to below 50 percent in 1990. The VAT was extended to cover most services, and the tax point systematically extended to the retail level on luxury and durable goods, motor vehicles and construction materials. VAT rates on many luxury goods were reduced, and raw materials were all taxed at the standard VAT rate. To rationalize the overall structure of consumption taxes, excise duties have been harmonized with the VAT. Excise duties are charged over and above the standard VAT rate on such goods as alcoholic beverages, tobacco products, and soft drinks.

In the area of the income tax, the base was expanded and tax rates were lowered. The top individual marginal tax rate was gradually lowered from 65 percent in the mid-1980s to 35 percent effective in 1996. Starting in 1990, the company tax rate was reduced in four equal steps from 45 percent to 35 percent effective in 1993. Self-assessment, installment taxes, selective audits and taxpayer numbering systems among other administrative innovations were introduced. Tax structures were reformed to support economic structural adjustment. In the area of capital market development, a system of tax deductible pension contributions for employer-based and individual-based plans has been phased in since 1991. The legislative framework for unit trusts was reformed and the tax biases against equity financing were significantly reduced by removing the double-taxation of corporate profits distributed as dividends. A dividend tax account and compensating tax was introduced to ensure corporate taxes are fully paid. In the area of trade policy reform and export development, average tariff rates were lowered by more than 40 percent and the structure of tariff rates were significantly rationalized. All export duties were eliminated in 1994. In the early 1990s, a number of export promotion structures were introduced in Export Processing Zones and duty exemption for imported inputs with export production.

Tax Policy Formulation

A Tax Policy Unit (TPU), with an operational Computer Unit, was established within the Fiscal and Monetary Affairs Department in the Ministry of Finance. The Computer Unit maintains large microinformation databases on a Local Area Network. The data include tax collection information based on import/export data, import duties and taxes, excise duties, domestic VAT, and corporate and individual income taxes drawn from sources in the various revenue departments. The data are used for revenue monitoring, modeling, and forecasting, and the preparation of tax analyses and reports that are inputs into the tax policy formulation. The TPU also coordinates with the revenue departments in monitoring tax policy and the project implementation, and in developing and drafting new tax legislation.

To build up the technical capacity of the TPU and the policy experts in the revenue departments, HIID organized a number of short-term in-country workshops on tax policy analysis issues and techniques. Government officers were also sent on long-term graduate training in tax policy, legislation and administration, and public finance, while others attended short-term specialized courses or conferences in tax policy or computerization at Harvard University and elsewhere.

Customs and Excise Administration

Since early 1991, assistance was provided to the Customs and Excise Department to upgrade the organization, management, and procedures in order to achieve two major objectives: (1) revenue protection and enhancement, and (2) trade facilitation as part of the trade liberalization and export development programs. As more than 50 percent of revenues are derived from import and excise duties, the VAT collected on imports, and excise duties on domestic productions, the operation of the Customs and Excise Department is also central to Kenya's efficient economic performance. Furthermore, customs is key to trade facilitation and the implementation of export promotion programs that are part of the government's liberalization policies. Customs system reforms occurred in two phases. During the initial phase (1991–1993), the overall system was reviewed and a number of basic systems reforms were introduced. A wide range of basic and specialized training was also delivered. During the second phase (1993–1994), a radical new pre-shipment inspection program was designed and implemented, and some preliminary microcomputer systems were introduced.

TMP Outcomes Through 1995

The TMP can be evaluated in terms of five standard criteria for tax systems: (1) revenue performance, (2) economic efficiency costs of tax collections, (3) equity impact, (4) stability of revenues, and (5) the sustainability of the tax system. First, in terms of revenue yields the TMP has been highly successful, particularly since 1993/1994 when ordinary revenue yields rose to 27 percent of gross domestic product (GDP), and revenue targets for 1994/1995 exceeded that level. These are the highest revenue yields ever achieved in the history of Kenya. Typically, during the late 1980s and early 1990s, ordinary revenues have hovered in the range of 22 percent of GDP. Through 1994, the revenue target of tax reform was 24 percent of GDP. Macroeconomic stabilization demands arose in 1993, which required a markedly increased revenue effort. Fortunately, the combination of all the improvements in the tax system had already built up sufficient capacity to enable the system to respond and meet the higher revenue target.

Second, the economic efficiency costs of revenue collections appear to be markedly lower as a result of the reforms. The general lowering of top and average tax rates, and the rationalization of rates on all major tax bases in combination with higher revenue yields argues that significant economic efficiency gains have been achieved. Perhaps the most surprising result has been in the area of import duties. While the simple average official duty rate has fallen over the period, from 46 percent in 1989/1990 to 26 percent in 1994/1995, import duties, after initially falling as a share of revenues to a low of 10 percent in 1991/1992, have risen to 17 percent in 1994/1995. Similarly, import duties relative to GDP dropped to a low of 2 percent in 1991/1992, but reached nearly 5 percent of GDP in 1994/1995 even though tariff rates were being slashed. The longer run efficiency of the tax system is also being enhanced through shifts in the tax structure to rely more heavily on domestic consumption taxes (the VAT and excises) and through the removal of the double taxation of income from corporate equity investments. These shifts in tax structure favor higher levels of investment and economic growth.

Third, the equity of the tax system has been enhanced at least on the horizontal dimension. The expansion of the VAT and income tax bases by legal measures and by tighter administration has resulted in a broader base of Kenyans paying tax. Before the taxpayer identification numbering system was introduced in 1993, less than 200,000 companies and individuals filed tax returns. By the end of 1994, some 1.6 million identification numbers had been assigned, which will translate into a rapidly growing number of tax filers. The impact of the tax reforms on vertical equity is less certain. While top income tax rates have fallen, there have been significant expansions in the taxation of employer-provided benefits, which largely accrue to high income earners. The efforts to improve compliance have also been largely targeted at high-income persons. For example, the in-depth tax audits primarily target those with higher income and, therefore, produce the higher tax yields from this added enforcement effort.

Fourth, the stability of revenues has also been enhanced. The record revenue yields in 1993 through 1995 have been achieved in low growth rate years of the Kenyan economy.

Fifth, the tax reform efforts generally are expected to be sustainable. In terms of tax structure reforms, the improvements to date would have to be actively reversed by legislative changes. Policy pronouncements are generally foreseeing a continuation of the structural reforms. In terms of new administration techniques and systems, the gains made to date should be consolidated and strengthened by the formation of the Kenya Revenue Authority in 1995, which should relax constraints on resources, professional personnel, and appropriate work incentives. Where systems such as the pre-shipment inspection of imports have been contracted out, these are funded by local charges. The dependence of long-term expatriate advisors is not high. While these experts have played important roles in initiating, coordinating, and guiding the reforms, their numbers have been limited to between five and twelve at various times between 1990 and 1995. These numbers are small as compared to the over 4,000 employees of the revenue departments and Treasury involved in implementing the TMP. Much of the success of the TMP can be attributed to the coordinated approach of introducing reforms that took detailed consideration of the administrative capacity requirements as well as the policy structures. Many tax reforms underperform for lack of coordinated policy and administrative development.

Malawi: Tax Reform

The HIID project began in 1987 for an initial two-year period, and was extended periodically until 1995. Staffing included residents (usually at least one resident was in the country during the entire project), and short-term advisors and individuals (who spent from one to three months in the country working on specific aspects of the program). The project followed on a major study by the World Bank of tax structure and administration in Malawi.

Tax reform in Malawi started with a major effort to redesign the basic tax systems, including the trade taxes. In the area of indirect taxation, a VAT was implemented that was extended to the manufacturing level. This tax was a replacement for a prior multiple-rate system of sales tax. With the introduction of the VAT, the tax base was extended from goods to some services. Initially, the introduction of the VAT did not unify the multiple-rate system. Over time, the VAT was greatly simplified so that the basic rate of the VAT covered most services. The excise tax system was also overhauled. The system of unit taxes, which had to be continuously updated to adjust for the effects of inflation, was replaced by a set of tax rates. Further, the rates were rationalized with the domestic protection elements removed from their structure. This enabled the excises to be focused on their ability to raise revenue, while the tariff system was in place for the protection of the domestic industry, where necessary, and for revenue purposes.

In the area of income taxation, the base and rates of personal income taxes were rationalized and significantly reduced. The system of withholding taxes was greatly expanded, and the taxation extended to cover fringe benefits. The personal tax system and the corporate tax system were designed so that they became integrated. In the area of corporate income taxation, the rates and the base were adjusted to be compatible with the personal income tax system. The depreciation system and corporate and tax incentives were also rationalized, so that any incentive provided was contained in a single expensing provision. Furthermore, a border withholding tax and branch profits tax were implemented.

In the area of trade taxes, there was a radical reduction of the tariff import structure in 1990. To complement this trade reform, a duty drawback system was developed and implemented along with a move to commodity classification based on the new harmonized system.

Tax administration became a key element in the implementation of the Malawi tax reform. One of the first areas in which HIID provided assistance was to develop a unique taxpayer identification numbering system that is now used by all taxpayers. A new taxpayer audit examination effort was developed for all aspects of taxation. New collection procedures were designed and implemented, along with a field audit program covering both the income tax and the VAT systems.

Malawi is one of the first countries in which HIID participated in assisting the government to begin computerizing its administrative functions. Assistance was provided in the selection, installation, and operation of a new computer system and in the development of software. This software was developed in a modular fashion, using high-level languages that could be maintained by the Malawians with a minimum of external assistance. The initial systems were devoted to developing master files, taxpayer numbers, and receipt documentation in the surtax income tax area. The system was expanded to include such functions as stopfilers, delinquent notices, billings, and, more recently, efforts on import procedures and border control of the goods flowing into Malawi.

The major objectives of the tax reform effort were realized and, relative to expectations, the effort has been largely successful. It was stated early in the process that no one should expect Malawi to have a stand-alone tax system within five to seven years. Human capital is scare, resources in the country (particularly personnel and senior officials) were expected to (and did) change, and institution building requires significant time. The implementation of the surtax credit system (or VAT) is a significant achievement even with revenue shortfalls and other difficulties. These efforts, followed by administrative and structural reform in the income tax, were considered a credit to the Malawian staff who worked on the effort.

There was an intentional strategy to reduce rates, and to reduce revenues measured as a share of GDP, in the post-1990 period. Malawian officials were concerned about short-term revenue needs during the late 1980s and were constrained by donor performance requirements. However, Malawian officials agreed to support publicly a program whereby taxes would increase, measured as a percentage of GDP, which would be followed by rate reductions. Revenue enhancements included: introducing the VAT at a rate of over 30 percent (lowered to 20 percent after a few years), speeding income tax payments, introducing an advanced installment payment system, and increasing the corporate and individual rates. Tax revenues increased, both adjusted for inflation and as a share of GDP.

These increases were to be down payments for the reductions that came later. Reductions resulted largely from rate reductions of all major taxes.[8] These reductions were planned and anticipated. In particular, there was general agreement that the share of revenues to GDP would return to the pre-1988 level as the reforms proceeded. In fact, the original reform package (presented in a report prepared for the World Bank entitled *Tax Reform for Malawi*) was designed to be revenue neutral, in terms of GDP shares. By a sheer random event, this fall has been accomplished. Recent revenue falls have been attributed to foreign exchange shortfalls related to dramatic changes in political circumstances, events not predicted as the work program was developed.

Relevance of HIID Experience

HIID's prior tax efforts were reinforced and expanded in Malawi. Some examples of the lessons learned illustrate the continuity of HIID's experience in the Malawian context.

There is no such thing as a simple tax system. HIID had learned elsewhere that policy and administration must be closely coordinated. Essentially, it is not worthwhile to design policy without looking at the tax administration because such policies will fail. The HIID approach might be described by the admonition: Don't make a policy recommendation unless you are prepared to administer it yourself. While perhaps too broad, the tone is reflective of the approach. This approach is, in turn, reflected in Malawi in policies such as simple rate structures, expanded withholding, the application of dividend tax accounts as a method of corporate integration, restricting the VAT to the manufacturing level during the initial phase, and harmonization of excise rates. Each policy, taken individually, is a simplification; taken together, these policies are part of a framework for comprehensive taxation.

The practice in Malawi, as elsewhere, is that HIID tax advisors write long proposals and studies only under duress. These advisors prepare short targeted memoranda almost exclusively. As in the case of the Indonesian tax work, hundreds of memoranda were drafted during the Malawi reform. Each was targeted to a specific topic and did not reflect overall policy. For example, memoranda were drafted on such topics as foreign exchange gains and losses, repealing a minimum tax, repealing the tax exemption for certain interest income, and unifying VAT rates. Each memorandum contained recommendations, along with their justification. The memoranda are not comprehensive in the sense that all aspects of either the targeted problem or the solution is addressed. However, their purpose has been to define the agenda for debate and to serve as a springboard for the development and refinement of policy applications. Taken together, the memoranda serve as an important historical record of relevant issues, of how debates evolved. (More than one memorandum was drafted on the same topic at different points in time as a policy was deferred, mistakes were made and corrected, and circumstances changed.) The memoranda illustrate how tax policies were changed and how proposals were implemented.

Decision-makers in emerging economies tend to believe that computerization will be a significant boon to their collections and admission. However, computerization without administrative training, reform, and structural change is doomed to failure. The approach adopted in Malawi, and elsewhere, by HIID advisors has been to blend computerization into the reform process. Computers are introduced incrementally and only after initial policy decisions have been made. Computers cannot be used for anything other than data storage without reasonable tax policies, without the management of the tax system having a clear understanding of tax administration procedures, and without a sufficient level of human capital accumulation in the tax administration to implement change.

The costs of the incremental approach include longer implementation periods and the risk of foreign advisors becoming permanently attached to computer departments. These costs can be mitigated, to some degree, by having local staff involved from the beginning and by shifting programming responsibilities to local staff through time.

The HIID assistance program for Malawi has illustrated a number of important issues. First, it may be difficult to change tax policies, but changing tax policies is much easier than changing bureaucratic and administrative systems. In the area of tax policy, Malawi completely transformed its revenue system. In terms of administration, major improvements were made, but the task is far from finished. A low level of donor support toward technical assistance and, at the same time, a fluctuating economic and political environment all served to slow down and disrupt the process of administrative reform. Significant gains, however, have been made. A large number of the senior officers of the tax departments and the Ministry of Finance have been trained both in Malawi and abroad through HIID's efforts. With the conclusion of this project, a solid management structure for policy process and the administrative functioning of the tax systems have been put in place.

In comparing the Malawi efforts with those in Kenya and Indonesia, one finds a number of similarities and some contrasts. These reforms are similar in that they are comprehensive, dealing with all aspects of the tax system. They are also similar in that major changes have been made to improve the structure and the legislative foundation of the tax systems. Given the precarious state of public finances in Malawi and the lack of commitment of donors to the tax reform effort, the process of implementing and routing the administrative reform of the fiscal system was not developed to the same degree as is found in Kenya and Indonesia.

Dominican Republic: Tax and Customs Reform

HIID's work on tax and customs reform in the Dominican Republic began in late 1989, with the support of the United Nations Development Programme (UNDP). To initiate the program, a detailed analysis was carried out of the existing tax system, including taxes on income, sales, excise, and trade.

The tax reform work in the Dominican Republic has been somewhat unique because, compared to other efforts to date, a much greater proportion of the work has been spent on the reform of the customs system and on the preparation of a modern legislative framework. As part of the assistance HIID provided, a modern management information system was created for the operation of customs. The introduction of this information system was accompanied by a restructuring of the procedures of customs, and a major tariff reform.

Due to the disorganized state of the legal system for taxes in the Dominican Republic, the decision was made to prepare a tax code that would integrate all the taxes and administrative procedures and put the tax code into a single legal document. This tax code was the object of considerable discussion among both policy makers and the legal community in the country, and ultimately was passed into legislation by the government. From 1991 to 1994, HIID had a resident advisor in the Dominican Republic, who coordinated the activities of the consultants and focused on enhancing the administrative capability of the tax departments. There were many opposing political forces to a modern tax reform both within the government and among the donor communities. As a consequence, considerable time and effort were spent in the analysis and preparation of proposals which, in the end, were not implemented. A major step taken by the government was the introduction of a separate tax court. The tax court judges were trained by a graduate student of Harvard's International Tax Program who had done extensive research on the Dominican Republic's tax laws and the reforms implemented. Another major outcome of the project was the computerization of the entire Central Bank and its linkage to the Ministry of Finance. This was a subcomponent of the overall tax reform work and by contrast, was implemented smoothly and professionally.

HIID's work in the Dominican Republic served to bring together a large group of people who have continued to develop HIID's capacity for providing technical assistance to Latin America. Many of the core group from that project are now engaged in other HIID projects providing technical assistance in the area of taxation and, in addition, several of these people have played a key role in the reform of the tax systems in the countries of the former Soviet Union.

A significant side-output from the work in the Dominican Republic was the development of an integrated tax covering all the major taxes and administrative functions applicable to the tax system. Later, this tax code would be revised and published as the *Basic World Tax Code*. Since 1992, this publication has been further updated and published in various languages, receiving worldwide distribution.[9]

Zambia: Tax Reform

Since 1992, HIID has had a macroeconomic reform project in Zambia. As part of the initial project work, several tax policy measures were proposed and implemented. At that time it was realized that the sales tax system, as well as the administration systems for customs and income taxes, were in critical need of reform.

The work has progressed along three directions. First, the sales tax was converted into a VAT. Second, in the area of administrative reform, a major effort was undertaken to computerize the information system for the income tax administration. Third, tax and customs administrations were converted into a semi-autonomous revenue authority. At the beginning of these efforts, other tax advisory organizations took over the task of assisting in their implementation. HIID has concentrated on assisting the Ministry of Finance on formulating a tax policy in the context of the national budget preparation and on developing information systems in the ministry for monitoring the performance of tax systems through time. Although Zambia has suffered greatly from both political and economic instability during this period, as of 1995 a solid foundation of tax policies and administrative institutions has been put in place.

Nepal: Tax Reform

In 1993, HIID was asked to undertake a mission to Nepal to evaluate the state of the country's indirect tax system and to determine whether conditions were suitable for the implementation of a VAT. Throughout 1993 and 1994, HIID sent a series of missions to Nepal to prepare the government for the eventual implementation of the VAT. Extensive work was done to prepare legislation, and also to develop the administrative systems for the operation of such a tax. The issues addressed included the restructuring of the human resources of the existing sales tax administration, and the design of a computerized management information system for the operation of the tax. The legislation prepared in 1994 was passed by the Parliament in 1996.

As regards the policy reform process in Nepal, major steps have been taken over the past few years to improve the indirect tax system in ways that will make it easier to implement a full VAT system. For each successive budget since 1993, major steps have been made to reform an obsolete excise tax system into a modern tax system. By 1996, the number of tax rates had been reduced from several hundred to just one rate of 15 percent. These policy changes appear, at this point, to have paved the way for the movement from an excise tax system into a full-fledged VAT. The fundamental administration of the tax system in Nepal is perhaps one of the most archaic in the world today. Major efforts are being made by the government to modernize how revenue authorities operate and service the taxpayers. Currently, HIID is assisting the government in all aspects of tax administration, from taxpayer education to computerization, with the objective of introducing a modern VAT system in early 1997.

Short-Term Advisory Projects

Since 1990, HIID has participated in a number of missions to countries and entities to provide assistance on specific tax policy or administration issues. Assistance has been provided to the following: Bolivia, Peru, Sri Lanka, Lesotho, Costa Rica, the Palestinian National Authority, and The Gambia.

Bolivia

From 1990 to 1992, HIID assisted the government in evaluating measures to improve the structure of both the VAT and the taxation of corporations and individuals. During 1993–1994, a series of missions were carried out to advise the government on the implications of introducing a cash flow tax, instead of a corporate income tax. In these efforts, a complete draft law was prepared by a lawyer from Harvard's International Tax Program. In addition to this tax work, other missions were carried out to determine an effective strategy for the reform of the customs system, including its preshipment inspection system.

Peru

In 1992, HIID conducted a series of missions to Peru to advise the government on how to develop a modern management information system for customs. Advice was provided also to the government on the design of a system for pre-shipment inspection of goods entering the country through customs.

Sri Lanka

During 1992–1994, a series of missions were carried out to Sri Lanka to advise the government on the reform of the corporate income tax system. This involved considerable tax analysis, including the development of a tax calculator model for the corporation income tax system. During this time, a small project was developed to assist the Inland Revenue Department in establishing a research and planning unit. The work involved developing the terms of reference for the unit, and training the staff in tax analysis. In 1994, two missions were carried out to develop revenue forecasting models for the indirect tax system that could be used to assist the government in planning for the introduction of a VAT. These models were built and used in the deliberations carried out in early 1995 on the structure of the VAT to be introduced in Sri Lanka.

Lesotho

HIID's association with Lesotho began in early 1992, with a mission to review the institute's potential contribution to the general tax reform efforts being initiated by the government. From 1993 to 1995, HIID carried out a small-scale advisory project that assisted in the analysis and development of the indirect tax systems, both sales tax and customs.

The core issue in the fiscal policy of Lesotho was its dependence on the customs and excise duties it receives under the revenue sharing arrangements of the Southern African Customs Union (SACU). Typically, some 50 to 60 percent of its revenues have been derived from the SACU revenue pool. With the democratization of South Africa and the general political and economic changes in the region, it was clear that the revenue sharing arrangements would be fundamentally renegotiated within the medium term. Accordingly, the project had two major thrusts: (1) advice on ways of strengthening the domestic revenue capacity, and (2) analyses of issues related to the SACU structure and revenue sharing arrangements.

HIID applied a multifold approach to assist the government in strengthening Lesotho's revenue-raising capacity. Initially, a major review was conducted on the structure and administration of the sales tax, along with a minor review of the capacity of the customs service. As a result, Lesotho has adopted a revised sales tax law in preparation for adoption of a VAT. The second area was to assist in developing the concepts and mechanisms of a bilateral transfer arrangement for the collection of the sales tax or the VAT on trade with South Africa. The third area of assistance consisted of a review of possible strategies for computerizing Lesotho's customs and sales tax administration, taking into consideration the trade and taxation relationships with South Africa. Another major area of assistance in strengthening the indirect tax system was to review the SACU arrangements, focusing on the revenue-sharing formulas. Reports were prepared on the economic basis for revenue sharing within a customs union, the need for and approaches to improving the trade data required for cost-benefit analysis of different arrangements for Lesotho, and different formulas for sharing customs and excise revenues among SACU members.

Costa Rica

In 1994, a request was made to HIID to assist the government in evaluating a number of proposals for restructuring the country's tax system. This work was completed in two missions, which led to a further request for assistance in the area of customs reform. A mission was carried out which evaluated the various proposals for customs reform and recommended the use of pre-shipment inspection services as part of an overall reform of the customs system.

Palestine National Authority

In late 1994, HIID undertook a mission to the West Bank and Gaza to assist the Palestine National Authority in the formation of a tax administration for the West Bank and Gaza Bank region. In 1995, two additional missions were conducted, focusing on the development of a modern information system for tax administration and on the administrative procedures for the assessment and collection of taxes.

The Gambia

From 1993 to 1995, HIID assisted the Central Revenue Authority of The Gambia in the modernization and computerization of its tax administration. During this time, a number of reforms were undertaken to streamline the tax administration and modernize its information system.

The Central Revenue Department's information system for the income tax administration was computerized, including the development of a taxpayer numbering system. As a further development of this system, progress was made to link the income tax system to other government departments, including sales tax administration and customs.

Conclusion

Over the past twenty years, HIID has undertaken a wide range of advisory and research projects in the area of tax reform. Many of these efforts have been highly effective in changing how governments both design tax policies and administer tax systems. HIID has also learned a great deal from this work, and an entire cadre of HIID staff and professionals associated with the work has become experienced advisors in this field.

With the reduction of international assistance and the disintegration of the Soviet Union into many independent countries, the demand for professionals in the area of tax reform and tax system design in developing and transition economies has never been greater. Political stability and political will, which are so important for effective tax reform, are often not in large supply in these transition economies. It has been clear from HIID's work that political will and political leadership are necessary ingredients for the effective implementation of modern tax systems. High quality tax studies can be prepared and published, but without the political will needed for implementation the potential practical benefits to a country will not be realized. From HIID's work in this area, it is clear that thoughtful advisors can assist in building the political will for reform in the ministers and counterparts with whom they work. An understanding by the advisors of what is politically impossible, and what is politically difficult, is critical. It is the politically difficult measures, not the politically impossible ones, which should be the focus of the advisors' work. If a government can first take small steps that are successful, political support for bolder measures is likely to follow.

It also is critical for the advisors to appreciate the political sensitivity of the taxation function for any government. Effective taxation is at the heart of defining the legitimacy of a government. If a tax measure becomes publicly identified as the proposal of an advisor or an international organization, there is almost no hope for its effective implementation, even if it is legislated. To be effective, the advisor must be heard by the decision makers, but not heard (or seen) by the other interest groups in the society. It has been HIID's experience that if a tax advisor chooses to take public credit for advising a government on tax policy, it is likely the government will have to ignore the advice. Taking public credit for tax policies while successfully implementing such policies is not the privilege of a foreign advisor.

Notes

1 From the 1950s and 1960s the proposals by Shoup on the VAT, Kaldor for self-reinforcing tax structures, Musgrave on income tax design, and Harberger on corporate taxation are examples of such tax innovations. From the 1970s came further examples, with the proposals for rent re-

source taxation and fiscal contracts. In the 1980s and 1990s, environmental taxation has been a prime catalyst for such experimental tax design activity.

2 Gillis (1978).

3 Gillis and Beals (1980).

4 For more information about the work of these commissions, for Canada, see Canada Royal Commission on Taxation (1966); for Colombia, see Musgrave and Gillis (1971); and for Sri Lanka, see Kaldor (1980).

5 See, for example, Gillis (1985); Gray (1986b); and Hart (1987).

6 *Indonesia Sourcebook*, National Development Information Office, Jakarta, Indonesia, and *Government Finances Yearbook (1984–1994)*, International Monetary Fund, Washington, D.C.

7 See Rosengard (1992). Also, see Kelly (1989, 1992, 1993a, 1993b, 1993c, 1994, 1995).

8 Administrative reforms could be expected to make up some, not all revenue loses. The tax administration in Malawi is small, inexperienced, and lacking in sufficient infrastructure for anyone to claim that rate reductions could be self-financing.

9 See Hussey and Lubick (1992, 1996).

8 Food and Agricultural Policy and Rural Development

John M. Cohen, Charles K. Mann, and Pauline E. Peters[1]

Introduction

HIID has an established reputation as an institute primarily focused on assisting government ministries of finance and planning to address fiscal and monetary policy issues. Yet from the institute's establishment in 1974 through the mid-1980s, much of its project work was in food and agricultural policy and rural development. For example, in 1978 projects in these areas accounted for 65 percent of HIID's overseas funding and 57 percent of total funding, though these areas were not central to the professional interests of its core staff. As late as June 1982, projects in these areas accounted for 31 percent of the overseas project funding and 25 percent of total funding. Yet by the early 1990s, projects on agricultural and rural development, including agro-forestry but excluding health and education activities, comprised only 7 percent of HIID's overseas funding and 5 percent of total funding.

Despite this decline in funding relative to HIID's overall programming, projects on agricultural and rural development have comprised an important core of the institute's activities and have been central to the academic and teaching focus of a number of its professional staff. These projects can be divided into three kinds of activities, each of which is separately reviewed in this chapter. The first section provides a brief overview of the Harvard-generated macroeconomic perspective that has guided the food policy analysis exercises carried out under various projects. The next section reviews several types of institute activities: large-scale projects based in central ministries and implemented by advisory teams seeking to strengthen governmental capacity to address agricultural and rural development issues, field-based projects carried out by technical personnel guided by HIID professionals, and small-scale policy related research projects carried out either in the field or in Cambridge. The third section reviews HIID's efforts to train economists and planners who work on agricultural and rural development issues in the sectoral ministries and marketing parastatals. The chapter concludes with a summary of the lessons learned from the projects and research activities reviewed.

Food and Agricultural Policy in a Macroeconomic Context

HIID's advisory approach to food and agricultural policy grew out of the work of John D. Black, a Harvard University professor who established a theoretical focus known as the economics of agriculture. This focus was distinct from that of agricultural economists working in land grant colleges in the United States. Grounded in macroeconomics, Black's theory influenced HIID's early projects in Pakistan and Indonesia. Harvard graduate students trained in Black's tradition went on to do professional work in food and agricultural policy at HIID and at the Rockefeller Foundation. Publications by specialists are influential, particularly in consolidating and extending analytical frameworks for understanding and formulating food and agricultural policy.[2]

Black's focus on interrelationships between macroeconomic policy and the agricultural sector has characterized much of HIID's work in government ministries of finance and planning. It also influenced more applied work on food and agricultural policy in other ministries and institutes, as illustrated in the cases of Malawi, Indonesia, and Kenya, which follow.

HIID Activities in Rural and Agricultural Development

Malawi

Food Security and Nutrition Policy (FSNP), 1987–1991, Food Security Monitoring and Policy Department, 1992–1996

Beginning in 1987 with World Bank funding for a part-time consultant, the Food Security and Nutrition Policy project has provided technical assistance to the Food Security and Nutrition Unit (FSNU), a section within the Ministry of Economic Planning and Development

(MEPD). (Before 1994, the Ministry had been a department within the Office of the President and Cabinet.) When the World Bank funding ended in 1991, the Government of Malawi asked the United States Agency for International Development (USAID) to continue support to FSNU, converting the recurrent consultancies of the food security advisor to a full-time resident position. USAID agreed, and HIID entered into a cooperative agreement with the government and USAID to support this position through October 1996.

The FSNU was established in 1987, following a 1986 research conference that replaced the government's prevailing image of Malawi as a food exporter in temporary distress with the chilling reality that over half the nation's pre-school-aged children were chronically malnourished. The FSNU was created to help define the underlying causes of malnutrition and to design and implement policies to address the nation's nutritional needs. With positions for economists and nutritionists, FSNU monitors policies and projects affecting food security and nutrition; develops strategies for identifying and addressing food security and nutritional needs, including early warning systems and managing food reserves; and coordinates the government's activities to improve nutrition and food security, including chairing the Interministerial Committee on Food Security and Nutrition.

HIID has assisted FSNU to address issues such as the liberalization of grain trade, aggregate food supply/demand balances and resulting food aid requirements, management of the strategic grain reserve to buffer shortfall and surplus and to help stabilize prices, and development of means to increase food security of the poorest households. FSNU staff and HIID's food security advisor played an important role in the development of Malawi's *National Food Security and Nutrition Strategy Statement: Supplement to the National Statement of Development Policies.* This document focused on the fundamental need to reduce the grinding poverty of most households in order to achieve an enduring improvement in their food security and nutrition. Both its objectives and its multisectoral approach presaged the current government's central theme of poverty alleviation.

Drought and political liberalization had profoundly affected Malawi's food security environment. The growth in maize production had derived largely from a rapidly expanded credit program that provided seed and fertilizer to farmers. The combined effects of rapid expansion, drought, and the dissolution of the ruling party's coercive repayment enforcement apparatus led to the collapse of the credit system. Simultaneously, the government's on-going commitment to economic liberalization dictated a complete change in the policy framework of agricultural marketing of both inputs and outputs.

HIID's project assisted the government to manage its food system through this difficult transitional period. A joint HIID-MEPD analysis correctly projected that the collapse of the credit system would result in a sharp drop in the use of both hybrid seed and fertilizer. Having this early-warning prior to the planting season, the government and the aid agencies were able to devise an input-based drought recovery program which provided a high-yield input package for 0.2 hectares to over half of Malawi's smallholder families. The increase in maize production due to this program represented the difference between a national catastrophe and a hardship that could be relieved through moderate food aid. The following year, HIID's analysis projected a low uptake of inputs, this time due to steep increases in domestic fertilizer prices and a liquidity squeeze in the smallholder sector. The government and the aid agencies responded again with a targeted smallholder input recovery scheme, which eventually may help to close the anticipated national food demand/supply gap.

As for the agricultural policy framework, HIID consultants have worked with the government and the major marketing parastatals to develop a comprehensive approach to decontrol both input and output markets. Special attention has been given to transitional arrangements that will stimulate rapid growth of the private sector and still assure a degree of price stability and reliability of national supply for both maize and fertilizer.

As for the micro-nutrient aspects of nutrition, a team of HIID consultants made an important contribution in 1995 to reducing the high incidence of iodine deficiency disease (IDD) in Malawi. While accepting the need to assure that all salt consumed in Malawi contains iodine, the team analyzed the salt market and proved the need for major revision in the government's planned approach to achieving this objective. The team also demonstrated that the original approach would have led to the inadvertent creation of a private salt monopoly and to sharply higher prices. On the basis of the analysis, an alternate approach has been adopted that promises to bring iodinated salt to the populace without the adverse side-effects and costs of monopoly control.

The market study was supplemented by a household-level survey that measured salt consumption by individuals over a three-day period for a national sample of about 800 households. At modest extra cost, the scope of the survey was expanded to collect complete information on all food consumed by each household member over the three days. This information base is providing Malawian analysts and policy-makers with the nation's first-ever national food consumption information (as distinct from expenditure surveys). With the diversification of the food supply as an explicit national goal, this survey is providing urgently needed information on the nutritional composition of the Malawian diet by region, urban/rural, by age and gender, and by expenditure class. Because part of the sample included households already surveyed in the recent National Statistical Survey of Agriculture, links between nutrition and other household variables can be explored.

Through other HIID connections, five FSNU staff members gained analytical skills at HIID's African Workshop on Food and Agricultural Policy Analysis, three MEPD staff benefited from the HIID Workshop on Macroeconomic Adjustment and Food/Agricultural Policy, and one senior MEPD staff member is currently completing a Master's degree at Harvard while working with HIID staff who contributed to the policy studies described.

The value of HIID's work at the macro level of the food security system is enhanced by its link with its village-level studies in Malawi. These village studies, described below, provide a way to assess the impact of macro policy changes on household welfare and decision-making. The linkage between the macro-level projects and micro-level projects has produced significant insights and led to adjustments that have made national policy more effective in reaching its objectives. This conceptually linked macro-micro combination has been termed HIID's "Malawi approach." The groundwork on the micro side was set in place by the project described in the following section.

Agricultural Commercialization and Nutrition Project (1986–1988)

With funding from USAID, a team of HIID researchers carried out the Malawi Agricultural Commercialization and Nutrition project based on in-depth household-level surveys. The team investigated the effects of agricultural commercialization on food consumption and nutrition among smallholders in Malawi. The field research, which was carried out from July 1986 to August 1987, investigated the inter-relations among crop production, income, consumption, and nutrition as these vary across rural households differentiated by household structure, land size, and cropping patterns.

A central focus of the research was the degree and determinants of household food security, a matter of concern to many African countries. During the 1970s, high aggregate growth caused Malawi to be considered an economic success. However, a series of papers demonstrated that the aggregate picture masked declining incomes and welfare for rural producers and preferential policy treatment for the estate sector at the expense of smallholder agriculture. Severe economic downturns, external shocks (especially from the increase in the oil price), and poor management of estates all combined to worsen the situation by the early 1980s. At the time the research began, Malawi had one of the lowest income levels on the continent, and high levels of deprivation (high infant mortality and undernutrition).

HIID's team, comprised of an anthropologist, an agricultural economist, and a nutritionist, studied patterns of production, income, and consumption in the southern region's Zomba District. The team was affiliated with the Center for Social Research at the University of Malawi and worked closely with members of the university faculty. Zomba was selected as the locus of the project because of its high person-to-land ratio, produced maize, vegetables, and tobacco, and because some of its population engaged in self-employment and wage labor. The area, located between two large urban centers, had long been part of a commercialized economy with extensive cash cropping in the colonial period and numerous local markets. The results of the project were based on data for 210 households in six village clusters through multiple methods of repeated agro-economic and nutrition surveys and intensive ethnographic studies.

This study documented that rural families in the crowded southern region are not self-sufficient in their staple food, maize.[3] It supported arguments that, despite the widely touted assertion that Malawi had a national record of maize surpluses, substantial numbers of farming families were chronically in food deficit. The study findings argued that it was misleading to classify rural households as either subsistence producers growing only crops for consumption or commercial producers growing cash crops for sale, since all households follow both strategies. What differs is the scale or relative proportions of agricultural production that is sold. Moreover, the research found a positive association between commercialized production and maize self-sufficiency.

The relations among cash-cropping (or more precisely the production of non-food cash crops), household food security, and nutritional status have been a central focus of the HIID research. Much of the higher income and expenditures of the better-off households were shown to come from tobacco sales. The research established a positive, though not strong, correlation between total income and child stature. Although tobacco-growing households, on average, enjoyed higher income, they did no better or worse in their children's stature as a group than other households. This throws doubt on a simple correlation between "cash-cropping" and food insecurity, which has been suggested elsewhere. The HIID findings reflect the heterogeneity among tobacco growers. When they were divided by income level, the top third had a higher caloric intake at the household level though not at the individual-child level. This suggests that it was the level of overall income, rather than tobacco-growing itself, that had more influence on children's nutritional status. The lack of influence on the individual child's intake even in households with higher levels of caloric intake suggests that the particular form the increased intake took was less productive for children. Also, the lack of influence of higher income on levels of morbidity indicates that the positive effects of higher income and higher household caloric intake can be swamped by the persistent drain of illness in small children. Such findings do not pinpoint a particular effect of tobacco-growing as contrasted with other rural income activities on nutritional status.

On the other hand, when the small group of seven households growing tobacco on land holdings of one or less hectares in 1986–1987 was compared with non-growers with similarly sized land, the tobacco-growing households were found to have lower maize harvests and higher expenditures on maize, but lower child energy intake during the deficit pre-harvest period. The small number gives little statistical confidence and the correlations were not found in the 1990–1991 research (described below), suggesting variability in tobacco production and income. However, these findings suggest that research should look carefully at those growing non-food cash crops, like tobacco, on small-land holdings, as well as at the effects of a "lumpy" income source as compared with a more spread income, the ways in which increased income is translated into different patterns of expenditures, and possible shifts in expenditures between men and women within a household.

Finally, the research showed that "malnutrition" is best seen as the outcome of a synergistic relation between seasonal and/or chronic food shortage and incidence of illness, especially malaria, diarrheal, respiratory, and intestinal disease. To that extent, addressing food insecurity and malnutrition requires cross-sectoral and inter-ministry strategies involving health, agriculture, and employment. This research conclusion helped to shape the multisectoral approach of the national food security and nutrition policy document mentioned above. The findings were also drawn on by major aid agencies, most notably the World Bank (for two policy documents on food security and poverty alleviation), USAID, and the United Nations International Children's Emergency Fund (UNICEF). The project demonstrated the value of such detailed village-level research in helping to inform the national policy formulation process.

Assessing Market Liberalization among Smallholders (1990–1992)

Because of the demonstrated usefulness of the above research to policy-makers and to donor agencies, in 1990 USAID and the World Bank supported field research to restudy the same sample of households studied in 1986–1987. In this case the focus of the investigation was to assess the impact of grain market liberalization on production, income, food security, consumption, and nutrition of smallholder farm families in the southern part of the country, using the 1986–1987 data as a base line since the grain market liberalization policy was initiated in mid-1987. The first pilot stage of extending burley growing as a legal option for smallholder farmers was carried out in 1990–1991. The area of the study sample was one of the sites selected.

The most significant results for food security are as follows: (1) household income levels increased substantially for those in the top 25 percent of income but dropped for the bottom 50 percent (in terms of real income as deflated by the consumer price index for urban Zomba poor); (2) although the poorest 25 percent (like all sample households) increased the proportion of household maize supply provided from their own harvests, as well as increased the percentage of cash expenditures spent on maize purchases, they obtained less total maize per capita than in 1986–1987; (3) although the number of traders in maize and other food crops had increased substantially since liberalization in 1987, virtually all were engaged in post-harvest buying (and reselling), whereas very few were selling maize in the food-deficit, pre-harvest period; and (4) the vast bulk of maize purchased by households in the pre-harvest season (October–February) came from the parastatal marketing board centers.

The implications of these findings are that allowing smallholder farmers to grow burley tobacco legally has had the clear and positive effect of increasing income of participating households. Also, in a year like 1993 when there was no shortfall in crops, this burley income was, to some extent, spread among non-grower households through the tobacco growers' increased demand for local services and products. However, only a few households are able to participate in the burley scheme and the HIID research showed that the tobacco income earned between 1986–1987 and between 1990–1991 increased the income differential between the richer and poorer. This raises questions about monitoring whether wage levels offered by the tobacco growers will increase over time, and about the need to identify other options for income-earning crops or other income opportunities for rural families.

A second implication is that the liberalization of markets is a long and complex process. The absolute dependence of a large majority of households on the government's agricultural parastatal for maize in the deficit period indicates that it is unrealistic to expect the agricultural parastatal to close down its food supply operations within a few years. The lack of capital, skill, and management expertise among traders is reflected in the proliferation of small-scale, opportunistic traders with few specialist traders and an absence of reliable, consistent, and flexible marketing systems on which rural families can rely for food.[4]

Monitoring Food Security among Smallholder Families (1993–Present)

With the value of the micro-macro feedback now well established and demonstrated to both government and donors, a follow-on series of studies was funded by USAID, under the same cooperative agreement with Harvard that supported the food policy advisor. In 1993, the first of a four-year cycle of short (three to four months) monitoring exercises was initiated. In each year, monitoring on selected policy-related issues is conducted among (subgroups of) the same households sampled in 1986–1987 and 1990–1991. In addition, a sample of households from a different area was added to provide comparative insight over the period of study. The changing policy built upon the information and analytical insights provided through the earlier multi-method studies. The singular advantage of repeated studies of a same set of households is that they can respond to questions as these arise in the changing policy and social contexts of the country. Recent examples where village-level information has fed into decision-making are the appropriate delivery mechanisms for relief and inputs packages, the effects of burley tobacco production, and the availability of sources of maize in the deficit season. The "Malawi approach" of linking micro-level research with macro-level policy advising demonstrated its usefulness over a wide range of policy domains.

Indonesia

Development Policy Implementation Studies (1979–1992)

The Development Policy Implementation Studies (DPIS) project, which was funded by the Indonesian Government, was a comparative, interdisciplinary study of four major service delivery programs that were national in scope and extended to the village level. One of the programs selected for study was rice intensification (the others were family planning, primary education, and decentralized village public works). The primary sites for the research were in the provinces of West Java, East Java, South Sulawesi, and South Sumatra. Brief comparative studies were also carried out in five other provinces. The DPIS research was carried out in collaboration with five Indonesian universities, and the overall program included training for academicians at those institutions.

Research components included: (1) organizational analysis of service delivery systems, from the capital city to the village; (2) anthropological analysis of the impact of service delivery in selected villages and subdistrict capitals; and (3) economic analysis of program costs and the distribution of benefits. This research sought to understand what the programs were intended to accomplish, how well they were implemented by the government bureaucracy, whether they reached intended users, and on the basis of study results what advice could be given to policy-makers on how to improve implementation of successfully conceived programs and reform those not achieving their objectives. (The DPIS is discussed in more detail in Chapter 3.)

Center for Policy and Implementation Studies (1982–1992)

The successful activities of DPIS gave way to a new project, which began in mid-1982 when the government funded the Center for Policy and Implementation Studies (CPIS) and asked HIID to provide technical assistance to the new center. The CPIS was designed to carry out interdisciplinary research, policy advising, and training. It comprised some twenty Indonesian researchers acting under the directorship of an official in the Ministry of Finance.

The major foci of research undertaken by CPIS included: (1) rural savings and banking; (2) rice intensification, particularly the effects of government policies on use of purchased inputs, such as insecticides and fertilizer; (3) smallholder production of tree crops, such as rubber, coconuts, coffee, and cloves, particularly addressing policy measures that could raise smallholder income; (4) efficiency, and export earnings, given the existing stock of trees; (5) identification of ways to get smallholders to plant higher quality tree crops; (6) the government's village development program; (7) the establishment of a village database for longitudinal studies of selected development activities and broader social and economic changes at the village level; and (8) trade deregulation policies for agricultural commodities. Excluding HIID Development Discussion Papers, a number of HIID staff published academic articles on these DPIS and CPIS studies.[5]

By 1992, when HIID technical assistance to CPIS ended, the center had a much larger professional staff, including fifty researchers representing a variety of disciplines and carrying out research on such wide-ranging topics as informal sector urban employment, higher education reform, health sector issues (such as health technology, community health, malaria control, and nurse education), and regulatory reform in manufactured goods. Some HIID publications resulted from this work.[6] (The CPIS is discussed in more detail in Chapter 3.)

Integrated Pest Management (1985–1993)

An important field action project emerging from the CPIS research on rice intensification was an innovative program that introduced new methods of pest management and facilitated a huge decline in the amount of pesticides used on rice. The green revolution programs of rice intensification had resulted in large increases in yields so that national self-sufficiency had been achieved by the mid-1980s. However, in the face of fears of increasing attack by pests, especially the rice brown planthopper, researchers began to show that the decrease in the number of rice varieties bred for distribution to farmers entailed the danger of genetic uniformity and, in turn, increased susceptibility to pest damage. In addition, researchers concluded that the heavily promoted and subsidized pesticides were being overused, with the effect of killing the natural enemies of the rice brown planthopper. Starting in 1985, HIID researchers worked to develop a system of integrated pest management. By 1990, pesticide subsidies had been abolished and there was a fifty percent drop in pesticide use, while rice production stabilized at a level of fifteen percent above that of 1986. Pesticide subsidies had been associated with trade distortions, caused large government expenditures and, along with aggressive promotion in agricultural extension, had facilitated the proliferation of pests and high levels of crop losses as well as caused environmental contamination.

Indonesia's National Integrated Pest Management Program was launched in 1989 with funding from USAID and the Food and Agriculture Organization of the United Nations (FAO). This program was based on a new approach to farm extension, involving close working relations between farmers and field staff, who were trained in new Farmer Field Schools, and the development of agro-ecosystems management. The latter was based on ecological methods and, in particular, on habitat studies that analyzed insect population dynamics within specific ecosystems or "micro mosaics" of rice cultivation. Such studies were able to draw on the knowledge and practices of rice farmers as well as on insect and plant ecology. The studies, in turn, led to recommendations about particular pests in particular places and involved the field staff working through a mass effort on the part of literally millions of farmers. For example, during a 1991 outbreak of white stemborer in a large rice region, the program mobilized and trained 80,000 school children and over 350,000 farmers to collect egg masses and monitor moth flights. As a result the outbreak was brought under control without the use of chemicals. The integration of research and extension, actually in the fields with the farmers, makes it possible to move much faster in investigation, diagnosis, and action than in the more conventional mode.

To date, some of the methods developed in this Indonesia program have been taken up in a number of countries in the region, including Bangladesh, China, India, Korea, the Philippines, Sri Lanka, and Vietnam. The results and developing procedures of integrated pest management warrant careful attention in coming years as their potential for other countries is substantial. (The subject of integrated pest management is discussed in more detail in Chapters 3 and 13.)

Rural Electrification Project (1981)

Following the government's decision to bring electricity to as many villages as possible by 1983 and at the most reasonable costs, the Rural Electrification project was designed to study the prospects for productive rural uses of electricity. Alternative sources of energy, such as mini-hydropower and geothermal projects, were among the prospects considered, since these are well-suited for isolated areas where electrical energy is either very difficult to provide or extremely expensive. The Rural Electrification project was a spin-off from the HIID executed Training and Technical Assistance project located in the Ministry of Finance, and served as a link between HIID's work on macroeconomic policy and rural development.

Kenya

The Technical Assistance Pool Project (1977–1992)

One of HIID's major efforts to assist a late developing country to improve the planning capacity in agriculture and livestock ministries is the Technical Assistance Pool (TAP) project, which was implemented in Kenya between 1977 and 1992. It sought to provide advisory services in two sectoral ministries, the Ministry of Agriculture and the Ministry of Livestock Development, while training senior managers, economists, and planners working in those sectoral ministries or representing those sectors in the Ministry of Planning and National Development (MPND). Funded by shifting coalitions of aid agencies over its life, the TAP project was intended primarily to strengthen senior administrative and budgetary management systems in the sectors of focus, while giving additional gap-filling and systems building advisory support and training to economists and planners located in the Planning Departments of the two ministries.

The TAP project is discussed briefly here, because it is described in detail in Chapter 4. From 1977 to 1980 the project was dominated by agricultural economists who focused on strengthening the government's capacity to formulate long-term agricultural and livestock strategies and policies, design and evaluate programs and projects targeted on those sectors, and analyze and formulate price and marketing policies. On the training side, the project sought to promote the capacity of agricultural and livestock sector managers, economists, and planners through long- and short-term overseas training, in-country seminars and workshops, and counterpart work.

While these types of activities continued over the history of the project, by the 1980s the dominant activity focused on strengthening budgeting in the target ministries. To a large extent the emergence of a management and budget focus resulted from the project's successful experimentation with microcomputers in the budget area. This shift in focus was reinforced in 1992 when the TAP project ended and was replaced by the budget component of a new two-year project launched by the World Bank, the Agricultural Sector Adjustment Operation (ASAO II) program. Under this phase of the original TAP project, HIID advisors continued to provide gap-filling advisory services in the areas of economic policy analysis, financial management reform, and computerization.

In terms of capacity building, the TAP project was largely unsuccessful in building a strong, self-sustaining planning and policy unit in the agriculture and livestock development ministry. [7] To a large extent this was due to low salaries, inadequate benefits, poor senior manager leadership, and ample employment opportunities in the higher paying private sector. Still, most of those trained under the TAP project remained in Kenya, making contributions in the public sector, if not directly, then as consultants. The project also sent a number of officers to short-term external training courses ranging from budgeting and finance management to agricultural and food policy formulation. Further, the project encouraged counterpart training efforts by advisors, organized specialized in-house seminars to strengthen economic and microcomputer skills, and worked to strengthen the teaching of agricultural policy analysis and project design skills in national universities.

Evaluating the impact of advisor work is difficult, in part because throughout the project's history the Government of Kenya formulated good policies but failed to implement them. As discussed in detail in Chapter 4, there is no question that advisors contributed to agricultural sector components of several five-year national development plans and to several potentially important policy papers, most significantly, the 1981 Sessional Paper on Food Policy and the 1986 Sessional Paper laying out a Renewed Economic Growth Strategy.[8] Other major policy contributions include: a maize market policy study evaluating the benefits and costs of various policy instruments aimed at achieving market liberalization within a price stabilization framework; commodity specific policy studies ranging from cotton marketing and processing to issues associated with slow payment from cooperatives to coffee farmers; and a major study of food security policy. The TAP project also helped to establish a more timely and systematic annual price review of commodities whose price, by legislation, was set by the government. Also, over the project life advisors helped to strengthen project design and evaluation capacities in the target ministries.

Finally, advisors assisted the target ministries to improve their the annual and forward budget preparation activities by introducing budget rationalization principles and computer-based budgeting and management information systems. Indeed, it was this success in management that led to both the budget rationalization activities carried out by three projects described fully in Chapter 4: the budget component of the ASAO II program that in effect extended the TAP project, the Budget and Economic Management Project (BEMP), and the computerization activities of the Resource Management for Rural Development (RMRD) project.

District Level Planning and Resource Management (1976–1992)

Two related and sequential HIID projects in Kenya sought to strengthen the Kenyan Government's decentralized planning and management systems: the Rural Planning (RP) project, which ran from 1976 through 1985, and the follow-on Resource Management for Rural Development (RMRD) project, which was carried out from 1986 to 1992. Both projects were funded by USAID and interacted closely with the earlier described TAP project. Over this long period, the projects provided, on average, a team of four to six advisors. (See Chapter 4 for a detailed description of the projects' activities.)

The major objective of the RP project was to assist planners in the planning ministry to design and implement sustainable systems and procedures for the preparation of five-year district plans, annual work plans, and budget proposals in support of those plans. Further, the project's design charged advisors with assisting government professionals to develop systems for disaggregating governmental data to the provincial and district level, enhancing program and project monitoring and evaluation procedures, and strengthening the coordination of integrated development projects that were being carried out in arid and semi-arid land areas.

Toward the end of the RP project, advisors built on the successful introduction of microcomputer and spreadsheet technology by the TAP project management advisors and further assisted the government to computerize the national budget and the district planning processes.

The RP project also worked with government economists and planners on a number of policy papers and implementation problems related to the rural sector. Perhaps the most significant of the successes occurred when advisors worked with senior government officers to formulate a crisis program aimed at ensuring that the dramatic fall in maize production resulting from the 1983 drought did not lead to famine conditions. Working with TAP project advisors who focused on tracking production and shortfall as well as on options for obtaining overseas food grains, the RP project advisors developed a microcomputer system to track the import and distribution of food grains throughout the country. As a result of the advisory work and other government interventions, Kenya experienced virtually no famine.[9]

Recognizing the success of the project in strengthening district-level planning, USAID funded the follow-on RMRD project that gave increased emphasis to building the MPND's cadre of skilled economists and planners, both for headquarters and field positions. Briefly, the RMRD project assisted the government to: (1) formulate strategies to promote the efficient and effective management of scarce domestic resources; (2) design policies and programs aimed at rapidly increasing productive employment opportunities in rural areas and small urban centers; (3) ensure compatibility of district-level planning with the government's Budget Rationalization Program; (4) identify linkages between increased agricultural productivity and expanded employment in urban-based manufacturing, commerce, and service centers, thereby creating opportunity for private investment; and (5) continue institutionalization of the district planning and management information systems developed under the RP project. Of all of these activities, the project's work on rural-urban balance strategies contributed the most to the academic literature.[10]

The RMRD project's human capacity-building objectives were to: (1) accelerate the long- and short-term training of economists, planners, and statisticians working in the MPND or in sectoral planning units of operating ministries, particularly through a special program administered by Cornell University's Department of City and Regional Planning; (2) expand in-country training of district development officers through seminars and workshops; and (3) empower economists, planners, and statisticians through training in the use of microcomputers and selected software, largely through an end-user strategy that involved extensive microcomputer training at a project-developed course at the Kenya Institute for Administration.

The RP project trained fifteen economists to the Master's level but, for reasons similar to those faced by the TAP project, only five of these individuals were in the targeted Rural Planning Department of the planning ministry at the end of 1994. Because of a change in training strategy, which is described elsewhere,[11] RMRD had greater success, with twenty-three of the forty-one officers trained remaining in the targeted ministry units in 1994, many of whom were working in the field as provincial and district planning officers or as the head of district-wide integrated rural development projects. Perhaps because of this greater retention, Kenyan officers produced all 1994–1998 district development plans, using the microcomputer-based systems introduced by the RP and the RMRD projects.

In sum, the RP and the RMRD projects demonstrate that HIID has the capacity to strengthen district-level planning in rural countries. One reason for the success of this venture is that while advisors spent a considerable amount of time in the field, they were based in the target ministry's headquarters office and could use that logistical base to work with senior government decision-makers and aid agency officials to accomplish their objectives.

Other Agricultural and Rural Development Projects

In addition to the projects carried out in Malawi, Indonesia, and Kenya, HIID has also implemented agricultural and rural development projects in a number of other countries, only some of which will be covered here, largely because they are described elsewhere in this volume. Two of these projects, the Abyei Integrated Rural Development project in Sudan and the Local Development Associations project in North Yemen, are among the few activities HIID has carried out under difficult field conditions. The other projects reviewed here have been largely small-scale efforts carried out in capital cities or in Cambridge.

The Abyei Integrated Rural Development Project, Sudan (1978–1981)

Aside from the work on health and education described in Chapters 14 and 15 (respectively) of this volume, HIID has carried out only one completely field-based project: the Abyei Integrated Rural Development project. The project proved extremely difficult to implement because of the remoteness of the site, logistics, and local politics. Located in Sudan's North Kordofan Province, this USAID-funded project was executed though a series of complex components that required the institute to support a team of technical advisors who were not only located in a remote region but also cut off from HIID for months at a time during the long rainy season.

The Abyei project involved an experimental approach to integrated rural development. It was designed at the request of the Sudanese Government and sought to: (1) combine agricultural development, health, education, and other forms of assistance in a mutually reinforcing way to promote area development consonant with traditional cultural values; and (2) devise methods of rural development applicable in other parts of Sudan.

The project began with a research initiative carried out in collaboration with the Development Studies Research Center of the University of Khartoum and the Ministry of Health. This research involved anthropological field work and surveys of socioeconomic conditions, with special reference to cultivation practices and livestock marketing practices, as well as to health and nutritional status. Based on the research findings, a project was designed that would field a team of experienced rural development experts charged with improving local organization, promoting cooperative farm efforts, assisting government field agents to more effectively deliver health services and relevant education programs, and construct physical facilities for project staff and field agents of line ministries.

After the first two years of experience, the project was redesigned to focus on a more specific set of issues. In agriculture, technicians engaged in testing alternative tillage systems, ranging from full mechanization to digging sticks. Tests were made of new low-volume, herbicide-based zero tillage systems. Particularly interesting experiments were also carried out with ox-drawn equipment. In the area of water development, alternative drilling techniques and water pumps were tested as part of an effort to identify low-cost, low-maintenance systems that would meet the dry season needs of both people and livestock. Innovative experimentation with hydroplanes was carried out to see if transportation between the isolated project area and the outside world could be improved. Finally, efforts also continued to improve the delivery of health services and construct housing for staff and school facilities.

HIID involvement in the project's field work ended in April 1981, when USAID suspended funding. To a large extent this was because the project, as designed and implemented by HIID project staff, was too experimental, slow-moving, and inflexible to satisfy the complex political interests of the powerful Sudanese politicians, who lobbied for the project, and United States Embassy officials, who funded it through the USAID mission. The decision to stop funding was also made because HIID had lost credibility with USAID officials and the project's Sudanese supporters.

The only evaluation done of the Abyei project deemed it unsuccessful and criticized both HIID's project design and implementation activities.[12] Briefly, that review concluded that HIID staff had failed to perceive and predict the enormity of the problems the project sought to address, the activities undertaken were not technically feasible in the harsh environment of Abyei, the technical staff was inexperienced, project activities were inadequately planned and funded, and grass-roots participation in the project was minimal. There is some truth to these criticisms. Still, substantial lessons were learned about the difficulties of implementing rural development projects in remote areas of late developing countries. These lessons are reviewed in a book written by two of the senior members of the Abyei team.[13]

Local Development Associations (North Yemen 1978–1983)

As a subcontract to Cornell University's USAID cooperative agreement on Rural Development Participation, HIID staff worked with Cornell colleagues to carry out baseline studies of rural development in North Yemen. The specific focus of the research was local development organizations led by the local elite, funded by high remittance earnings of Yemeni workers in the Arabian Gulf, and engaged in building rural roads, schools, clinics, and water systems on a participatory, self-help basis. The objective of the research, which involved considerable field work, was to describe the under-studied local government system of North Yemen and recommend how USAID could more effectively assist local associations to increase the development potential of the remittances channeled through the associations. The North Yemen case raised an interesting question about the economic strategies that might be followed by poor rural countries in which capital is relatively abundant and labor is relatively scarce. The project's research products contributed to both this question and the general database on rural development in North Yemen.[14]

Agriculture and Rural Development Policy Studies (Venezuela 1981–1982)

In 1981, HIID began to assist the Venezuelan National Institute of Agricultural Credit (ICAP) in carrying out research on agricultural and rural development policies and programs. The two priority research topics selected were: the economic and distributional consequences of government subsidization of four important food products; and determinants of the performance of communal and cooperative farm production organizations (OECs) established by the government under its land reform program. These studies were carried out in collaboration with the Venezuelan Foundation for Development of the West-Central Region (FUDECO), and the results were presented at a seminar held in January 1982.

A number of papers, largely prepared by Cambridge-based HIID professionals, were presented at this seminar.[15] These papers focused on comparative international experience with agricultural and rural development policies and programs. Seminar discussions led to a recommendation that ICAP carry out two additional studies, one on the utilization of ICAP's new computerized information system to evaluate credit programs, and the other on the proposed food stamp program in Venezuela. Discussion about further HIID work with ICAP did not bear fruit and the project ended in 1982.

Women, Widows, and Household Livelihoods (India 1988–Present)

A study of a village in the Indian state of Gujarat, conducted in 1988–1989 and partially funded by the Ford Foundation, analyzed how different classes of households cope with seasonality and drought. Two critical dimensions of household-coping strategies received particular attention: the significance of women's work and of gender in understanding household behavior, and the centrality of non-market resources, relations, and institutions in the struggle for survival. The study findings were published and led to a larger scale study of widows in rural areas.[16]

On the basis of that record, a new project was initiated in 1990, funded by the World Institute for Development Economics Research (WIDER) at the United Nations University and the MacArthur Foundation. The project was designed to analyze the vulnerabilities of different types of widows in India, and to promote appropriate policy responses. Working closely with nine Indian partner institutions, research has been carried out in two villages in each of seven states:

Andhra Pradesh, Bihar, Kerala, Rajasthan, Tamil Nadu, Uttar Pradesh, and West Bengal.

The interim findings from North India suggest five basic sources of vulnerability for widows: patrilocal residence, patrilineal inheritance, remarriage practices, employment restrictions, and social isolation. These factors have been discussed in detail in papers, and a book based on comparative historical and anthropological studies is currently in progress.[17]

Priorities for Rural Development Research (1983–1984)

A Cambridge-based research project, entitled Priorities for Rural Development Research, addressed a question of central concern to USAID, namely: "In a decade, what social science topics of relevance to rural development will we wish we had begun research on today?" The project, funded by the Office of Rural Development, Bureau of Science and Technology, had three main objectives: (1) to identify a future-oriented agenda for social science research on rural development; (2) to review the research output produced by nine cooperative agreements between AID and universities and/or consulting firms; and (3) to make recommendations about the cooperative agreement as a mechanism for uniting basic and applied research with technical assistance to USAID missions.

In response to the project's central question, a team of HIID professionals issued a report that suggested twenty-eight issues in which important research investments should be made to enhance understanding of rural development needs and processes. This report provided the basis of a workshop held in Washington, D.C. in June of 1983, where participants discussed five key topics (of the twenty eight) that merited consideration for future research investments by AID: (1) understanding government decision-making; (2) expanding markets and equity concerns; (3) overcoming rural insecurity and unemployment; (4) building local institutions between the public and private sectors; and (5) managing complexity in an environment of uncertainty.

In addition, the team reviewed a number of cooperative agreements USAID had carried out with universities and institutions, such as Cornell University's Rural Participation Project, University of California–Berkeley's Decentralization Project, Ohio State's Rural Credit Program, and Michigan State's Agricultural Production Project. The resulting report focused on: (1) the quality of research produced under the cooperative agreement mechanism; (2) the dissemination of research output; and (3) the management of cooperative agreement institutional relations.[18] This final product of the HIID project was also reviewed at a workshop with USAID officials held in Washington, D.C. in December 1984. At the conclusion of this final workshop, USAID officers stated that the project had done much to stimulate discussion and debate about the contributions of the social sciences to rural development policies, programs, and projects in late developing countries.[19]

The World Hunger Media Project (1984–1990)

The World Hunger Media Project, hosted by HIID and with early support from The Rockefeller Foundation, was designed to develop teaching and informational materials on successful rural development programs and on how to make donor funds more effective in reducing hunger and poverty in developing countries. The project was designed and managed by an award-winning journalist who worked closely with HIID and other professionals to help shape the focus and select the cases. These were in eight countries: Bangladesh, Bolivia, Burkina Faso, Kenya, Malawi, Mexico, Pakistan, and Sri Lanka. The development programs were selected for their success in reducing the vulnerability of villagers to shortages of food and water and for their participatory approaches.

The book produced under this project, entitled *Breakthroughs on Hunger*, focused on improvements in the economic climate in which rural development occurs, farming systems research, efforts to overcome political obstacles to small farmer advancement, and issues of environmental sustainability.[20] The television documentary, entitled *Local Heroes, Global Change,* was broadcast in the United States nationwide on the Public Broadcasting System in 1990. It won three national media awards and has been translated into Japanese, Spanish, and French and broadcast in a number of countries. Both the book and the video series are used for educational purposes by teachers in schools, universities, and church groups.

Population Growth, Renewable Resources, and Environmental Policies (1986–1987)

USAID's Bureau of Program and Policy Coordination funded this project of research on the complex relations among population growth, land tenure systems, and agricultural resource management in Kenya and other African countries with densely settled agrarian populations. Among the questions asked were how rapid population growth effects tenure systems, and how the issuing of private land titles to small-scale farmers affects their farming practices. More specifically, this research project assessed attempts to introduce private property in rural land in densely settled areas of Sub-Saharan Africa. It sought to compare the effects of these directed interventions with the changes in tenure systems occurring spontaneously. Ethnographic analyses were combined with large-scale survey findings and aerial photography to evaluate new hypotheses on African responses to rural crowding.

The basic findings of the study are: (1) population growth, cash cropping, and other causes are producing discernible movements toward stronger individual claims to rural land in the more crowded rural areas, regardless of state attempts to transform tenure; (2) rising densities contribute to agricultural intensification and local resource conservation, though not necessarily enough to ensure productivity keeps pace or to stop resource depletion; and (3) governments and international agencies cannot easily control or speed up privatization. Strong similarities were found among the outcomes of twentieth-century attempts at tenure reform across the continent. They were slower, more superficial, and more ephemeral than planned. They failed to provide secure title. More often than not they merely introduced new temptations for poorer farmers to sell to richer ones. These reforms also failed to ensure means of keeping land registers up-to-date or to develop workable systems of loan collateral. The Kenyan case, examined in some detail, is the most ambitious and emblematic: an expensive nationwide titling scheme is producing a register that is quickly becoming obsolete. But the registration process can radically affect the distribution of rights, concentrating these in the hands of some at the cost of others and of men at the cost of women, and introducing new kinds of confusion about titles, transfers, and mortgages.

Directed tenure reforms, the study concludes, will be inappropriate for most of the densely settled areas where they are likely to be attempted in coming decades. For most areas, scarce program and project resources are better spent on other initiatives that are more realistic, less contentious, quicker to implement, less deleterious in their socioeconomic effects, and more lasting in benefits. These results have proved useful to USAID and produced publications.[21]

Technological Improvement in Agriculture (Bolivia 1990)

Launched with World Bank funding in 1990, this research project seeks to measure the macroeconomic impact of improving the production technology of essentially non-tradable (potatoes, maize) and tradable (soybeans, wheat) crops in Bolivia. The findings indicated that non-tradable staples produced a larger spill-over effect on the economy than tradable crops, because the former affected real wages, consumption of intermediate inputs, and demand for nonagricultural goods and services. Despite the superior returns from improving the production technology of staples, most of Bolivia's producers of export crops, though fewer in numbers, wield more political influence and are better organized than producers of staples. Partly as a result of this research, the government and the donor community have started to pay more attention to improving the production technology of non-traded staples. Several reports and academic publications have emerged out of this study that have direct relevance to Bolivian policy-makers and aid agency professional.[22] These publications have led the government to give higher priority to agricultural research. Towards this end, the government has set up a blue-ribbon Presidential Panel to study agricultural research issues and report back to it by mid-1995. The project's publications have also induced the government to set up an National Science Foundation type-foundation with its own endowment to finance graduate overseas training and agricultural research.

Thailand Rural Industries and Employment Project (1988)

This short, eighteen-month research project sought to explain the existing pattern of industrial activity, particularly in regard to rural employment. The industrial sector of Thailand had been growing rapidly for the few years prior to the launching of the project. Growth was heavily concentrated in the greater Bangkok Area. Yet nearly two-thirds of the labor force still worked in agriculture and there were large rural-urban differentials in income and productivity. Agricultural development, which was also rapid, was thought to be exhausting its potential for growth along the extensive margin. Hence, the government, through the Thailand Development Research Institute, was interested in research that might lead to possible policy measures to promote the regional dispersion of industrial activity in Thailand during the 1990s. Toward this end, the study sought to illuminate the existing pattern of industrial activity in Thailand, the implications of current trends, and the costs and benefits of alternative policies.

Based on this research, the project report concluded that, although the concentration of industry and economic activities in Greater Bangkok does create social costs, industrial firms derive significant advantages from agglomeration, and many possible policies intended to alter the locational pattern are likely to be either ineffective or very costly.[23] Thus, while in effect not a rural development study, the paper directly addressed the issue of regional industrialization and rural-urban balance. The recommendations, relative to the rural sector, included decentralization of government authority and services, provision of information, training, and technical services, accelerated infrastructure development, modified property taxation, restructured minimum wage regulations, and reduced credit restriction combined with efforts to strengthen rural credit markets. These recommendations were probably useful to those Thai policy-makers favoring strong government measures to promote economic activity outside Bangkok. But the study's influence on the debate over where Thailand's manufacturing investments should be made is not known.

Agricultural Policy Analysis Project II (1988–1993)

In 1988 USAID awarded the second phase of the Agricultural Policy Analysis Project (APAP) to a consortium that included HIID. During this five-year project, HIID was involved in implementing technical assistance, carrying out policy research, and training policy-makers. Responding to a request from the Government of the Philippines, HIID placed a resident advisor economist in the Department of Agriculture's Planning Division. During his two-year tenure, extensive work was carried out on pricing policy, improving the technical framework for forecasting market prices, and on issues relating to maize price stabilization. HIID foreign and Filipino consultants carried out a number of studies including the implications of possible GATT agreements on prospects for the Philippines sugar economy. Short courses on aspects of agricultural policy analysis were held in the Philippines, including a three-week Workshop on Macroeconomic Policy and Agricultural Sector issues. This workshop, which was taught by both senior Filipino economists as well as specialists from HIID, involved about two dozen participants invited by the Department of Agriculture and representing a wide range of public and private sector agencies whose activities interrelate and are affected by macroeconomic and sectoral policy reforms.

HIID also carried out a series of policy studies in Pakistan. Research papers were completed on edible oil policy, calling attention to issues related to Pakistan's largest food commodity import, and on livestock feed. HIID also developed the Pakistan research agenda carried out by other members of the APAP consortium. HIID conducted two training courses in Pakistan that included a program on pricing policy analysis for staff of the Pakistan Agricultural Price Commission (one week) and a three-week course for university faculty members and economists in the Ministry of Agriculture and the Agricultural Research Council on a wide range of agricultural and food policy issues.

In 1993, HIID organized a large symposium in Harare, Zimbabwe, on agricultural transformation in Africa. Participants in this three-day meeting included thirty senior agricultural economists, research managers, and policy-makers from a number of English and Francophone countries. An extensive proceedings was produced.

Under the APAP, HIID also carried out various research studies in Cambridge. A short text on open-economy macroeconomics was produced to support training programs on economic adjustment and agriculture. Papers on the political economy of agricultural policy reform, on policy issues relating to informal sector development, and on macroeconomic adjustment and agriculture were also produced. Longer studies on African land reform issues, on agricultural productivity in Africa, and on comparative approaches to managing price stabilization programs using Indonesia and the Philippines as cases were also produced. Finally, the institute completed papers on agriculture demand management and food consumption in Pakistan and in Indonesia, as well as a comparative paper on South East Asian, South Asian, and Near Eastern countries.

Training Activities

Many of HIID's field projects couple the provision of gap-filling advisors with extensive training activities. These range from Master's degree programs and short-term external courses on specific topics to in-country seminars and workshops. Only one of HIID's agricultural and rural development projects has led to a Cambridge-based training activity in these areas: the Workshop on Macroeconomic

Adjustment and Food and Agricultural Policy (1985–1994). This workshop was established in two stages: the African Workshop on Food and Agricultural Policy Analysis, and the Workshop on Macroeconomic Adjustment and Food and Agriculture Policy.

African Workshop on Food and Agricultural Policy Analysis (1987–1991)

In the summer of 1987, HIID introduced a five-week African Workshop on Food and Agricultural Policy Analysis. Reflecting the Harvard tradition of economics of agriculture discussed earlier, this workshop was based at the Agriculture Resource Centre at Kenya's Egerton University. The African workshop was offered once a year for five years. Each session attracted about twenty-five participants from nine to eleven African countries. Students were generally young economists with recent Master's degrees who worked as analysts in planning units or food security units. The aim of the workshop was to introduce participants to practical techniques for conducting food and agricultural policy analysis in an environment where data and time for analysis are scarce. The course focused on using the basic foundation concepts in economics to define and analyze policy problems and to guide in the use of simple estimating techniques that can substitute, when necessary, for more sophisticated applications. The major topics covered in these workshops were: (1) making demand and supply projections; (2) agricultural pricing policy issues; (3) measuring the costs, benefits, and distributional impact of food and input subsidies; (4) assessing policy impact on food consumption patterns; (5) exchange rate impacts on agricultural growth; and (6) food security analysis. Participants applied lessons learned from these topics in phased policy analysis based on an important commodity in their own countries and using workshop developed databases for these countries. In addition, the workshop introduced microcomputer-based exercises based on spreadsheet software.

Workshop on Macroeconomic Adjustment and Food/Agricultural Policy (1990–1995)

Since the Cambridge-based Workshop on Macroeconomic Adjustment and Food/Agricultural Policy was introduced in 1990, an average of thirty participants have attended this annual six-week program, representing countries from Africa, Asia, Eastern Europe, and Latin America. The program also attracted employees of aid agencies. The workshop employed a number of the training approaches developed under the African workshop, but the objectives were very different. This workshop was aimed at more senior policy managers and sought to facilitate a more sophisticated understanding of the conceptual frameworks underlying the design of adjustment strategies. The core of the course was based on an innovative introduction to open-economy macroeconomic ideas and policy implications. The workshop also covered agricultural sector issues in a macroeconomic context, implications of international agricultural trade negotiations, and design of safety net programs to protect vulnerable groups during adjustment programs. The workshop also contained a module on computer-based economic models in policy analysis.

Lessons Learned

The projects reviewed suggest that HIID contributes best to agricultural and rural development through the provision of economic and planning policy advice to ministries of finance and planning or agricultural and livestock planning departments in line ministries. There are two exceptions to this lesson. First, the experience reviewed suggests that the institute can also carry out advisory work on agricultural and rural development issues at the middle-level of sectoral ministries or with local research institutions and universities (for example, the RP and RMRD projects in Kenya and the CPIS in Indonesia). Second, the experience reviewed suggests that experienced, field-oriented HIID professionals can carry out influential research in rural areas (for example, India, Indonesia, Malawi, and North Yemen). In particular, the Malawi projects suggest that while HIID's experience in the use of village- and household-based research in the formation and monitoring of agricultural, food security, and nutrition policies has been limited, there is much potential for significant contributions, especially when they are combined with national level analysis—the so-called Malawi approach noted earlier.

The only case where HIID attempted to implement a field-based project (Abyei in Sudan) suggests that the closer the institute gets to applied field-level activities and the further its staff is from the capital city, the greater the probability that the project will be troubled. To a large extent this is because implementing advisory and training projects outside the capital city require a far more effective support system than HIID has developed for the centrally located teams it supports in the capital cities of countries where it carries out advisory services. There is, however, a major exception to this lesson: the Malawi food security activities described earlier demonstrate that experienced field professionals, particularly anthropologists, can effectively implement HIID activities in remote areas, whether connected to a project in the capital city or not.

A negative lesson from the review presented here is that there has been little direct relationship between the individual fields of expertise of HIID professionals and the kinds of agricultural and rural development projects HIID carried out overseas. That is, the academic publications of HIID professionals on agricultural and rural development topics have generally not been generated by, or directly related to, the HIID projects just reviewed.[24] For example, during the historical period covered, several HIID staff members have made contributions to the literature on land tenure reform; yet the institute carried out no projects in that area of technical assistance. This gap between research publications and areas of project activity suggests HIID staff should make greater effort to identify and implement projects that relate to their academic expertise.

Finally, despite the publications documented in the endnotes of this chapter, the contribution of HIID's agricultural and rural development projects to the development literature have not been substantial. Only the CPIS, Malawi, and the RP and RMRD projects have made contributions commensurate with the advisory and financial resources invested in the projects reviewed. The lesson here is that if the institute is to use its agricultural and rural development projects to contribute to knowledge building, it must find better ways to translate advisory or research experience into academic publications.

Notes

1 Based in part on conference papers by John M. Cohen and Richard Goldman; and by Charles K. Mann and Pauline E. Peters.

2 See, for example, Timmer et al. (1983), and Mann and Huddleston (1984). Contributors to the latter volume include four current HIID staff members: David Dapice, Charles Mann, Malcolm McPherson, and Theodore Panayotou.

3 The basic report on the project was coauthored by Pauline E. Peters, M. Guillermo Herrera, and Thomas F. Randolph in 1989 under the title "Cash Cropping, Food Security and Nutrition: the Effects of Agricultural Com-

mercialization Among Smallholders in Malawi." For academic publications resulting from this research see: Peters and Herrera (1994) and Kennedy and Peters (1992).

4 Publications, apart from reports and memos written for the Government of Malawi and aid agencies, include: Tomich et al. (1994), a book in progress by Peters on "debating commercialization," Kennedy, Peters, and Haddad (1994), Peters (1995), and Peters (1996).

5 Among these publications are: Godoy and Bennet (1989, 1990,1991,1992a, 1992b); and Godoy and Feaw (1989, 1991). Aside from these focused studies, Godoy's work has entered into a number of more general articles and book chapters published on agro-forestry, including Robinson et al. (1993b). See also Tomich and Barlow (1991) and Tomich (1991, 1992). Among the numerous studies by C. Peter Timmer not covered elsewhere in this chapter, see Timmer (1986a, 1986b, 1986c, 1987, 1989, 1990, 1991b, 1991d, 1992, 1993); and Timmer with Falcon (1991).

6 Most notably: Robinson et al. (1993b).

7 The difficulties of capacity building in the Kenyan public sector in general and the TAP project, in particular, are reviewed in detail in Cohen and Wheeler (1997).

8 Republic of Kenya (1981, 1986). For an analysis of Sessional Paper No. 4 of 1981, see Cohen (1984).

9 Cohen and Lewis (1987, pp. 269–296).

10 Jones, B. G. (1986); Lewis (1991); Gaile (1992); Evans (1992); Smoke (1992a, 1992b).

11 Cohen and Wheeler (1997).

12 Development Alternatives, Inc. (1981).

13 Cole and Huntington (1997).

14 Cohen and Lewis (1979a, 1979b,1980, 1981, 1983).

15 One of the most useful of these studies was Michael Shifter's analysis of non-economic factors that influence the behavior of land reform communes and cooperatives, especially with respect to credit repayment. Based on field interviews and work previously carried out by rural sociologists in the country, he concluded that most small farmer organizations were passive clients of paternalistic government service delivery systems, each pursuing quite different objectives, and that most individuals farmers participated little in running the organizations to which they belonged.

16 Chen (1991).

17 Chen (1989a), Chen and Dreze (1992), Chen (1995a), Chen and Dreze (1995).

18 Cohen, Grindle, and Thomas (1983).

19 The only academic publication to result from this exercise was: Cohen, Grindle, and Walker (1985).

20 Harley (1990).

21 The publications of the principal researcher, Parker Shipton, include: Shipton (1988, 1990,1992b).

22 Godoy and de Franco (1993); Godoy et al. (1993). As with most of his project-related work, Godoy incorporated some of the lessons of this exercise into: Godoy and de Franco (1992a, 1992b).

23 Biggs, Brimble, Snodgrass, and Murray (1990).

24 Selected examples of books by HIID professionals on agricultural and rural development that are influential in the field but not generated by work related to institute projects are: Perkins and Yusuf (1984); Grindle (1985, 1988); Robinson (1988); Cohen (1987); Shipton (1989); Godoy (1990a); Timmer (1991a); Goldman (1991); Peters (1994); Grindle, Mann, and Shipton (1989); Mann, Grindle, and Sanders (1990).

17. [illegible]

18. [illegible]

19. [illegible]

20. [illegible]

21. The implications of [illegible]

22. [illegible]

23. [illegible]

24. [illegible] to industrial projects and [illegible]

9 ECONOMIC POLICY REFORM STUDIES

Clive S. Gray[1]

INTRODUCTION

This chapter covers four HIID projects, each concerned with a range of economic policy reform issues. Three projects—in Sri Lanka, Bangladesh, and Morocco—were activities confined to a single developing country, each spanning about three to four years. In all three cases the project contract was fulfilled but not renewed. (Consultations that took place in each case concerning the possibility of extension are described below.) The fourth project, Consulting Assistance for Economic Reform (CAER), a worldwide activity that involved HIID and four subcontractors, supported policy studies in thirty-three countries, along with a handful of studies covering entire regions.

Two of the country projects involved teams of resident advisors, numbering eleven in Bangladesh and two in Morocco, complemented by consultant visits. The Sri Lanka project involved only consultant visits, which, in the opinion of the participating HIID staff, weakened its impact. Table 9-1 gives a breakdown of the HIID-recruited participants in all four projects by HIID staff, Harvard faculty, Harvard students, local consultants, and others. As shown in the table, the two projects that used only consultants, Sri Lanka and CAER, involved the largest numbers of Harvard faculty members.

The Sri Lanka project addressed a wide range of problems at the top of the government's policy agenda; the Bangladesh project focused on issues of industrial development and trade; and the Morocco project was designed to help transform a price control unit into a policy studies group. Given these differing terms of reference, this chapter summarizes the origins, modalities, concerns, accomplishments, and shortcomings of each project consecutively, followed by a

TABLE 9-1
Personnel Engaged by HIID in Sri Lanka, Bangladesh, Morocco, and CAER Projects

Project	HIID Staff[a]	Harvard Faculty[b]	Harvard Students	Local	Others	Total[c]
Sri Lanka						
Consultants	4	5	1		2	12
Bangladesh						
Resident	1			7	8	
Consultants	3	1	1	37	7	49
Morocco						
Resident	1			1	2	
Consultants			4	1	5	
CAER						
Consultants	27	13	1		41	82

a Comprises HIID fellows and institute and research associates. Cambridge backstoppers are not included unless they visited the field as consultants.

b Some Harvard faculty are also HIID Faculty Fellows.

c Excludes personnel engaged by HIID subcontractors. Staff who made multiple visits are counted only once.

comparative look at the issue of project renewal, and the institutional aspects of the three country projects, especially capacity building.

SRI LANKA

Origins and Objectives

Of the three country projects, Sri Lanka is the only one where the initiative originated with the host government. The 1977 elections had installed the United National Party (UNP), which was committed to curbing state control over the economy. In 1979, the Minister of Finance and Planning, acquainted with HIID's work in Malaysia and Indonesia,[2] visited Cambridge and requested technical assistance to help his ministry analyze a range of policy issues. These revolved around the government's attempt to stabilize the economy and stimulate exports while retaining the country's social safety net.

The Malaysia and Indonesia projects provided the model to be followed, except for the absence of resident advisors. The United

Nations Development Programme (UNDP) agreed to fund 24 person-months of consulting services; project activity began in January 1980 and ran through 1982.

Modalities of Technical Assistance

The exclusion of resident advisors raises special issues in reviewing the Sri Lanka project's implementation. Three factors appear to have underlain the government's decision:

- While seeking to upgrade its staff, the Ministry of Finance and Planning (MoFP) wanted to avoid a *modus operandi* in which foreign advisors might dominate their counterparts.
- The government was concerned about criticism for allowing foreigners to influence policies that, by reducing direct controls and subsidies, would undercut Sri Lanka's social safety net. Relying on short-term consultants who would work in Sri Lanka for a few weeks at a time would reduce the political risks.
- UNDP funding for 24 person-months of advisory services would either support a single resident for two years or multiple consultants with expertise in different fields. The latter option appeared to offer more benefits.

As shown in Table 9-1, the project provided twelve foreign consultants, some of whom made multiple visits.[3] Typically several researchers would visit Colombo during the summer and return during the winter academic break to follow up on data collection and otherwise continue the work. To complement the written reports, which might not be read at senior levels, an effort was made to conclude each visit with a briefing for the minister or his senior staff.

A counterpart team was established as the project began, with members being assigned to the respective consultants. The MoFP expressed a strong desire to have them fully integrated into the work program, but their involvement proved episodic. With the availability of consultants determined to a considerable extent by Harvard teaching schedules,[4] lack of a resident HIID presence made it difficult to ensure the staff's availability to work with their foreign counterparts. Moreover, any interest and relationship built up during a consultant's visit tended to be dissipated once he had departed, and the local staff faced other demands, making for a "stop-go" pattern of project implementation.

Inflation and fiscal stress, by depressing real compensation in Sri Lanka's civil service, had made it difficult for government to recruit skilled economists. Hence the MoFP suggested that HIID involve independent Sri Lankan research institutes. The ministry promised to pay for these services out of its funds, but in the end no such financing was forthcoming. Notwithstanding numerous interchanges of ideas, meetings, and informal sharing of information with staff of the institutes, formal research collaboration did not take place.

At the UNDP's request a project steering committee was established, with a number of senior officials agreeing to serve on it. However, it met only once and failed to provide much support in resolving project implementation problems.

Apart from on-the-job training the HIID consultants held seminars in the MoFP and central bank, to report on their research and explain the analytic techniques used. One of the more fruitful project activities was a day-long seminar on legal and economic issues in negotiating with foreign private investors, given by Harvard faculty members—one each from the Law and the Business Schools—to an audience that included senior Sri Lankan officials.

Substantive Project Concerns

The study agenda focused on the UNP government's central concerns—to create jobs by liberalizing the economy, and to relieve fiscal stress by reducing income subsidies while protecting incomes of the poorest segments of society. The work program eventually agreed upon by the MoFP and HIID stressed the following issues:

- The impact of a set of capital-intensive public investments—so-called "lead projects"—on the balance of payments and macroeconomic stability (for example, a high dam and accompanying irrigation network). Most of the projects had been studied but were not yet fully funded. The donor community's favorable disposition to the UNP government raised the possibility of additional funding.
- How to make the food stamp program more cost-effective while protecting the welfare of the poorest.
- The relative merits of input and production subsidies versus food subsidies on agricultural efficiency and income distribution.
- The performance of state-owned enterprises.

- The "explosion" of concessions requested by, and often granted to, industrial promoters without serious economic evaluation, and their impact on income distribution.
- Development of a flow of funds table in collaboration with central bank staff as a basis for analyzing the monetary system and identifying sources of inflation.

An underlying theme of all the topics was concern with the welfare effects of government policies and programs.

Project Accomplishments and Shortfalls

Notwithstanding the stop-go pattern of activity, the project produced new insights into Sri Lanka's economic situation, along with policy implications. There was an unusual degree of inter-relatedness among the studies. For example, reflecting the government's high priority for employment creation to offset reduction or abolition of food subsidies, the study of the "lead projects" computed the employment impact of such investments.

On protecting the income of the poor, the project measured the food stamp program's contribution and confirmed its key role in the social safety net, but it warned that continued inflation was jeopardizing the program's efficacy as an income redistribution measure. The papers on stabilization noted that fiscal and trade reforms had only begun to remove the distortions inherited by the UNP government, and that efforts to protect the poor and to increase employment would fail without better macroeconomic management. In the area of food policy, what was probably the first attempt to develop a comprehensive model of Sri Lanka's food production sector provided evidence that a rise in rural incomes served to increase labor demand, but that a disproportionate rise of paddy prices in the more productive areas would likely induce the use of tractors with a negative impact on labor use.

The government valued the studies' conclusions and saw HIID's input as providing an independent view of required reform measures. Despite his desire for the project to maintain a low profile, the minister used HIID's involvement to counter press charges that policy reforms were dictated by the donor agencies. For example, to counter donor pressure to trim the lead projects, he announced that government at first wanted its own advisors to review the issue. This led donor agency staff to complain that HIID was merely duplicating their own work.

Through the Sri Lanka project HIID tested a service modality (short-term consultants) that turned out to have both pros and cons. It allowed HIID to integrate institute staff and Harvard faculty in a strong team, but the long gaps between visits to Colombo (by militating against any ongoing program of research and analysis) ruled out institutional development.

Moreover, the absence of a resident advisor limited the impact of the project reports. HIID staff could neither become familiar with the bureaucracy and the personalities involved in policymaking, nor obtain timely feedback on the work done. This made it difficult to determine which part of the analysis might be flawed and what further work might be useful. The wrap-up meetings following each round of consultant visits were no substitute for an ongoing dialogue about the work program and follow-up to policy recommendations.

Bangladesh

Origins and Objectives

Starting in the 1970s the donor community was pressing the Bangladesh Government for policy reforms as a condition for continuing foreign aid, which financed about half of the country's imports. The Minister of Finance, taking office during an economic crisis in 1982, agreed with the World Bank to undertake the Trade and Industry Policy (TIP) project under an International Development Association (IDA) credit.[5]

The project's objectives were to strengthen policy planning and analysis in key government agencies and to recommend reforms particularly in regard to import taxation, exchange controls, export promotion, industrial investment incentives, and improvement of statistics. With Arthur D. Little, Inc. (ADL) as a subcontractor, HIID was selected in a competitive bidding process, and had advisors on the ground during 1982–1986, with some consultant activity continuing until mid-1987.

Modalities of Technical Assistance

Reflecting the fragmentation of responsibility for trade and industry policy in Bangladesh, the TIP project had seven units, set up under the aegis of four separate government agencies: the Tariff Commission (one unit); the Planning Commission (two units); the Department of Industries, or DoI (three units); and the Bureau of Statistics (one unit). Arthur D. Little, Inc., the subcontractor, assisted the units responsible for industrial investment and export promotion, while HIID worked with the others. An HIID Institute Fellow served as resident director of the project.

Responsibility for coordination was assigned to a project management unit located in the Planning Commission and to a high-level governing body composed of some twenty agency representatives and chaired by the central bank governor. The governing body was supposed to sort out bureaucratic conflicts and review policy reform recommendations, but was rarely able to assemble a quorum. A proposal to delegate responsibility to smaller working committees was blocked by a key member's unwillingness to share authority.

As in Sri Lanka, inflation and fiscal stringency had depressed real compensation in the civil service, entailing a scarcity of qualified counterparts. However, in contrast to Sri Lanka, the project foresaw hiring local consultants with funds from the IDA credit, rather than the government budget; at one time or another, a total of thirty-seven local consultants were engaged, the most important source being Dhaka University. Some worked over extended periods and effectively became the foreign advisors' counterparts. The shortage of qualified government staff did, however, impose more managerial and coordination responsibilities on the foreign advisors than was expected or desirable.

The resident advisor format allowed the foreign staff to invest substantial time in training. Series of seminars were held on effective protection analysis and project appraisal; staff were trained in the use of personal computers; and Arthur D. Little, Inc. staff organized training in fundamentals such as accounting, finance, and project analysis. Conferences at which TIP studies and recommendations were discussed with senior officials and local professionals, while organized mainly to disseminate project work, also served training purposes.

Substantive Project Concerns

The TIP project's terms of reference called for industrial assistance policy studies of some ninety-two subsectors of the Bangladesh economy, based on the assumption that available data would permit effective protection analysis at the subsector level. This turned out not to be the case, and since the Bureau of Statistics was otherwise engaged, the other units had to do extensive field research as a basis for the subsector studies.

With no guidance forthcoming from the TIP governing body, the HIID field director and his counterparts in the Planning Commission had to decide which sectoral reforms were most likely to gain support and thus merited project attention. For example, noting the opposition of private ship-breaking and steel re-rolling interests to the high protection enjoyed by the state-owned steel monopoly, the staff decided to target the steel and engineering sector. Three other sectors highlighted were cotton textiles and garments, agroindustries, and chemicals.

Hoping to attract support for more outward-looking policies from domestic manufacturers of textiles and other intermediate products, the staff also targeted incentives for the backward integration of export activities. By suggesting that nontraditional exporters be offered a choice between using a bonded warehouse or receiving duty drawbacks, the advisors even sought to foster rent-seeking competition within the bureaucracy.[6]

The shift of focus to broad sectoral policies also reflected the staff's judgment that micro-managing protection of each individual product or firm was not the best way to promote industrial growth. The preference was to help develop more general "rules of the game," reducing the scope for administrative discretion.

This shift involved not only rationalizing and simplifying industrial assistance, but also analyzing fiscal and exchange rate policies. Early on it became evident that official reluctance to lower import duties, comprising 55 percent of total government revenue, was largely motivated by concern over the budget deficit—in most countries a source of tension between would-be trade liberalizers and macroeconomic stabilizers. Project staff also watched closely the trend of the real effective exchange rate as Bangladesh moved away from controls and multiple exchange rates toward a single rate system. At the micro level, as it became evident that the impact of government policies and controls depended as much on modes of execution as on their design and intent, TIP project work focused on issues of policy implementation.

Project Accomplishments and Shortfalls

The TIP project can be viewed as an outgrowth of the literature on industrial policy and analysis of the effective rate of protection as it existed by the early 1980s. While not making innovative technical contributions to this literature, the project did provide insights into the political economy of trade and industry policy reform in an economy heavily controlled by a centralized bureaucracy.

From the viewpoint of Bangladesh, the project helped to disseminate concepts of rational trade policy analysis to a broad constituency of officials, business groups, and academics. This resulted from the training program as well as from distribution of over one hundred papers, which were discussed in lectures, seminars, and conferences. Institutionally, the evolution of the Tariff Commission provides the best example. From a bureaucratic, quasi-judicial body it evolved into a more professional agency employing modern techniques of analysis. This transformation was aided by the World Bank, which relied on TIP studies to negotiate industrial sector credits and continued to provide technical assistance to the Commission after HIID's departure.

It is difficult to disentangle the impact of TIP work on government policy from that of the International Monetary Fund (IMF), the World Bank, and the Asian Development Bank, who were conveying similar policy messages backed by aid leverage. Whatever the correct apportionment of influence, numerous measures recommended, *inter alia,* by the advisors have been adopted. These include liberalization of investment and exchange controls; development of new revenue sources to compensate for lowered import tariffs, notably a trade-neutral value added tax and excise taxes on consumer durables; simplification of import tariffs; and reduction of nominal protection (the unweighted average rate had dropped from 94 percent to 30 percent by 1994–1995). Still, much remains to be done: convergence of tariff rates to avoid anomalies in incentives, recommended by the TIP project, is incomplete, and administrative discretion still plays a large role in policy implementation, notably in determining presumptive c.i.f. prices as a basis for assessing import duties.

On the minus side, the project suffered from several design flaws:

- failure to initiate the statistical component at least a year in advance, so that data would be available for the industrial assistance studies;
- macro policy was virtually ignored, despite the fiscal and monetary implications of altering industrial protection and strengthening incentives for investment and exports;

- lack of attention to policy implementation, notably administration of import licenses, passbooks, foreign exchange allocations, bonded warehouses, duty drawbacks, back-to-back letters of credit, and the like; and
- a bureau staffed by civil servants had no chance of attracting skilled business professionals to promote private investment.

Flexibility to revise the terms of reference along the way might have enabled some of these flaws to be overcome, but once the project started, everything was locked in place. This rigidity was exacerbated by the wide dispersion of project units among four government agencies, each trying to protect its turf and resources. Each agency controlled the budget of its TIP unit and had its own work agenda that advisors were expected to help carry out independently of the project's terms of reference.

Morocco

Origins and Objectives

The initiative for this project originated with USAID's then Near East/North Africa bureau, which in the mid-1980s was seeking openings for economists from the United States to influence national policymaking in client countries, both by current advising and local capacity building. USAID/Morocco invited an HIID economist in late 1984 to solicit interest on the part of Moroccan agencies. Out of half a dozen contacted, only one responded positively: the Ministry of Economic Affairs (MEA), whose head had been chief counterpart to a University of Michigan team in the early 1970s, and had a clear vision of how an HIID team might help him to institutionalize policy analysis.

Within a few months this individual had been promoted to Minister of Health, and his MEA successor turned out to lack such vision. However, USAID continued to prepare a resident advisory project, and the new minister signed a project agreement envisaging the transformation of MEA's Directorate of Prices (DoP) from a price control unit into a team of analysts dealing with issues ranging from economic stabilization, with particular attention to commodity subsidies, to competition policy. Together with Associates for Resources and Development (AIRD), a private firm with links to Tufts University, as subcontractor, HIID won a competitive bid for the project.

Modalities of Technical Assistance

During 1986–1990 HIID fielded the two resident economists in the DoP, an institute fellow serving as senior advisor, while AIRD provided short-term consultants and training in consumption analysis.

Early after project inauguration it was evident that most of the DoP counterpart staff, while holding local undergraduate degrees in economics, lacked the aptitude and motivation necessary to absorb and apply training in policy analysis. HIID concluded that, to achieve the project's capacity building and policy research objectives, it was necessary to recruit new local staff with potential for policy analysis, and to engage economics lecturers at local universities as part-time research consultants.

Its access to the minister blocked, HIID appraised the USAID mission director, who stimulated the minister to consult the advisors. Authorization was eventually given to hire one new staff member in whose recruitment HIID would participate, and to contract with a team of university economists to study the impact of removal of price controls on Moroccan industry. Through independent contacts with the University of Rabat's and the University of Casablanca's economics departments, HIID identified candidates, and after interviews in which the minister took part, contracts were signed with three Rabat university economists. Subsequently a Casablanca university law professor on contract to HIID advised on the drafting of a competition policy law.

The project design had envisaged assignments by independent foreign consultants, but owing to the lack of MEA interest, only one short visit took place. As an extra-contractual arrangement HIID enlisted participation by the French competition authority (DCCRF[7]), several of whose officials led workshops in Morocco for staff from DoP and other agencies, and provided internships in France.

The project envisaged no foreign degree training but provided short-term training both in the country and abroad. One or both of the HIID advisors held regular (in principle, weekly) sessions in microeconomics and computer applications for up to ten DoP staff, and AIRD led two summer workshops in consumption analysis for inter-ministerial teams. Foreign training comprised two short-term programs in the United States and six brief internships with the DCCRF in Paris. The project financed English training for several DoP staff members, but none attained sufficient comprehension to qualify for an anglophone course.

Substantive Project Concerns

Key policy issues faced by the Morocco project included the following:

- Whether removal of price controls had led the industries concerned to raise prices above competitive levels, if so what to do about it, and if not, how best to gather evidence and attract public support for completion of the liberalization process.
- What degree of concentration existed in Moroccan industry, whether traditional price control should be replaced by legislation against restrictive business practices and the establishment of a competition authority, and if so, how best to go about it.
- How the transfers involved in government price subsidies for soft wheat, sugar, and edible oils were distributed among different income groups, how reducing or eliminating the subsidies would affect both public finances and vulnerable groups, and how consumption subsidies could be targeted more efficiently to those groups.
- What criteria and procedures should be used to compute prices or price ceilings for nonfood items remaining under control, notably pharmaceuticals and utility rates.
- How best to implement the privatization program entrusted to the MEA near the end of the project, including how to establish market values for public enterprise assets.

Project Accomplishments and Shortfalls

The Morocco project was first and foremost designed to create analytical capacity in the host ministry and its directorate of prices (MEA/DoP), a goal which it largely failed to achieve. With rare exceptions the HIID advisors and consultants did not succeed in motivating or inculcating economic intuitions in DoP staff. Only about half the complement even absorbed computer technology into their regular work procedures. The project was allowed to recruit only one new staff member, who put a sound academic training to good use in spite of being largely ostracized. Through HIID intervention the individual secured admission and funding in a Canadian doctoral program and has already become a significant asset to Moroccan economics education and research; the MEA made no effort to lure him back.

Conversely, the project gave a significant boost to capacity for competition policy research and innovation in economics teaching material and methodology in Morocco's two major universities, Rabat and Casablanca. The project's most significant published output was a volume of twelve sectoral studies, appearing after the project ended, authored by the local university team that HIID recruited over bureaucratic opposition.[8] The volume provided convincing evidence that abolition of price controls, far from accelerating inflation, made the sectors concerned more efficient and competitive, in several cases enhancing export potential.

Notwithstanding the clear benefits to MEA (USAID/Morocco's counterpart agency) of engaging university researchers on a part-time contract basis, the ministry's management ignored HIID's entreaties to make provision in the MEA budget to enable such an activity to continue after USAID funding ended. Apart from the early intervention that enabled HIID to launch the University of Rabat team's study and bring a local economist into the MEA, USAID's leverage was not sufficient to enable it to pursue this and other project implementation issues with the minister.

With significant input from subcontractor AIRD, the project advanced Moroccan economists' awareness of scientific consumption analysis and its potential role in policy-making. By far the project's biggest public splash was a three-day symposium on consumption modeling held in December 1988, featuring over one hundred participants debating thirty papers by university and government staff. Unfortunately, lacking support from MEA management, the interagency working group launched with great enthusiasm to manage a follow-up program soon petered out.

The staff economist recruited by HIID, using Morocco's industrial census to calculate the country's first indices of industrial concentration,[9] demonstrated the use of the data for analysis of industrial structure. Basing a Master's thesis on this work, the analyst became the first graduate of a new master's program in applied economics at the University of Casablanca.

With a strong assist from the French government, the project advanced awareness of competition issues and generated a workable competition bill, drafted initially by another local HIID consultant. The business community, however, was suspicious of a new regulatory intervention, and the Moroccan government, reacting partly to this concern and partly out of reluctance to come to grips with a jurisdictional conflict among three ministries (economic affairs, commerce and industry, and interior) bidding to implement competition policy, put the matter on hold.

Partly in response to persistent weaknesses in its host organization, HIID devoted substantial effort to networking and training in other agencies, notably the universities and five ministries. However, initiatives to establish both a policy research network and an interagency committee on macroeconomic modeling, and to organize a symposium on competition policy, were stillborn due, in all three cases, to the lack of MEA interest supplemented, in the first case, by a lack of flexibility on the part of USAID.

No startling discoveries were made on technical issues. However, it had not previously been documented in a North African context (as thoroughly as the Rabat University team's research showed) that government attempts to control prices of manufactures are inherently anti-growth because they discourage investment and exports, divert managerial resources, and depress efficiency and competition. Coming after decontrol had largely been carried out, the findings can be regarded as after the fact. Yet some observers feel these findings have contributed to a stock of intellectual capital that reduces the chances of a future Moroccan administration reimposing price controls as a populist reaction to inflation.

The Consulting Assistance for Economic Reform Project

Origins and Objectives

The CAER project was established to provide USAID headquarters and field missions with advice on the economic reform agenda that has guided the program of U.S. foreign assistance over the last decade. Its structure provided a flexible vehicle for USAID field missions to recruit and fund consultants out of their own budgets. Terms of reference of the majority of studies were agreed with host governments, and CAER consultants reported both to them and to the AID missions. In a minority of cases consultants advised missions alone on their policies and programs. The project also funded several policy studies at the initiative of USAID/Washington D.C.

Of the four projects discussed in this chapter, the decision to bid for CAER entailed the most soul-searching in HIID. The institute had long shied away from contracting to perform ad hoc studies, feeling this was a task better suited to consulting firms and that HIID's comparative advantage lay in establishing multi-year relationships that would include training counterparts and building capacity. Ad hoc studies also provided limited scope for HIID's research vocation. For these reasons HIID had never responded to any of USAID's numerous requests for proposals for so-called indefinite quantity contracts (IQCs).

Three considerations tipped the balance in favor of a bid: (1) CAER's explicit research component, (2) the view that policies for economic reform offered sharper focus within a major field of HIID interest than previous IQC projects, and (3) the expectation that the contractor winning CAER would have an inside track with USAID missions and counterpart agencies for follow-on projects consonant with HIID's traditional *modus operandi.*

HIID, together with three consulting firms (Development Alternatives International or DAI, AIRD, and International Management Communications Corporation or IMCC) and with Williams College as subcontractors, won the CAER bid in 1989. Work took place during 1989–1994.

Modalities of Technical Assistance

The CAER studies involved widely varying inputs by the eight-two researchers of the five cooperating institutions. Most were economists, but anthropologists, lawyers, political scientists, tax administration specialists and others also took part. Numbers engaged in a single study ranged from one to fourteen.

Stays in cooperating countries varied from ten days to three months. Work on one of the Africa regional studies proceeded intermittently over a period of three years, although most of the projects lasted less than a year. Some of the activities produced a training spin-off, as consultants gave seminars to discuss their findings and communicate research techniques to clients and counterparts.

Areas of Emphasis

Of the sixty-nine CAER activities concerning single countries or regions, just over half dealt with Africa, 25 percent with Asia, 14 percent with Latin America, and 9 percent with Central and Eastern Europe. One project was a comparative study of development in Asia and Africa.

A few concentrations emerged among the four participating institutions: IMCC dealt with financial and monetary reform in Latin America, the Philippines, and the transition economies of Europe; AIRD focused on trade patterns and reforms in Africa, particularly the Sahel region; DAI covered a wider range of topics, with notable contributions to the impact of economic reform on poverty in Africa and Latin America; HIID's four largest projects (and some smaller ones) dealt with economic adjustment and development strategy in Africa, but the institute also worked extensively on tax reform and environmental economics.

USAID's economic reform agenda has deep historical and intellectual roots that set the framework for CAER. The project's primary aim was to provide USAID and its client governments with expert studies applying principles of the reform agenda to specific policy choices. There were areas of emphasis, as summarized below. [10]

- **Macroeconomic stabilization.** Studies that explored macroeconomic stabilization and recommended specific policy approaches included: (1) a comparison of macroeconomic policy in Asia and Africa; (2) one monograph each on monetary and exchange rate management in Africa; (3) an assessment of the CFA franc exchange rate[11] and the need for devaluation; (4) a volume on economic recovery in The Gambia; (5) several studies on monetary and financial policy in Central America (IMCC); (6) five country reports on the macroeconomic conditions for financial reform in Central and Eastern Europe (DAI and IMCC); and (7) a review of the monetary impact of counterpart funds (Williams College).

- **Greater dependence on market forces.** CAER's initial design stressed market liberalization. Papers contributed under this heading dealt with: (1) foreign exchange liberalization in Sri Lanka and the Philippines (IMCC); (2) monetary and exchange rate management in Africa; (3) trade regimes in West Africa, especially the Sahel region (AIRD); and (4) financial liberalization in Central America, the Philippines, and Eastern Europe (IMCC and DAI).

- **An outward-looking incentive structure.** The importance of outward-looking reforms as a development strategy was the central theme of CAER studies on: (1) the legacy from Asia for Africa; (2) economic reform and industrialization in The Gambia; (3) trade and investment incentives in Morocco and Rwanda (DAI); (4)

incentives in livestock trade in the Sahel; (5) trade regimes in West Africa (AIRD); (6) institutional constraints on nontraditional export growth in Africa (AIRD); and (7) the exchange rate studies mentioned above.

- **Augmenting markets through institutional development.** Proposals on this topic figured in CAER's work on: (1) monetary policy in Africa; (2) financial markets in the Philippines, Central America, and Eastern Europe (IMCC and DAI); (3) legal, regulatory, and judicial reform in financial markets (IMCC and HIID); (4) small-scale credit schemes and small-saver financial instruments; (5) institutional barriers to nontraditional exports in Africa (AIRD); (6) regional trade integration in West Africa (AIRD); (7) export houses in Sri Lanka (IMCC); (8) the development legacy from Asia for Africa; and (9) economic recovery in The Gambia.
- **Government reforms.** These were implicit, and often explicit, in most of the studies, but particularly in tax reform work in Sri Lanka as well as a major tax project in Nepal that is so far HIID's only resident field project to emerge from CAER.

While helping to bring about stabilization and economic growth, such reforms also entail social costs. In recent years the economic reform agenda has been amended significantly to ameliorate these costs and to further a process of democratization seen increasingly as necessary to sustain economic growth in the long term. In this connection CAER featured three additional emphases:

- **The impact of economic reforms on the poor.** A major product of CAER was to assess changes in living standards of the poor in both Latin America and Africa during the 1980s (DAI). It also contributed a study of macroeconomic, sectoral, and investment policies to reduce poverty in Africa, and a review of other USAID-sponsored research on adjustment and the poor in Africa (AIRD). Several financial market studies looked at the impact of reforms on the poor, including a survey of the informal credit market in Honduras, two reviews of small-scale credit programs, and the design of a small-saver financial instrument for the Philippines (IMCC).
- **Sustainable development.** CAER studies of the economics of environmental degradation, environmental liability in Russia, and

water resource management have addressed issues of ecological sustainability.

- **Democracy and participation.** CAER's first major activity—a workshop on the political economy of reform—anticipated this concern. The study on The Gambia's economic recovery concluded that the government's democratic base gave it a major advantage in instituting sweeping economic reforms. And the volume on lessons from Asian development highlighted the elements of governance that seem to have been essential in promoting economic reform and rapid development in both democracies and authoritarian regimes of East and Southeast Asia.

A Summary of Key Findings

The work accomplished by CAER researchers and consultants has been within the mainstream of neoclassical development economics, affirming through close observation in a variety of countries the efficacy of the orthodox economic reform agenda. However, some CAER studies have broken new ground. Taken as a whole, the body of CAER work points to linkages among reform policies that counsel in favor of adjustment on a broad front. Key findings are summarized below.

A decade of economic reform has not, despite widely held views to the contrary, been especially damaging to the poor. During the 1980s, although average incomes in Africa and a few countries elsewhere fell, social indicators show an improvement of living standards for the poor. Adjusting and non-adjusting countries performed similarly in regard to social indicators. Nonetheless, sound reform programs offer scope for further measures to protect incomes of the most disadvantaged. The long-run promise of reform is, of course, more rapid growth and reduction of poverty.

The efficacy of an outward-looking approach to development is justified by results from Asia and elsewhere. A range of strategies can be called "outward-looking," some interventionist, others closer to *laissez-faire.* Within that range, the mixed but more market-oriented approaches of three Southeast Asia countries are probably better models for Africa and elsewhere than is recognized in the literature.

Stabilization in general, and fiscal and monetary policy in particular, deserve a central place in development strategy. Distortion of monetary policy to finance large budget deficits entails controls, distortions, and inflationary expectations that discourage investment and reduce its productivity. For financial and foreign exchange markets to function productively, fiscal and monetary policy must be under control.

Financial deregulation (that is, the abandonment of interest rate control and credit allocation) is essential to allow other reform measures to stimulate investment and growth. However, it also requires stronger and more efficient prudential regulation of financial institutions.

Deregulated financial markets can serve microenterprises through minimalist credit schemes charging market rates of interest and offering deposit facilities. Many of these schemes—notably the Bank Rakyat Indonesia program assisted by HIID—are financially viable and manage to reach considerable numbers of small-scale borrowers.

Foreign exchange reforms should aim at flexible, market-determined exchange rates, and close to full currency convertibility. Gradualist reforms, contrary to expectations, may do little to reduce the pain of reform and may well inflict higher costs.

West African trade regimes discriminate against exports and inhibit intra-regional trade, which many strategists wish to see promoted. The CFA franc's 1994 devaluation and currency reforms in other countries will not promote dynamic export industries unless the tax, quota, and institutional barriers to trade—formal and informal—are vigorously reduced.

African countries wishing to encourage nontraditional exports, especially of manufactures, should adopt an "export enterprise" approach, reducing exporting costs by curbing effective protection and diminishing costs of nontradables, especially government services.

Progress can be made toward environmental sustainability by eliminating obvious price distortions and causing market prices to reflect environmental costs and benefits.

Project Evaluation and Termination

A technical assistance project's destiny as contract terms expire provides indicators of its contribution, or at least the perception of that contribution by interested parties. This analysis is subject to ambiguity inasmuch as a fully successful project, by definition, creates local capacity to carry out, at much lower cost, the policy analysis functions initially entrusted to the advisors. Thus the most successful advisor is one who works him/herself out of a job within the term of his/her contract.

On the other hand, both policy makers in the less developed countries (LDCs) and funding agencies now accept that capacity for policy analysis is rarely established within the initial term of any technical assistance project. (The question of how far the policies and practices of LDC policy makers, donor agencies, and technical assistance providers, including HIID, may have delayed the coming into being of capacity for policy analysis beyond what might have been achieved in the absence of technical assistance is discussed, *inter alia,* in a companion HIID volume.[12])

In cases where adequate capacity was not expected to come into being during the initial contract term, a request by the host agency to extend the contract, and acceptance of that request by the same or a different funder, amount to telling the contractor that he has done a good job and there is no better way of continuing to work toward project goals than to have him continue for another term. Many projects described in other chapters of this volume were extended for at least one additional term, and some, particularly those in Indonesia and Kenya, were extended several times over, leading to an HIID presence of twenty years or more in one or the other country.

Such was not the case with the three country projects described in this chapter.[13] Apart from brief extensions, facilitated by the presence of unexpended project balances or pursuant to a funder's request to HIID to help it carry a particular individual over an otherwise unfunded gap pending start of a different project, each of these projects ended upon expiration of its initial contract period. This section describes the circumstances of each case.

Sri Lanka

As this contract neared its term in 1982, HIID and MoFP discussed the issue of extension. HIID indicated willingness in principle to continue, while pointing to the problems caused during the first contract period by the lack of a resident advisor. MoFP management took under advisement the possibility of such a posting, but Sri Lanka's political climate was clearly becoming hostile to the move. Discussions dragged on to mid-1983, when MoFP expressed the view that the time for significant reforms had passed. Indeed, a few weeks later civil unrest broke out in Colombo, presaging a period of instability.

On the funder's side, the UNDP had become less supportive of the project in light of the donor complaints mentioned earlier. While this would have complicated an eventual extension, it would not have been fatal had the government made a firm request for continued assistance from HIID, which it refrained from doing.

Bangladesh

As this project neared its term in 1986, there was a consensus that technical assistance, such as that HIID was providing, would be most effective in future if concentrated in the Tariff Commission. However, the possibility of HIID's continuation as contractor became tangled with bureaucratic politics, and the government made no request to HIID or to the World Bank. IDA-financed assistance to the Tariff Commission continued under other auspices.

Morocco

Of the three country projects, Morocco raises the most interesting issues here because it alone was subject to a formal mid-term evaluation, pursuant to USAID procedures,[14] and because a request for extension by both the MEA and USAID, eventually turned down by HIID, was a subject of controversy in the institute.

The mid-term evaluation, carried out by staff from two consulting firms (from the Washington D.C. area), was categorized by the project field director as a "whitewash." While noting some of the problems cited in HIID's semiannual report to USAID and MEA management, and suggesting corrective measures (nearly all of which had been tried unsuccessfully), the evaluators reported that the project was achieving its key objectives. Meeting twice with the minister, the evaluators could not bring themselves to question him on such issues as why he was ignoring HIID's requests to discuss its semiannual report and consider its recommendations for personnel actions to build capacity for policy analysis in the DoP. Nor did they take seriously the evidence presented by HIID on DoP staff potential.

Sharing most of these criticisms of the evaluation, USAID/Morocco agreed with HIID that no policy analysis unit worth the name could be developed in the MEA under its current management. Hence its forward planning envisioned ending the project at its term in September 1990. However, in the project's final year King Hassan launched a privatization program, adding it to the MEA portfolio. The minister asked USAID to continue the services of one of the HIID advisors, a public enterprise specialist, for that purpose. In May 1990, considering it strategic to support privatization, USAID offered HIID a contract extension to this end.

The HIID field director argued that, while USAID was justified in seizing the occasion to support privatization, HIID should decline the invitation to continue serving a minister who had spurned its efforts to build capacity in the MEA. He maintained that such a stand would enhance the institute's integrity in the eyes of responsible local professionals who were familiar with the situation in the MEA, and thus better serve HIID's long-term interests in Morocco.

The opposing position, seeing privatization as a core issue in HIID's concern with economic reform, was that the institute should not reject an opportunity to work on it in Morocco simply due to dissatisfaction with the past performance of the minister concerned. In the end HIID management deferred to the field director's position. No new opportunity for HIID field work in Morocco has arisen in the six years since the project ended.[15]

The CAER Project

This project was reviewed formally during its fourth year, preparatory to a decision by USAID whether to extend it under competitive bidding. The evaluators described CAER as having delivered timely, professionally sound products to USAID missions and host countries, and to have developed an effective management system. Based on the evaluation, in June 1995 USAID offered the consortium a second phase with an expanded core research program and provision for US$25 million worth of mission buy-ins over five years.

Lessons for Institutional Development from the Projects

Morocco, as the one project out of the three with the strongest mandate for institutional development, is discussed first in this section. The project highlighted five points, none of which is new:

- Not every counterpart provided to an advisory team can be motivated or trained to the point where he/she is capable of performing analytical staff work; once this is clear, the investment of additional training resources in such individuals is not only wasteful but counter-productive.
- Similarly, not every manager can be motivated to take an interest in creating a durable staff capacity in his/her agency.

- Where such managers abound, capacity for policy analysis may have to be created as a floating pool, with a base in the academic and/or consulting community ready to be tapped when an agency temporarily comes under competent management.
- If and when it becomes clear that the assigned counterpart staff is essentially untrainable and management is uninterested, advisors concerned with capacity building should explore options such as recruiting temporary staff, involving outsiders on contract, and networking with other agencies, including educational institutions and independent research institutes, that offer more fruitful staff development opportunities.
- Given stringency and rigidity in counterpart agency budgets, it is vital that donor budgets for technical assistance projects allocate funds for hiring local contract staff.

The Sri Lanka and Bangladesh experiences reinforce several of these judgments and, compared with Morocco, both countries had undergone more rapid inflation, had seen real compensation levels of civil servants decline further, and were facing larger gaps between compensation inside and outside the civil service.[16]

In Sri Lanka both the MoFP and HIID recognized the need to involve research institute staff, but the ministry failed to come through on a promise to finance their services. Interestingly, a 1991 CAER study in Sri Lanka concluded that industry studies for improved competition policy could only be conducted by short-term contract staff from universities and other nongovernmental institutions, and urged that aid donors finance such work.[17]

Facing similar constraints in regard to counterparts in the Bangladesh civil service, the TIP project made greater use of local consultants than any HIID resident field project before or since. Noting that barriers to human resource development in the public sector cripple many technical assistance projects, HIID's TIP field director has urged that technical assistance agreements make regular provision for local contracting, funded if necessary out of aid proceeds.

Notes

1 Based in part on conference papers by Clive Gray; by Richard Mallon; by Michael Roemer; and by Joseph Stern.

2 The Indonesia projects are described in Chapter 3 of this volume; the relevant Malaysia project ended in 1980.

3 Apart from involving Harvard University's Department of Economics faculty, the project also brought two graduate students to Colombo. Both eventually used their work in dissertation research.

4 In other words, many consultants were available for periods of longer than a week only during December–January and the summer vacation.

5 The International Development Association is the soft-loan affiliate of the World Bank.

6 This strategy is described in Mallon and Stern (1991).

7 Direction de la Concurrence, de la Consommation et de la Répression des Fraudes (in the Ministry of Finance).

8 Nasr Hajji, Larabi Jaïdi, and Mekki Zouaoui, *Prix et Concurrence au Maroc*, Ministère chargé des affaires économiques, Rabat, 1992.

9 Specifically, CR4, the proportion of total output accounted for by the four largest producers, and the Herfindahl-Hirschman index, a more refined coefficient that sums the squares of each producer's percentage contribution, taking on values between 0 and 10,000.

10 Studies mentioned here and not identified with one of the subcontractors were carried out by HIID.

11 The exchange rate between the French franc and the currency of the Communauté Financière Africaine comprising most of France's former colonies in West and Central Africa.

12 See Grindle (1997, Chapters 4, 5, and 14).

13 HIID's CAER contract was recently renewed for two years with an option to extend for three additional years, but given the nature of that project as a flexible mechanism for responding to requests from USAID missions, its extension does not raise the issue of perceived value to a particular host government.

14 CAER was also the object of a formal evaluation.

15 Two minor qualifications to this: HIID subcontractors AIRD and DAI subsequently have conducted research in Morocco under CAER, and one of six country studies under the UNDP Capacity Building project concerned Morocco.

16 For example, ratios of consumer price indices for each project's final year (Bangladesh: 1987; Morocco: 1990; Sri Lanka: 1982) to the level of ten years earlier are 3.0 for Bangladesh, 2.75 for Sri Lanka, and 2.0 for Morocco. World Bank *World Tables—1992*, respective country pages.

17 Gray (1991).

10 The Public Enterprise Program

Richard D. Mallon[1]

Motivated by a growing concern with the performance of state-owned businesses in less developed countries, HIID presented its first Public Enterprise Workshop (PEW) in the summer of 1973. The workshop has continued every year since (with the exception of 1975), growing from a small number of participants to an average of thirty to forty students from many developing countries. After the first few years, the workshop became financially self-sustaining and generated a variety of other training, research, and technical assistance activities in the field. Indeed, the PEW has provided the thread of continuity for all of HIID's public enterprise activities.

The six-week workshop is a practical, multidisciplinary course relying heavily on the case method of instruction. Many original cases and other teaching materials have been prepared specifically for use in the PEW. These cases and materials have been updated regularly to keep abreast of new developments in the field, such as the growing emphasis on the privatization of public enterprises and the related subjects of regulation and pricing of public services. Currently, the last two weeks of the workshop are devoted exclusively to privatization issues.

Over the years the PEW has attracted participants not only from a wide spectrum of developing countries but also from international organizations. All participants have been funded from outside sources, most of them by their own governments or organizations. Many of them have remained in contact with HIID and have sponsored subsequent participants in the workshop; on occasion they have also promoted other public enterprise activities in their countries.

It is difficult to measure the results that have flowed directly from the PEW, except that it has served as a major innovating vehicle for several other summer workshops later undertaken by HIID. The continuing interest of PEW alumni in the program indicates that they consider it useful, and workshop faculty were charter members of the Boston Area Public Enterprise Group (BAPEG).

THE BOSTON AREA PUBLIC ENTERPRISE GROUP

The Public Enterprise Workshop was initiated with staff drawn mainly from HIID and Harvard, but it soon became evident that non-HIID personnel would have to be relied on more extensively to develop necessary teaching materials and to establish the professional credibility required to attract outside funding in this new field.[2] BAPEG was, therefore, set up in 1977 under a three-member steering committee composed of an HIID fellow, the director of the Harvard Center for International Affairs, and the director of the recently established Program in the Economics and Management of Public Enterprise at Boston University. The group also included faculty from the Massachusetts Institute of Technology, Northeastern University, and other local universities. The stated objective of BAPEG was to create a critical mass of expertise in the field and to become a repository of public enterprise experience and top notch research on the subject.

BAPEG approached the Ford Foundation for seed money, and in 1978 succeeded in obtaining grants in excess of US$100,000 for HIID and a larger amount for Boston University, which had inaugurated a three-course specialization in the field as an integral part of the university's graduate degree programs in economics and management.[3] The Ford Foundation grants were used mainly to finance the development of teaching materials, biweekly forums and special seminars, visiting researchers, preparation and distribution of a BAPEG brochure and an annual newsletter, and the development of a specialized library and data bank.

In 1979–1980 BAPEG organized two international conferences on state-owned enterprises (SOEs) with financial support from various sources. The first conference dealt with SOEs in industrialized, mixed economies and was held at the Harvard Business School. The second was on SOEs in less developed countries and was conducted off campus in Boston. Papers from both conferences were subsequently published in two separate volumes.[4] During this period, BAPEG members also attended a number of conferences and meetings on SOEs sponsored by other organizations such as the World Bank in Washington, D.C., the Government of Pakistan in Islamabad, the International Development Research Council (IDRC) in Ottawa, Corporacion Venezolana de Guayana, in Caracas Venezuela, the National Institute for Public Administration (INTAN) in Kuala Lumpur, the National Management Institute in Cairo, and the National Bureau of Economic Research (NBER/FIPE) in Sao Paulo.

In addition to the two conference volumes, a few other books and many journal articles have been published by members of BAPEG on different aspects of public enterprise.[5] Perhaps the most notable research output has been the development of a computerized system for evaluating SOE performance, the formalization of so-called performance contracts to enhance the autonomy and accountability of SOEs, and more recently the analysis of costs and benefits of privatization. With few exceptions, this very applied and multidisciplinary type of research has not captured the attention of peer-reviewed journals.

Some funding for professional activities continued to be provided on an institutional basis, such as the Tinker Foundation grant to HIID for carrying out a study of SOEs in raw materials industries in Latin America; but institutional support for financing public enterprise research became increasingly scarce. Important funding organizations, such as the World Bank, preferred to contract individual experts directly, rather than through institutions such as HIID, for conducting SOE research and technical assistance projects. BAPEG funding thus dried up, and its activities, especially after the chairman of the steering committee took up long-term residence abroad in 1983, virtually came to an end.

Other Training Activities

Perhaps the best example of the continuing interest of PEW alumni in HIID's public enterprise program is the relationship that has been established between HIID and its workshop alumni association and the Fulbright Commission in Egypt. For the past several years the commission has funded three or four participants annually in the PEW, and in 1992 it requested HIID to organize and teach a three-week workshop in Cairo. PEW alumni collaborated actively in the workshop, which was considered so successful that another one was held in January 1995. HIID has received a number of other requests from alumni for holding local workshops on public enterprise issues in their countries, but it has proved difficult to round up the necessary funding and local organizational support.[6]

An exception was the workshop carried out in May 1987, in collaboration with the Catholic University in the Dominican Republic and financed by the local USAID mission in that country. Funds were provided for field research to prepare a case on the national sugar corporation, which was used in teaching the workshop. The five-day event was attended by top government dignitaries, including the Vice President of the country, as well as by senior public enterprise officials. Unlike the Egyptian experience, however, there has been no further follow-up.

The local workshop taught in The Gambia in October 1989 also included a case (on the national public utility enterprise) that was prepared especially for the occasion. This workshop emanated not from PEW alumni initiative but from technical assistance on SOE performance contracts provided to the National Investment Board (NIB) of The Gambia, as part of HIID's ongoing advisory project in the country. The workshop was co-sponsored by the national training institute, in whose locale the event took place, and NIB staff participated in teaching several sessions.

In contrast, the public enterprise seminars in Vietnam in July–August 1992, conducted by HIID and funded by the World Bank, did not emanate either from PEW alumni initiatives or from an ongoing technical assistance relationship. No preparatory field work was carried out, and no local institutions or counterparts participated actively in preparing materials or teaching the seminars. It is, therefore, difficult to ascertain how much useful knowledge was communicated to the participants, especially since that teaching was conducted entirely through interpreters who were not familiar with many technical terms.

TECHNICAL ASSISTANCE

Most of HIID's technical assistance on public enterprise matters has been carried as a component of broader projects. The project with the Central American Institute of Business Administration (INCAE) during 1973–1974 was set up to help with earthquake reconstruction in Nicaragua, and HIID also assisted the development of training courses in public management because of the importance of SOEs in implementing reconstruction programs. In 1979–1980, HIID's ongoing project with the Economic Planning Unit in Malaysia provided special assistance for analyzing the role of SOEs in the country's Five Year Plan then under preparation. A study of public enterprises in 1980, under a broader HIID project in Sri Lanka, was short lived because of a jurisdictional dispute, but the public enterprise component of HIID's advisory project in Bangladesh continued from 1983 to 1986. Similarly, technical assistance to the NIB on SOE performance contracts was carried out from 1987 to 1989, by short-term consultants under the existing project in The Gambia; in Indonesia a resident HIID advisor provided similar advice from 1990 to 1992.

HIID's only technical assistance project devoted exclusively to public enterprises was conducted in the Bolivian Ministry of Planning and Coordination, from 1989 to 1993.[7] This project involved designing a novel system of performance contracts between government and large, "strategic" SOEs, for the purpose of transforming them into more business-like, competitive, and efficient firms. After the proposed system was accepted, assistance was then provided for identifying and negotiating specific changes—both in SOE organization, control, and information systems, and in government regulatory regimes—that needed to be included as reciprocal obligations in the contracts. Beginning in 1990 several contracts were actually negotiated and implemented, and HIID consultants then turned their attention to assisting in the monitoring and evaluation of results. The results of the contract with the national electricity company were considered successful enough to merit the organization of a World Bank seminar in Washington, D.C. to discuss the case.

Despite initial accomplishments, further progress in Bolivia was blocked by jurisdictional disputes and the politicization of the process in anticipation of national elections in 1993. The new performance contract system was criticized for abuses that occurred (mostly as a result of slack contract enforcement), but opposition came primarily from an ideological shift in favor of the privatization of SOEs. The argument that performance contracts, far from being an obstacle to privatization, could in fact be used to make SOEs more competitive and efficient, to enhance their sales value, and to reduce government regulation of their operations, proved to be of no avail. The project, therefore, came to an end in 1993.

Although not dealing primarily with public enterprise, HIID's technical assistance for improving public services such as transportation, where public enterprises often play an important role, has addressed related issues. One example is the project begun in 1993 to evaluate and summarize a collection of World Bank studies on restructuring transportation in Russia, Belarus, Ukraine, and Kazakhstan, where many opportunities exist for breaking up old integrated SOEs, encouraging greater competition, and replacing central commands with market-oriented regulatory structures. Project consultants concluded that in this setting the most effective way to facilitate the restructuring of the transport sector was to rely more on privatization than on the corporatization or other types of public enterprise reform.

A considerable amount of technical assistance on public enterprise matters has also been provided by HIID/BAPEG personnel on an individual basis: for example, to the Korea Development Institute in Korea; in Venezuela for the Inter-American Development Bank; in Ecuador for USAID; in Mongolia for the United Nations Development Programme (UNDP); and for the introduction of performance contracts in India. In recent years the focus of these activities has shifted increasingly from improving SOE performance to privatization, an area in which HIID does not have comparative advantage.

As for tangible results flowing directly from this technical assistance, some accomplishments can be listed, such as the improvement in performance of the Bolivian electricity company mentioned above and the alleged success of SOE performance evaluation systems introduced in Korea and Pakistan. But it would be disingenuous to claim that a professional consensus has been reached on how best to deal with public enterprises in developing countries. The most that can be said is that ideas developed on the subject by HIID and BAPEG have been widely circulated, and that several colleagues have gained an international reputation in the field.

Evaluation

If HIID's public enterprise program is judged according to the support received—as measured by the human and financial resources it has attracted and by the professional recognition it has achieved—then it cannot be considered very successful. The program could no doubt have benefited from stronger intellectual leadership and entrepreneurship, but it also had to face other major constraints.

First, from the outset there was little, if any, prospect that public enterprise could be recognized at Harvard as a legitimate subject for scholarly specialization. Applied research on public enterprises did not favor the use of rigorous tools of analysis rewarded by academic departments, and no professional school felt comfortable fitting this vaguely defined, multidisciplinary subject into its curriculum. At Boston University the situation was different in the 1970s, and the study of public enterprise was recognized as an academic field for specialization in its graduate degree programs in both economics and business.

Second, the academic institutionalization of public enterprise as a field of specialization enabled BAPEG colleagues at Boston University to devote most of their time to the subject. They could rely on the human resources and institutional commitment that HIID lacked to attract funding and carry out research and other projects, and they could also count on their graduate alumni to turn to them for technical assistance once they returned home. Boston University colleagues recognized that continued participation in the PEW under the Harvard label was mutually convenient, with the result that the quality of instruction and reputation of the PEW was enhanced. But the net result was that Boston University became the main beneficiary of BAPEG.

Third, funding for overseas training seminars and workshops was usually linked to existing technical assistance projects on public enterprise. For these projects major funders generally preferred to hire experts directly, instead of contracting with institutions like HIID, unless the project was devoted exclusively to privatization. In this case, international banking and accounting firms became the chosen instruments, because most privatization projects did not require economists and management specialists so much as experts familiar with the valuation and sale of existing business assets.

HIID's public enterprise program, therefore, succeeded only in carving out a tenuous institutional niche for conducting funded research and overseas projects. Even those technical assistance projects that HIID succeeded in obtaining frequently encountered problems to which this field seems especially prone. Responsibility for public enterprises in most countries is diffuse and controversial: SOEs are agents with plural principals, who not only have conflicting goals but are frequently engaged in jurisdictional disputes. In this situation no single government agency is able to provide an undisputed home for public enterprise projects. Furthermore, if the environment in which SOE reforms take place is ideologically charged, as is typical when privatization is under discussion, technical considerations tend to be submerged in political controversy.

The difficulties described above do not, however, justify HIID's abandoning its concern with SOEs in less-developed and transition economies. The Public Enterprise Workshop apparently continues to attract enough participants to make it financially self-sustaining, and some day HIID may find the intellectual leadership and entrepreneurship needed to create a more solid foundation for a public enterprise program.

Notes

1 Based in part on conference papers by Richard Mallon; and by John Meyer and John Strong.

2 At HIID only Richard Mallon was available to devote a major part of his time to public enterprise teaching and research. The Harvard graduate students upon which the PEW initially relied soon moved on to take academic positions in other Boston area universities.

3 It was not possible to institutionalize the public enterprise program at Harvard in this way, although a course was sponsored by the Government Department and taught at the John F. Kennedy School of Government for several years.

4 See Vernon and Aharoni (1981), and Jones et al. (1982).

5 See, for example, Vernon (1988); Trivedi (1990); Ramamurti and Vernon (1991); Mallon (1981, 1984).

6 Participation by a local organization, such as a university or research institute, is considered necessary to help prepare teaching materials and cases based on local experience so as to differentiate such workshops from the PEW. Indigenous collaboration would also facilitate the development of local capacity to carry out similar training programs and to help to fulfill HIID's commitment to institution building.

7 HIID also carried out two projects with SOEs in Venezuela, with the Corporacion Venezolana de Guayana, Caracas Venezuela, from 1976 to 1979, and with the Agricultural Credit Institute, from 1981 to 1982, but in neither of these projects did the technical assistance concern specific public enterprise issues.

11 Work on Small-Scale Enterprise

Donald R. Snodgrass[1]

Overview

Most of HIID's work on small-scale enterprise (SSE)[2] took place between 1980 and 1991 under four projects: the Small Enterprise Development Project (SEDP) in Indonesia, from 1980 to 1985; the Employment and Enterprise Policy Analysis (EEPA) project, from 1984 to 1991; the Assistance to Resource Institutions for Enterprise Support (ARIES) project, from 1985 to 1990; and the Thailand Rural Industries and Employment project, from 1988 to 1989. The SEDP was financed by the World Bank, while the other three projects were sponsored by the United States Agency for International Development (USAID).

Support for small enterprise promotion is an almost universally accepted value among developing country governments, which have backed their verbal commitments to SSEs with promotional programs that provide credit, technical assistance, training, and (sometimes) business facilities (such as shops, market stalls, and factory sites in small industry parks) and materials (such as fabrics used by cloth or garment manufacturers).[3,4] Many international assistance bodies promote these activities, eagerly supported by hundreds of private voluntary organizations that make it their business to assist SSEs. A small group of specialists based at the World Bank, the International Labor Organisation (ILO), and a few universities dominate research on SSEs. The widespread enthusiasm for SSE promotion flows from a variety of value orientations and objectives, ranging from a desire to promote petty capitalism and build political support for market economies, to humanitarian desires to assist the poor and strengthen the economic base of women and other disadvantaged groups. Yet paradoxes abound in the field.

One of these paradoxes is that while developing country governments often favor the development of SSEs through verbal pronouncements and promotional programs, many of their policies are detrimental to the welfare of small-scale entrepreneurs and to the growth and transformation of these firms. Government interventions in capital and foreign exchange markets often favor larger firms that compete with small and microenterprises. Scale-related biases in labor market, fiscal, and regulatory policies may partially offset this effect, either by exempting small firms from, for example, minimum wage laws and sales taxes applicable to larger enterprises, or by loosely enforcing regulations on small firms. On balance, actions by developing country governments in this area often belie official statements.

A second paradox is that while SSEs provide employment as well as goods and services to the poor in low-income countries, national economic development involves a decline in the importance of these factors over the long run. The average scale of business operations invariably rises as countries develop and dualism declines, with smaller firms eventually resembling larger ones in technology, factor proportions, and productivity. Nor do significant numbers of SSEs grow in time to become medium- or large-scale enterprises. A very few do, but most are devoted to family subsistence and have little developmental potential.

It has also been suggested that explicit consideration of gender is important in analyzing SSE programs.[5] When the impact of such programs on women is considered, what may appear at first to be only welfare-oriented activities may also be developmental activities. This is especially true in a country like Bangladesh, where social restrictions on female participation in other economic roles create a low opportunity cost for female labor and thus a high rate of return to capital in small businesses that employ women.

The objectives of governments and aid agencies in SSE development thus merit careful analysis. Welfare objectives may not be consistent with developmental objectives, and much depends on whether policies are aimed at solving short- or long-run problems, at redistributing income, or at raising total income over time.

A third paradox is that SSE promotion programs continue, undaunted by substantial evidence indicating these programs are seldom effective and, still less often, cost-effective.[6] Many directed and subsidized SSE credit programs have proven not to be viable in the long run because of poor loan repayment records, and the social benefits of these programs are difficult to establish.[7] Firm-level technical assistance to SSEs is unlikely to be cost-effective because of the numerous and widely varying characteristics of these enterprises. At best, such activities may be cost-effective if confined to a few relatively progressive and somewhat larger firms; in most cases they are better undertaken by private, rather than official, bodies.

In sum, there are substantial doubts about whether SSEs should be promoted and, if so, by what means. The conventional view is that they should be supported and that government-sponsored programs are the best means—either through full technical assistance packages (as recommended by Staley and Morse[8]) or (according to some recent advocates) through credit unsupported by technical assistance. The contrary position argues for more scale neutrality in policies, less reliance on promotional programs, and efforts to extend the financial system into rural areas and the informal sector in line with the new paradigm of small-scale lending.[9]

Amid all these controversies and uncertainties, HIID's position, as expressed through the projects in which it has been involved, has been eclectic, not to say inconsistent. Two of the four SSE projects—SEDP and ARIES—tacitly accepted the orthodox ideology and approach espoused by most developing country governments and aid agencies, while the other two projects—EEPA and rural industrialization in Thailand—were more inclined to challenge accepted views.[10]

Small-Scale Enterprises in HIID's Work Before 1980

While the four projects mentioned above represent the bulk of HIID's work on SSEs—or on microenterprises or on small and medium enterprises (SMEs)—a few scattered precursors deserve brief mention. Some research and policy advising relative to SSEs was done under projects carried out by Harvard's Development Advisory Service (DAS)—HIID's predecessor—in Malaysia (1966–1975)[11] and in Ethiopia (1970–1975), as well as under the Public Sector Programs project in Indonesia (1978–1979). In both Malaysia and Indonesia, work on SSEs was motivated by concern for the fate of small, indigenously-owned firms that were struggling to compete with larger, better-organized enterprises operated by ethnic Chinese, and by a desire to find effective ways of promoting entrepreneurship among the indigenous group. Although Malaysia especially enjoyed considerable success in increasing the participation of indigenous people in business, small enterprise promotion programs contributed little or nothing to this achievement. In Ethiopia, the main theme of Harvard's work was that small-scale industry should be given a part to play in the overall industrialization effort.

The Small Enterprise Development Project in Indonesia

The Indonesian Small Enterprise Development Project (SEDP) was a massive lending effort aimed at small- and medium-scale enterprises owned by indigenous Indonesians. The project grew out of a 1973 government decision to improve financial services for the numerous SMEs which provided most of the country's nonagricultural jobs. Of the several credit programs introduced to serve SMEs, the largest was that known in Indonesia as KIK/KMKP, which began lending in 1975.[12] Its purpose was to mobilize commercial banks to provide medium-term credits to SMEs nationwide in virtually all economic sectors. KIK/KMKP was subsidized by Bank Indonesia through a low-cost rediscount facility. In addition, 75 percent of the credit risk was borne by ASKRINDO, a government-owned insurance company created expressly for this purpose, in return for a compulsory 3 percent premium, of which Bank Indonesia paid half. The banks themselves (principally the five government-owned commercial banks but with limited participation by private banks) were generally responsible for identifying and screening customers.

KIK/KMKP soon became bogged down as a result of banker reluctance to lend to an unfamiliar SME clientele. As a result, Bank Indonesia initiated the SEDP to help the banks develop the capacity to expand the quantity and improve the quality of KIK/KMKP loans. In 1978, the World Bank agreed to support the project with a US$40 million project loan. Part of this funding was to be used for technical assistance, while the remainder was to be on-lent to KIK clients through the commercial banks. The stimulus provided by the SEDP revitalized KIK/KMKP lending. By 1980, the World Bank regarded KIK/KMKP as the largest program of its type in the world.

Most of the technical assistance associated with the SEDP was supplied by the World Bank on a direct-hire basis, but in 1979 HIID was asked to provide a resident advisor to carry out various analytical and managerial tasks associated with the operation of the project.

The main tasks envisaged were to support the handling banks in the provinces, to broaden and deepen the scope of the project, and to satisfy reporting and evaluation conditions set by the World Bank for renewal of its funding. Technical assistance teams set up in a number of provinces were supposed to report on KIK/KMKP operations and evaluate the program's economic and social impact. The weakness of much of the teams' work led to a situation in which impact evaluation became the principal activity of the two successive HIID resident advisors who worked in Bank Indonesia between 1980 and 1985.

The most substantive achievement of the project was the implementation of a well-designed study of the economic impact of the KIK/KMKP credit program. This represented a conscientious effort to solve the difficult—some would say impossible—problem of measuring the actual impact of a lending program on such variables as sales growth and employment expansion among firms that had borrowed under the program. The methodology developed for this study can stand as a model for evaluating SSE credit programs.[13] Substantively, the study found that the program yielded substantial benefits in terms of incremental effects on fixed investment, job creation, production, and value added. In the end, Bank Indonesia felt that the results of the impact study did not suit their policy needs. Evidently, the estimated net impact was not large enough to justify the subsidy element in the credit program for domestic political purposes.

Thus another impact study was initiated in 1986. Based on a simple before-and-after methodology, this study produced (improbably high) estimates of the program's impact. The results were criticized by the World Bank, which then withdrew support for the SEDP. In 1990, KIK/KMKP was terminated, a victim of the moral hazard inherent in below-market interest rates, subsidized funding, and pretenses of credit insurance.[14] Whatever its social impact may have been during its lifetime, this credit program failed the test of long-term sustainability and thus proved unable to provide economic benefits in the long run. Other subsidized SSE credit programs nevertheless continued in Indonesia, largely as a symbol of the government's pledge to assist "weak economic groups." Learning gradually did take place. It may be no coincidence that the managing director of Bank Indonesia in charge of the SEDP went on to launch Indonesia's highly regarded KUPEDES (General Rural Credit) loan program shortly after his appointment as president director of Bank Raykat Indonesia.

As discussed in Chapter 12, HIID's experience with KIK/KMKP was followed by a more innovative and constructive involvement in the development of the KUPEDES loan program, which grew out of the work of two other HIID activities in Indonesia: the Development Policy Implementation Studies (DPIS) project of 1979–1982, and the Center for Policy and Implementation Studies (CPIS) project of 1982–1992. KUPEDES was based on commercial principles and was able to generate most of its funding internally through the rural savings program (SIMPEDES), which HIID also helped to design. Introduced by Bank Raykat Indonesia at the end of 1983, KUPEDES lends to small rural producers in all sectors at an interest rate high enough to earn a profit for a (not-very-efficient) state-owned commercial bank, yet low enough to be attractive to borrowers whose main alternative source of credit is borrowing at even higher rates from informal sources of finance. KUPEDES has registered substantial achievements over more than a decade, both as an effective means of channeling credit to small, productive rural enterprises and as a major profit center for Bank Raykat Indonesia. The economic and social impacts of KUPEDES are more difficult to determine than its financial performance, but it has been established that the program reaches a wide cross-section of the rural population and finances important small-business needs for both fixed and working capital.[15] The social and commercial success of KUPEDES and the new paradigm of small-scale lending that it exemplifies have important implications for financial development (see Chapter 12).

The Employment and Enterprise Policy Analysis Project

In its proposal request for the EEPA project, USAID emphasized that it regarded SMEs as important sources of employment creation in developing countries, which should be actively promoted for equity and efficiency reasons. According to USAID, in many developing countries the larger, more formally organized enterprises were creating jobs at too slow a rate; SMEs could be part of the solution. Furthermore, the proposal request hypothesized, more attention should be given to the effects of economic policies (trade, monetary, fiscal, labor, price, and regulatory policies) as a hitherto overlooked influence on the development of SMEs. The project was asked to gauge the potential for adopting policy reforms that would stimulate the growth of SMEs, or at least eliminate existing "policy biases" that reduce the competitiveness of SMEs relative to large-scale enterprises.

EEPA was both a research and a technical assistance project. It was intended to improve understanding of potential SME contributions to development objectives and to create methodologies for analyzing those contributions; it would also help USAID missions and bureaus to guide client countries toward the promotion of SMEs through both short- and long-term advisory assistance. The project was planned originally to last five years. Core funding of US$2 million was provided by USAID's Bureau of Science and Technology in Washington D.C. In addition, there was a "buy-in capacity" of US$ 6 million that could be tapped by USAID missions and bureaus to fund activities within EEPA's terms of reference without the need for further competitive bidding.

To improve its chances of being awarded the project, HIID invited both Michigan State University (MSU) and Development Alternatives, Inc. (DAI) to join its bid as subcontractors. HIID's main contribution to this consortium was conceived as its broad policy and advisory experience, while MSU was thought to bring expertise in SSE research and DAI the capacity to respond to short-turnaround consulting requests that might not interest the two universities or would be difficult for them to fulfill. The structure of the consortium probably contributed to the success of HIID's bid, but it created operational problems after the project was won.

The EEPA project was run by a full-time HIID project manager, under the guidance of a part-time project coordinator. The subcontractors appointed their own coordinators. The project was given two no-cost extensions by USAID and eventually ran seven years (1984–1991).

Over the life of the project, long-term advisory activities were undertaken in Bangladesh (by HIID), in Sri Lanka (by DAI), and in Rwanda (by MSU). Short-term consulting took place in nineteen countries, and three USAID bureaus other than Science and Technology bought services from the project. Although all these activities fell within EEPA's broad and somewhat vague terms of reference, their actual content varied widely, depending both on the interests of the respective clients and on the interests and abilities of the consortium members that supplied the services in question.

After lengthy discussion early in the project about what EEPA's research focus should be, HIID eventually decided to emphasize analysis of the changing role of SMEs in manufacturing at different levels of economic development. The institute attempted to develop an understanding of SMEs consistent both with the research on patterns of economic development conducted by Simon Kuznets, Hollis Chenery, and others[16] and with industrial organization theory. One important component of HIID's research under the EEPA project focused on the sharply contrasting roles played by SMEs in Korea, where they rapidly gave way to large-scale enterprise, and in Taiwan, where SMEs played a more significant and lasting role. Meanwhile, MSU used its part of the EEPA research budget to further its ongoing research program, which documented the substantial dimensions of SME and informal sector activities in many developing countries (particularly in Africa) and argued that many of these small firms were efficient, at least relative to Africa's notoriously inefficient large-scale enterprises. MSU also contributed analysis of the differential effects of various economic policies on firms of different scales.

The operations of the EEPA project were conflict-ridden. Sharp differences in opinion and self-interest emerged among the three contractors. In particular, the MSU group sought to defend its established position as an advocate for SME promotion measures, while HIID devoted itself to a critical analysis of the established viewpoint. As the project proceeded, HIID increasingly rejected one of USAID's basic premises for the project—that the number and employment size of SMEs should be "promoted"—and put forward alternative views that were challenging and somewhat unpopular with both USAID and HIID's subcontractors. However, the EEPA research did verify USAID's other basic hypothesis: that government policies have a significant and often deleterious effect on the development of SMEs and that these policies should thus be given greater emphasis relative to SME promotion programs.

In view of these operational difficulties, what can be rightly claimed as accomplishments of the EEPA project? The project produced several pieces of high-quality research and advisory work, but probably had little immediate influence on policy in any of the countries in which it worked. In some countries (for example, the Philippines and Somalia), excellent advice went unheeded. In others (for example, Bangladesh), the advisory impact was limited by questions about the quality of the advice given and the research on which it was based. Of the three resident missions, the one in Rwanda was probably the most influential, but subsequent turmoil in that country would have rendered any benefits highly transitory.

The EEPA project did result in numerous papers and publications. An EEPA discussion paper series eventually included thirty-one titles. Most of these discussion papers were later published. The major intellectual product is a book, *Industrialization and the Small Firm: Patterns and Policies*, published in 1996.[17] This book extends past analysis of patterns of economic development to include the changing role of SMEs in manufacturing at different levels of per capita income, analyzes how policies enacted for reasons unrelated to enterprise scale impact significantly on the competition between small and large firms (generally to the detriment of the SMEs), critically examines past evaluations of SME promotion programs, and concludes with a series of case studies on the role of SMEs and their policy implications in several low-income countries (in Sub-Saharan Africa and Bangladesh), middle-income countries (in Latin America and the Philippines), and newly industrializing countries (Korea and Taiwan).

While it is too early to assess EEPA's cumulative intellectual impact, those involved in the project hope that EEPA will significantly modify the way people look at SMEs, especially through the book and subsequent research done at the World Bank by two former EEPA researchers. Rather than regarding SMEs as a "good thing" that should be "promoted" in countries at all levels of development, *Industrialization and the Small Firm* argues that the role of SMEs changes radically and generally diminishes as development proceeds. In all countries, SMEs become far less important as per capita income rises, while surviving SMEs come to resemble large enterprises in all respects other than scale. In most high-income countries SMEs employ only about one-quarter of workers in manufacturing, and resemble larger firms in capital intensity, technology, labor productivity, and wages paid. There are, however, a few deviant cases—notably Japan and Italy—where SMEs still employ about half the manufacturing workforce. These countries are not exceptions to the rule that average plant size rises and scale-related differences diminish, but they do retain higher levels of industrial dualism, for reasons analyzed in the book.

It is the conclusion of the EEPA studies that most of the programs and policies undertaken to "promote" SMEs are ineffective and inefficient. To the extent that they do have an impact, they may cause undesirable distortions—as they have in India, the country that has pushed SSE preferences most vigorously. In general, scale-neutral policies are best. However, limited interventions aimed at reducing the transaction costs faced by SMEs may be beneficial, especially in capital markets.

The ARIES Project and HIID's Role

While the EEPA project dealt with small and medium enterprises and was primarily concerned with their development potential, the ARIES project involved small and microenterprises and was more concerned with poverty alleviation. An earlier USAID project called PISCES (Program for Investment in the Small Capital Enterprise Sector) had tried to demonstrate the feasibility of providing credit and technical assistance to microenterprises. The ARIES project was intended to take the next step of providing resources to nongovernmental organizations (NGOs)—such as private voluntary organizations, chambers of commerce, and management training centers—that work with small and microenterprises.

The project had three substantive components: research, training, and technical assistance. HIID participated, as a subcontractor to Robert Nathan Associates, with responsibility for the project's applied research component; HIID was not involved directly in the training activity or at all in the technical assistance. The institute had three specific tasks: (1) to prepare a strategic overview paper that would identify the major problems facing SSE support organizations; (2) to develop a series of teaching cases focused on strategic decisions shaping important development institutions; and (3) to develop a textual database called AskARIES. The case-writing activity developed cases on various aspects of SSE promotion that could be used to train trainers by the case method. The overview paper and cases were published in a book entitled *Seeking Solutions: Framework and Cases for Small Enterprise Development Programs.*[18] The innovative AskARIES knowledge base was issued as software (on sixteen diskettes plus a *Users' Guide*) that those involved in SSE promotion could use to obtain information from the literature on recurrent problems in SSE promotion activities. Both the book and the knowledge base have been widely praised and used by organizations working with SSEs.

While the ARIES project implicitly supported the existing approach to SSE development, those involved in the project emphasized that the work was neutral in terms of choices among alternative policies and program designs. The purpose was not to determine which policies were best, let alone to advocate specific policies. Rather, it was to provide practitioners with useful materials and to stimulate thinking so that they could reach informed decisions on actions to be taken.

The Thailand Rural Industries and Employment Project

This small, eighteen-month project on rural industrialization and employment in Thailand was designated as a minority business set-aside by USAID and therefore could not be carried out as a buy-in to the EEPA project, as originally planned. Instead, HIID, working as a subcontractor to the Honolulu-based consulting firm PACMAR (Pacific Management Resources, Inc.), helped the Thailand Development Research Institute (TDRI) to carry out a study aimed at developing proposals for promoting industrialization in areas other than Bangkok and its five surrounding provinces. The study was motivated by the rapid industrialization of Thailand in recent years, the extraordinary concentration of industrial growth in the Bangkok region, and the severe urban environmental problems that this concentration was believed to be causing. The study was designed to illuminate the existing pattern of industrial activity in Thailand, the implications of current trends, and the costs and benefits of alternative policies.

Because of USAID contracting delays, the Thailand rural industrialization project was well under way within TDRI before the HIID team arrived on the scene. TDRI had seconded an academic from one of the Thai universities to direct the study and contracted with several other Thai economists to carry out component studies. However, the debatable nature of some of the project's terms of reference and the limited time availability of the best of the Thai economists involved combined to reduce the usefulness of most of these component studies to a low level. As a result of these problems, the HIID team was eventually asked to prepare a "synthesis report," which was a virtually independent effort to analyze the problem.

In its report,[19] the HIID team reviewed the basic facts, analyzed these patterns and trends to understand their major determinants, and considered alternative policies for achieving the government's aim of promoting industrialization outside the Bangkok region. The analysis criticized perceptions about the role of industry in Thai economic growth, the reasons for geographic concentration of existing industry, the relationship between industrial concentration and inequality, and the potential effectiveness of policies intended to produce regional dispersion of industry. It urged the government to seek a better understanding of the market forces that cause firms to select their locations, to appreciate the limited nature and potential of rural industry, and to decentralize more of its own authority and services if it wished to promote regional balance. Other actions urged in the report included accelerated provision of infrastructure outside the Bangkok region, modification of property taxation, restructuring of minimum wage legislation, removal of restrictions on terms of credit contracts, and strengthening of rural credit markets.

Whether to take strong measures to promote economic activity outside the Bangkok region has been a long- and much-debated issue in Thailand. The HIID report was well received by those sympathetic with its policy line and was no doubt dismissed by those with opposing views. Its influence on the long-term course of the debate is unclear.

Conclusions: Small-Scale Enterprise in HIID's Past and Future

Work on small-scale enterprise was not a major portion of HIID's activities over the period 1980–1995. Nor was the institute a truly major participant in the field, which, as noted at the outset, tends to be dominated by a well-defined group of firms and private voluntary organizations working on programs for international development and by a small group of research specialists. Nevertheless, HIID has made important contributions. Through the SEDP, it provided a methodological model for evaluating the firm-level impact of a credit program. Through its work on rural banking in Indonesia, HIID made a significant input into the development of the new paradigm of small-scale lending, which may prove to be of great importance for small enterprise development. Through the ARIES project, it produced teaching and reference materials that are widely used by agencies supporting SSE development. Through the EEPA project, it advised on policies that impinge on the development of SMEs and contributed new research findings and views to the on-going controversy about the role of SSEs in economic development. These are not negligible contributions.

Except for recent exploratory work in a number of countries aimed at spreading the new paradigm of small-scale lending exemplified by KUPEDES, HIID has not undertaken any further projects concerned with SSEs or SMEs since 1991. A new USAID project concerned with evaluating the impact of microenterprise promotion programs, in which HIID will be a subcontractor to Management Services International, was awarded in late 1995. It thus appears that HIID will continue to be involved in work on small scale enterprise, at least to some degree.

Notes

1 The author wishes to thank Bruce Bolnick for a draft report on the Small Enterprise Development Project (SEDP) and Martha Chen and Marguerite Robinson for comments on an earlier draft of this essay.

2 There is no totally satisfactory definition of small-scale enterprise (SSE). Most often, the number of employees is used as a measurement scale, if only because employment data are readily available. Reference is usually made to establishments or plants, rather than firms, although among SSEs these are usually the same thing. SSEs may be defined as establishments with twenty or fewer employees. Related categories are small and medium enterprises (SMEs), which may go up to fifty or one hundred employees, and microenterprises, which may be defined as those with five or fewer employees. The microenterprise usually includes individual proprietors who work alone or engage only family labor.

3 This subject is discussed at length in Snodgrass and Biggs (1996).

4 Assistance to SSEs typically follows a model based on agricultural extension and worked out in India in the late 1950s and early 1960s. The classic text is Staley and Morse (1965). However, Staley and Morse, whose treatment was sophisticated and discriminating, cannot be blamed for the many failings of subsequent SSE promotion programs in numerous developing countries.

5 The importance of gender considerations in analyzing small-scale enterprise programs has been suggested by Martha Chen, among others.

6 See Snodgrass and Biggs (1996, Chapter 4) for a discussion of these issues.

7 The "new paradigm" of small business lending is more promising, however. See Chapter 12 of this volume for more information.

8 See Staley and Morse (1965).

9 A well-known World Bank study denies that enterprise scale in manufacturing tells one anything useful for policy-making purposes. See Little et al. (1987).

10 Innovative work on small-scale credit programs was also done under HIID's Center for Policy and Implementation Studies (CPIS) project in Indonesia, which is discussed in Chapters 3, 12, and 17 of this volume. CPIS also studied microenterprises in the urban informal sector (pedal rickshaws, trash collectors, and sidewalk vendors).

11 This refers to the first phase of Harvard's DAS activities in Malaysia financed by the Ford Foundation. HIID also worked in Malaysia in 1977–1981, under funding from the United Nations Development Programme (UNDP).

12 For the credit program KIK/KMKP, the letters stand for the Indonesian words for small investment credit (KIK) and permanent working capital loans (KMKP).

13 See Bolnick and Nelson (1990).

14 See Bolnick (1987). This paper interprets Indonesia's small-credit program as having positive net effects in the 1970s, but concludes that major liberalization was overdue by 1983.

15 KUPEDES does not, however, make very small loans or reach the "poorest of the poor," mainly because of the proportionately high transaction costs of such loans.

16 See, for example, Kuznets (1971); Chenery (1979); and Chenery et al. (1986).

17 See Snodgrass and Biggs (1996).

18 See Grindle et al. (1989).

19 See Biggs et al. (1990).

12 Sustainable Microfinance

Marguerite S. Robinson[1]

The Shift from Subsidized Credit to Commercial Finance

This chapter is about the history of an idea. It reviews the evolution of a concept through multiple HIID projects over more than fifteen years. The idea—that the massive demand for microfinance in developing countries[2] can be supplied by sustainable institutions providing financial services commercially, and that these services can have important effects on social and economic development—has been well demonstrated on a large scale. HIID's role in the formulation of the initial hypotheses is addressed here, as are HIID's contributions in planning and coordinating the underlying research, advising on the policies and implementation strategies that put concept into practice, analyzing the results, and disseminating the findings.[3]

The shift in microfinance presently underway in the developing world is marked by the change from government and donor-funded[4] subsidized credit to sustainable financial intermediation.[5] This has occurred because of the work of many people in many countries.[6] This chapter, however, is limited to discussion of HIID's contributions. The primary focus here is HIID's role, from 1979 until the present, in advising the Indonesian Ministry of Finance and the Bank Rakyat Indonesia (BRI) on the development of BRI's nationwide system of profitable local banking.[7] The chapter also reviews briefly HIID's wider role in Asia, Africa, and Latin America, in assisting governments and financial institutions to adapt relevant aspects of the Indonesian model to the conditions of their countries.

During the 1980s BRI, one of Indonesia's five state-owned commercial banks, developed a viable system of microfinance, combining institutional profitability with wide coverage of lower-income clients throughout Indonesia, the world's fourth most highly-populated country. The shift there from government-subsidized credit delivery to profitable financial intermediation at the local level enabled, for the first time in the developing world, the demand for microfinance to be met on a large scale.

It was not obvious that this shift would occur. In the early 1980s, there were no large-scale examples of commercial microfinance in any developing country. Derived from supply-leading finance theory, the old paradigm of subsidized credit for lower-income borrowers in rural areas was then well-entrenched in Indonesia, as in most of the developing world. Microfinance, as a commercial institutional activity, was generally perceived by policy makers and by the formal financial sector to be unimportant for the economy, unprofitable for financial institutions, and unnecessary for the poor. This remains the prevailing view in most developing countries today. However, the "new microfinance" pioneered in Indonesia—non-subsidized, commercial financial intermediation with services delivered at the local level—is beginning to be adapted in many other countries. The new ideas are spreading rapidly.

Banks and other financial institutions in Bangladesh, Bolivia, Cameroon, Chile, Colombia, Costa Rica, the Dominican Republic, Ecuador, Egypt, India, Jamaica, Kenya, Mexico, the Philippines, Senegal, Tanzania, Vietnam, and others—in addition to a number of institutions in Indonesia—have either established commercial microfinance programs or are in various stages of actively learning about the principles and practices of sustainable microfinance. Many have visited BRI in Indonesia.

What has been called the "microfinance revolution,"[8] however, is at an early stage of development. Despite the widespread demand for financial services at the local level—for both credit and savings facilities[9]—it is estimated that institutional finance is still unavailable to over 80 percent of all households in developing countries.[10] This includes most of the poor people in the developing world.

The examples of BRI and of other self-sufficient institutions that provide finance to large numbers of lower-income households are important globally for four reasons. First, the cost of credit to the borrower is usually significantly lower than credit obtained on the informal commercial credit market. Substantial evidence exists to show that financial institutions can profitably provide microcredit, delivered locally to large numbers of borrowers, at 5 to 15 percent of the interest rates, and below 10 to 20 percent of the total costs, that are normally paid by lower-income borrowers for informal commercial credit. Thus, informal commercial lenders in Indonesia, and in many developing countries, typically charge lower-income borrowers a flat monthly interest rate of 10 to over 40 percent on the original loan balance.[11] They may charge lower rates to better-off and more influential borrowers, but in general the higher rates are charged to the poorer borrowers, who have the fewest alternatives. In contrast, BRI's nationwide local banking system provides loans profitably at the local level at or below a flat monthly interest rate of 1.5 percent on the original balance of the loan. No additional fees are charged to borrowers who repay on time.

BRI's interest rate on its small loan program is equivalent to an annual effective interest rate on the declining balance of about 32 percent[12] for a twelve-month loan with monthly installments. It should be noted that this is significantly higher than the commercial rates of urban Indonesian banks, reflecting the fact that the provision of microfinance services at many small, scattered locations is considerably more expensive than providing relatively few clients in an urban bank with larger loans and deposits. Therefore, the term "commercial" as used in microfinance denotes interest rates sufficient to cover all costs associated with the provision of the financial services, including non-cash costs such as depreciation, bad loan provisions, inflation losses in the real value of equity, and the full commercial cost of raising funds. The resulting rate is invariably larger than prevailing market loan rates in commercial banking for larger customers.

The crucial point, however—which is not widely understood—is that the interest rates of self-sufficient microfinance institutions are highly attractive to borrowers at the local level in developing countries because they represent a small fraction of the rates charged on the informal commercial market. In addition, sustainable microfinance institutions make concerted efforts to make procedures simple, locations convenient, and staff trained and motivated to be helpful to clients; this keeps the transaction costs of clients relatively low.

The second reason for the importance of commercial microfinance for development is that the demand for institutional microcredit worldwide is far too large to be met by donor or government funds. The global demand for small loans can be met only by licensed commercial institutions that are able to mobilize local savings, leverage commercial investment as necessary, and provide small loans in large volume.

Third, the demand for appropriate savings services at the local level is massive, typically far larger even than the demand for microcredit.

Fourth, it has been demonstrated that commercial institutions can provide microfinance profitably in very different institutional structures and in widely varying socioeconomic contexts.[13] The necessary—although not sufficient—conditions are an enabling macroeconomic and regulatory environment, an adequate degree of monetization, a reasonable level of political stability, and sufficient population density.[14]

Development of Sustainable Microfinance in Indonesia: Background

Each of Indonesia's five state-owned commercial banks has traditionally held particular responsibilities in addition to general banking activities. The special assignment of BRI has been the provision of banking services to the rural areas, with emphasis on agricultural credit. BRI's unit banking system[15] was originally created as a channeling agent for BIMAS,[16] the credit component of Indonesia's multipronged drive to reach national rice self-sufficiency.[17] The unit banking system is a division of BRI; the bank also provides commercial, corporate, and international banking services in addition to local-level banking.

In the early 1970s, BRI established over 3,600 unit banks at the sub-district level; these functioned primarily as channeling agents for the BIMAS program and other subsidized rural lending programs. Beginning in the mid-1970s, TABANAS,[18] the national savings program of Bank Indonesia (the central bank) was offered in BRI's unit banks. However, annual interest rates set by the government at 12 percent for loans and 15 percent for most deposits discouraged the bank from undertaking active savings mobilization.

In 1979, HIID was asked by Indonesia's Ministry of Finance to advise on the national rice intensification program, one of four programs reviewed by HIID's Development Policy Implementation Studies (DPIS).[19] A large-scale interdisciplinary study of the rice program at national, regional, district, sub-district, and village levels in four provinces of Indonesia, with additional, less intensive, work in other provinces, was carried out from 1979 to 1983. The DPIS rice intensification study involved six HIID advisors (three anthropologists, two economists, and a sociologist) and over fifty Indonesian researchers. HIID's role was to design, coordinate, and analyze the research and to prepare policy recommendations based on the conclusions of the study. The advisors worked closely during the four-year period with the Minister of Finance and other Indonesian officials.

HIID's 400-page report found that the dramatic rise in rice production was made possible by a combination of factors: an appropriate and effectively implemented price policy; available and affordable inputs; rapid learning among rice farmers; improvements in infrastructure, especially irrigation and roads; and the continuing development of new high-yielding, early-maturing rice varieties at the International Rice Research Institute (IRRI) and the provision of these seeds to Indonesia.[20] The credit component of the rice intensification project was conspicuously absent from the list of forces driving the success of Indonesia's rice seed-fertilizer revolution.

The report concluded that BRI's approach to financial intermediation at the local level was similar to that found in many developing countries: institutional credit was subsidized, the credit program was poorly planned, the low-interest BIMAS loans typically bypassed the poor, arrears and losses were high, and deposits were low. During 1983, BRI gave serious consideration to closing down its unit banking system. As a high-level BRI official commented at that time, "The unit banking system gets in the way of our real banking activities." (Had the unit bank network been closed down, this would have ended the provision of banking services in over 90 percent of the locations in Indonesia where formal banking services were available.)

The HIID report recommended that the subsidized unit banks be transformed into a sustainable system of commercial banking at the local level, and that a program of general rural credit at commercial interest rates be implemented through the unit banking system. The recommendation for the shift from credit delivery programs to financial intermediation was based on five basic hypotheses, all of which have since been proven correct:

- There is massive demand for institutional commercial microfinance—both credit and savings—at the local level.
- Because of its volume, this demand can be met only through financially viable institutions.

- Meeting microfinance demand and building sustainable financial institutions are mutually reinforcing goals.
- Mobilization of voluntary public savings is required for the large-scale financial intermediation that is necessary to meet the demand for commercial institutional microcredit at the local level.
- Microfinance can be both socially and economically profitable.

After extensive, wide-ranging discussions over a number of months, HIID's recommendation to restructure BRI's unit banking system was accepted by the Ministry of Finance. At that time, the Indonesian Government was planning a series of major financial reforms. The first of these, announced in June 1983, permitted state-owned banks to set their own interest rates on most loans and deposits. Among other purposes, this deregulation served to provide an enabling environment for the transformation of BRI's unit banks that began in early 1984.

Policy Issues

Why did the Indonesian Government decide to build BRI's local-level banking system? In the early 1980s, the government anticipated (correctly, as it turned out) a possible significant decline in the real value of oil revenues, and began to seek alternative sources of government revenue and to undertake wide-ranging financial reforms. In this context, it was recognized that a competitive economy and new sources of investment would be required. The private sector would have to become responsible for a significantly larger share of savings and investment than had been possible in the 1970s, and the state-owned banks, instead of serving primarily as channeling agents for government subsidies, would have to become commercial banks. As part of the wider financial deregulation process, banks were given more autonomy in decision making and encouraged to expand their products and services. These reforms provided the background to the 1983 decision to convert BRI's "rice banks" into "real banks." Commercial microfinance in the unit banks began in 1984 in the rural areas; in 1989, the unit banking system was extended to urban areas. Therefore, the term "local level" as used here refers to bank services delivered both in rural areas and in lower-income neighborhoods of urban areas.

Emphasis on Voluntary Savings Mobilization

Why did BRI decide, unlike many other financial institutions serving the local level in developing countries, to emphasize voluntary savings mobilization? Although there were suggestions in 1984 that the new commercial loan program could become self-sustaining even without substantial local savings, that approach was rejected. There were three reasons the government and BRI decided to plan and implement the credit and savings components of the program together.

First, they intended to finance the country's demand for small loans delivered at the local level with locally-mobilized savings. The Indonesian Government, expecting lower oil revenues and actively seeking increased private sector savings and investment, decided that extensive long-term funding for a nationwide microcredit program could not be committed from Bank Indonesia, the central bank. The idea behind the new credit program, called KUPEDES,[21] was to meet local credit demand using a loan instrument suitable for all types of small productive activities, with interest rates that would enable long-term institutional viability. It was correctly anticipated that meeting the country's demand for microcredit would eventually require a substantially greater amount of financing than had been required for the total amount of all previous rural credit programs combined and that this demand could be financed by local deposits.

Second, the risk was considered too high for a long-term commitment of central bank funds. It was well-known that many local-level credit programs in Indonesia and in other developing countries had a history of high arrears. There was no successful model of financial intermediation on a significant scale at the local level that could be found in any developing country. Indonesia's economics ministers recognized the potential for a large-scale banking system serving customers at the local level and supported its introduction with government funding; they also recognized the importance of limiting government risk.

The third motivation was to encourage the mobilization of local-level savings in the unit banking system. As part of its wider policy of encouraging private savings, the government wanted to meet what was accurately estimated as a large potential demand for savings services in financial institutions at the local level. It was thought that an approach offering deposit instruments appropriate for local demand could both provide customers with generally positive real returns and help to build the long-term viability of the unit banking system. Both results would contribute to economic development at the local level.

RESTRUCTURING BRI'S UNIT BANKING SYSTEM

The first stage of HIID's advising on BRI's unit banking system under the DPIS project (1979–1983), which involved assessment of the system as it was then constituted, resulted in advice that the system be transformed from a channeling agent for subsidized government credit into a commercial banking network. In the second stage of its work with BRI (1984–present), HIID has advised BRI on the many phases of development of its unit banking system.[22]

Establishment of the New System

In 1982, some of the HIID advisors in the DPIS project formed a Rural Credit Working Group to advise the Ministry of Finance on the policy implications of the DPIS study findings on rice intensification. Following the June 1983 financial deregulation and the approval of the recommendations in the DPIS rice report that BRI's unit banking network be converted to a commercial system, the Rural Credit Working Group, augmented by several others from HIID, began working closely with the Ministry of Finance and BRI to provide policy briefings and to prepare detailed recommendations for the new local banking system. In August 1983, a new BRI president-director was appointed to lead the transformation of BRI's local-level banking system.

The Minister of Finance was the key decision maker in the policy changes, with critical initial support to BRI provided also by Bank Indonesia. The interest rate on lending was set to enable the unit banking system to break even—if credit outstanding could reach $220 million and if loan losses could be held to 4.5 percent or lower. The rates set assumed that the major source of funding would be savings raised at the TABANAS interest rate of 15 percent per year. The interest rate on the new KUPEDES loans for working capital was stated as 1.5 percent per month flat rate on the original balance.[23]

It was estimated that this interest rate would enable the bank to cover all the costs of a local level banking system and to earn a profit. Although high in comparison with market rates for urban banks, it was well known to the decision makers in the Ministry of Finance that the KUPEDES interest rate represents a small fraction of the rates typically charged to lower-income borrowers by informal commercial lenders. This fact was learned in part as a result of the extensive fieldwork on local finance carried out during the preceding years under HIID's DPIS project.

Bank Indonesia agreed to provide seed money to BRI at 15 percent per year, the same rate that BRI's unit banks paid depositors for TABANAS savings. The intent was to avoid giving BRI an incentive to rely on Bank Indonesia liquidity credits as the major long-term source of funds for lending at the units rather than to mobilize savings. When the KUPEDES program began in February 1984, the main sources of funds for the loan portfolio were about $140 million of liquidity credit from Bank Indonesia; and about $65 million from government funds that BRI had received earlier and was permitted to retain, even though Kredit Mini, the subsidized loan program for which the funds had been originally provided, would now be ended.[24] The Ministry of Finance agreed to continue to subsidize BRI's operating losses on the units until the system broke even—which was expected to take two years. The intent behind the initial capitalization of the KUPEDES loan program was to provide a "subsidy to end subsidy." BRI's newly transformed unit banking system broke even on a monthly basis by late 1985, a little under the two years that had been estimated, and the units showed a profit for the year 1986—and for every year since.

Development of the Instruments

Shortly after the June 1983 financial deregulation, BRI, with advice from HIID, began to design the new credit instrument in detail. This was accompanied by the retraining of unit bank staff aimed at changing them from passive channeling agents of subsidized credit to active agents of financial intermediation at the local level. In February 1984, BRI began its new program of general rural credit, offered throughout the unit banking network. KUPEDES retained both the methods of appraising the creditworthiness of loan applicants and the basic repayment schedules that had been successfully developed under two earlier unit bank credit programs: Kredit Mini, which had provided subsidized loans up to a maximum of $220 primarily for off-farm activities and Kredit Midi, which had offered subsidized loans up to $550 to Kredit Mini "graduates." The main difference between Kredit Mini/Kredit Midi and KUPEDES was the setting of a KUPEDES interest rate that would cover all costs including the non-subsidized cost of raising funds. No new loans were given under Kredit Mini/ Kredit Midi after 1983 and in 1985 the subsidized BIMAS agricultural loan program was also phased out.

KUPEDES loans are provided for any viable productive activity. Since most Indonesian households have multiple income sources the loan is, in fact, often used for financing several economic activities within the household. While longer-term agricultural loans are available under KUPEDES, many borrowers with seasonal incomes from crops prefer to repay in monthly installments from other household income (petty trading, services, small industry, etc.). KUPEDES loans were originally available up to a maximum of $975. The ceiling was gradually raised, and the loans are now available from about $11 to $11,000. Borrowers may re-borrow as many times as they wish, so long as they have a good repayment record and continue to be creditworthy borrowers. Thus, lower-income borrowers who begin with small loans, and whose enterprises grow and/or diversify successfully, can qualify over time for increasingly larger loans and can gradually raise themselves out of poverty.

KUPEDES loans include a "prompt payment incentive:" the borrower pays 2 percent flat rate a month of which 1.5 percent is interest. The additional 0.5 percent per month is returned to the borrower in a lump sum at the end of the loan period, or at the end of 6 months (whichever is shorter), if all payments have been made in full and on time.

By December 31, 1985, nearly two years after the introduction of KUPEDES, the loan portfolio totaled about $205 million. It had become clear that there was a market for credit at an interest rate that would cover all costs, and that the units could successfully make and collect back such loans. However, the Ministry of Finance had emphasized from the start that additional government funds for KUPEDES loans would not be available; for further expansion of the loan portfolio, savings would have to be mobilized by the units.

Extensive research conducted in many parts of Indonesia from 1983 to 1985 had assessed local demand for institutional deposit instruments. This activity was carried out by BRI, with advice from HIID and the Center for Policy and Implementation Studies (CPIS), a government-supported foundation that developed out of HIID's DPIS project with the Ministry of Finance. The studies on the demand for deposit instruments were carried out to understand local savings habits and to learn what types of deposit accounts would meet the different kinds of local demand for savings instruments.

HIID worked with CPIS and BRI to learn the forms in which ordinary people save (such as hoarded cash, gold, animals, agricultural products, raw materials, and construction materials), and to understand the purposes for which they save in these different forms. Institutional deposit instruments were then designed to provide significantly better savings options, judged by the peoples' own standards, than the savers could accomplish by themselves. The research on demand showed that a fully liquid deposit account, not then available at the units, was greatly in demand. In addition, it became clear that a package of several instruments would be needed to meet savers' multiple requirements.

During 1984–1985, new deposit instruments were designed for the unit banks. These were then tested in a two-stage pilot project in selected units. By mid-1986, a set of new deposit instruments was offered throughout BRI's unit banking system that provided, for the first time at the local level, a combination of security, convenience, liquidity, confidentiality, and returns. Since 1985, three main types of savings instruments have been featured in all unit banks: (1) a fully liquid account, which pays interest and features a lottery (SIMPEDES and SIMASKOT);[25] (2) a fixed deposit account, which is the least liquid of the accounts but normally pays the highest interest rates; and (3) the national savings program (TABANAS), which generally falls between the other two instruments in both the degree of liquidity and the interest rate paid. Thus all accounts offer security and convenience, and customers can choose among instruments offering different ratios of liquidity and returns. Many households hold different types of accounts and use these for different purposes. All savings are voluntary; no compulsory savings are required to obtain loans.

Reorganizing BRI's Unit Banking System

The transformation of the BRI units into a financially viable local banking system—covering both rural and urban areas—required fundamental changes in institutional organization and management. These included changes in the organization of the unit banking system, in accounting and reporting procedures, in allocation of responsibilities, and in staff training and incentives.

Accounting

Before 1984, the units were more similar in structure to a branch window than to a local bank with its own accounting system. With the beginning of the new system, each unit was required to maintain its own balance sheet and its own profit and loss statement. Transactions at the units were no longer posted as branch transactions. Each unit was provided with equity of about $18,675. Units with more than that amount outstanding were shown as borrowing from the branch, and the unit was charged a monthly interest at a transfer price set by the head office. Reserves for bad debt were set aside based on arrears. Remaining assets and liabilities were transferred to the branch books, with the units acting as collection agents for the branch.

Under the system introduced in 1984, interest paid on KUPEDES loans is retained by the unit. Savings mobilized by the unit are shown as a unit liability; they are not transferred to the branch, as was the case previously. Reserves for payment of interest on savings at the end of the year are set aside each month. Accrual of income earned but not yet paid was stopped; only interest paid is recognized as income. Units with excess liquidity can deposit funds at the branch and earn interest on their deposits, while units with a higher loan amount outstanding than total deposits must borrow from the branch. In 1986 the interest rate for liquidity credit from BRI branches to units was raised to 17 percent, to encourage the units to raise savings by making it cheaper to do so than to borrow from the branch.

The profit and loss position of each unit is available monthly, enabling unit staff to take timely actions to help the unit to reach, or to increase, profitability. Also, the supervisors of the units at the branch offices can review monthly the performance of the units they supervise and can take immediate corrective action when necessary. Head office staff can review the overall monthly progress by unit, branch, and region. Poorly performing units can be visited to learn the problems and to institute corrections, while unusually well-performing units can be visited to learn successful techniques that might be replicated or adapted by other units.

Management Information Systems

When the new unit banking system began in 1984, the thirty-two types of reports that were previously (and excessively) required were reduced to five: a balance sheet, a profit and loss statement, a credit report that shows loan arrears over time, a savings report, and a unit progress report. The unit progress report provides twenty-five indicators of the units' condition; in addition, the head office conducts periodic sample surveys to obtain information that is not collected on a regular basis. At first the units had manual systems; later the unit banking system was gradually computerized.

Allocation of Responsibilities

The new unit banking system was necessarily accompanied by fundamental changes in the allocation of responsibilities. Since 1984, the unit staff have been held directly responsible for the financial results of their banking decisions. Thus, the unit bank head and the field officer responsible for examining credit applications (mantri) are accountable for the quality of the loans they make. Loan losses can be easily tracked from the unit's monthly profit and loss statements, and unit staff are evaluated on the basis of the financial performance of their unit. Staff promotions and incentives, or the lack thereof, are allocated accordingly.

Branch managers are also held accountable for the financial performance of the units they supervise. In the beginning, many had misconceptions about the new system and needed considerable supervision by the head office. In general, higher-level supervisors tended to find it more difficult to accept the far-reaching changes being made in the unit banking system than did the unit staff themselves.

At the branch level, one unit business manager (UBM) is assigned to supervise a maximum of four units, and one unit desa officer (UDO) supervises about ten units. The job of the UBM involves supervision of all aspects of the unit's activities, including checking with customers to ensure that the unit's loan and deposit records are correct. UBMs are required to talk with all borrowers who are in arrears; this serves the double purpose of assisting in loan collection and identifying cases of collusion between unit staff and borrower.

As the unit banking system grew, new organizational components were created at regional and central levels to supervise unit bank business activities. At the regional level, a business unit desa (BUD) section (or village business unit section) was created, with responsibility for the oversight and support of unit activities. The regional BUD section is charged with reviewing, and correcting as necessary, the unit bank activities of the branches under its supervision. This role is especially important in cases in which the problems have been caused by branch error. The BUD section does not have responsibility for most of the support functions for the unit banking system (such as personnel, logistics, and computerization); rather, its function is to ensure that such support is provided by the various sections responsible.

At the BRI head office in Jakarta, supervision of the unit banking system is provided by the BUD division whose head reports to a BRI managing director. The BUD division head supervises the various sections of this division and also coordinates the unit banks' activities with BRI's support divisions. The BUD division head does not have authority over these divisions; inter-divisional issues are referred to the responsible managing directors.

Staff Training and Incentives

At first, training of the unit bank staff was concentrated on teaching staff the elements of the new banking system, including accounting, bookkeeping, and financial analysis; on studies of local markets, networks, and income flows; and on developing staff capabilities in customer relations and publicity. The trainers were an ad hoc assortment of BRI directors, regional and branch staff, CPIS staff, and HIID consultants. By 1986–1987, however, BRI began a systematic re-training of the entire unit bank staff; the purpose was both to upgrade the staff and to ensure that unit practices became standardized throughout the system. Five unit bank training centers, located in different parts of the country, have a combined capacity of 780 students. Full-time instructors provide three types of training: training for new staff, courses for those being promoted to new positions, and annual refresher courses. The curriculum consists of over twenty different courses designed especially for the unit banking system.

The main incentive for good staff performance is a promotion system based in considerable part on merit. In addition, there are two other types of unit bank staff incentives. Ten percent of each unit's annual profits is distributed to that unit's employees as an incentive bonus, with caps up to 2.5 percent of monthly salary. An additional incentive system is based on a weighted combination of the unit's increase in deposits, increase in loans outstanding, decrease in arrears, profitability, and quality of administration. In this case the incentives, given to the staff of the unit, are partly cash awards and partly in the form of recognition within the bank. Units that meet their goals, as well as those that are the best in the branch, region, and nation are publicly recognized in various ceremonies. The national winners have been sent abroad to observe local banking systems in other Asian countries.

Unit Bank Performance

Over a twelve-year period (January 1, 1984 to December 31, 1995), BRI's unit banking system extended about $10 billion in 16.6 million KUPEDES loans. As of December 31, 1995, there was about $1.4 billion in KUPEDES credit outstanding to about 2.3 million borrowers; the average KUPEDES loan balance as of the same date was about $625.[26] The KUPEDES long-term loss ratio at the end of 1995 was 2.3 percent.[27] The low rate of arrears is attributable primarily to the fact that borrowers repay promptly because they want to retain the option to re-borrow; the prompt payment incentive is also important in this regard.

From the early 1970s until the financial deregulation of June 1983, the unit banking system had mobilized deposits of only about $17 million nationwide in over 3,600 unit banks. This was widely attributed within the government and the formal financial sector to the lack of local demand for financial services, absence of "bank-mindedness," and mistrust of banks that were assumed to characterize Indonesia's rural population. These assumptions were wrong. The unit banking system holds deposits of about $2.7 billion in about 14.5 million deposit accounts (as of December 31, 1995). The SIMPEDES and SIMASKOT instruments, which permit an unlimited number of withdrawals, are the most popular and account, together, for 77 percent of the total amount of unit bank deposits. Because the new instruments and services were designed with the extensive knowledge of local financial markets that had been acquired by BRI staff, the deposit instruments were immediately in demand and have been so continuously. Unit bank deposits, a highly stable source of funds, finance all KUPEDES loans. The average deposit balance in 1995 for all types of accounts was about $186.

In addition to the activities of its unit banking system, BRI supervises and in some cases provides loans to capitalize about 5,000 village-owned banks, known as Badan Kredit Desa (BKD). The BKD system, which is itself profitable and self-sufficient, was begun in 1897; as of December 31, 1995 it serves over 750,000 clients in Java and Madura. At the BKDs, as of the end of 1995, the average loan was about $80. Compulsory savings range from 8 to 10 percent of the loan. Most loans are short term, usually for ten to twelve weeks. Interest rates, set by the respective local governments, are typically at least double the unit bank rates.

Financial services are thus widely available through BRI and the BKDs to lower-income clients throughout Indonesia. A 1993 BRI study found that 24 percent of KUPEDES loans were below about \$242, and 38 percent were between about \$242 and \$484. At the same time, 86 percent of unit bank deposit accounts were below \$242, while 46 percent were below \$12. A 1988 KUPEDES impact survey found that of its 192 respondents, 92 percent had never before received a loan from a bank or a government agency. One-third of the respondents reported monthly household incomes of below \$78.[28]

Since late 1985 when BRI's unit banking system broke even, it has been profitable every year. As the unit banking system grew, its profits have been more stable than those of the rest of the bank and have grown substantially and increasingly as a percentage of BRI profits. In 1995, BRI was able to reduce KUPEDES interest rates for some loans.[29] The unit banking system that the bank wanted to discard in 1983 has now become its most profitable activity. In 1995, 95.7 percent of its 3,569 units were profitable; the others were largely new units.

BRI's unit banking system has become internationally recognized as the leading sustainable microfinance program in the developing world. Many central banks, financial institutions in developing countries, donor agencies and foundations, and nongovernmental organizations (NGOs) send representatives to visit BRI each year. Since 1995, HIID has worked with BRI to develop an instructional program for BRI's many international visitors. This has brought HIID advisors together with people interested in developing commercial microfinance from over thirty countries. Several HIID projects have been undertaken to help banks and other financial institutions in developing countries to learn and adapt the lessons of the new institutional commercial microfinance developed in Indonesia. Some of these projects grew out of discussions with BRI visitors. A number of publications have resulted from HIID's work with BRI, including a book in 1993 that was authored jointly with BRI's managing director responsible for the unit banking system and the (then) general manager of the village units division.[30]

Bank Dagang Bali

During the 1990s, HIID began to discover that many smaller private financial institutions found it difficult to learn directly from BRI. As a division of a large state-owned bank, the structure of BRI's unit banking system cannot be easily compared with that of small private institutions. Therefore, a study of the Bank Dagang Bali (BDB), a private bank in Indonesia, was carried out during 1994–1995.[31] This study was undertaken to document and make available the history of what may be the oldest licensed, full-service bank in the world providing extensive and continuous commercial microfinance services.

BDB was opened in 1970 by a husband and wife team who had long previous experience as microentrepreneurs and informal commercial lenders. As insiders to the microfinance market in Bali, they understood that there was large, unmet demand for commercial credit and savings services among lower-income people; they used this knowledge in creating BDB. Unlike government banks at that time, a private bank could provide microfinance profitably, since interest rates at private banks did not come under the same regulations as those of state banks. BDB opened in September 1970 with about $55,000 in capital, a small office, and a small staff that included three retired BRI staff members who were hired to help manage BDB. The bank grew steadily over the years, and as of December 31, 1995, BDB—still solely owned by its founders—serves over 350,000 clients, and has about $95 million in deposits and about $82 million in credit outstanding. At the end of 1995, BDB assets, excluding those held in the name of the owners, were about $115 million.

Since the early 1980s, HIID advisors have visited BDB on numerous occasions. With the permission of BDB, some of the principles and methods of sustainable microfinance developed there were adapted into BRI's unit banking system, as the latter developed during the 1980s.

At BDB, the annual effective interest rate on most small loans is about 30 percent, and repayment rates have been consistently high. Loans in arrears over three months were well below 1 percent at the end of 1995. BDB has been profitable every year since it opened, and is fully self-sufficient. During the 1990s, annual before-tax profits have ranged from about $1 million to about $1.7 million. BDB is extremely active on the savings side of its microfinance activities and provides many services, including the maintenance of daily routes to customers' homes or places of work where deposits are collected and withdrawals processed. Savers of all income groups, including the lower levels of the working poor, save regularly—often daily—in BDB. As of December 31, 1995, the average deposit account, including all types of accounts, was about $267.

Representatives of financial institutions from other countries have visited BDB increasingly, as international interest in the development of sustainable microfinance grows, as more institutions want to learn about the design and implementation of voluntary savings instruments for lower-income people, and as the role of private banks in commercial microfinance expands.

Adapting the Lessons from Indonesia

Indonesia's enabling macroeconomic and political environment has been crucial to the development of its institutional commercial microfinance. In addition, the development of sustainable microfinance on a large scale there is based on a number of achievements of the implementing institutions. These include: (1) knowledge of local markets; (2) convenient, secure bank locations at the local level; (3) provision of loans to all segments of the local population (rather than providing, for example, agricultural credit, credit for women, or credit for local industry); (4) provision of a set of deposit instruments designed to be appropriate for local demand; (5) a spread between loan and deposit interest rates that covers all costs and enables institutional profitability; (6) a system under which each bank unit operates as a profit center; (7) staff accountability for financial performance; (8) simple, uniform, and transparent reporting procedures; (9) careful and continuing attention to staff training and motivation; and (10) an effective institutional organization and management structure.

By the early 1990s, many financial institutions and governments in other developing countries, foundations and donor agencies, and NGOs had begun to learn that BRI's unit banking system, the BKDs, and BDB were contributing to the underpinnings of a new microfinance paradigm. It became evident that, given enabling macroeconomic, political, regulatory, and demographic conditions, commercial institutions could be developed to provide financial intermediation, delivering services at the local level profitably and without ongoing subsidy.

This view challenged the widespread assumptions that subsidies are required for local-level lending in developing countries, and that lower-income people do not save or will not save in banks. Both BDB and BRI have demonstrated that formal financial institutions can deliver services profitably at the local level in developing countries. In contrast, the many institutions worldwide that on-lend government or donor funds at subsidized interest rates, that combine social and financial services, and that do not mobilize voluntary savings effectively have not (and cannot) become self-sufficient. Some, such as the well-known Grameen Bank of Bangladesh, are highly effective at providing credit to poor people and recovering loans. However, institutions of this type are dependent on continuing donor or government injections of low-cost funds. Unless these institutions raise interest rates on loans to cover all costs, mobilize voluntary savings, and separate social and financial activities, they cannot become sustainable.

The demand for institutional microfinance can be met only by commercial financial institutions. There are not enough donor and government funds to meet a significant proportion of the worldwide demand for microfinance. The Grameen model is not globally affordable. The Indonesian model can be both adaptable and affordable for some institutions in many developing countries. It is likely that, when one or more institutions in a particular country have demonstrated that microfinance can be profitable, the formal banking sector will begin to enter the market. This has already occurred in Indonesia.

HIID continues to advise BRI, both on its unit banking system and on the development of its program for the many international visitors who visit the unit banks. The program is jointly sponsored by the United States Agency for International Development (USAID) and BRI.

Recent HIID activities relating to the spread of commercial microfinance in other developing countries include:

- advisory services to USAID and its mission in India to provide information about sustainable microfinance to the Government of India and private training and advice to the country's regional rural banks;
- advisory services to BancoSol in Bolivia, a private bank which opened in 1992, specializing in microfinance;

- advisory services to the Kenya Rural Enterprise Program (K-REP) to make the transition from an NGO providing credit to lower-income borrowers to a self-sufficient financial intermediary;
- exchange of information about commercial microfinance by HIID personnel with financial institutions and donor agencies in numerous other countries including Bangladesh, China, Mexico, the Philippines, South Africa, Tanzania, and Vietnam; and
- dissemination of the principles and experiences of the new microfinance paradigm through invited lectures, workshop participation, and course teaching for government departments, central banks, financial institutions, universities and donor agencies in the United States and Europe, and many parts of the developing world.

The Indonesian approach to microfinance is adaptable in different ways to many different conditions. There are, of course, special circumstances that provide both constraints and opportunities for the development of commercial microfinance in different countries. However, HIID's work in other institutions and other countries indicates that the broad principles of sustainable microfinance have been shown to work. BancoSol in Bolivia serves as a good example.

Countless NGOs provide microcredit to borrowers in the developing world. Usually, these institutions do not collect voluntary savings. In some cases, this is because the NGOs are not permitted to do so; in others, it is because NGOs have no incentive to mobilize savings since they are provided with continued injections of low-cost funds from governments or donors. Among financial institutions that want to become self-sufficient, there is a large demand for technical assistance in order to learn how to add voluntary savings to an already-existing loan portfolio.

BancoSol in Bolivia is the first bank in Latin America to provide financial services for microenterprises on a large scale. BancoSol was created out of PRODEM, an NGO that provides credit to microentrepreneurs. Although PRODEM successfully delivers and recovers microcredit provided at commercial interest rates, it is donor-funded and thus capital constrained. Studies of PRODEM's activities indicated that the credit program reached less than 2 percent of the estimated number of Bolivia's microenterprises. Yet, as an NGO, PRODEM is legally restricted from seeking funding from client savings, commercial debt, or central bank loan. To mobilize other sources of funds, expand the volume of lending, and provide full financial services to microentrepreneurs, PRODEM's board of directors decided to open a private commercial bank serving microenterprises. In 1991, members of the PRODEM board and its managers visited BRI. Since PRODEM already had an excellent small loan program, its main interest in visiting BRI was to learn about the mobilization of voluntary savings.

BancoSol was opened in 1992 with the NGO, PRODEM, as its major shareholder. Unlike PRODEM, BancoSol is permitted to mobilize voluntary deposits and to access commercial debt. In 1992, at the request of BancoSol, USAID, and the USAID-funded Gemini Project of Development Alternatives, Inc., an HIID advisor began to advise the bank on its development as a financial intermediary, with particular emphasis on deposit mobilization. Studies of demand for savings among lower-income households and enterprises were conducted, using techniques for staff training and field research adapted from those developed at BRI. BancoSol then began two pilot projects in savings mobilization, adapted in part from the BRI experience with pilot projects. The three main deposit instruments of the BRI units were modified to suit Bolivian conditions and were offered in the pilot projects where they achieved good results. Deposits in the two pilot branches increased from the $28,000 in compulsory savings the branches held at the time they began offering the new voluntary savings instruments (in August and November, 1993, respectively) to about $187,000 as of August 31, 1994, a one-year increase of over 550 percent.

In 1995, BancoSol began to expand its new savings instruments and services to its other branches. The bank has also been able to access commercial loans to finance its rapidly increasing loan portfolio. This is probably the first bank to gain access to capital from prime international investment firms based on the security of loans to microenterprises, such as shoemakers, food vendors, carpenters, and tailors.

In 1992, when the bank opened, it inherited from PRODEM a loan portfolio of $8.8 million. By 1995, BancoSol was lending about $80 million a year in small, short-term loans to low-income borrowers. The outstanding portfolio in 1996 was about $35 million, of which about one-fourth was funded from savings. BancoSol, now self-sufficient and operating without subsidy, serves nearly 70,000 clients—about 40 percent of all the clients in Bolivia's banking system.

The Reserve Bank of India (RBI) provides a contrasting example, that, along with BancoSol, illuminates the different types of lessons that can be drawn from the Indonesian experience. In 1995, India's central bank brought a high-level team to visit BRI primarily to learn about successful lending methods for rural areas. The visiting team was interested in reforming India's regional rural banks –which, in aggregate, have high savings, but also very high arrears in their subsidized loan programs and large losses. Therefore, RBI's interest was concentrated on learning from BRI about its KUPEDES loan program, as well as about the organization and operations of the bank. In 1996, India deregulated interest rates and began to restructure its regional rural banks to become commercial financial intermediaries that would serve low-income clients in the rural areas. HIID is currently advising the RBI and the National Bank for Agriculture and Rural Development (NABARD) on this process.

As HIID's work on commercial institutional microfinance expands, it is becoming clear that some aspects of microfinance programs can be replicated almost unchanged; some can be adapted; and some probably cannot be transferred. A good example of easy replicability is provided by the use of lotteries as a feature in the design of savings instruments. Lotteries were begun in Indonesia's BDB in 1971. The owners of BDB, who grew up in poverty, have an extensive understanding of the psychology of lower-income people. They know that poor people tend to gamble, since many see this as the only potential route out of poverty. BDB sought to satisfy this widespread interest in gambling, but to remove the risk for the participants while simultaneously encouraging them to save in BDB. Therefore, every BDB saver receives free of charge one lottery number per month for each $4.50 in the account's minimum monthly balance. The lottery is held four times a year, and is enormously popular. Earlier the highest annual prize was a motorcycle, then an automobile, and finally a house. Smaller prizes are also given at each lottery drawing. The underlying psychology was valid: the lotteries that began in BDB were adapted by BRI for their liquid accounts in 1984, and by BancoSol for their liquid and semi-liquid accounts in 1993. Transferred without basic changes, the lotteries enjoy huge popularity with customers in all three banks.

At the next level of adaptability, financial instruments, services, and staff training methods seem to be adaptable to different environments. At another level, there are aspects of institutional microfinance that do not appear to transfer well. Organizational structure, institutional management, and supervision are examples. However, it has been well established that sustainable microfinance can flourish in very different institutional settings.

Numerous lessons from microfinance in Indonesia, Bolivia, and elsewhere are presently being adapted in countries in Asia, Africa, and Latin America. The process is not one of replication, but one that combines adaptation, indigenous tradition, and innovation.

Sustainable Microfinance: Policy Implications

There are important policy implications of the new microfinance, and HIID is actively involved in analyzing and advising on these. Lessons for governments, donor agencies, banks, and NGOs can be briefly summarized:

Governments

For institutional commercial microfinance to be successful, the primary responsibilities of governments are to: (1) control inflation; (2) establish appropriate regulations that permit institutions to charge the interest rates and fees needed to cover all costs, to return profits, to open multiple outlets, and to select their own borrowers; (3) institute effective and appropriate supervision of institutions providing microfinance; and (4) educate the bureaucracy and the public about the importance of large-scale sustainable microfinance for the economy and for development. Some issues related to microfinance, such as the relatively high loan interest rates required for the profitable delivery of financial services locally, are politically sensitive. Government leaders who understand the potential social and economic benefits for the country that can derive from commercial microfinance should consider how such issues can be best addressed in their countries and guide the political processes accordingly.

Donors

Social services programs, such as health, nutrition, family planning, literacy, and training, are often combined—for both funding and implementation purposes—with credit and compulsory savings activities. This makes it impossible for the program to become self-sufficient. Both social and financial services are needed for development, but in the new microfinance approach these are funded and implemented separately and differently. Many donors now believe that the latter should be financed commercially. The former, where appropriate, should continue to be funded by donors through grants and concessional loans.

Donors can help the emergence of commercial microfinance in particular countries through the use of grants and subsidies to fund the start-up equity required by selected institutions that are qualified and committed to attaining full self-sufficiency. These are the institutions that will provide the example for the country's formal financial sector. Therefore, in addition to providing equity, grants and low-cost loans can be provided to such institutions for specific purposes, such as start-up costs, staff training, technical assistance, and the development of appropriate management information systems.

Banks

The banks that learn that institutional microfinance can be profitable, and that there is huge unmet demand in both rural and urban areas, are likely to have a strong comparative advantage in the coming decades. Also, banks that prove themselves profitable in the home microfinance market in the near future are likely to be sought after for joint ventures in other countries as well.

Non-Government Organizations Providing Microcredit

NGOs have made major contributions to the development of microfinance in various ways, especially by demonstrating clearly that lower-income people can be good borrowers. Some NGOs have also played an important role in the shift from subsidized credit to commercial microloans. However, NGOs are dependent on donor funding and, as NGOs, they are unlikely to play a large role in the long-term future of microfinance. Once the profitability of microfinance is more widely understood, the formal financial sector is likely to take the lead in meeting microfinance demand. NGOs whose boards and managers perceive the larger trends will be able to make the choices that are appropriate for their institutions in the coming decades. Some may become licensed financial institutions in the PRODEM-BancoSol model. Others may choose to turn to social services, such as health, family planning, education, the environment, and human rights.

HIID's Role in Sustainable Microfinance: Summary

HIID has worked in Indonesia with Bank Rakyat Indonesia, the largest and most successful bank in the world providing sustainable microfinance, and with Bank Dagang Bali, possibly the first licensed, full service bank to supply microfinance profitably. It has worked with BancoSol, the first bank providing large-scale sustainable microfinance in Latin America; and with the Kenya Rural Enterprise Programme (K-REP), an NGO that aims at becoming the first sustainable microfinance institution in Africa. In India, HIID has worked with the Reserve Bank of India and the National Bank for Agriculture and Rural Development (NABARD), to improve the country's regional rural banks. HIID is also currently engaged in policy discussions about sustainable microfinance with policy makers and banks in many developing countries in Asia, Latin America, and Africa.

In summary, HIID works with NGOs that want to create banks, with banks that want to enter the microfinance market, and with governments and donor agencies that want to learn about commercial microfinance. HIID is also advising BRI on its program for international visitors. In addition, HIID is analyzing and teaching—in universities, government ministries, financial institutions, and donor agencies—the principles and the results of the new microfinance paradigm.

The role of institutional commercial microfinance is best expressed by its clients. A customer of Indonesia's Bank Dagang Bali for over two decades said:

> I grew up poor and without education. I learned, though, that I could improve myself, and that the bank [Bank Dagang Bali] would help me. The president of Bank Dagang Bali is a great man. Why do I say that? Not because he is a bank president; there are many bank presidents. Because he knew that poor people fear banks, and he taught us not to be afraid. BDB taught us something important that we never knew before. BDB taught us that the bank is not a king, the bank is a servant.

HIID continues to work, as it has for more than fifteen years, to help to create, develop, and disseminate the idea that institutional commercial microfinance is crucial for social and economic development, and that it can be implemented widely by sustainable institutions throughout much of the developing world.

Notes

1 Based in part on conference papers by Marguerite S. Robinson; and by Richard H. Patten.

2 Lack of access to institutional finance by lower-income people in developed countries is also widespread, and also has major effects on both society and economy. However, discussion of microfinance in developed countries is outside the scope of this paper.

3 The research on which this paper is based was supported primarily by the Ministry of Finance, Government of Indonesia. Other support was provided by the Coordinating Minister for Economy, Finance, and Industry, Government of Indonesia; Bank Rakyat Indonesia; the Center for Policy and Implementation Studies (CPIS) in Jakarta; Bank Dagang Bali; PRODEM and BancoSol; the Kenya Rural Enterprise Programme; the World Bank; USAID; the USAID-funded Gemini Project of Development Alternatives, Inc.; the Calmeadow Foundation; and the Ford Foundation. The author acknowledges with gratitude both the financial support and the extensive assistance provided by the management and staff of all these institutions.

4 The term donor is used as in Rosenberg (1994, p. 1): "'Donor' is used here as shorthand for any group or individual who invests money in microfinance efforts, and whose investment is motivated primarily by concerns of poverty reduction and/or economic development, rather than maximizing the investor's financial return."

5 See Robinson (1995a; 1997b) for analysis of the paradigm shift in microfinance currently occurring in developing countries.

6 HIID work since 1979 in developing and analyzing the concepts and practices of microfinance builds on earlier work by many authors, especially Dale Adams, Claudio Gonzalez-Vega, Robert Vogel, and J. D. Von Pischke. It is also influenced by recent ideas and publications by those authors and others, including Robert Peck Christen, Michael Chu, Maria Otero, Elisabeth Rhyne, and Richard Rosenberg. See Robinson (1992, 1994a, 1997a, 1997b) for microfinance bibliographic references.

7 For the development of BRI's unit banking system, see Development Program Implementation Studies Report on Rice Intensification (1983); Robinson and Snodgrass (1987); Patten and Snodgrass (1987); Sugianto (1989, 1990a, 1990b); Robinson (1992, 1994a, 1994b, 1995a, 1995b, 1995c, 1995d, 1997a, 1997b); Bank Rakyat Indonesia (1990, 1994); Patten and Rosengard (1991); Snodgrass and Patten (1991); Patten (1995); Schmit (1991); Sugianto, Purnomo, and Robinson (1993); Martokoesoemo (1993); Gonzalez-Vega and Chaves (1992); Boomgard and Angell (1994); Hook (1995). For comparative studies including BRI's unit banking sys-

tem, see Yaron (1992a, 1992b); Otero and Rhyne, eds. (1994); Rhyne and Rotblatt (1994); Christen, Rhyne, and Vogel (1994); Brugger and Rajapatirana, eds. (1995).

8 Maria Otero, Chair of the International Microfinance Network, at their annual meetings, held in South Africa in 1994.

9 Other financial services may also be provided by local banking units, such as channeling customers' payments for taxes and for electricity and telephone bills, as well as channeling payments of salaries and pensions to bank clients.

10 See Christen, Rhyne, and Vogel (1994); Rosenberg (1994); Robinson (1997b). This point was also made by Jean Francois Rischard, Vice President of Finance and Public Sector Development, The World Bank, in his keynote address to a workshop on The Efficient Promotion of Small Enterprises, organized by the Fundacion para el desarrollo sostenible en America Latina (FUNDES) in Interlaken, Switzerland, September 18, 1993.

11 See, for example, Reserve Bank of India (1954); Nisbet (1967); Ladman (1971); Bottomley (1983, first published 1975); Mundle (1976); Tun Wai (1977, 1980); Kamble (1979,1982); Marla (1981); Adams and Graham (1981); Singh (1983, first published 1968); Roth (1983); Chandavarkar (1987); Hossain (1988); Robinson (1988); Bouman (1989); Varian (1989); Von Pischke (1991); Germidis, Kessler, and Meghir (1991); Chen (1991); Floro and Yatopoulos (1991); Aleem (1993); Bravermann and Guasch (1993); Siamwalla et al. (1993); Ghate et al. (1993). For a classic study, see Darling (1978, first published 1928). In Indonesia, based on the findings of CPIS field research from 1982 to 1990, people in many areas of Indonesia reported that the monthly rates they paid to informal commercial lenders ranged from about 3 percent to over 35 percent flat rate on the original balance, with monthly rates from about 6 percent to about 15 percent being most common. However, the lower-income borrowers commonly reported paying flat rates of over 15 percent per month, with many paying 25 to 40 percent per month, especially on short-term loans. Interest rates lower than this range are also reported, and the rates in some areas have decreased over time; see, for example, Tun Wai (1977, 1980); Chandavarkar (1987); Fernando (1988); Bouman (1989); and Von Pischke (1991).

12 This assumes a 1.5 percent per month flat interest rate on the original balance, the highest rate charged on the small loan program.

13 In their study of eleven of the best microfinance programs on three continents, Christen, Rhyne, and Vogel (1994) found that institutional commercial microfinance can occur in widely differing institutional structures and country environments.

14 It is possible that in the future the population density requirement may be overcome through developments in technology.

15 The term "unit bank" has a special meaning in Indonesia. BRI's sub-district-level banks were originally called "village units" (unit desa); when urban units (unit kota) were added in the late 1980s, the term "unit bank" came to be used for all BRI's local banks, both rural and urban. The unit banking system, as it is known, operates at the sub-district (kecamatan) level, serving the villages of each rural sub-district, as well as selected urban neighborhoods; the unit banks are under the supervision of the BRI branch, regional, and head offices.

16 Improved National BIMAS (an acronym for Bimbingan Massal, or Mass Guidance) was begun during the 1970–1971 wet season.

17 Indonesia achieved self-sufficiency in rice in 1985.

18 Tabungan Nasional (National Savings) is a government savings program available nationwide.

19 For discussion of the Development Policy Implementation Studies (DPIS) and its successor, the Center for Policy and Implementation Studies (CPIS), see Chapter 3 in this volume.

20 HIID's 1983 Report on Rice Intensification (DPIS, 1983) also called attention to the alarming decrease in the Indonesian rice gene pool, and recommended immediate further study. The recommendation was accepted by the Indonesian Ministry of Finance. The ensuing study, carried out first within CPIS and then by an HIID advisory project on rice seeds and pesticide use, led to identification of the use of resurgence-causing pesticides as a major cause of pest attacks in Indonesia and to the development of a national integrated pest management program. This aspect of HIID's work in Indonesia is discussed in Chapter 3 of this volume.

21 KUPEDES is an acronym for Kredit Umum Pedesaan, or general rural credit.

22 This phase of the work with BRI was carried out in part by HIID advisors based at the Center for Policy and Implementation Studies (CPIS) in Jakarta, a foundation funded by the Ministry of Finance; and in part by HIID advisors working at BRI under USAID and World Bank funding.

23 During the period under discussion here (1984–1995), inflation remained below about 10 percent.

24 In 1987 funding for the units was made available from the World Bank at BRI's own cost for interest bearing deposits. However, since 1989 unit bank savings have been higher than KUPEDES loans outstanding.

25 SIMPEDES is an acronym for Simpanan Pedesaan or rural savings; its urban equivalent is SIMASKOT, an acronym for Simpanan Kota or urban savings. Both permit an unlimited number of withdrawals.

26 BRI does not have data on the average loan size of its total KUPEDES portfolio, so the average loan balance of the credit outstanding on December 31, 1995 is given here instead. The average loan size for loans made in 1995 was about $900. Many borrowers are long-term clients who, having started with small loans, have expanded their enterprises and gradually increased the loan sizes for which they qualify.

27 BRI's unit banking system uses two measures of long term arrears. The long term loss ratio (2.3 percent as of December 31, 1995) is the ratio of the cumulative amount due but unpaid since the opening of the unit, to the total amount due. Portfolio status (3.5 percent as of the same date) is the ratio of the aggregate amount of overdue principal installments on loans that have not reached their final due date, to the total principal outstanding.

28 This study, consisting of two surveys, was conducted by BRI's Planning and Research Department, with Ann Dunham Sutoro as Principal Investigator (Bank Rakyal Indonesia, 1990); see also O'Rourke (1993).

29 In 1995 the KUPEDES interest rate for loans over about $1,335 million was reduced. Rates depend on the loan amount, with the lowest rate set at 1.2 percent flat rate per month. The Prompt Payment Incentive continues.

30 Sugianto, Purnomo, and Robinson (1993). HIID authors who have written on BRI's unit banking system include: (DPIS 1983), coordinated by Robinson; Robinson and Snodgrass (1987); Patten and Snodgrass (1987); Robinson (1988, 1992, 1994a, 1994b, 1995d, 1997a,1997b); Patten and Rosengard (1991); Snodgrass and Patten (1991); Patten (1995); Hook (1995).

31 Robinson (1997a).

Part IV

Environment and Social Sector Programs

HIID's largest group of projects in the 1990s involved efforts to help design environmentally sensitive policies and laws that were consistent with concurrent economic reform programs, particularly in the transition economies of Central and Eastern Europe and the Former Soviet Union. HIID programs in the social sectors, health and education, began in the late 1970s and have involved research and action projects in Asia, Africa, and Latin America. Issues related to gender were a particular focus of much of the social sector work.

13 The International Environment Program

Theodore Panayotou and Jeffrey R. Vincent

Background

Natural resource management, environmental economics, and environmental policy increasingly have become focal areas of HIID's international development work. The role of natural resources in economics can be traced to classical economists, who considered land and natural resources indispensable for production and were concerned with resource rent at the micro level and with increasing resource scarcity at the macro level. Even in neoclassical economics where natural resources appear to fade into the background with the two-factor (labor and capital) aggregate production functions, natural resources remain an important form of capital, albeit an easily substitutable one. In development economics, "vent for surplus" and competing theories explain the role of natural resources in economic development as a source of investable surplus for industrialization.

More recently, beginning with Hotelling's 1931 seminal article on optimal resource depletion, natural resource and environmental economics has emerged as a distinct subdiscipline of economics. At the micro level, the key issue is the exploitation and management of limited renewable and non-renewable resources to maximize the owners' or society's welfare. At the macro level, the normative issue is how to achieve sustainability and growth in the face of depletable resources; the positive issue is the macroeconomic and growth implications of heavy dependence on natural resources. An abundance of natural resources has been a mixed blessing: many resource-dependent economies have found it difficult to remain internationally competitive in other sectors (for example, the "Dutch disease") and have experienced slower aggregate growth rates.[1]

On the normative side, the reinvestment of optimally extracted resource rents has been prescribed for sustainability and higher rates of savings and investment for sustainable growth.[2] At the global level, technical progress and high rates of substitutability have been found to mitigate the scarcity of non-renewable resources;[3] in contrast, open-access renewable resources (such as fisheries and forests) have suffered from excessive rates of depletion.

As concern for growing resource scarcity began to recede, new issues on the environmental impact of economic activity emerged. The use of the environment as a sink for the waste byproducts of production and consumption has reduced its amenity value and resulted in health and productivity losses. While these losses are external to the generator of the waste, they are internal to society and reduce social welfare. This has led to new research aimed at assessing the damages through non-market valuation methods, estimating abatement costs, determining the optimal rate of pollution abatement, and selecting cost-effective instruments of environmental policy to achieve these aims. At the macro level, concerns have been increasingly raised about the environmental consequences of structural adjustment programs in developing countries, market reforms (such as restructuring and privatization) in transition economies, and the globalization of the world economy. Here, the security of property rights, the enforcement of contracts, the rule of law, and the use of cost-effective instruments for the internalization of environmental costs largely determine the direction and magnitude of the environmental impact of economic reforms.

Yet another inquiry concerns the long-term relationship between economic growth and environmental degradation. For natural resources and for most (but by no means all) pollutants, an inverted ∪-shaped relationship (a Kuznets curve) has been observed between environmental degradation and income per capita. This is due to the depletion of resources and the degradation of the environment during the take-off process of development, followed by structural change (less heavy industry and direct cleanup activities), as willingness-to-pay for environmental amenities rises with income growth.[4] However, this relationship may not be observed in the absence of policies that remove distortions and correct for market failures.[5]

Finally, with the increase in the scale of global economic activity, concerns are being raised about the impact of human activity on the so-called global commons, the global climate, and biological diversity. The growing atmospheric concentrations of carbon dioxide (CO_2) and other gases resulting from fossil fuel consumption and land-use change could lead to climate change (notably global warming) and a rise in the sea level by the middle of the twenty-first century, and could significantly damage certain regions of the world, including many developing countries. Many of the contemplated global policy responses (such as the restriction of fossil fuel consumption to stabilize concentrations) would have a more immediate detrimental effect on the growth of developing countries. No-regret policies and internationally tradable CO_2 emission permits are contemplated as potential cost-effective interventions that would allow economic growth to continue while slowing down greenhouse gas emissions.[6]

Purpose and Scope of the Program

Against this backdrop of issues and of a rapidly changing body of knowledge, HIID's International Environment Program (IEP) has sought to contribute to the environment-development debate and to assist developing and transition economies in dealing with environmental concerns while tackling the development challenge. For these economies, the concern for the environment is a concern for the sustainability of the development process at sufficiently high rates of economic growth to alleviate poverty and to achieve economic convergence with the more developed world. With few trained ecologists and environmental economists, developing and transition economies are ill-prepared to assume the environmental challenge in addition to the already difficult economic development challenge—especially when the two challenges appear to be in direct conflict.

The IEP was created to help developing and transition economies reconcile and meet these challenges synergistically and holistically, by identifying and assessing tradeoffs and complementarities, setting priorities, and selecting cost-effective policy interventions. The IEP has launched a major capacity-building effort in environmental economics and policy analysis for developing and transition economies, to expand their local capability for environmental management.

The IEP has employed the following instruments:

- technical and policy assistance to developing and transition economies, through the placement of resident advisors, the recruitment of short-term consultants, and the creation of local policy analysis working groups (think tanks);

- collaborative research involving HIID, other Harvard faculty, and researchers from institutions in developing and transition economies, on issues of immediate or long-term concern to these economies;
- the development of pilot or demonstration projects that can be generalized, transferred, and replicated beyond the project site;
- the development of long-term research sites and research capability in tropical forest management, with collaborating research institutions in developing and developed countries;
- course instruction in tropical forest management, natural resource economics, environmental policy, and sustainable development at various Harvard schools and departments, to disseminate lessons from applied field research and policy formulation to undergraduate and graduate students and to integrate these lessons with Harvard's curricula in ecology, development, and environment;
- short-term training through annual summer workshops in environmental economics and policy analysis, to train practitioners (mainly from developing and transition economies) and to retrofit the skills of policy analysts with the concepts and methods of environmental and resource economics; and
- policy seminars in developing and transition economies, to sensitize policy makers to emerging issues and to enlarge their knowledge of the menu of available policy options through case discussion and analysis.

IEP's work covers a broad range of issues, including common property resources, the determinants of deforestation, tropical forest management, water pricing economics, valuation of natural resources and environmental impacts, pollution control through market-based instruments (for example, the design of tradable pollution permits and environmental tax reforms), environmental financing, resource-based industrialization, structural adjustment and the environment, and environmental accounting. Activities include policy research, implementation, and training projects, most of which have been done in the field and in collaboration with local institutions, working groups, and individuals.

For the purpose of this chapter, HIID's environmental work can be divided into two periods: work before the mid-1980s, and work after the mid-1980s. During the first period, the work focused mainly on natural resource management, especially forest and mining policy and, to a lesser extent, on land, water, and energy. The second period has built on the earlier work, broadening the scope to include all natural resources, environmental policy, and global issues.

The major projects of the post-1985 period include:

- Natural Resource Management in Thailand,
- Tropical Forest Management,
- Environmental Economics and Policy Analysis in Central and Eastern Europe,
- Environmental Economics and Policy Analysis in the Newly Independent States of the former Soviet Union,
- Economic Analysis of International Forestry Issues,
- Asia Environmental Policy Analysis and Training,
- Structural Adjustment and the Environment,
- Middle East Water Technical Assistance,
- Natural Resources, Environment, and Development in Malaysia, and
- Capacity Building in Environmental Economics and Policy Analysis.

The balance of this chapter reviews the institute's environmental work before the mid-1980s and that of each of the above projects since 1985, some of which are still in progress. The discussion covers the activities, successes and limitations, and the lessons learned that will influence the institute's future work on the environment.

Environmental Work Before the Mid-1980s

The bulk of HIID's work on the environment began after the mid-1980s, but there were important precursors as part of its development efforts on resource-based sectors such as agriculture, mining, and forestry. Most early research and policy advising on resource management was done in Indonesia, under the long-standing project on Customs and Economic Management (CEM) and related projects. (HIID's work in Indonesia is discussed fully in Chapter 3.)

Most notable is the work on integrated pest management (IPM), which was motivated by growing pest damage to agriculture (especially rice) despite the use of increasing quantities of pesticides. Like many developing countries in the 1970s, Indonesia's heavy reliance on the use of chemical pesticides proved to be self-destructive. Excessive use of agrochemicals killed natural predators and caused herbivorous insects to multiply in unprecedented numbers. Devastating outbreaks of destructive insects—particularly the brown planthopper—occurred with increasing frequency. By the mid-1980s, Indonesia realized that heavy chemical use created more problems than solutions. HIID worked with Indonesian and Food and Agricultural Organization (FAO) experts to analyze the problem and to identify effective policy responses. The subsidization of pesticides was reduced and eventually phased out, over fifty types of broad-spectrum pesticides were banned, and the national Indonesian IPM program was launched. The program promoted the balanced use of chemicals through national pest management strategies, based largely on biological control rather than chemical control. As part of the program, HIID helped to develop educational programs for farmers. Thousands of field schools were established to train farmers to analyze conditions in the rice fields. Within a decade, pesticide use was reduced by 70 percent from 1986 levels, while rice production was increased by 15 percent. Partly as a result of the program's success in Indonesia, IPM is now internationally accepted and promoted as an essential ingredient of sustainable agricultural development.

The taxation of natural resource extraction was another area of HIID's early work in natural resource management. In Indonesia, as part of the CEM project, HIID analyzed and provided advice on forest tax reforms for reducing high-grading and deforestation while increasing rent capture and government revenues from logging. In a related study, HIID analyzed the Indonesian trade policy toward timber and rattan, as well as the economic and environmental implications of the export ban on logs and raw rattan and related incentives for domestic processing, and proposed optimal export taxes as superior alternatives.

During 1981–1982 HIID worked with an Ecuadorian state-owned oil company to design fair and efficient production sharing agreements with multinational investors for oil and gas exploitation. This involved the use of computer-simulated models, comparative international studies of the terms and conditions of international oil and gas contracts, and market studies of oil and gas. The results of these activities—the structuring of contractual arrangements, an oil production tax system, and revenue-sharing arrangements—have had impacts beyond Ecuador in influencing the taxation of the mining sector.

Environmental Work After 1985

Natural Resource Management in Thailand

In 1985, HIID began a major research and development advisory project with the Thailand Development Research Institute (TDRI), funded by the United States Agency for International Development (USAID). HIID assisted TDRI in its early formative years to develop a research program in which natural resources and the environment was a main thrust. At that time, Thailand was undergoing a rapid rate of deforestation and soil erosion while urban centers, especially Bangkok, were suffering from growing rates of traffic congestion and air and water pollution. In terms of the growth-environment relationship, Thailand was ascending the rising part of its environmental Kuznets curve as it was taking off economically.

The collaboration between TDRI's natural resources and environment program and HIID's environmental economics team succeeded in putting together a strong research program that attracted funding from a variety of sources. More important, the program anticipated many of the country's environmental crises of the late 1980s—for example, deforestation-related floods and landslides, a series of hazardous chemical accidents, water shortages—which changed the political landscape of environmental policy-making in Thailand. The output of this five-year collaborative research project has had a significant policy impact on fisheries management and land reform policy, among others. The fact that natural resource management was a component of a larger project (which included macroeconomics, industry and trade, science and technology, agriculture, and the social sectors) enabled provision of consistent and integrated advisory services in research design and institutional development and also mutually compatible policy recommendations.

In recognition of the successful TDRI-HIID collaboration on natural resources management, HIID was awarded a new three-year cooperative agreement to work with TDRI on a major policy research project, as part of a larger assistance program to Thailand on the Management of Natural Resources and Environment (MANRES). Under this project, carried out from 1989 to 1995, HIID and TDRI formed a close partnership, studying the following issues: the role of property rights and security of ownership in land use and forest policy; economic incentives for water use and conservation; energy policy, air pollution, and global climate change; the impact of Thailand's industrial and investment policy on the environment and possible remedial policy reforms; environmental management of mining; and urban environmental infrastructure and hazardous waste management. The products included collaborative policy research monographs and pilot project designs for possible implementation.

The first phase of the project (1989–1991) culminated with eleven co-authored monographs presented at a national conference on Industrializing Thailand and the Impact on its Environment. For Thailand, this was the first major policy research conference on environmental issues, with stakeholder-wide participation at the decision-making level. The policy studies and the conference marked a new era in Thai environmental policy as the country was recovering from major environmental disasters and was seeking more lasting solutions to unchecked resource depletion and environmental degradation.

The TDRI-HIID studies sought to identify the root causes of environmental degradation and to formulate systemic solutions. Undefined or insecure property rights, pervasive externalities, underpricing, and environmentally harmful subsidies were found to cause many of Thailand's environmental problems. The studies recommended: (1) the removal of environmentally harmful subsidies (for example, investment incentives for hazardous waste-generating industries); (2) the issuance of secure land titles to farmers; (3) full-cost water pricing and transferable water rights; (4) the expansion of conservation forest from 15 to 25 percent of the country's area, and the engagement of local communities in its protection and management; and (5) for industry, the establishment of a system of presumptive waste charges combined with waste-delivery bonds and central treatment for hazardous waste.

The study results were widely publicized in the Thai press, and meetings were held with policy makers to disseminate findings and develop proposals for implementation. Some of the proposed policy changes and new initiatives have been adopted by policy makers, albeit in a modified form. The protected forest area was expanded to 25 percent, the issuance of land titles was accelerated, and a differential tax between leaded and unleaded gasoline was introduced. The concept of an environmental fund was adopted, but without the elements of presumptive charges and waste-delivery bonds that would have made it efficient and consistent with the polluter-pays principle.

During the project's second phase (1993–1995) three studies were also undertaken: (1) the economic valuation of Khao Yai National Park, (2) watershed management in the Mae Taeng River Basin, and (3) water pricing in Phuket Island. Under the first study, a joint TDRI-HIID team conducted a large-scale survey to determine the willingness-to-pay of visitors to the Khao Yai National Park, using travel cost and contingent valuation methods to guide the pricing of park entrance and to identify the desired level of service. Visitors to the park were found to be willing to pay sufficiently high entrance fees to finance both the current and an even higher price for improved levels of service, and to contribute to a fund for the protection of the park.[7] The second study examined the downstream impacts of watershed protection programs in the Mae Taeng River Basin in northern Thailand. Contrary to common thought, these programs (which included reforestation) were found to generate downstream costs in the form of reduced agricultural output and higher water supply costs because of reduced water yields. As an alternative, the study recommended incentives to promote more efficient water use in the basin.[8] The third study surveyed water users in Phuket Island, to establish the degree of their satisfaction with the existing level of service and to ascertain their willingness-to-pay for an improved level of service. The study concluded that water users are willing to pay substantially more than they currently do for the public supply of water, provided the water is clean and the service is reliable. Thus better service and higher prices would provide escape from the low equilibrium trap in which both the water utility and the water users find themselves with the existing subsidized low-quality, low-coverage service. The results of the three studies were presented at a high-level seminar and debated among policy makers, policy analysts, and activists from nongovernmental organizations (NGOs).

The project also had its share of disappointments. Most notable among these was the inability of the second phase to build on the success of the first phase in hazardous waste management. A successful partnership failed to emerge between HIID's subcontracted consultant and the Thai counterparts. As a result, the outcome had less policy relevance than that of other studies. Evaluation of these results revealed the risk of subcontracting arrangements in areas requiring rigorous policy research, especially with non-academic institutions—a risk also evidenced in other (non-environmental) projects. The evaluation of the overall project also indicated the importance of close collaboration with local counterparts, and the timely exploitation of political windows of opportunity to influence policy change.

The first phase of the project had a much greater impact on policy reform than the second phase, because of the presence of the HIID resident advisor. The main impacts of the second phase appear to have been capacity building and the preparation of the ground for later policy reforms. The question of whether these reforms actually might have occurred with a resident advisor to push them through will never be answered.

Tropical Forest Management

Despite the efforts undertaken over the past decade to protect and better manage tropical forests, for the early 1990s the World Bank estimated that, worldwide, these ecosystems are disappearing at the rate of 13 million hectares per year.[9] Such trends in deforestation, coupled with a generalized forest degradation, are alarming because of the implications such modifications have on the welfare of local populations and the global community. At the local level, tropical forests provide goods such as timber and various animal and plant products. On hilly landscapes, forests provide on-site and off-site protection against soil erosion and damage to watercourses and downstream ecosystems. For the global community, tropical forests provide benefits by regulating global climate and by hosting an extremely rich biological (and often cultural) diversity.

Still, there are many open questions about the management of these complex ecosystems. Not only has the concept of tropical forest management largely focused on timber production (thus ignoring other forest products and services) but also management prescriptions, even when conceived for timber production, generally neglect industrial responses to ever-changing markets. Market acceptance of smaller diameter logs and species, once considered non-marketable, requires a re-analysis of current management systems. There is a need for management systems that are sustainable and economically feasible and that take into account the whole array of services and values of tropical forests.

Since 1990 a team of researchers—from Harvard, the Center for Tropical Forests Science of the Smithsonian Tropical Research Institute, and collaborating institutes in developing countries—has been implementing a long-term, multidisciplinary research project on the management and valuation of tropical forests. Under this project, longer-term forest dynamics plots have been established (or are planned) in Cameroon, Ecuador, India, Malaysia, Panama, the Philippines, Puerto Rico, Singapore, Sri Lanka, Thailand, and Zaire. Drawing on this unique biological database, the project addresses the issue of sustainable management of tropical forests by developing appropriate site-level simulation models. With expertise from both the social and natural sciences, the multidisciplinary project is modeling the interaction of natural and economic systems.

The project has three goals. First, it seeks to assess the total economic value of representative forest samples by taking into account marketable products and non-marketed products, non-use values, and environmental services. Second, it aims to identify the biological and socioeconomic determinants that influence this forest economic value. Third, the project seeks to provide guidelines and design schemes for economically viable and sustainable management of tropical forests.

The simulation models developed by HIID describe the interdependencies between relevant forest stand components, predict the impact (in biological and economic terms) of various degrees of human intervention, compute the net present value of current and future forest uses, and evaluate the tradeoffs and opportunity cost of promoting alternative forest uses and/or various levels of conservation.[10] Through economic valuation studies HIID is assessing the relative value of various forest products and services included in the models. The studies consider both products with market value and products and services that are ignored by conventional markets.

Field experiments are the ultimate tools for assessing the impact of alternative management schemes on tropical forests' dynamics and economic potentials. However, experiments are extremely costly in terms of time and effort. Expediency in finding solutions is necessary, and data collection should be targeted to that information which exhibits the highest benefit-cost ratio. HIID's modeling efforts have provided information on which critical data are currently lacking and deserve attention. The research sites and forest facilities established by the collaborating institutions, under the leadership of the Smithsonian Institute and the partnership with Harvard, are being used for research by an increasing number of agencies, including the Center for International Forestry Research, the Global Terrestrial Observing System of the United Nations Environment Program (UNEP), and a consortium of Japanese universities.

The project's major challenge has been the maintenance of the long-term interest of donor agencies in work that has a long gestation period and is primary data–intensive. The biological modeling work, which began several years earlier, has yielded substantial output that is being used as input to the socioeconomic modeling. This work benefited from an abundance of biological and ecological data generated by the research sites, but it was constrained by the paucity of socioeconomic information. Collection of primary socioeconomic data and valuation information are underway, but at a slower pace than ideal for the purpose of the optimization models.

HIID, however, has conducted significant primary research to better understand the effects of markets and trade on indigenous people's use of the rain forest in countries such as Bolivia, Honduras, and Sri Lanka. A team of researchers comprised of natural and social scientists (working in Bolivia and Honduras and supported by the National Science Foundation) has tested hypotheses about the likely effects of trade on foraging specialization, the value of the forest measured by non-timber forest products extracted, and the area of forest cleared. They have combined methods from social anthropology (for example, time allocation) and from household economics. The research focused partly on the household and community determinants of land clearance and the adoption of improved agricultural technologies. Research is directed at the role of human capital in the decision to deforest and adopt new farm technologies. Preliminary results suggest that education lowers pressure on the forest, though perhaps not in the short run.

A major lesson from this effort has been that the collection of primary data from indigenous people and forest dwellers is necessary for understanding local behaviors which, under one set of circumstances, lead to deforestation and, under another set, lead to careful management and conservation. Such data collection requires the patience and long-term commitment of both researchers and funders.

Environmental Economics and Policy in Central and Eastern Europe

The failure of the centrally planned economies of Central and Eastern Europe and the former Soviet Union to generate sustainable economic prosperity was paralleled by an equally devastating failure to protect their people and natural assets from serious environmental damage. This was experienced in the form of health and productivity losses of an unprecedented magnitude. Since the early 1990s, the countries of this region have faced the challenge of (simultaneously) generating environmental recovery and economic recovery despite a severe scarcity of financial resources. There is a need to remove environmental liability constraints to privatization and foreign investment, to maximize the environmental synergies with economic reforms, and to introduce cost-effective environmental policies.

To this end, HIID—with the support of USAID and in close consultation with the region's governments—has carried out the Central and Eastern Europe Environmental Economics and Policy project. The project sought to introduce environmental economics as a basic policy development tool for use by these transition economies at a crucial stage in their histories. The project took advantage of a unique period of strong interest by governments and their citizens in large-scale public policy reform and of high receptiveness to economic instruments for environmental protection.

Specifically, the project:

- identified and analyzed critical environmental policy issues in Central and Eastern Europe and proposed policy responses that would enhance environmental quality while contributing to economic growth and privatization;
- translated the proposed policy responses into concrete programs through the design of property-rights arrangements, institutional structures and mechanisms, financial and fiscal policy instruments, and pilot projects for implementation;
- enhanced access to foreign capital for environmental investments by governments and enterprises through policy reforms that fostered the development of local capital markets and enterprise-level project preparation activities; and

- trained a critical mass of economists, political scientists, and policy analysts in environmental economics, environmental policy reform, and natural resource management, through formal training, policy seminars, and collaborative research.

The project was carried out in Albania, the Baltic States, Bulgaria, the Czech Republic, Hungary, Poland, Romania, and Slovakia. For most of these countries, long-term HIID advisors specializing in environmental economics and policy or in environmental finance served for two to four years; short-term expatriate consultants supplemented this expertise. In addition, for each country the advisors established a local think tank, called the Policy Analysis Working Group (PAWG), where local environmental and economics professionals could contribute to the project's analytical work and overall direction.

Most advisors operated from within government ministries, which afforded them daily contact with host-country policy makers. The advisors collaborated with their host-country counterparts to set the agenda for project work, which was usually undertaken in close cooperation with the PAWG and local staff and with expatriate consultants. In each country, the project's collaborative mode was crucial to the advisors' acceptance into the policy development process. In the countries where the project did not place an advisor, project activities were carried out by short-term consultants and/or by subcontractors. These individuals generally focused on specific projects, as opposed to the multiple policy interventions of the advisor-based program.

Overall, the advisors were successful in promoting economic approaches to environmental policy. Given the legacy of environmental damage and extreme under-investment in pollution control, together with strong public demand for rapid growth, the advisors emphasized the development of environmental policies that would contribute to economic growth and privatization.

Successful policy interventions by HIID advisors included:

- use of the contingent valuation methodology for the pricing of public services, such as water supply and solid waste management;
- creation of pilot projects to demonstrate the utility of tradable-permit systems in reducing the overall costs of pollution control;
- use of cost-benefit measures for assessing proposed policies and the use of economic principles and empirical analysis for evaluating policy effectiveness;

- use of environmental audits to address information problems relating to past environmental damage that had restrained the progress of privatization;
- reform of the system of pollution charges to restructure incentives and thus internalize the cost of environmental damage and reduce abatement costs to a minimal level; and
- development of environmental funds to enhance the availability of capital for environmental investments as a stopgap measure until capital markets are better developed.

The project faced many challenges, such as rapid (and occasionally radical) shifts in political directions as the transition economies became parliamentary democracies. Long lead times were needed to gain the trust of host country counterparts before meaningful advisory work could begin, which led to many advisors being involved in the policy development and legislative drafting phases, but not in the crucial activities of implementation. Also, the lack of facility in the local language may have slowed progress in a few areas.

The project yielded valuable lessons in the application of environmental economics to economies in transition. It demonstrated that environmental policy can contribute to economic growth and privatization, even in the context of rapid economic growth and a difficult political situation. The project also demonstrated the possibility of using market-based instruments, such as effluent charges, product charges, and tradable permits, even in the context of economies and governments that were recently non-market and non-democratic.

The project also generated lessons in the management of large, multicountry policy advising projects and the potential synergy that such projects could generate. The use of long-term advisors was central to the project's success, and the relationships formed by the advisors with the government counterparts could not have been replicated by other organizational forms. The project also showed that, even within an outwardly similar group of countries, there is large variance in host-country government and enterprise acceptance of specific policy approaches and desired policy endpoints.

Another lesson is that the successful transition to local expertise and long-term sustainability is not an achievement that can be planned for during a project's phase-out period, but must be anticipated, planned, and structured from project inception. The establishment of the local PAWG in each country proved to be a wise decision and an invaluable asset for the quality of advice provided and for the smooth transition to long-term sustainability. The institutionalization or integration of these local groups into existing institutions is the next major challenge of the project.

Environmental Economics and Policy in the Newly Independent States

The Newly Independent States of the former Soviet Union face the formidable task of reversing the severe environmental degradation created by decades of unsound economic policies and ineffective environmental regulations. As these states move toward market-based economies and democratic forms of government, they need to take environmental considerations into account to avoid undermining the processes of political and economic reform. At the same time, severe budgetary and institutional constraints call for policies to minimize the costs of achieving environmental objectives.

The Newly Independent States Environmental Economics and Policy project, modeled on the project on Environmental Economics and Policy in Central and Eastern Europe, was initiated in late 1993. HIID advisors have worked with government decision makers in Russia and the Central Asian Republics (primarily Kazakhstan) to identify and promote cost-effective environmental and economic policies that foster sustainable development, democratization, and the transition to a market-based economy. The project has four goals: to improve the prioritization of environmental problems; to identify and evaluate strategies for cost-effective pollution abatement and efficient natural resource allocation; to promote public participation in the decision-making process; and to build local capacity to conduct environmental and economic policy analysis.

With limited resources available to address pervasive and severe environmental problems, these countries need to prioritize the problems and risks as a prerequisite for sound environmental and economic decision-making. The project has helped to improve prioritization by conducting assessments of pollution health risks in several Russian cities and by identifying strategies for cost-effectively reducing those risks, by jump-starting the process of developing a national environmental action plan for Kazakhstan, and by working with regional administrations in the Russian Far East to set priorities for forest sector development.

The project team has worked with national and regional governments to identify, analyze, and implement policies and strategies for cost-effectively reducing pollution and improving the allocation and pricing of natural resources. Achievements include the development of a pilot program for permit-trading air emissions in the city of Almaty (the first functioning program outside the United States), and cost assessments of the damages to human health caused by air pollution in Almaty, Tashkent, and several Russian cities.

Public participation in environmental decision-making is crucial to ensuring that policy decisions benefit the public and secure community support. Through its efforts to establish local water users' associations in Kazakhstan, the project created a national forum in which farmers and other water users could contribute to national decisions on water allocation, irrigation management, and agricultural privatization.

Through extensive collaborative research and analysis with local colleagues as well as formal training workshops, the project has helped to strengthen the skills of a core of local economists and environmental specialists in Moscow, the Russian Far East, Kazakhstan, and Uzbekistan.

As in the Central and Eastern European project, long-term resident environmental policy advisors have built strong relationships with senior policy makers at the national, regional, and local levels. These relationships have been critical to the project's success. From their bases in Moscow, Almaty, and the Russian Far East, the advisors have strengthened local institutions and built professional capacity through joint policy research with local colleagues, seminars and workshops, and the establishment of expert working groups. Efforts at the local and regional levels have been designed to improve policies and approaches at those levels, and simultaneously to provide models and lessons for national policy and to contribute to environmental and economic reforms nationwide.

Not surprisingly, the challenges encountered and lessons learned in the project parallel those of the Central and Eastern European project, given the similar experiences of the two regions under central planning. The project in the Newly Independent States has had a greater impact on policy reform in Kazakhstan than in Russia, a consequence of unusually strong language skills and the catalytic capabilities of the advisory team in Almaty, the political difficulty of influencing policy reform in a country as big and as politically and administratively "fragmented" as Russia, and the greater autonomy afforded the advisory team in Almaty by the donor organization. In both countries, the continuation of the project hinged on the support of the local USAID missions, which faced ongoing cost-cutting pressures from Washington D.C. (At that time Russia was the focus of certain anti-foreign-assistance elements in the U.S. Congress.) This highlighted the practical need not only to have a positive impact on environmental policy reform and capacity-building efforts, but also to communicate this need effectively to USAID in a way that did not jeopardize the relationship between the HIID advisory teams and their host-country counterparts—for example, by avoiding the impression that HIID or USAID, and not government officials, deserved the credit for reforms.

Economic Analysis of International Forestry Issues

The traditional role of the U.S. Environmental Protection Agency (EPA) has been to deal with domestic "brown" (pollution-related) issues within the United States. In the late 1980s, the EPA became involved in the formulation of the U.S. Government's responses to international forestry issues—particularly issues related to global climate change. These issues included deforestation as a source of CO_2 emissions and forestry projects as a means of sequestering carbon. EPA was instrumental in the development of the "Forests for the Future Initiative," announced by then U.S. President Bush at the Earth Summit in Rio de Janeiro in June 1992.

Given its limited experience with international forestry policy issues, EPA requested, in mid-1992, analytical support from HIID on the evaluation of the issues and potential policy responses. Under a cooperative agreement with EPA, HIID carried out economic analysis of international forestry issues, focusing on the causes of deforestation (especially macroeconomic policies), on innovative mechanisms for stemming deforestation and degradation, and on one performance of existing multilateral forestry programs. Three activities have been carried out under the project: (1) an appraisal of the effectiveness of bilateral and multilateral forestry assistance programs, (2) a review of methods for analyzing the impacts of intersectoral and macroeconomic policies upon forest degradation in tropical countries, and (3) an economic evaluation of carbon-offset projects.

The institute's activities on forestry assistance programs involved the preparation of a review paper that synthesized information in existing documents and suggested ways of making forestry assistance more effective. Donor assistance in the forestry sector has expanded in magnitude and scope over the last twenty years. The focus of projects has shifted from commercial timber production to the protection and provision of a broader range of forest values, as well as to the use of projects to leverage forestry policy reforms. The donor and host-country organizations involved have become more diverse—for example, there has been greater NGO involvement. Efforts to coordinate the increased donor activity have attempted to use available funds more efficiently—for example, the Tropical Forestry Action Plan. Despite the increased effort, the results of the forestry assistance programs are generally disappointing. The review paper compared success rates across programs and identified the institutional and programmatic reasons for the differences.

The second set of activities pertained to the analytical work on the general policy environment in which the assistance programs have occurred. Most studies of forest degradation in developing countries have examined immediate causal factors, such as agricultural encroachment, fuelwood collection, and commercial logging. Over the last few years, several economists have undertaken studies of impacts of policies in other sectors (for example, agricultural subsidies) and of broader macroeconomic policies (for example, exchange rates and international debt). These intersectoral and macroeconomic policies have indirect but significant impacts on the use of forest resources. HIID's work involved reviewing existing studies to distill lessons for appropriate policy reforms and to develop an analytical framework for guiding future empirical work in this area.

The third set of project activities had the narrowest focus and involved the most basic research. The work is directly related to EPA's core interest in global climate change issues. Although numerous general guides to project appraisal exist, none contain case studies on carbon-offset projects. These are projects in which a carbon emitter in one country invests in carbon sequestration activities in another. A number of appraisal issues related to these projects have remained unresolved, such as the selection of the discount rate, the treatment of co-benefits, and the composition of additionality. HIID surveyed existing carbon-offset projects and used this information (supplemented by site visits and interviews) to develop a manual that provided an analytical framework for evaluating carbon-offset projects. The manual aimed to assist EPA, other agencies (such as the U.S.

Department of Energy), potential investors (usually northern power utilities), and host-country counterparts with the evaluation of prospective offset projects.

In one sense, the study of carbon-offset projects was ideal: it involved research in a new policy area, with an output of mainly analytical models and inputs of policy simulations to both policy formulation and peer-reviewed journals. In another sense, it proved to be difficult: the research focus was a constantly changing and evolving field. New carbon-offset projects and new research studies are being announced frequently, while the uncertainty persists as to whether any carbon-offsets across borders would receive any credit under the Global Climate Convention. Closer cooperation and interaction with the sponsoring agency would have benefited the project, especially the carbon-offset component.

Asia Environmental Policy and Training

As much of Asia accelerated its industrialization and economic growth during the 1980s and 1990s, resource depletion and environmental degradation also began to accelerate, reflecting the region's ascent on a steep-sloping environmental Kuznets curve. A combination of policy failures, market failures, and population pressures, already at the root of many of Asia's creeping environmental problems during the 1970s, were magnified in countries attaining double-digit or nearly double-digit rates of economic growth. Even the much slower growing economies of South Asia experienced a rapid growth in deforestation, soil erosion, water shortages, urban congestion, and pollution because of poverty and high rates of urbanization. Asia found itself ill-prepared to deal with many of these issues, because past human capital investments were mainly directed at attaining high economic growth rates and little attention was paid to environmental protection. Environmental economics, the main discipline dealing with development-environment tradeoffs, was new to developing Asia, and there was practically no local expertise in this area.

Responding to the urgent need for increased analytical capacity in environmental economics in the Asia region, in the early 1990s HIID, under a cooperative agreement with USAID, began providing training, research, and advisory services. The institute developed a new training workshop for policy analysts (held annually since 1993), organized policy seminars for policy makers, and carried out policy studies on issues of both pedagogic and policy value, such as economic valuation of environmental impacts, formulation and assessment of market-based instruments, and resolution of resource conflicts.

The annual policy seminar, a three-day program for some twenty to thirty senior decision makers from the public, private, and NGO sectors, aimed to raise consciousness about the economic costs of environmental degradation, the environmental impacts of economic policies, and the economic implications of environmental policies. Above all, these seminars aimed to enlarge the set of available options considered by decision makers, and to promote a dialogue and eventually partnerships between the private sector, the public sector, and the civil society. As of late 1995, three policy seminars have been held, bringing together some eighty senior policy makers, business leaders, and NGO activists to interact in an informal setting and to begin a dialogue on developing innovative solutions for integrating environmental protection and economic growth. Eleven case studies prepared for the seminars were developed and discussed at length. They covered a variety of issues, including water pricing, pesticide subsidies, industrial pollution charges, carbon-offset projects, and greening the budget and the national accounts.

As judged by the demand for technical assistance and training by participating institutions, the project succeeded in creating effective demand for environmental economics expertise. HIID met part of this demand through the development of an annual environmental economics and policy analysis workshop, first under the sponsorship of the Asia project and then as an independent, self-financed workshop for all regions. This workshop is discussed in more detail later in this chapter.

Another component of the Asia project has been the preparation of major policy studies on industrial pollution control in India, the Philippines, and Thailand; on coal mining in Indonesia; on the use of market-based instruments in Asia; and on sustainability in small open economies. The study findings were made available to USAID and other development agencies, to Asian policy makers, and to the community of environmental economists and advisors through discussion papers, case studies, and policy briefs.

The Asia project has demonstrated the synergies of policy research, policy seminars (for decision makers), and training workshops (for policy analysts) in creating demand for analytical capability as an input to policy formulation and in expanding the supply of analytical capacity. Unlike training, which can become self-financing, policy seminars aimed at raising awareness and creating demand are not always self-financed; their return is yielded later in terms of willingness to send staff for training, to use their expertise upon their return, and generally to employ environmental economics and policy analysis in policy formulation and assessment.

Structural Adjustment and the Environment

Structural adjustment programs generate fundamental changes in the economies of developing countries, by changing relative prices, increasing the role of exports, and reducing the role of government, among others. Adjustment programs deepen the linkages between national economies and the world market. Such fundamental changes have profound impacts on a country's environmental and resource base, but such impacts vary widely across countries. Even the direction of these effects cannot be determined with simple or partial analysis. For example, while adjustment can increase the efficiency of consumption of depletable resources, increased efficiency may lead to increased depletion if increasing scarcity does not induce substitution and conservation.

To better understand and quantify these impacts, HIID, with the support of the World Wildlife Fund (WWF) International, worked collaboratively with local research institutes in five countries: El Salvador, Jamaica, Pakistan, Venezuela, and Vietnam. The project had three objectives: (1) to document the impact of adjustment programs on the major environmental problems of these countries, (2) to analyze the impact of macroeconomic reforms on the long-term sustainability of the countries and to propose policy alternatives to promote sustainable development, and (3) to strengthen the analytical capacity of local research institutes to continue research and maintain a policy dialogue with policy makers.

The common environmental concerns analyzed were deforestation, soil erosion and land degradation, industrial and urban pollution, environmental degradation from extractive industries, and loss of biodiversity. The main structural adjustment or economic reform policies studied were trade liberalization, tax reform, the curtailing of public expenditures to reduce public sector deficits, and price reforms, including adjustments of exchange rate and interest rates to better reflect market conditions.

The project studies found little evidence that the governments of the countries studied (or the donor agencies that assisted them) had genuinely considered environmental impacts in formulating economic reforms or development policies, or had properly considered the role of natural resources and environmental services in economic growth. Yet the impacts on the environment were mixed: increased efficiency reduced pollution and resource depletion per unit of output, while the expansionary effect of trade liberalization tended to increase total levels of resource depletion and pollution. Factors influencing the environmental outcomes included institutions (for example, security of property rights) and environmental policies (the presence of effective incentives to internalize environmental externalities). Structural adjustment programs, which generally constrain government spending in the short run, often led to cutbacks that fell disproportionately on environmental programs. In the long run, adjustment programs appeared to be essential for mobilizing additional fiscal resources for public environmental investment and for raising individual demand and willingness to pay for environmental amenities; yet such programs contained no provisions for ensuring that additional resources would be channeled into environmental investments of high social benefit.

The studies reached a number of policy recommendations for improving the design and implementation of structural adjustment programs:

- Environmental policies should accompany improved economic policies for the potential benefits of the latter to be maximized and sustained.
- The link between environmental planning and macroeconomic policy should be integrated into public policy and in the selection of development options.
- There should be a clear shift of concern from the physical aspects of the environment to the socioeconomic dimensions of environmental problems (health and productivity losses).
- Where negative impacts have been identified, appropriate environmental adjustment policies should be built into the economic reform package.
- Structural adjustment programs can best ensure sustainability by promoting the reinvestment of rents from the depletion of natu-

ral resources in natural, human, and man-made capital to maintain and expand the productive capacity of the economy.

A general conclusion of the studies was that conditionality and compliance schedules, though capable of generating some environmental sensitivity among economic policy makers, are weak substitutes for the integration of environmental policy into economic reforms and development policies.

The project faced serious limitations because of the restrictive three-sided contractual arrangement among WWF International, HIID, and the local institutions. While HIID was made responsible for the quality and timeliness of the studies, it was directed to keep its input just below that of a fully collaborative partner. This limited the mutually beneficial exchanges and capacity building accomplished by the project. Furthermore, the type and quality of research output varied significantly among countries, as did the influence of the project on policy makers. Another lesson is that despite the advances in electronic communications, brief visits cannot replace a residency when capacity building is an essential objective, even in research projects. The dominant role of the sponsoring organization in the selection of countries and the direction of research in some cases may have limited the extent to which some of the project's results can be generalized.

Natural Resources, the Environment, and Development in Malaysia

The project on natural resources, the environment, and development in Malaysia was initiated in 1992, as part of a larger HIID study on Malaysian economic development. It was conducted in cooperation with the Malaysian Institute of Strategic and International Studies (ISIS) and funded by the Malaysian private sector. The study highlighted differences between the Malaysian example of rapid economic development and the better known East Asian cases—differences which may make the Malaysian case a more relevant example for other developing countries. The natural resource and environment component of the study focused on the contribution of natural resources to sustainable economic development and the impacts of development on environmental quality.

This work represented the first comprehensive economic study on resource and environmental issues in Malaysia. Malaysia offers a nearly ideal situation for research on the relationships among natural resources, environment, and development, as it has rich endowments of natural resources, rapid industrialization experience, and regions that have pursued different economic and environmental policies. The study provided a retrospective economic analysis of policies during the 1970s and 1980s, and this analysis, in turn, provided lessons for future policy-making. The study sought to answer to two broad questions. The first was, "How has the utilization of natural resources contributed to economic development?" Research on this question addressed both macro-level issues—in particular, ones related to sustainability—and issues in specific resource sectors, including minerals, forestry, fisheries, and freshwater. The second question was, "How has economic development affected the quality of the environment?" As with the first question, both macro-level and sectoral issues were addressed.

Although the study was not part of a policy advising project, it succeeded in conveying an economic perspective on natural resource and environmental policies to relevant government agencies through regular meetings and occasional workshops and seminars, including a 1993 conference at ISIS's Centre for Environmental Studies. It contributed significantly to capacity building in environmental economics in Malaysia, with more than a dozen local researchers involved in the work. The study results were published in 1997 in a collaborative volume by HIID and ISIS researchers.[11] The unequivocal success of this project in terms of both effective collaboration and capacity building contrasts with the unduly constrained collaboration under the WWF-International-sponsored Structural Adjustment and Environment project.

The Harvard Middle East Water Project

HIID's International Environment Program assisted collaborating research teams in the Middle East in collecting and analyzing data on water supply and demand; the work was done under the sponsorship of the Institute for Social and Economic Policy in the Middle East (ISEPME) of Harvard's John F. Kennedy School of Government. This activity provided input for ISEPME's collaborative development and use of an economics-based approach for analyzing the issues of water ownership rights and water use in the Middle East. The goals of the Harvard Middle East Water project are to facilitate the negotiations on water issues, and to promote regional cooperation in water usage, infrastructure development, and management. The Harvard

Water Allocation System (WAS), and the preliminary findings on the model's application to the study of water issues in several areas of the Middle East, have attracted the interest of the region's policy makers, planners, and negotiators.

Capacity Building in Environmental Economics and Policy Analysis

Mounting environmental problems in Asia, ranging from deforestation and soil erosion to urban congestion and industrial pollution, coupled with a growing environmental awareness, have created a demand for policy reform and for the introduction of environmentally sound policies and projects. Yet the supply of trained environmental economists, policy analysts, and resource managers has been slow to respond, partly because of an information lag and partly because of the long gestation of skill development to meet the new needs of environmental policy and sustainability. Unlike the prevailing view in the 1970s and early 1980s that environmental protection was a luxury few developing countries could afford, the new ethic of sustainable development required reconciliation and synergy of environmental protection and economic growth. Environmental economics possesses the tools for valuing the benefits from environmental protection and improvement compared with the opportunity costs. Policy analysis holds the promise of low, zero, or negative costs of environmental protection provided that distortionary policies are replaced by corrective ones.

In response to the increasing need for analytical capacity in environmental economics and policy analysis, HIID, through its International Environment Program, offers courses, workshops, seminars, research apprenticeships, and assistance in curricula design and institutional development. Foremost among these efforts to expand capacity in developing countries has been the summer workshop in Environmental Economics and Policy Analysis, offered annually since 1993. The workshop's goal is to retrofit the skills of economists and other scientists with a background in economics and an interest in environmental matters. It aims to convey quantitative skills necessary for analyzing, from an economic perspective, the environmental aspects of policies, projects, and business decisions. The workshop emphasizes the integration of economic and environmental considerations—opportunities to protect the environment without restricting economic growth—and innovative approaches (incentive systems) for environmental management in both the public and the private sectors.

While the workshop activities include case studies, group discussions, hands-on computer exercises, and individual projects, HIID realizes that few graduates have had opportunities to implement in practice what they had learned in training and that an apprenticeship program is needed to allow them to learn by doing and by interacting with more experienced researchers and policy analysts. Unfortunately, with the exception of the Canadian Economy-Environment Program for Southeast Asia (EEPSEA), which provides research grants for aspiring environmental researchers, there is a paucity of opportunities for on-the-job training. Of the 200-plus graduates of HIID's environmental economics workshops, only about one-half are actually engaged in the direct application of techniques learned in the workshop. Thus, the challenge for HIID's future capacity-building work is to develop opportunities, in collaboration with donor agencies and other institutions, for participants to use and further enhance the skills acquired during their formal training.

Equally important are policy seminars to establish effective demand for environmental economics input to policy analysis, as it has been practiced for the past three years in Asia. Similar efforts are needed in other regions. A worldwide network of policy makers and environmental economics professionals is beginning to emerge from the capacity-building efforts of HIID and other institutions.

Conclusions

The International Environment Program (IEP) is an evolving program in a rapidly evolving field. The program's ten years of active involvement in designing and managing international advisory projects in capacity building and in policy research has generated important lessons for its future development. Applying environmental economics in combination with development economics is a rich source of knowledge and insights for a development institute operating within a research university. In retrospect, the most productive engagements were those driven by the confluence of intellectual interest in the subject and an opportunity to help build local analytical capacity. Less successful were projects that were carried out with limited freedom to innovate and to interact with local counterparts, as the Structural Adjustment and the Environment project demonstrates.

In other cases, such as the Central and Eastern European project, research opportunities afforded by advisory projects were not fully utilized because of time constraints imposed by day-to-day management and urgent, short-term policy advising. Now that the IEP is well-established, it is possible to be more selective and to help set the agenda of donor agencies rather than be driven by short-term priorities. The ideal project would be one with a substantial research component, field residency, and close interaction with local counterparts, with direct lines of communication with policy makers—and with the necessary independence and flexibility to be entrepreneurial and innovative.

Despite some obvious limitations, the IEP has succeeded over the past ten years, and especially the last five years, in influencing environmental policy (in some cases economic policy) in a large number of developing and transition economies. As a result of HIID's environment work, the process of privatization in Central and Eastern Europe and in the Newly Independent States faces fewer constraints; environmental policies are more incentive-based than command-based; and Asia has a network of policy makers and analysts that interact regularly on environmental policy matters. As HIID intensifies its involvement in environmental issues in Latin America and Africa in the coming years, both the experience gained in Asia and Europe and the network of workshop alumni should prove to be valuable assets. Drawing on lessons learned over the past decade, HIID's International Environment Program is in an ideal, if not unique, position to help tackle the environment-development challenges of the new century through research, technical assistance, and capacity building.

Notes

1 Sachs and Warner (1995).

2 Hartwick (1977).

3 Slade (1982).

4 Grossman and Krueger (1995).

5 Panayotou (1996).

6 Nordhaus (1993).

7 The study is discussed fully in Kaosa-ard, Desharo, and Panayotou (1995).

8 Vincent et al. (1995b).

9 World Bank (1992).

10 Microeconomics theory suggests that the optimal production mix results from the interplay of two tradeoffs: the production tradeoff, determined by feasibly combining products and services that can be offered by a forest; and the consumption tradeoff, determined by the relative values of these products. The problem of selecting the best attainable combination of products and services is solved at the point where the biological and technical rate at which the forest can trade off production of one output for the other equals the rate at which consumers are willing to make such trades. The development of a "bioeconomic" model involves the derivation of the tradeoff curves between different products and services (the "production possibility frontier") and the identification of the slopes of the isovalue curves. Optimization analysis and economic valuation techniques are being used for this purpose. Through optimization analysis involving the development of predictive models that simulate forest dynamics and the forest's capability to provide various products, HIID has empirically derived tradeoff curves that describe the set of feasible combinations of products that can be produced by the forest. For more detailed information, see Boscolo et al. (1996).

11 Vincent and Rozali et al. (1997).

14 The Health Program

Charles N. Myers and Jonathon L. Simon [1]

Introduction

The links between health and economic development are multifold and multidirectional. Macroeconomic theory postulates that improvements in health status contribute to development through the improvement in the quantity and quality of labor. Healthy populations are reported to use the factors of production more efficiently. Economic growth also contributes to rising government and household incomes if the growth is spread somewhat equitably across the various sectors of the society. These additional resources generated by growth can be invested in improvements in education, nutrition, or the environment, which in turn will improve health status.[2]

The links between health and development are most clear in the area of epidemic infectious diseases. Epidemics—particularly acquired immune deficiency syndrome (AIDS), resurgent malaria, or cholera—are threats to the economies of some developing countries. The AIDS pandemic has shown that countries' development plans can be dramatically affected by the impact of the disease on labor markets—particularly the urban, highly educated sectors of the labor market—and by the extraordinary health care costs associated with the disease. Epidemic diseases not only reduce domestic labor availability and productivity, but also can have negative impacts on trade and tourism, which are major sources of foreign exchange in many countries.

Economic development (growth) policy, however, can also have detrimental impacts on health. Choices in terms of which agricultural industries or industrial products are encouraged can dramatically affect the health of populations. Support for commercial flood field rice production in western Kenya led to increased rates of malaria and eventually constrained the availability of local labor.[3] The well-documented negative health impacts of increased tobacco production led United Nations agencies and the World Bank to suspend development assistance for further support of this agro-industry.[4] The mining industry of South Africa and its associated induced labor migration of unaccompanied men is associated with the rapid spread of the human immunodeficiency virus (HIV) and sexually transmitted diseases (STDs) throughout the countries of southern Africa.[5] Recent scholarship continues to debate the health impacts of economic stabilization and structural adjustment programs.[6] Though immediate impacts in terms of increased morbidity and mortality may not be measurable, the effect of reduced "flows" of social expenditures on health and reductions in income for vulnerable sections of the population may be reducing the health "stocks."[7] The impact of the stabilization programs may be temporarily hidden, like the latency period of an infectious disease.

One of the great strengths of HIID is the bringing together under one institutional roof the various disciplines that can contribute to research, advising, and teaching on development. HIID's Health Office has worked on a broad range of issues since its inception in 1978. These include: capacity strengthening; health system reform, especially the development of health management information systems; economics of health (including the costs of illness) and health care finance; and other high priority public health problems such as AIDS and micronutrient malnutrition. The work has included both policy research and implementation projects. The vast majority of the work has been done in the field.

This chapter descriptively reviews the activities undertaken between 1978 and 1995, comments on the successes and limitations, and offers conclusions on the lessons learned that will guide HIID's efforts for the coming years.

Capacity Strengthening

All of the HIID Health Office project activities sought to strengthen the skills and capabilities of the national counterparts with whom HIID personnel worked. Training and capacity strengthening are essential elements of development work, and attention to these components is the expression of HIID's commitment to development in addition to its analytic work. The largest project in the history of the HIID Health Office, Applied Diarrheal Disease Research (ADDR), focused largely on strengthening scientific capacity in a number of countries. This effort, continued as the recently awarded Applied Research on Child Health (ARCH) project, is an attempt to conduct high-quality child health research while strengthening national health research capacity and contributing to rational, data-based health policy reform. With these three interlinked goals, the ADDR project explicitly reflects the purpose of the Health Office projects: to collaborate with international colleagues in high-quality research and the development of appropriate solutions to important international public health issues. This section describes the ADDR project and other projects which focused more narrowly on training and capacity strengthening.

The Applied Diarrheal Disease Research Project

The ADDR project was initiated in September 1985 through a cooperative agreement between HIID and the United States Agency for International Development (USAID). The New England Medical Center and the Johns Hopkins University School of Hygiene and Public Health were collaborating institutions. In 1991 the project was refunded for a second, five-year cycle of support that ended in May 1996.

The ADDR project had three interlinked goals: (1) to support an applied research program that would produce and disseminate high-quality, data-based information through systematic research on high priority child health questions; (2) to improve the use of research findings in the formulation of health policies and programs; and (3) to strengthen national capacity in both the social and the biomedical sciences to identify key research questions, conduct, analyze, and use applied health research.

The fundamental premise of the ADDR project was that scientists from less developed countries (LDCs) could be trained to conduct better research by involving them in a structured experiential learning process, in close consultation with their national policy and program personnel, and with technical collaboration with external scientists. A corollary belief was that the local scientists would be better able to disseminate the research findings to the policy makers and program personnel responsible for implementation and therefore to improve the linkage between research and policy. The explicit linkage of science with development distinguishes the ADDR project from most other international research programs.

Though initially focused solely on diarrheal diseases, at the time the largest killer of children less than five years of age, the ADDR project soon expanded the scientific mandate to include pneumonia, micronutrient deficiencies, and a special focus on the first cholera epidemic in the Western Hemisphere in almost one hundred years. Research activities were supported in sixteen countries, with large scientific portfolios in Nigeria, Pakistan, and Peru.

The ADDR project developed an innovative research training methodology. The process, which was modified by experience over time, consisted of five phases: (1) participation in a proposal development workshop, (2) an iterative proposal review and revision process, (3) the provision of technical assistance to funded studies, (4) participation in a data analysis workshop, and (5) provision of technical assistance to foster dissemination by assisting with the development of scientific manuscripts, policy reports, and support for special meetings.

By the end of the initial ten years of the project, over 150 research studies had been funded. An additional fifty small grants had been awarded for workshops, conferences, and dissemination activities. Over 350 local scientists participated in the program as investigators. Their skills as researchers improved as demonstrated by their heightened ability to compete successfully for other research funds. Their utility to national programs also appears to have improved as measured by the scientists' increasing involvement in government health committees and as technical experts in national debates on health policies. By mid-1996, over 220 scientific papers had been published in the international and national journals. Many more papers continued to be reviewed and revised. Most important, the research results had led to health policy and program improvements in most of the countries where the ADDR project was active.

The ADDR project supported research intended to change health practices and policies at all levels of the health system. Some research was supported that addressed global policy questions; other studies were meant to improve policies and practices at the local facility level. At the global level, ADDR-supported research, in collaboration with the World Health Organization (WHO), funded a multicenter trial for a revised nutritional therapy for persistent diarrhea. The results of this work form the technical basis for the global recommendations from WHO and the United Nations International Children's Emergency Fund (UNICEF) for appropriate diarrhea case management. Similarly, ongoing work on reducing the sodium content (and osmolarity) of oral rehydration salts (ORS) has the potential to alter global efforts at controlling diarrheal disease by changing the composition of the 900 million ORS packets purchased by UNICEF yearly. On a national level, ADDR-funded research provided information for the Government of Pakistan to select its first-line antibiotic for management of pneumonia given its unique antimicrobial resistance pattern. Research in Mexico led to the President of the country initiating a national program to combat malnutrition based on the weaning foods tested by local scientists in the ADDR project network. Examples of research having impact on provincial, district, and local levels abound. The project strongly encouraged the research teams to take the results of the studies back to the communities from which the data were generated in order to identify how the information could be used by the people who contributed to the generation of the scientific knowledge.

The Pakistan Child Survival Project

The training component of the Pakistan Child Survival project was part of the larger child survival program that included the development of the health management information system (discussed in detail later in this chapter). For both activities, HIID worked as a subcontractor to Management Sciences for Health. The objectives of the childhood illness case management training were fourfold: (1) to develop the training curriculum, (2) to establish training units for an integrated child survival training program, (3) to assist the Ministry of Health in strengthening the supervisory system, and (4) to assist the ministry in establishing a continuing education program.

The decision to develop an integrated child survival training program was a bold one. Vertical disease control programs were the standard approach. At the time of the initial discussions within the Ministry of Health, WHO and UNICEF were promoting separate training in case management of the main childhood health problems: diarrheal diseases, acute respiratory infections, immunizable childhood diseases, and malnutrition. Their main argument was that disease-specific approaches are necessary to maintain acceptable training quality. These separate training activities were not only costly in terms of staff time but, most important, they alienated the care providers from the concept of integrated and comprehensive child health care delivery. A long and tedious consensus-building process launched by the HIID project team resulted finally in a national agreement on the training strategy. A training curriculum was designed and pre-tested, and twenty-six integrated Child Survival Training Units (CSTUs) were established. Over the life time of the project (1990–1993), about 1,500 health professionals were trained in the integrated case management approach, including 100 supervisors. The establishment of continuing education cells was well underway in the four provinces. Both WHO and UNICEF eventually supported the program and the Pakistan Child Survival project experience was one of the country case studies that convinced them to promote the integrated child survival training strategy worldwide. By the mid-1990s, four or five years after the innovative training program was tried in Pakistan, the integrated management of the sick child approach had become the global policy recommendation of WHO, UNICEF, and USAID.

The Djibouti Health Management Training Project

The Djibouti project, conducted from1987 to 1988, aimed to strengthen the health care system through focused training to improve managerial capacity of key personnel within the Ministry of Health. Seven management training courses were developed, covering such topics as health planning, budgeting, financial management, inventory control, personnel management and supervision, organizational development, computer training, and applied research methods and utilization. Two senior health managers were sent to the United States for study on new training methods. The Djibouti project, though focused solely on the provision of short-term training, assisted the health systems development process by improving the technical skill base of the senior professionals within the Ministry of Health responsible for much of the primary health care system programs.

The Togo Health Sector Support for Child Survival Project

The Togo project, conducted in 1991, sought to assist the Ministry of Health in improving its planning and budgeting capabilities at regional and district levels. This skill building was seen as essential for the development of the decentralization process as part of the health reforms. Thirty-four regional and district program managers participated in a series of workshops on health planning and management.

A training manual customized to the issues facing the Togolese managers of the public health system was developed along with Togo-specific case materials. The workshops' topics included: needs assessment, priority setting, definition of objectives, choosing strategies, resource-allocation issues, budget development, and the skills needed for monitoring and evaluating programs. Each participant had to develop a district health plan. At the completion of the workshops, health plans had been prepared and budgeted for all twenty-seven prefectures in the country.

The Zaire School of Public Health Project

The Zaire project, from 1986 to 1991, helped to create the first school of public health in the history of Zaire. For this activity, HIID worked as a subcontractor to the Tulane University School of Public Health. The effort included curriculum development in primary health care, teaching, and the initiation of an applied research program on the AIDS epidemic. Students and faculty collected and analyzed primary data on the epidemic, interviewed AIDS patients and members of high-risk groups, and developed policy options. The applied research program was an integral part of the teaching curriculum and also generated useful information for health policy officials. Great effort was made to introduce and sustain the use of computers in both the teaching and the research activities. In addition to the activities in Kinshasa, twelve Zairian faculty members were supported for doctoral studies in the United States. All twelve subsequently returned to assume positions as instructors and researchers within Zaire's School of Public Health.

Health System Reform

Health system reform has become the catchall term for a series of activities that seek to improve the functioning and financing of national health systems. In the early 1980s, based on the acceptance of the 1978 Alma Ata Declaration of Health for All by the Year 2000 (the basis for the primary health care movement), the reforms were largely to institute and improve primary health care at peripheral levels of health systems. Community participation and the use of paramedical workers to expand access to health care were seen as key health system reforms.

The reform process changed course, accelerating in the 1990s because of three interrelated dynamics in many health systems throughout the world. First, the financial crises faced by many LDC governments throughout the late 1980s and early 1990s, and the concomitant introduction of structural adjustment programs, mandated a reduction in social sector expenditures. This led to a reduction in government services, a stagnation in maintaining or improving the quality and breadth of services, and increasing interest in new financing mechanisms to pay for health care delivery. Second, the end of the Cold War, the demise of the Soviet Union, and the retrenchment of socialist political systems worldwide fostered a greater openness to market economy principles. This dynamic created conditions for the simultaneous reduction in governments' efforts and increases in the role of the private sector in the production and delivery of health care in the developing world. Third, the international donor community, particularly with the ascendancy of the World Bank as the major actor in health sector development assistance, drove governments toward embracing health system reform and particularly toward accepting the privatization of health services. Failure to do so would force governments to face the risk of reductions in foreign development assistance. USAID also shifted its emphasis to greater support for and reliance on private sector provision of health services. The types of reforms initiated included the reorganization of primary health care systems with management training to improve efficiency of services delivered, and technical training of health workers at the primary health care level to improve the quality of the services. The reforms highlighted experiments in new financing systems and the use of markets to contain health care costs while improving health outcomes. The development of health management information systems that could be used to improve health planning was another key element of the reform process and became one of the focus areas of HIID's Health Office.

The Health Office has been involved in health system reform through projects in eleven countries (Bolivia, Burkina Faso, Cameroon, Chad, Djibouti, Mali, Pakistan, the Philippines, Senegal, Thailand, and Togo) between 1978 and 1995. Most of these projects were supported in whole or in part by USAID development assistance funds. United Nations agencies also contributed to some activities. The main goal of these projects was to provide policy and management support for national, regional (provincial), or district health services. The health care financing components of projects in Bolivia, Burkina Faso, Cameroon, the Philippines, and Thailand are covered later in this chapter; here acknowledgment is made of their essential role in the reform efforts of some of the countries with which HIID worked. Similarly, the capacity strengthening through management and service delivery training efforts in Djibouti, Pakistan, and Togo has been discussed above. The following section, therefore, focuses on reform and health information system development efforts in Mali, Chad, Pakistan, Costa Rica, Senegal, and Cameroon.

The Mali Rural Health Project (Projet de Santé Rural)

The Mali project was initiated in 1978 with two objectives. The first was to design, implement, and evaluate a demonstration rural health system which would: provide health services (including health promotion and disease prevention services) to the village level; integrate with other community and economic development activities (especially efforts in the agriculture and education sectors); and provide the services described above for within an annual operational cost of less than US$2 per capita. The second objective was to serve as a demonstration project that would encourage Mali to develop an improved rural health system, and to assist the Ministry of Public Health in preparing to implement this new system nationwide.

The Mali rural health system was designed to use Community Health Workers (CHWs) as the primary provider of basic curative, health promotive, and preventive services. The CHWs (a total of 240 workers) were supposed to be selected by the villages, trained by the project, and supported by small fees paid by the villagers for services provided. The demonstration project was implemented in three counties (arrondissements) in three different non-adjacent regions. The project was meant to provide services to 60,000 people living in 120 villages. In addition to providing services, CHWs were responsible for the management of a revolving drug fund. They were provided a seed stock of pharmaceuticals and basic supplies considered necessary for the functioning of CHWs. The project assumed that the sale of the drugs would generate US$1 per capita, with proceeds used to support the replenishment of the fund and additional supplies for the CHWs.

By project end in 1982, only 70 of the 120 villages had selected CHWs, covering potentially less than 60 percent of the target population. Community acceptance and support were extremely limited; in no village did the CHW receive remuneration. In the villages that selected CHWs, attrition was a major problem with 7 to 33 percent of the trained CHWs abandoning their efforts within the four-year project period due to out-migration and lack of community support.

The revolving drug funds also suffered from lack of support. Revenue was estimated at US$0.06 per capita.[8] Recurrent costs to manage the funds were greater than anticipated largely because of higher than projected re-supply and supervision costs. The basic package of drugs emphasized child health problems, while health service utilization patterns were more likely to require health services and commodities for adults.

The Ministry of Health showed limited support for this donor-designed project. National counterparts never materialized. The lack of community support and financial sustainability precluded the project from being replicated as a model for nationwide adoption. The problems and pitfalls of attempting to implement cost recovery programs in state-funded primary health care programs in resource poor countries are described in *Primary Health Care in Africa: A Study of the Mali Rural Health Project.*[9]

The Chad Health Planning Restoration Project

The Chad Health Planning Restoration project was a subactivity of the Chad Relief and Rehabilitation project, which began in 1985 with funding from USAID and the United Nations Development Programme (UNDP). The goal of the project was to assist the Ministry of Health to restore the health planning function through the recreation of a health planning unit. Health service delivery and health planning had largely ceased to exist during the twenty years of civil war. The main activities of the project became the formation of a health management information system (HMIS) and the development of policy to provide the legal basis for the family planning program.

The development of the HMIS began with an initial study that documented how the health system had been seriously damaged by the war. Health centers were barely functioning, and there was little formalized collection, dissemination, or use of health information. The priority was thus to design and implement an HMIS which would provide the Ministry of Health the tools necessary to plan health services and to institutionalize that system by training national health professionals to carry out the work.

The system designed was management-oriented and facility-based, with routine data collection and reporting from both public and private health facilities. The data collected in three types of reports were to be analyzed with the aid of microcomputers by the Ministry of Health's Bureau of Statistics, Planning and Studies (BSPE). To implement the system, the project organized seminars for health professionals throughout the country and provided training in computerized data entry and analysis for the staff of BSPE.

By project end in 1988, most health facilities in Chad were reporting, and BSPE was providing feedback reports and analyses to all levels of the system. The utility of the information system was shown in a meningitis epidemic in 1988, during which BSPE became the center for data management and for successful management of the epidemic. The system has also produced a statistical year book on health in the country each year since 1988.

The Chad experience showed the feasibility of transforming a weak, centrally-focused, disease-oriented reporting system into a management information system addressing needs at differing levels of the health system. Several countries in the region became interested in replicating the effort.[10]

The other major component of the Chad project was to develop the policy environment to allow the delivery of family planning services and training efforts, and to organize the provision of contraceptive commodities. The project's population advisor helped to form a viable coalition of family planning advocates from across the various sectors of the government. This coalition advocated the repeal of the Pharmacy Law, which legally forbade the use, distribution, and advertisement of contraceptives and precluded official support for family planning services. Two hundred and fifty Chadian professionals were trained in clinical, administrative, and social aspects of family planning programs. This preparatory policy reform and training work set the stage for an International Family Planning Conference in N'Djamena in October 1988. This was the first time Chad had hosted a conference on family planning. Twenty international experts and over two hundred Chadian participants representing the political, religious, and technical institutions in the country attended. The conference recommendations encouraged the government to adopt a family planning policy that took into account the ethnic, sociocultural, and religious diversity of Chad and to abrogate the Pharmacy Law. The conference also recommended greater collaboration between the public and the private sectors to ensure the development of a Chadian family planning program. One result of the conference was the formal establishment of the Chadian Family Planning Association.

The training and policy development work, undertaken as a subcomponent of the Chad Health Planning Restoration project, was crucial to the development of family planning services as part of the package of essential health services provided to the population. HIID Health Office personnel, as external advisors and catalysts, were able to stimulate the formation of a coalition of Chadian professionals sufficiently committed and technically prepared to overcome the initial religious and cultural biases against the development of a family planning program.

The Pakistan Child Survival Project

The Pakistan Child Survival project, conducted initially from 1990 to 1993 and extended to 1994, was responsible for, among other tasks, helping to establish a health management information system for first-level care facilities (HMIS/FLCF). The new system was to replace an existing reporting system of little use for management or planning. The objectives of the health information systems component were: (1) to assist the Ministry of Health in the design and implementation of a comprehensive HMIS/FLCF that would replace the existing routine reporting system; (2) to provide training to public health managers in using the information generated by the system for planning and management of child survival interventions; and (3) to assist the ministry in institutionalizing the new HMIS/FLCF.

The system was designed through a national broad-based consensus-building process, involving future users in all provinces. The system indicators were based on a package of first-level care activities, taking into account decision-making at three management levels of the health system: the patient/client level, the health unit level, and the health system level.

A set of data collection instruments for each level was designed and pre-tested. For the first time in Pakistan, data processing was computerized. This resulted in more effective information feedback to decision makers at all levels in the health system. At the end of the initial project (in September 1993), nationwide implementation was well underway: more than one third of the 10,000 first-level care facilities in Pakistan were using the system after a brief training course in the new data collection procedures. Thirty computer centers had been set up and the staff had been trained in data entry and processing. Unfortunately, at the initial project completion date, the institutionalization of HMIS/FLCF was only in an embryonic stage: the Ministry of Health's system's management capability was weak; no budgetary support for the recurrent costs of the system had been committed; and, since data had been collected for only a short time, very little training in the use of the information had taken place. It was therefore decided to extend the HMIS component of the Pakistan project for an additional eight months, this time with HIID as prime contractor. Additional funds for the further implementation of HMIS/FLCF were provided by USAID and UNICEF.

The HMIS/FLCF extension covered more than five thousand first-level care outlets. About forty percent of the districts were reporting regularly. The computerized data processing system was further developed and fine-tuned to produce and disseminate a variety of user-friendly feedback reports to managers at all levels in the health system. About 400 supervisors and managers had been trained in using the information generated for planning and management of the health services, particularly related to child survival interventions. The institutionalization of HMIS/FLCF was well underway: most provinces had finalized the necessary (and complicated) administrative procedures to budget for the recurrent costs of the system. Most important, the Ministry of Health would receive the necessary support from other donors, such as UNICEF and the World Bank, to complete HMIS/FLCF implementation and to ensure its institutionalization.

The development of HMIS/FLCF in Pakistan showed the importance of selecting indicators based on the needs of care providers. Careful selection improved both the quality and the use of the information. Also, the results of the HMIS reform depend largely on the administrative support and sociocultural context. Implementation of the technical aspects of the health information system is only one part of a comprehensive health system reform effort.

Costa Rica: Lot-Quality Assurance Sampling

The Costa Rica project was the first field test of Lot-Quality Assurance Sampling (LQAS) in health. LQAS is a technique developed in industry to inexpensively assess, using a relatively small sample, whether or not an inventory lot meets a threshold standard of quality.

The technique was used to identify rural health centers performing below threshold norms for immunization coverage, identification and referral of neonates and pregnant women, competency in the use of oral rehydration therapy (ORT), and maintenance of vital records. There was a trade-off in the use of LQAS for this purpose. Information was obtained quickly and priorities were easily set, but because the information was binomial—one, or at most two thresholds are used—there was no way to know the overall distribution of performance (statistically or geographically). After initial tests, the technique was introduced and institutionalized in the national system of primary care. A new supervisory system—using LQAS information—was developed for primary care, and primary care services improved.[11]

The Senegal Rural Health Care II Project

The Senegal project was the second phase of an effort to develop the primary health care system in two rural districts—Kaolack and Fatick—in the country's Sine-Saloum region. As with the Mali effort, USAID funded a set of activities in selected areas of the country to develop a demonstration primary health care system, hoping that the model could be expanded throughout the country. Tulane University and John Snow Inc. were subcontractors to HIID on this effort.

The overall objective was to improve child survival in Senegal. Specific technical areas were selected based on the disease patterns of the area. The primary technical goal was to establish a model ORT control program in the two districts. Appropriate use of ORT is essential for reducing the deaths due to diarrhea in children less than five years of age. The ORT program also included growth monitoring, nutrition intervention, and nutritional counseling services; a diarrheal disease control component was part of the primary prevention of the disease. The ORT programs in Kaolack and Fatick were to serve as the basis for the planned national ORT program. Malaria control and treatment were the second major disease priority.

The establishment of disease surveillance capability was the third major component of the project. The surveillance was intended to improve health planning and also to improve the ability of the government's health services to respond to disease outbreaks. The development of the surveillance systems was part of a broader effort to improve the health management information system.

The development of the primary health care services was linked to an extensive training effort. Both in-country training for health workers and external Master's of Public Health (MPH) degree training for Senegalese Ministry of Health officials were supported.

Originally conceived as a four-year effort, the project was curtailed in 1987 after two years. The high turnover of personnel responsible for this effort within the Ministry of Health made it difficult to maintain government interest and support. In addition, changes in both project and USAID/Senegal personnel caused serious problems with continuity in project implementation.

The Cameroon Maternal and Child Health Project/Projet Santé de l'Enfant au Sud et dans l'Adamaoua (SESA)

Project SESA was initially conceptualized as a standard maternal-child health (MCH) project. Using the best of the known maternal and child survival interventions, the project was intended to improve the health of women of reproductive age and children less than five years of age in two provinces, Adamaoua and South. The six key interventions selected for improved implementation were: (1) infant immunization against measles, polio, pertussis, diphtheria, tuberculosis and tetanus; (2) maternal immunization against tetanus to prevent neonatal tetanus; (3) diarrheal disease control including extensive support for expanding ORT use; (4) growth monitoring and nutritional counseling and rehabilitation; (5) malaria control; and (6) provision of improved family planning services. These interventions were to be delivered by CHWs as mutually reinforcing vertical interventions. (As was later learned, projects designed to achieve quick, measurable improvements in health status indicators may not be the best way to strengthen and sustain health system development and foster health system reform.)

Within two years of the project's implementation in 1987, the Cameroon Government embarked on an overhaul of their health policy. Three dynamics fueled the desire for reform: (1) the CHW-based strategy was failing to provide high quality health services to the rural population; (2) the government was increasingly unable to finance the recurrent costs of the public health system and desperately needed to identify new sources of financing; and (3) donor pressure to comply with structural adjustment conditionalities required greater decentralization and reduction of public health services and promotion of the private sector. The new health policy became known as the Reorientation of Primary Health Care in Cameroon.

The new policy was based on three central tenets: (1) the fostering of decentralized decision-making that included the right to raise and retain funds at the community and provincial level; (2) the imposition of user fees to increase cost recovery; and (3) the encouragement of community participation in financing and organization of the health services. A new institution—Provincial Solidarity Fund for the Promotion of Health (or Provincial Health Funds)—was created to implement the new policy, and the project SESA staff were asked to provide technical assistance for this new initiative.

The project transformed itself from a service delivery management effort to an analytic effort advising the government on the reformulation of the national health policy. In addition, the government became more interested in the development of a functional health information system.

The project developed the legal and institutional framework for the Provincial Health Funds. Focus groups were carried out to monitor acceptance of the new policy and to provide guidance on appropriate levels of drug prices. The financial effect of the introduction of fee for service was analyzed. The communications component of the team actively supported the new policy through the production of brochures, videotapes, and television advertising.

Training teams were created at the provincial level to train health workers in the new procedures called for by the reorientation, and supervisory manuals were developed. The performance-based incentive system, with supervisory data and support through premiums paid into the revolving drug funds, was initiated. By project end in 1994, the decentralization of activities from the provincial to the district level had been completed in one pilot district of Adamaoua province.

Based on the findings of an assessment study undertaken in 1991, project SESA assisted the Ministry of Health to design a pilot health management information system. The new system focused on information support for district-level management of health services. The HMIS recurrent costs were financed by the newly established, community-managed cost recovery system described above. This financing mechanism, relatively uncommon elsewhere in Africa, provided the HMIS with a better chance of being sustained after the withdrawal of the external advisors and donor funds.

The Economics of Health

Health economics has been a central focus of HIID's work in health and an integral part of many projects, including the Thailand Development Research Institute (TDRI) and the Unidad de Analisis de Politicas Sociales (UDAPSO)–Bolivia projects, not usually classified as health projects. Understanding the economic incentives and disincentives to changes in the supply of and demand for health and health services is crucial to the reform process. HIID's work on the economics of health has included: (1) the development and analysis of national health accounts, (2) demand analysis and pricing policy, and (3) the analysis of options for health care finance. The analyses of the costs of illness (for AIDS) and of the cost-effectiveness of health interventions (for Dengue fever) are discussed in the next section.

National Health Accounts

National health accounts address central questions for health sector reform: how much is being spent, by whom, and for what? The usual form of the accounts is a matrix of sources and uses of funds in health. Governments, households, nongovernmental organizations (NGOs), and foreign donors are among the sources. Preventive services, and primary, secondary, and tertiary care are among the users.

HIID helped to document and analyze national health accounts in Thailand, the Philippines, and Bolivia. The principal finding in all three cases was that households accounted for more than half of all national health expenditures and that government health ministries accounted for less than a third. There are two important policy implications of this finding: that there must be analysis of demand as well as of supply; and that there is the option to create incentives—such as insurance schemes—to alter and enhance household demand in ways consistent with public health priorities. [12]

Demand Analysis and Pricing Policy

HIID helped to analyze demand in Bolivia, Burkina Faso, and Thailand. The objective in each case was to estimate the effect of client characteristics and service characteristics (particularly price) on the choice of services and providers.

In Thailand, price and cross elasticities of demand for family planning methods and services were estimated for a sample of married women. The estimated elasticities were then used to simulate the consequences of price changes on the methods selected and of the increases in the number of nonusers. The consequences for both cost recovery and the cost effectiveness of the national family planning program were evaluated. Results indicated that repricing of two methods, pills and injectables, would reduce the aggregate subsidy of family planning by 25 percent with no decrease in the contraceptive prevalence rate, suggesting that the existing public subsidies were both inefficient and excessive.[13]

In both Burkina Faso and Bolivia, the purpose of the analyses was to understand adult decisions to use health services and parents' decisions about care-seeking for their children. In the urban areas of Bolivia, the results showed that for adults, age, education level, gender (males were more likely to seek care), household income and morbidity, and waiting and travel time, strongly affected demand, while changes in user fees (up or down) did not. For children, the situation was different. Age, household income, travel time, and price affected demand. Price elasticities for children were much higher than for adults. In rural Burkina Faso, the results were similar. [14] Households were found willing to seek care for working adults but much less likely to seek care for infants and young children.

Thus in both settings there was an important disparity between household demand and public health priorities—between treatment of sick adults and attention to children less than five. Among the policy implications was the need for differential pricing for adults and children and other incentives for care of children. For example, simulations in Bolivia indicated that a decrease in user fees for children from a median of US$1.25 per visit to zero would increase demand for care of children by an average of 30 percent.

Options for Health Care Finance

The HIID Health Office has helped to analyze and test various options for financing health services, including cost recovery and community financing experiments, prepayment health card schemes for both rural and the urban informal sectors, and social insurance.

Cost Recovery and Community Financing Experiments

Demand analysis and simulations are first steps in analyzing the prospective effects of the introduction or changes in user fees and the feasibility of cost recovery. Field testing is the only way to know for sure. Three HIID projects (Thailand, Mali, and Cameroon) helped to design, field test, and analyze cost recovery schemes.

In Thailand, HIID helped TDRI and the Thai Ministry of Public Health to design and conduct family planning repricing experiments in four provinces over an eighteen-month period. The repricing scheme tested was similar to, though less comprehensive than, the changes in the simulations. The results were similar to what was predicted by the simulations. There was no decrease in contraceptive prevalence or effectiveness and cost recovery for pills and injectables increased by 50 to 80 percent.[15]

In the Mali Rural Health project, one objective was the establishment of revolving drug funds to generate sufficient sales (on the order of US$1 per person per year in the catchment areas) to restock the funds and to provide modest compensation to the CHWs, which the project also trained during the four-year period. This seemingly modest objective was not attained for at least three reasons. First, project sites were remote and re-supply costs were high—fifty times higher than pre-project estimates.[16] Stock-outs were common. Second, drugs for sale were mainly for the care of children, for example antimalarials and ORS packets; household demand (as in Bolivia and Burkina Faso) was more likely to have been for treatment of adults. Third, the project's four-year life (1978-1982) coincided with a steep decline in per capita income, government revenues, and government funding of health. Any one of these shortcomings was serious. All three together were fatal; revolving funds sales were equal to only US$0.06 per person per year.

In Cameroon, HIID helped to undertake one of the largest field tests in Africa of cost-recovery through revolving drug funds with built-in cross subsidies. Drug fund sales (and small users' fees for other services) were to cover 100 percent of all non-salary recurrent costs of primary care. Provincial health funds with local fund committees were established and acquired legitimacy. Fund pharmacies were established with a range of products for sale for adults as well as children, overseen by the local fund committees, with performance-based compensation of managers and a secure resupply system based on bulk purchase of generic drugs on the international market.[17] By project end in 1994, cost recovery had reached 70 percent of non-salary recurrent costs and was increasing. Demand had gone up in general, and the greatest increase was found in the lowest quintiles of the income distribution.

In Thailand, HIID's Health Office helped to conduct a national evaluation of community finance experiments including: revolving drug funds, construction funds, and nutrition funds. The characteristics of the most successful funds—the revolving drug funds—were many of the same as those later developed in Cameroon: community health fund control, performance-based compensation of managers and a commercial orientation in pricing and operations.[18] Critical issues in the design of community finance programs identified in the study included: options for tie-ups with NGOs and government; requirements and incentives for membership; pricing policy, scale and scope; and incentives for good management.

Health Cards

Prepayment health card programs are potentially important for workers and households outside the formal sector of developing economies. In the absence of some form of health insurance, the medical care options for these workers and families are to use subsidized public sector services which charge fees and are rationed by both the fees and queues, or to use fee-for-service private providers. In either case there is the risk of deferred or no care, and if loans are taken to pay for care of serious illness or accidents, then there is the risk of prolonged indebtedness or landlessness due to the high cost of hospitalization. Voluntary prepaid health insurance schemes for rural households and self-employed workers can reduce the risk, provided the scheme is both affordable and sufficiently appealing that the risk is pooled and adverse selection problems, inherent in any voluntary system, are minimized or controlled.

The HIID Health Office professionals helped to conduct an analysis and evaluation of the health card program in Thailand—a voluntary prepaid rural health insurance scheme—initiated by Thailand's Ministry of Public Health in 1983. A family health card valid for one year could be purchased at harvest time in rural areas. It covered four to six named family members who received free MCH and preventive medical services and treatment of six illness episodes a year. First-contact curative care was to be given at the local sub-district health center. A referral slip from the health center was required to receive treatment at a district or provincial hospital. Waiting time in hospitals for card holders with referral slips was to be reduced. Money from the sale of the cards was held for one year by the health card funds and, during the year, short-term loans were made to card holders to encourage entrepreneurial activities. At year end, the money collected from the sale of cards—but not the profit—was used to reimburse health centers and hospitals for the services the health card holders received.

The study showed that about 30 percent of recurrent expenditures of the services provided to health card holders were reimbursed by the health card funds—about the same as reimbursement from fees, and equivalent to non-salary recurrent costs; that there were clear patterns of card use, including episode saving, episode pooling, and a spike in use of the card in the month preceding its expiration. There was evidence of the insurance effect and/or adverse selection—that is, card holders used more services than non–card holders. Critical design issues identified were: incentives for risk pooling, disincentives to adverse selection and moral hazards, extent and nature of benefits, extent of access to private providers, alternatives for reimbursement of providers, and cost containment measures. The Thai Government has subsequently redesigned the health card program, which eventually will be merged with a new national social security system covering health care and pensions.

Social Insurance

Social insurance reform was the principal objective of the Philippines' Health Development project. The project undertook longitudinal experiments of modifications in the Philippine Medicare Program. The experiments were designed to test the feasibility of expanding Medicare benefits to include out-patient health services under two alternative payment mechanisms: fee-for-service, and capitation—both with cost containment measures. The evaluation assessed and analyzed the consequences of the alternatives tested for the design of a national health insurance program.

These experiments and the evaluation were important for health policy and health sector reform in the Philippines. The absence of out-patient coverage in Medicare was thought to increase in-patient treatment and thus overall costs. Reimbursement patterns affect cost, efficiency, quality, patient satisfaction and, eventually, health outcomes. Which pattern, or mix of patterns, for reimbursement of providers might be best is a key issue in health reform (and in health economics) worldwide. Unfortunately, the evaluation ended abruptly because of budget cuts in the project.

Targeted Health Interventions for Public Health Reform

HIID's Health Office conducts research on specific diseases in local settings in order to generate information of potential global significance. This section will describe projects on three high priority public health issues—AIDS, vitamin A deficiency, and dengue fever—that contributed to global understanding of disease-specific public health programs.

AIDS

When HIID began its work in health in 1978, AIDS was an unrecognized and unnamed epidemic. It is now a major worldwide health problem, rapidly becoming a primary cause of adult mortality among selected groups. The epidemic is not spreading evenly: in some countries of Central Africa, it has ravaged the professional strata of society; in some countries in Southeast Asia it has only begun to appear, though its precursor—high rates of infection from the HIV virus—is already evident. In other countries, the epidemic has only begun. HIID's work on AIDS includes analyses of the economic costs of the epidemic, the development of needs assessment techniques, and the design and implementation of treatment and prevention programs.

Economic Costs of AIDS

AIDS is a threat to poor economies because of the direct costs of treatment and prevention and, more important, the indirect costs of the premature death of young adults. HIID conducted some of the first analyses of the economic costs of AIDS—estimating the indirect costs of AIDS in Zaire[19] and the direct and indirect costs in Puerto Rico.[20] The HIID Health Office helped to conduct a more comprehensive analysis of prospective costs in Thailand.

The Thai results showed that, without aggressive prevention measures, 3.4 to 4.3 million people out of a population of 70 million would be infected by the year 2000, and that the present value of costs to the economy would be on the order of US$8.5 billion. With vigorous prevention an estimated 3.5 million people could avoid infection and US$5 billion could be saved.[21] The value of such studies is their ability to convince governments that the purely economic case for preventive measures is overwhelming. The study had the desired effect on government policy and on the private sector, as Thailand undertook a major effort to educate its population about the epidemic and risk-reduction behaviors.

In Rwanda, HIID scientists helped to develop and field test a methodology for analyzing the cost of AIDS care in developing countries. The methodology focused on in-patient hospital costs, and included techniques for abstracting and analyzing patient records, and for estimating average costs per day and average costs per year for AIDS patients. Results for 1990 showed that 4.6 percent of the public hospital budget was devoted to AIDS. Projections indicated that this proportion would more than double in five years.[22] AIDS care in hospitals was not sustainable; other options for out-patient treatment and home care had to be developed.

Community-Based Needs Assessment Methods

Planning for out-patient and home care was one objective of an HIID project (with WHO's Global Program on AIDS) which developed practical needs assessment methods to plan for and cope with the epidemic. HIID helped to design and field test a set of quantitative and qualitative assessment guides adaptable to local languages and cultures. The guides were field tested in Malawi and Mexico. In Malawi, a combination of survey research, focus groups, and ranking groups were used to assess needs for home health care programs for AIDS. A report of results was provided to the National AIDS Control Program recommending that special home care programs not be developed in Malawi, but that the government should instead provide resources to and reinforce existing social networks of caretaking. In Mexico, the project developed Spanish-language training materials in needs assessment, and worked with the National AIDS Control Program to assess the ability of state-level AIDS programs to do qualitative needs assessments and to develop appropriate training materials for health staff. The qualitative manual resulting from the two field tests was subsequently formatted and distributed worldwide by WHO to district level AIDS program personnel to assist them in assessing the needs of people with AIDS.[23]

AIDS Treatment and Prevention: Puerto Rico

HIID's work on AIDS treatment and prevention in San Juan, Puerto Rico covered six years (1987–1993), encompassed three projects and multiple activities, and is the most comprehensive work done by HIID on AIDS to date. In 1987, the city of San Juan had the second highest

AIDS incidence and prevalence of any city in the Americas. There were no outreach or prevention programs and no strategic plan to deal with the epidemic. AIDS patients were treated as in-patients in the AIDS ward of the municipal hospital, which was dismal, underequipped, and understaffed. The city's budget for health was severely limited.

The first problem addressed in the work was the treatment of AIDS patients. In-patient hospital treatment of AIDS patients followed a pattern seen early in the epidemic in many countries. When the epidemic first appears, there are relatively few patients and medical practitioners have limited experience with the disease. They are not able easily to distinguish acute from chronic episodes or predict the course of the disease. There may be stigmas associated with this disease. For these reasons, initially it seems better to keep AIDS patients in the hospital. Yet psychologically and physically this pattern is detrimental to patients. Long stays in an AIDS ward are unpleasant for both patients and families, and a hospital is an unhealthy place for people whose immune systems are compromised. Eventually, the pattern becomes a burden to the public budget as it was by 1987 in San Juan.

A group of Puerto Rican specialists in public health and health services administration, with HIID Health Office assistance, proposed an alternative. Their objectives were to reduce hospitalization of AIDS patients, improve patient quality of life, reduce expenditures per AIDS case, and use the money saved for AIDS outreach and prevention. The proposal was that the city of San Juan would provide to a private, nonprofit institution—the San Juan AIDS Institute—the amount it spent on treatment of AIDS patients in 1987. This money would be provided yearly. In return, the AIDS Institute would provide treatment of patients at all stages of the disease. It would improve AIDS wards in the municipal hospital and open and staff outreach clinics. It would initiate prevention programs and conduct epidemiological surveillance of the epidemic.

The AIDS Institute began work in 1988, and since then has largely accomplished what it promised. It established a system for the care of AIDS patients which minimizes in-patient care and provides services on out-patient basis. Each AIDS patient is assigned a caseworker reachable twenty-four hours a day. As much treatment as medically possible is given in the out-patient clinics, adult daycare centers, at home, and in hospice sites. As a result of these changes, in-patient hospitalization of AIDS patients was reduced from an average of twenty-two days in 1987 to eleven days in 1993. Average annual cost of in-patient care was reduced from US$15,000 per patient to US$3,900. Overall average cost of treatment per AIDS case dropped by half, after correction for changes in case mix.[24] Between 1988 and 1993, the number of AIDS patients in San Juan increased from 837 to 5,277. The AIDS Institute has been able to cope with this increase without additional support from the City of San Juan. It has also been able to secure additional funds for outreach, clinical research trials, and prevention.

Most AIDS patients in San Juan in 1988 to 1989 were injecting drug users and the medically indigent, who typically have little or no contact with preventive health services. Their only contact with the health system (if any) is for acute curative services. With support from the Robert Wood Johnson Foundation and technical assistance from the HIID Health Office, the San Juan AIDS Institute established nine inner city clinics reaching over 10,000 people at high risk of HIV infection and AIDS. The clinics initiated programs of AIDS prevention, AIDS surveillance, and HIV testing. Seventy percent of the clinics' patients were injecting drug users. A very high rate of HIV positive sero-prevalence and morbidity was found in this population. Cost-effective criteria for HIV testing were developed and implemented. Those found HIV negative but engaged in high risk behavior were taught how to minimize their risk of infection. Those found HIV positive were referred to counselors and case workers at the San Juan AIDS Institute. Partners of HIV positive individuals were traced, notified and helped to protect themselves. Management information systems and training programs were developed. Surveillance efforts were strengthened and the data were added to the overall epidemiological surveillance of the epidemic. These efforts continue to date and make San Juan one of the most organized major cities in terms of the prevention and treatment of AIDS.

Vitamin A Supplementation

Vitamin A deficiency has long been recognized as an important cause of childhood blindness. Within the past decade, however, field studies reported that a few doses of vitamin A could lower mortality from measles in children, and that vitamin A might also lower mortality from all causes among this group. If the effect was real, and not accompanied by significant side effects, giving vitamin A supplements could be an important and inexpensive way to increase child survival worldwide.

To determine the impact of vitamin A supplementation on child mortality in developing countries, USAID developed study proposals for double-blind, randomized population trials in three countries including the Sudan. Such studies are extremely complex, requiring large sample sizes, careful assessment of baseline prevalence and severity of vitamin A deficiency, careful mortality and morbidity surveillance, and close supervision of these complicated fieldwork tasks throughout the study's life.

The Sudan project was carried out between 1988 and 1990 by HIID personnel and counterparts in the Sudanese Ministry of Health. More than 28,000 children were enrolled in the study from five rural councils in the north of the country. Children were randomized by household to treatment or placebo groups, and were given a large dose of vitamin A every six months for eighteen months. Six teams of local staff were trained in research methods and field measurements to increase their effectiveness and accuracy in collecting data in the field.

Data collection continued despite the Sudanese civil war, and the study was eventually published in the medical journal *Lancet*. The study found that vitamin A supplementation did not have any significant effect on child mortality in Sudan. The authors urged researchers to identify factors which might modify the efficacy of vitamin A supplements, including frequency of supplementation, severity of vitamin A deficiency, incidence and severity of specific infectious diseases, and concurrent nutrient deficits.[25] They concluded that reducing poverty, improving sanitation, and improving diets should continue to be the primary goals of efforts to improve child survival. War, civil unrest, and withdrawal of donor funding soon stopped all of the planned follow-up activities within the Sudanese Ministry of Health.

Of seven community studies of vitamin A supplementation reviewed in 1992, five found a significant impact on mortality, and two (including the study in the Sudan) did not. When brought together to discuss these results, the principal investigators of these various studies concluded that in areas where vitamin A deficiency is a problem of public health importance, vitamin A also reduces mortality in infants in the second six months of life and in young children, although there are variations between communities and regions in the extent of impact.[26] The results of this study contributed to one of the largest policy debates in international health in the past decade.

Cost-Effectiveness Studies of Dengue Fever Control

Dengue fever is a mosquito-borne, rapid onset, viral disease with fever, headache, body pain, lack of appetite, and various gastrointestinal symptoms. In its severe form, dengue hemorrhagic fever, case fatality rates are one to five percent. Most people who die of the disease are under age fifteen. Epidemic outbreaks of dengue fever hospitalized more than 110,000 people in Cuba in 1981, and recent epidemics have been reported in Brazil, Thailand, Venezuela and Vietnam, among other countries.

Current technologies exist which can be used to control dengue fever transmission. They include elimination of breeding sites for mosquitoes, or chemical controls to kill the mosquitoes themselves. Of these two, environmental controls to eliminate breeding sites seem more effective. Vaccines are under development but not yet ready for distribution. Improved case management from training personnel and improving facilities and equipment is a third option, useful for reducing mortality but not morbidity.

Given the multiple intervention possibilities and the lack of data on the cost-effectiveness of these measures, an HIID team and local collaborators collected the best available economic, clinical, and epidemiologic data on dengue fever from the literature and from case studies in Brazil and Puerto Rico. These data were used to develop a series of epidemiologic scenarios. Prognoses were made about the evolution of the disease in the absence of any control measure, the type of disease transmission, and previous population exposure to the disease. Models were also constructed to describe the evolution of the disease under a series of potentially feasible interventions. This modeling exercise required looking at the sophistication of the health care delivery system, whether vaccine was available or not, and what combinations of interventions (improved case management, immunization available, chemical control of vectors, environmental controls of vectors) were proposed. The models were used to project the results of applying each intervention policy to a population of one million people, expressed in the cost and benefits per year of application.

The study found that the two countries included as case studies placed most of their resources in an expensive and relatively ineffective strategy of chemical control of vectors (spraying for adult mosquitoes). Though short-term data showed an effect for this strategy, long-term data showed that mosquito populations increased again within a few months. Literature reviews showed that environmental controls of breeding sites were more promising, but this cost-effectiveness assessment showed that even environmental controls were only moderately cost-effective, and therefore appropriate only for a middle-income country. In the absence of a vaccine, the paper recommended case management as the most cost-effective.[27]

The project was not designed to provide policy advice to specific countries; rather it was intended to develop more general models of cost-effectiveness analysis using a few specific case studies for worldwide application. The dengue fever project highlights the importance of taking local capacity into account in designing policies and programs. The dengue fever project developed a systematic model combining information about health-delivery system quality, potential combinations of interventions, and possible availability of vaccines. This model could then be applied to specific countries, to help them decide where to devote their scarce resources.

Discussion

HIID's two decades of experience in designing, managing, and analyzing a diverse portfolio of international public health projects allow for some general statements of where the institute succeeded, where it struggled, and what lessons have been learned that will guide the further development of the HIID Health Office program.

Conclusions

The Health Office group has had some of its greatest successes in applied research and in strengthening local research capacity. Whether one looks at the scientific results generated by the extensive multicountry ADDR research network, the effect of the applied economics research on AIDS in Thailand and in Puerto Rico, or the vitamin A intervention trial in the Sudan, clearly the Health Office has played a crucial role in fostering collaborative applied research that contributes to both national and global public health policy debates.

The substantive scientific contributions of the Health Office on the management of priority health problems in developing countries are numerous. The ADDR project-supported research on the dietary management of persistent diarrhea forms the technical basis for the persistent diarrhea component of the Integrated Management of the Sick Child approach. The Pakistan integrated case-management training showed vertical training programs were both expensive and inefficient. Both efforts formed part of the technical basis for global recommendations by WHO, UNICEF, and USAID.

The San Juan AIDS Institute system for providing AIDS treatment in a humane and cost-effective fashion has been imitated elsewhere throughout the Americas and even in Asia. As a whole, the accomplishments of the HIID Health Office cover a broad range of important international public health concerns.

The development of health management information systems in Cameroon, Chad, and Pakistan are examples of where HIID professionals have developed successful programs and contributed to reform efforts that reach beyond the local focus of the effort. Health Office staff, in collaboration with WHO staff, are preparing a book on design and implementation strategies for routine health management information systems.

The Health Office's economic research has advanced knowledge and practice in the documentation of national health accounts, health care financing experiments, analysis and simulation of demand patterns, and cost-effectiveness and cost-benefit analysis as applied to health interventions. The work on AIDS in Puerto Rico, Rwanda, and Thailand was path-breaking on the social and economic impacts of AIDS prevention and treatment.

The Health Office has enjoyed less success in managing large-scale implementation projects. Lack of clarity of purpose or lack of commitment to the health reform process by host governments were major impediments to the development of successful reform efforts in several countries.

HIID, as an institution within a research university, is able to contribute useful research and policy advice that fosters international debate on policy direction. Its comparative advantage is the ability to analyze and disseminate the lessons learned from running operational systems in the health sector. Projects that are solely service delivery, without resources or opportunities for evaluation and research, probably should be avoided.

Health reforms are integrally related to broader national reform efforts and macroeconomic changes. Negative changes in international terms of trade for primary commodities in West Africa severely complicated health reform efforts in Cameroon, Mali, and Senegal.

Conversely, health reforms in Thailand were facilitated by macroeconomic reforms and rapid rates of growth in real per capita income for a large proportion of the society. HIID is attempting, when feasible, to field multidisciplinary teams (for Burkina Faso and Malawi advisory missions) where the linkages between social sector development and macroeconomic reform can de considered and designed into the effort from the beginning.

Health reforms and project accomplishments are also subject to political circumstance. Changes in the political economy, societal collapse due to civil unrest, and discontinuities in development work caused by political decisions of the donor agencies are often more important to the success or failure of efforts than the technical substance of the work provided. The Health Office has focused much of its work in areas of Africa and Asia where social stability has been lacking. These are the toughest countries in which to develop sustainable efforts but which reflect the real challenges of development assistance. Project accomplishments have been dissipated by political upheavals in Rwanda, Togo, and Zaire. Continuity of effort was impossible in Djibouti, the Sudan, the Philippines, Thailand, and Pakistan for reasons of a cessation of USAID development assistance, a civil war, the reduction in aid from the United States after the closure of the large military bases, a military takeover of a civilian government, and both the Gulf War and the cessation of USAID programming, respectively. The ADDR project alone suffered the abrupt closure of project activities in Brazil, Kenya, Nigeria, Pakistan, Togo, Thailand, and Zaire during its ten-year effort. HIID's experience is not uncommon among development organizations that have tried to address the difficult questions in unstable areas of the world.

The selection of resident staff and the inter-institutional relationships are essential for project success. Careful selection of resident staff fostered successful projects in Pakistan, Thailand, and the second half of the Cameroon project, while inappropriate selection of personnel damaged the efforts in Senegal and the early days of the Cameroon project. It is far better to be the prime contractor, rather than a subcontractor, except in those rare cases like the Zaire School of Public Health Project where the consortium operated as a real partnership. In all cases, it is better to have a cooperative agreement rather than a contract with the government. The cooperative agreement allows far greater flexibility in the determination of the pathway to project success.

Field research and advising activities can be brought back and disseminated to future development professionals through the teaching program at Harvard University. Classes at the School of Public Health on infectious disease, health management information systems, and research ethics have all benefited from HIID field projects. Similarly, courses at Harvard's Graduate School of Education and at the John F. Kennedy School of Government are based on the experience gathered through HIID Health Office professionals in the course of their activities.

Looking Ahead

Development assistance in the health sector continues to be a major area of activity for HIID. The health challenges, particularly those facing the African continent and South Asia, are profound and may be stagnant or worsening in the near term. In low-income countries, governments will remain the major provider of health services. In all countries, irrespective of income, government seems to be responsible for the provision of public health and health promotion services. Health sector financing issues are acute, as governments face increasing shortages in meeting the basic health care needs of their people. Reliance on the private sector for curative care and on NGOs for health service delivery is increasing, without a clear understanding of who will benefit and who will be left aside. AIDS continues to extract a huge toll, and neither a cure, a vaccine, nor an effective prevention program appears on the near horizon. Emerging and re-emerging infectious diseases created a new, only recently recognized, challenge as resistant strains of malaria and tuberculosis expand their range. Donor flows for health are increasing as the development banks invest major sums to face all these challenges.

The HIID Health Office, based on the experience gained since 1978, is well-placed to provide technical leadership and major substantive contributions for addressing the international public health needs of the twenty-first century through its advising, research, and teaching activities that are grounded in project experiences.

Notes

1 Based in part on conference papers by Richard A. Cash, Jonathon L. Simon, Johannes U. Sommerfeld and James A. Trostle; by Theo J. Lippeveld and Rainer M. Sauerborn; and by Charles N. Myers

2 Carrin et al. (1993).

3 Mukiama and Mwangi (1989).

4 World Bank (1993b, p. 89).

5 Hambridge (1990); Parker (1991).

6 Ugalde and Jackson (1995).

7 Anand and Chen (1996).

8 Gray (1986a).

9 Gray et al (1990).

10 Lippeveld et al. (1992).

11 Valadez (1991).

12 Myers et al. (1985).

13 Myers (1989).

14 Sauerborn et al. (1995a).

15 Myers et al. (1991).

16 Gray (1986a).

17 Bodart and Owona (1995); Sauerborn et al. (1995b).

18 Myers (1988).

19 Myers and Henn (1988).

20 Shepard (1990).

21 Viravaidya et al.(1993).

22 Shepard et al. 1992).

23 Simon and Trostle (1995).

24 Kouri et al. (1992).

25 Herrera et al. (1992, p. 270).

26 WHO/USAID/NEI (1993).

27 Shepard and Halstead (1993).

15 Work in the Education Sector

Noel F. McGinn, Thomas J. Cassidy, Fernando M. Reimers, and Donald P. Warwick

Over the past twenty years, HIID research on education and development has evolved from the identification of general principles to govern policy advice, to the development of processes to facilitate the construction of situationally-appropriate solutions by policymakers and stakeholders. This chapter describes the research and technical assistance activities that have contributed to the learning required for this transition. The discussion focuses on four major periods: (1) pushing traditional planning to its limits; (2) improving specification of models through the inclusion of contextual data; (3) developing techniques to capture and use operational statistics in policy formulation; and (4) creating methods to identify and involve stakeholders in policy analysis and formulation.

Background

The general failure of development assistance to enable countries to "take off" was, by the late 1970s, painfully evident in human resource development. In many countries plans were never implemented. In those cases where governments had mobilized support for reforms, outcomes were much less than expected. Worse, the costs of education provision grew more rapidly than government revenues. Development assistance had contributed to producing more (of lesser quality) education. Before 1970, little was known about how to improve the quality of the output of education systems. In the developing world, the concern was how to increase access to schooling. In the early-industrialized countries, education systems were organized and operated with no attention to issues of economic growth; research focused on explaining differences in learning of individual students. The first national studies to assess the impact of schools on student learning were carried out in the United Kingdom and the United States in the late 1960s.[1]

The results were shocking: differences in inputs to schools appeared unrelated to differences in student achievement. There were no policy options to improve schools that could be expected to make much difference in the amount of student learning. This erroneous conclusion (based on analysis that ignored contextual factors) may have contributed to the relative shift of development assistance funds from education and human resource development to other sectors—which extended into the late 1980s. At the same time, the U.K. and U.S. studies opened a new line of research: the use of production-function models to identify policy options to increase desirable outputs from education systems.

Educational Planning (1976–1981)

In 1976, the United States Agency for International Development (USAID) funded a large-scale, four-year project at the Harvard Graduate School of Education, to develop state-of-the-art models and techniques in educational planning. The project, directed by an HIID Faculty Fellow, produced a four-volume set of books on educational planning that remains the standard for developing countries.[2]

Others working on the project became aware that little was known about the processes by which students come to acquire or produce knowledge and, consequently, about how best to organize and operate education systems to maximize knowledge production and student learning. Planning was seen as an empty shell: manpower planning was critiqued as an inadequate instrument,[3] and an alternative, transactive model of planning was proposed.[4] These efforts prefigured the shift of HIID away from a mechanistic approach to the identification of policy options for the education sector.[5]

In 1979, HIID was contracted by the Government of Mexico to provide technical assistance to a center for long-range (or prospective) research. Resident HIID staff in the education sector contributed to the development of a computerized simulation model of an education system, and to a book describing the use of information by the Secretariat of Education in planning and budgeting.[6]

Formalistic use of the production-function approach continued, however. Development assistance agencies were under increasing pressures to find quick solutions. A Decade of Development had saddled poor countries with heavy debt, and had failed to improve governments and economies. Demand for education continued apace, but finance was increasingly constrained. If the theme in the 1960s and early 1970s had been "how to do more," the theme of the mid-1970s and early 1980s was "how to spend less." Efficiency replaced access as the Holy Grail of technical assistance in the education sector, and analysts searched for an equivalent to the economic miracles spotted in various countries.

At USAID, hope for improvement in education was raised by triumphs in two other sectors. First, USAID officials were enthused by the impact of RAPID, a simulation model used to motivate national officials to reconsider population policies. Reports circulated of on-the-spot conversions. The second triumph, of significance, was the success of the oral rehydration therapy (ORT) for the reduction of infant mortality. The ORT package of salts cost practically nothing, was easily transported and locally manufactured, and could be administered effectively by non-professionals. It was a "silver bullet," a magical answer to an enormous problem. USAID officials asked why they could not have a silver bullet in education. They believed that once they learned what works, they could then spread it around the world with a RAPID-like technology.

USAID officials' desire to learn about what works was also stimulated by advances in the technology of comparative research on education systems. An organization of European and U.S. scholars had banded together to conduct production-function studies in their respective countries, using common or comparable instruments to measure both inputs to education systems as well as student achievement. The project, still underway, became known as the International Educational Achievement (IEA) studies. Initial results of the IEA studies attracted wide public attention, as they showed U.S. schools lagging behind those of several European countries and Japan in terms of achievement scores. More importantly, the studies also purported to identify input policies significantly associated with variations in achievement. The method (of common exams and questionnaires) has been extended successfully to a number of developing countries.

Research to Describe Local Realities: The BRIDGES Project (1985–1992)

In 1985, USAID issued a call for proposals for a five-year, US$10 million project to carry out research on policies for effective education. Only universities could bid as prime contractors, and a secondary objective of the project was increased capacity for policy research in universities in the United States. The USAID project document emphasized dissemination and utilization of research, using the most modern technologies available.

HIID's proposal mirrored USAID's concerns, and promised work on the development of computer simulation models that could be used by policymakers to select those policy alternatives that research had shown to be most effective. The proposal also argued that research done in early-industrialized countries would have relatively little applicability in most of the developing countries. Not only are education systems at a different level of development, but all have centralized governance structures much different than those of the United States or the United Kingdom. On the other hand, the proposal argued, there is much research in developing countries that could be captured, compiled, and synthesized, in the search for what works.

The contract was awarded to HIID as prime contractor, in cooperation with the Harvard Graduate School of Education. The features of the winning proposal appear to have been the extensive experience of HIID and Harvard staff in policy analysis and consulting in developing countries, and the tight focus of the proposal on policy applications rather than on development of research knowledge.

The subcontractors in the HIID team also had impressive backgrounds. The two consulting firms were the International Institute for Research, and the Research Triangle Institute; the two universities were Michigan State University and Texas Southern University. The International Institute for Research had extensive experience in nontraditional forms of delivery of educational services, including programmed instruction and computer-assisted instruction. The Research Triangle Institute was well-known to USAID for their work on simulation models. Michigan State University had an extensive background of research on teacher training. Texas Southern University had experience in research on bilingual education but was included to further the capacity of U.S. universities to carry out education policy research in other countries.

After the contract was awarded, the project was named BRIDGES, for Basic Research and Implementation in Developing Education Systems. This acronym was chosen to reflect the structure of the project, which depended on close relationships with research counterparts and policymakers in the participating countries.

Basic Strategy

The BRIDGES project developed the following assumptions:

- Many policymakers are not clear about the educational goals they pursue. They often are more clear about their political objectives, and their policies are politically rational. Because they do not have a good understanding of what education is and how it contributes to development, their educational goals generally are too abstract to serve as guides in development of policies.
- There are many possible policy options for the improvement of the performance of education systems, but most policymakers are familiar with few of them. That is, policymakers generally lack information about what are the options from which they can choose to achieve their goals.
- Many policymakers have a limited understanding of how an education system works. Some policymakers are former teachers, with perhaps an excellent understanding of classrooms, but little or no grasp of the complexities of the organization required to support the work of teachers in classrooms. Other policymakers come from outside education, and incorrectly attempt to transfer their understanding of simpler organizations. Almost all education bureaucracies are structured so that only the top officials receive information from all the parts of the organization. The volume of information received is more than they can process. Most operational policymakers (such as heads of the operating divisions of primary, secondary, teacher training, and technical education) are uninformed about the other units with which they are linked.

Members of the BRIDGES project made four assumptions as to how to act to increase the use of research in the choice of policy options: (1) sharpen the understanding of policymakers of their own education goals; (2) disseminate widely information about options for the improvement of education systems; (3) improve the understanding of policymakers of how the various parts of the education system fit together and support each other; and (4) develop the trust of the policymakers in the BRIDGES project and its members to ensure the success of these actions.

Modalities

The project opened with internal discussion over whether to adopt the IEA approach. Those in favor argued for the identification of policy options (silver bullets) that USAID and other international assistance agencies could apply across the board in the countries where they were working. Common instruments were the best way to insure comparability of findings. Those against this approach insisted that education systems reflect fundamental differences in culture and level of development, and that only tailor-made research designs could fit the unique situation of each country. The IEA approach appeared to impose a Northern model of education on participating countries. Initial reviews of research from several countries revealed wide differences in concerns and problems: BRIDGES opted for a research strategy that would capture individual differences and allow for development of a model of education systems that can be generalized.

The project members decided their research would cover all possible factors that contribute to student learning. Literature reviews were designed to contribute to the development of a comprehensive model of school effectiveness. Given the relatively short time span of the project, it would not be possible to carry out experiments to assess the impact of each factor. Instead, all research would have to be an evaluation of the relative effectiveness of policies already in place.

Goal Clarification

The project began, in each of the countries in which it eventually worked, with an extensive process of identifying and clarifying the goals of policymakers. Initial visits determined whether there was a match between the policymakers' objectives, and the capacity and mandate of the BRIDGES project. BRIDGES eventually worked extensively with ministries of education in Burundi, Egypt, Honduras, Jamaica, Jordan, Pakistan, Sri Lanka, and Thailand. Brief projects were carried out in Cameroon and North Yemen.

Introduction to policymakers came through the USAID missions. Policymakers were asked to help BRIDGES identify persons and institutions that would participate in the project. As most of the later work was carried out in languages other than English, the national counterparts played a central role in the process described below.

Method

The most common method of working with policymakers was a series of interviews with not only the key decision-makers but also their staff and persons in other positions in the ministry of education. The interviews were long and mostly unstructured. Project staff prepared summary statements of the interviews and reviewed them with the persons interviewed. This was done more than once and as often as necessary until staff felt that both they and the policymakers had a clear understanding of goals for the work to be done by the project in that setting. Project staff assumed they had arrived at an understanding of the goals and objectives of the policymakers only when they could develop indicators of the achievement of the goals, with which the policymakers could agree. That is, only when operational definitions of goals were accepted by the policymakers were they assumed to be understood.

For example, interviews were carried out with more than 100 education officials in the federal and provincial governments of Pakistan, asking about their objectives for and concerns about the education system. Following analysis of the interviews, a second round was carried out with a smaller set of officials, asking them to indicate which of several lines of research would be most useful, and exploring their understanding of the factors that had influenced the implementation of earlier reforms. Consultants from Michigan State University made several visits to Burundi over a year's time to assist policymakers in the definition of topics and rules of procedure for a collaborative research project. In Sri Lanka, two HIID staff negotiated the creation of an educational research institute and the definition of first tasks.

This process was time consuming and expensive. In several cases, USAID's Washington D.C. staff complained that the BRIDGES project was behind in its research schedule. In general, the first 25 percent of project time was spent in this process of goal clarification through interviews and development of indicators. That is, if a particular research study took four years to complete, actual field research did not begin until after a year of clarifying goals.

Products

On the basis of this experience, HIID and the Research Triangle Institute developed a simple software package (OPES) designed to help policymakers reflect on their education goals, and on how these goals relate to policy options. The software program asks users to assign weights to five different goals for education. Many policymakers in education have never formally assigned priorities to goals; the task helps them to understand what they mean when they say they are in favor of increased access, or improved learning outcomes, or increased national identity, or improved internal efficiency. HIID staff also developed a spreadsheet application (POPEX) for projecting single-year population data using Sprague multipliers, and worked with the Research Triangle Institute in the development of an enrollment projection package (STEP) that uses promotion and repetition data. Each of these tools was tried out in the various countries in which BRIDGES worked. For example, USAID and the ministries of education staff in five Central American countries and in Belize were trained in the use of STEP.

Lessons Learned

This investment of time in the clarification of the goals and objectives of the policymaker improved the research carried out in several ways. Goal clarification sharpened the issues to be addressed in research, helped to develop conceptual models; and made interpretation of findings easier.

Goal clarification did not, however, always contribute to the utilization of research findings by policymakers. The very process of clarification of goals increases the time that elapses before research findings can be presented. The longer the period, the more likely it is that the policymaker will have changed his or her definition of priorities. In some ministries, policymakers have relatively short tenures; research that takes too long ends up presenting results to someone with a different set of goals than that for which the study originally was designed.

Simple software programs can contribute to efforts to enable policymakers to consider a wider range of factors in their decision processes.

Reviews of Existing Research

Method and Products

Regional research institutions were contracted to produce reviews covering research in Latin America, Jordan, East Africa, and seven countries in Southeast Asia. Building on the work of these groups, BRIDGES developed a collection of about 1000 abstracts of research reports from all parts of the developing world. Working with programmers from the Research Triangle Institute, HIID staff were major authors of a software package (SHARE) that can be used on any personal computer and which permits a rapid retrieval of abstracts. This software package is now being used in ministries of education and universities in a number of countries.

BRIDGES also produced a set of reviews of the state of the art of research on different topics, such as access, internal efficiency, teaching effectiveness, cost analysis, distance education, alternative forms of teacher training, administrative reforms, and determinants of promotion in school. Manuscripts submitted for publication were read by two or more blind external reviewers. The publications were designed to be seminal reviews, and to have a long shelf life in developing countries that have little access to reports of research. As late as 1996, BRIDGES reviews are still actively used by USAID and by ministries of education.

Lessons Learned

The reviews validated the earlier assumption that much more research has been done than is ever published. Each country has a fund of studies that are useful for understanding national idiosyncrasies. Yet little of this research is ever made available to policymakers, managers, or researchers in the country, let alone to outsiders. Furthermore, publications of bilateral and international assistance agencies are either limited in distribution or too complex for most ministry staff. As a consequence, ministries have little access to research-based information.

The BRIDGES project reviews also contributed to the correction of common misconceptions about policies to improve education. The review on access to education, for example, discovered that many of the family barriers to education of girls attributed to religious beliefs diminish as education of boys approaches 100 percent. The review suggests that, in some instances, the best strategy to insure expansion of access to education for girls may be to accelerate efforts to enroll all boys. A review of research on classroom management instructional strategies highlighted the importance of "time on task," or time devoted to learning, to student achievement. This finding was incorporated into later field studies (see discussion below) and replicated in a number of countries.

Field Research

Method

The IEA studies were primarily comparative. Their focus was on the development of a general model to explain differences between countries. BRIDGES research, in contrast, sought to explain variations in levels of achievement of schools within countries. The focus was on national policies to improve local schools. All field studies began with interviews with decision-makers, and observations in schools. The results of this work informed the construction of instruments to capture regional and local variations in inputs and processes thought to be linked to variations in student achievement. Earlier reviews supplied a master list of variables; local observation made it possible to focus on those factors most likely to operate in the national context.

Large sample surveys were carried out in Burundi, Honduras, Pakistan, Sri Lanka, and Thailand. In several countries, such as Pakistan, the BRIDGES study was the first national examination of the education system. Each study used nationally-developed measures of achievement. In Honduras, Pakistan, and Thailand the achievement tests measured knowledge of what was being taught in schools and therefore permitted a direct assessment of school effectiveness.

Products

The findings of BRIDGES research were reported in HIID's Development Discussion paper series (fifteen titles); in the BRIDGES Research Report series (fourteen titles); and as articles in refereed journals.[7] Books based on BRIDGES research are currently being published.[8]

Lessons Learned

There are no "silver bullets" in education. There are no universally-distributed problems that can be solved by a single remedy. For example, the introduction of textbooks in Burundi contributed to raising levels of learning not only because there had been a shortage of books, but also because the level of education of teachers was sufficient that they could make effective use of the books. In Thailand and Egypt, more textbooks would have no impact on learning outcomes. In Honduras, textbooks designed for urban children were not appropriate for those in rural areas.

The physical conditions of classrooms and school buildings have little or no impact on student learning outcomes. This was the case in all the BRIDGES countries, even though in some districts buildings were so deficient that teachers held classes outside, while in others schools were well-built and maintained.

In all the countries involved in the BRIDGES project, teachers are the major source of school-related variation in student achievement scores. The importance of the teacher reflects the use of curriculum that designates the teacher as the source of all information to be learned. Teachers who knew more, that is, were better-educated, had students who scored higher on achievement tests.

Students learned most when teachers used methods that increased student attention to instruction, in particular, and student time-on-task, in general. In some countries, frequent punishment by teachers had the effect of reducing student time-on-task and therefore learning. In other countries, punishment sometimes acted to increase student attention and learning.

In some of the BRIDGES project countries teachers were most effective in schools in which principals act as managers and maintain high standards of discipline and school traditions. In other countries, principals made no contribution to student learning, because they spent little or no time on actual management of the school. Contrary to a common viewpoint in the United States, students did not learn most in schools with principals who acted as master teachers or instructional leaders for their staff.

As reported in the IEA studies and other research, the factor most strongly related to levels of student achievement can be called "opportunity to learn." Students who attend school regularly, whose teacher attends regularly, and who spend their time in school working on learning the curriculum, learn the most. In one country, research found differences in the number of actual hours in school, ranging from 600 to 1330 hours for the year. The findings suggest that for many students there is a minimal threshold level of hours below which little or no permanent learning occurs. School principals who maximize teacher and student contact are those who make the greatest contribution to student learning.

Dissemination of Research-Based Information

Much of the effort of the BRIDGES project focused on the dissemination of research-based information about the costs and outcomes of policy options to improve access to education, to reduce repetition and dropouts, and to increase learning. In addition to the print materials described above, research findings were also disseminated through a bulletin (*FORUM*) aimed at policymakers in developing countries.[9] *FORUM* discussed the policy implications of research in a format intended to be immediately accessible to decision-makers.

The second medium for dissemination of BRIDGES work was software packages. Two of these (POPEX and STEP) were instruments to facilitate processing of the kinds of statistics regularly used in ministries of education. SHARE was designed to facilitate retrieval of research pertinent to 35 policy issues in basic education. OPES encouraged users to consult summaries of research in the process of deciding which kinds of policies were most likely to maximize achievement of education goals chosen by the user. The Educational Impact Model (EIM) allows users to set initial values for their own country, and then shows the likely effect of increases in education of girls on fertility rates, labor force productivity, and gross national product (GDP) per capita.

BRIDGES staff also developed a complex simulation of the resource allocation process in education that combines a computable model with heuristics. This "game," EPICS, has been used now in about fifty different training situations, in the United States and in twelve other countries, and has been translated into and used in French and Spanish. Two spin-off simulations have since been developed by colleagues in Latin America.

As part of its dissemination activities BRIDGES developed a set of ten training packages that include a manual for the trainer, and materials and workbook for participants. These packages encourage participants to interpret and apply research on 190 major policy issues in education (such as access, repetition, quality and management). The packages have been used in a number of training settings. The Spanish version is now being used by a firm in Chile that provides consultancy services to the Inter-American Development Bank.

Under the BRIDGES project, HIID organized its first Summer Workshop on Educational Planning and Policy Analysis. This workshop, now in its sixth year, attracts planners and high-level policymakers from a number of countries.

Finally, the BRIDGES project organized three international conferences in Bangkok, Cairo, and Cambridge, at which project staff discussed research findings with other researchers and with education policymakers from government ministries and bilateral and international assistance agencies.

Lessons Learned

The database of research findings and research reports (not surprisingly) were used principally by other researchers. For example, BRIDGES research studies are widely cited in a recent book by the World Bank summarizing policy options for primary education.[10] The eventual contribution of the research-based information provided is, therefore, through the actions of researchers other than BRIDGES staff. This effort seems justified to the extent that it contributes to changes in the definition of what research topics are important, and to improvements in methodology.

The project had no systematic method to assess the impact of the research bulletin on decision-makers, but anecdotal information suggests that it has an impact on those who actually read it. The form of impact is similar to that of most articles in newspapers or popular magazines, that is, the reader incorporates the facts presented in the article into an already existing conceptual framework. The research-based information in the article may add to the working knowledge of the policymaker, but seldom is sufficiently powerful in itself to produce a major change in thinking.

In each BRIDGES experience, the impact of the research began well before the final publication of the report. The report is a public document that governments screen to make certain they do not contradict official policy. In some cases the policy was changed before the publication to make sure there was no public contradiction. All BRIDGES research began with a review of the literature— a good scientific practice. Researchers see the review of literature from other countries as a source of hypotheses about what might be true in their own country. Policymakers see the review of findings from other countries as a means of validation of what has been found in their own country. They are more likely to formulate a policy change if what has been shown in their own country has also been found in other countries. And they are especially likely to change policy, if the experience in other countries has been positive.

The most useful form of dissemination of research, in terms of having an impact on the rationality of policymakers, has been through small conferences or seminars in which researchers and policymakers meet to discuss the implications of research. In the experience of this project, policymakers have little interest in research methodology. They want to be reassured that the findings are credible, and want to know sufficient details of sampling to be able to defend conclusions drawn from the studies. But their interest focuses primarily on what the findings mean. In most meetings policymakers dominated discussions once findings were presented, and showed much more imagination and creativity in their interpretation of results than did the researchers. This occurred most frequently in those cases in which the policymakers had prior experience in education—in which case they had more experience than the researchers—and where the policy question affected only part of the education system.

A similar process can be generated with the use of a well-designed management information system. Some of the most useful policy discussions were generated by presenting ministers and their staff with maps showing the uneven distribution of resources and/or outcomes across school districts.

In some instances, the policymakers drew conclusions not anticipated by the researchers. In Burundi, for example, a finding that primary school graduates do poorly in the examination for secondary school because it is given in French prompted policymakers to introduce French as a second language even earlier in the primary cycle. The researchers had thought it would be best to change the language of the examination. The researchers in this case were tempted to challenge the rationality of the decision of the policymakers; it should be clear that the discussion was not about scientific findings, but about educational and political goals, and that the policy chosen was rational within a given framework.

This procedure does not in itself guarantee success. HIID's first attempt to influence policy in Pakistan failed miserably. Project staff presented what they considered irrefutable evidence, based on a large national sample survey, that a national goal of increased learning would best be achieved by spending more on academic schooling for teachers, less on teacher training in normal schools, and less on material improvements in schools. Project staff spent sixteen hours reviewing findings with forty of the top education officials in the country. Many of these persons had been interviewed earlier about their goals for education. After a careful presentation of the results, the officials were asked to write a document recommending policies based on the research. To the dismay of the project staff, the officials' report challenged the validity of the study, and recommended policies contrary to what project staff had expected.

An initial reaction in this case might be to brand the decision-makers as irrational for having rejected scientific findings. An alternative explanation is that the decision-makers listened carefully to, and were shocked by, the findings, which contradicted many of the usual myths about the education system. In their attempt to assimilate these findings into their working knowledge, they found it necessary to revise some of their goals for education. They interpreted the data as indicating that their goals of a quality education for all were unrealistic, that they had to re-emphasize access to schooling as a fundamental objective, even though that would mean continuing a system in which children did not learn very much. It was a shift of goals—prompted by a presentation of facts—and not a rejection of the facts that led to their decisions so contrary to BRIDGES staff's expectations.

In a second round of discussions about research results, HIID staff had much more success. Conference participants were trained in simple techniques of data analysis and produced their own reports. Discussions focused on policy implications rather than on the validity of the findings.[11]

Specific Impacts on Policy

Among the immediate impacts on educational policies in the countries in which BRIDGES worked are the following examples. In Pakistan, research showed that the physical conditions of the school buildings and furniture make little or no contribution to learning, and that the primary factor is the quality of teachers. These findings contributed to a shift in the emphasis of the government from a program of construction of expensive schools, to emphasis on changes in teacher training programs. In Thailand, BRIDGES research contributed to a decision to expand preschool education to all children, especially those in rural areas. In Burundi, BRIDGES-funded research contributed to a change in policy with respect to the emphasis to be given to French as opposed to the national language, as the language of instruction. In Egypt and Honduras, research helped to persuade the ministries of education to look more closely at the extent to which centrally-mandated reforms were being implemented in schools and classrooms.

Development of Education Management Information Systems (1987–1995)

Making research context-specific greatly increases its impact on policy but limits its ability to be generalized. Good research is so expensive in time and resources that many developing countries can afford only one major study every five to ten years. But policy issues emerge constantly. As a consequence, many policies are formulated without an empirical understanding of the issues.

One strategy to alleviate this situation is to develop non–research-based information for use in decision-making. Systems of this kind have been used in the military and private enterprise for three or four decades under the rubric of "management information systems." These systems are often sold and bought with unrealistic expectations, but no major corporation today could operate without the flow of information, and analysis, that these systems now generate. HIID's work since 1987 has focused on how to develop and maintain information systems that allow ministries of education to do their own operations research, reducing their dependency on research that uses social science designs and data collection methods.

HIID has now amassed considerable experience in the development and utilization of education management information systems (EMISs). Work on such systems has been carried out in Colombia, Egypt, Honduras, Jamaica, Jordan, and Pakistan. Technical assistance has included training in database management and the use of geographical information systems. The research focus has been on the identification of the minimal elements for a functional information system, and on ways to present analyses to influence the policy process.

Work on education management information systems began with a review of the relevant literature on information systems development. Across all sectors, in both developed and developing countries, more projects have failed than have succeeded. Failure takes two forms: systems are not maintained after external funding and technical assistance ends; even when maintained, the information generated is not used in the policy process.

Failures are most often attributed to an overemphasis on technical concerns, i.e., on hardware and software issues, and reliance on traditional, more closed application development strategies. In most failures, potential users of the data and information generated by information systems were only peripherally involved in system development. Data provided by such systems were often not relevant or reliable. Critical elements of the organization and the broader institutional environment were often neglected. More successful interventions were found to be characterized by approaches that emphasized broad-based, end-user involvement, and which focused on organizational development.

HIID also reviewed literature on decision-making practices of education managers, planners, and policymakers. In education, as elsewhere, research-based information appears to have a minor role in decisions. Lack of use of rational data is explained by any or all of these factors: (1) data are not available when needed; (2) insufficient relevant data are available; (3) statistical analyses are beyond the comprehension of the decision-maker; (4) data conflict with data from other sources and no means of judging the validity of data is provided; (5) political and social realities often eclipse rational realities; (6) units expected to provide necessary data are often unaware of the types of issues decision-makers face and the types of data they require; and (7) systematic and effective dissemination of information often is not considered within the scope of responsibility of the data-gathering agency.

HIID's two longest experiences in EMIS development have been in Pakistan (Primary Education Development project) and in Egypt (Educational Planning Unit project). The Pakistan experience appears to have been the most successful. HIID advisors contributed to improving the institutional capacity of the Directorates of Primary Education in the Balochistan and Northwest Frontier provinces. The project targeted the improvement of data collection systems, development of routine reporting procedures, and the execution and publication of basic analyses of education statistics. In both provinces, the ministry of education now reports data within the year in which they are collected, for almost 100 percent of schools. In the past, reports had lagged two and sometimes three years behind data collection and did not provide an accurate estimate of total number of schools. Both provinces now publish attractive statistical reports that are widely distributed to politicians and other stakeholders. There is consistent anecdotal evidence that EMIS products are being used by policymakers. HIID consultants also contributed to the design and analysis of a human resource survey at the village level that identified opportunities to mobilize local labor for school construction. Survey data were also used in the preparation of a master teacher supply and training plan.

Three Harvard doctoral dissertations have been completed using data from the Pakistan project. One dissertation examines the utility of presenting education statistics in geographic form (that is, showing distributions on maps of the region) as opposed to conventional tables and charts. The research shows that policymakers extract more information in less time and with fewer errors, using the geographic-based information. A second dissertation examines threats to data quality. The study demonstrates how and to what extent education officials in Pakistan act to falsify data. The study will be of great help in future efforts to design data systems that cannot be corrupted. A third dissertation focuses on the relationships between female and male officials in the education system, and the impact this has on data collection.

HIID advisors worked in Egypt over a six-year period on all aspects of the design and development of an EMIS and provided extensive training to technicians, planners, and researchers in the Ministry of Education and the National Center for Education Research and Development. The objective of efforts in Egypt was to improve the quality of data available for policy analysis and planning. Data collection forms, a relational database, and applications were developed to facilitate the collection, storage, dissemination, and analysis of data on the more than 25,000 schools in Egypt. In the later stages of the project, emphasis was given to the development of the capacity of regional offices to collect, maintain, and use education data. Systems were put in place in twenty-seven regional offices. The project achieved close collaboration with potential users of the EMIS at all levels. The results were modification of the annual school census, greater coordination of data collection efforts across ministry units, and improved capabilities for tracking data on students, teachers, and the capacity and condition of educational facilities.

Projects in Jordan and Jamaica have focused on increased utilization of available data, abundant in both countries. Utilization has been limited because the officials in charge of data collection and storage have engaged in rent-seeking. HIID's work has focused on ways to break their monopoly, to develop a high demand for information, and to create an infrastructure capable of rapid distribution.

One emphasis has been on development of new ways to present information to potential users. In Jordan, statistical data were used to develop an attractive wall poster that describes the key education issues in the country. In Jamaica, routine data have been used to prepare briefs that describe critical problems facing the education ministry. In both countries, HIID has helped to develop a decentralized capacity for data collection and processing. Once again, a major lesson has been the relatively low importance of hardware compared to the development of management skills and organizational coherence.

Informing Politics with Research (1991–1995)

"Policy dialogue" refers to a set of procedures to increase the use of research-based information in policy formulation and implementation. Continuous improvement of education requires not just a one-time application of research findings to immediate problems, but also the construction of new processes and structures that anticipate problems and capitalize on opportunities for improvement. The process of dialogue is intended to foster this kind of organizational learning. In turn, efforts to learn how to dialogue have changed how HIID does research in education.

Beginning in 1991, HIID staff have participated in three major policy dialogues for education. The first of these took place in Honduras. HIID was asked by USAID and the Ministry of Education to help them understand the problem of repetition by children in primary grades. Repetition is a severe form of inefficiency in Latin America where, in 1990, governments spent US$2 billion more on primary education than would have been necessary if no children had failed and repeated grades.

Interviews with ministry officials helped to define the research question. Ministry staff participated in the design of the study, in the actual field work, and in the analysis of the data. Results were reported in early 1992 to ministry officials, and then to groups of teachers, supervisors, union officials, and newspaper and television journalists. Reports were written in Spanish, in a short and in an extended form. Meetings with various audiences stimulated a public discussion about factors related to school failure.

The study had two major policy impacts. First, the Ministry of Education changed its policy with respect to the assignment of new teachers: better and more teachers now are assigned to the sensitive early primary grades. Second, USAID redesigned its next education project to require the contractor to do research that would generate a policy dialogue.

From this experience HIID learned that ministry officials can be persuaded to make public even sharply critical research findings, if the presentation of these findings identifies the ministry as a participant in the design of the research. HIID also learned that to involve a wide number of groups, results must be presented in a variety of formats and on a number of different occasions.

HIID's second major experiment in education policy dialogue took place in Paraguay in fall 1992. HIID was asked by USAID to carry out a sector assessment that would inform future assistance programs in education. The institute proposed instead to do an assessment that would shape discussion of education in the upcoming presidential campaign. This was Paraguay's first contested election in thirty years. The previous government had created an Education Reform Commission that had, with limited empirical information, designed a major reform of basic education. HIID wanted an opportunity to see whether an injection of research-based information at this point could broaden participation in a discussion of alternative policies.

HIID staff met regularly with staff of Paraguay's only education research center, and with the Reform Commission to identify issues and design research. Working with counterparts, HIID staff carried out a review of problems and opportunities in all levels of the education system. Research methods included interviews and focus groups, and contacts with various political, economic and religious factions. Data analysis was limited to existing databases. Initial results were reviewed with the Reform Commission. The final product was published, in Spanish, as a low-cost non-technical book and as a pamphlet, both laying out policy options for education.[12]

The publications were distributed widely to many public officials, but also sold well in commercial bookstores and newsstands as the only study of what should be done in education. It was cited in political speeches and by newspaper columnists. The experiment demonstrated the feasibility of information "high stakes" political debates with technically excellent yet jargon-free research reports.

El Salvador: Promoting a National Debate on Education (1993)

In the summer of 1993 HIID responded to a request for proposal from the USAID mission to El Salvador. The request called for an assessment of the education sector aimed at identifying options and priorities for policy reform. HIID saw this request as another opportunity to test methods for expanding participation in discussions of education policy. After twelve years of civil war there was little space left for political dialogue and negotiation in El Salvador. HIID wanted to see if research could contribute to building the kind of interaction essential for a democratic society. The institute's proposal emphasized a highly participatory process of research design and analysis.

Preparation for the assessment began in September 1993. Twenty-two of the thirty-five technical advisors who wrote the assessment were citizens of El Salvador. Collaborating in the preparation of the assessment were two institutions with credibility among opposing political groups: Universidad Centro Americana (UCA), a prestigious private university that had been a source of criticism of government policies; and the Fundación Empresarial para el Desarrollo Educativo (FEPEDE), an education foundation set up by the business community. The Ministry of Education was a full participant but did not exercise veto power.

Each of the technical groups conducting the ten studies in the assessment organized focus groups to explore issues and conclusions regarding each subject analyzed in the assessment. For example, the group working on the non-formal education chapter organized a three-day seminar with more than thirty representatives of nongovernmental organizations (NGOs) active in non-formal education.

In coordination with UCA, FEPADE, USAID, and the Ministry of Education, HIID organized an advisory committee for the assessment. This committee included some fifty representatives of more than thirty organizations, including officials from the Ministries of Education, Planning and Finance, members of Congress, ex-insurgents, members of the Chamber of Commerce and the association of exporters, industrialists, teacher union leaders, administrators from public and private universities, and representatives from NGOs and other relevant groups. The committee met weekly, between September and December, with the professionals writing the chapters of the assessment. The weekly meetings served two purposes. They helped researchers to identify those issues most salient to the groups represented in the advisory committee, and the members of the committee were better able to ground their discussion on concrete issues and evidence as these were advanced by the researchers.

By the end of the process, members of the advisory committee endorsed the overall conclusion that education in El Salvador was in very bad condition.[13] Specifically, they concluded:

- The output of the education system of El Salvador was insufficient to support rapid economic growth, especially in export-oriented industries. A model to estimate the education requirements of the labor force to sustain growth rates at 5 percent per year demonstrated a shortfall in the annual number of graduates of basic and secondary education. Interviews with a sample of employers in the most dynamic sector of the economy concluded that, in addition to the insufficient number of trained personnel, there were deficiencies in the quality of education provided.
- The quality of the system was among the lowest in Latin America, primarily because of insufficient finance during the past ten years. As a percentage of government expenditures education declined from 14 percent in 1980 to 13 percent in 1992; as a percentage of GNP it declined from 3.6 to 1.5 percent over this period.
- Low levels of learning were attributed primarily to the lack of teaching materials and textbooks, and to rigid and formalistic teaching methods. This was the case at all levels of the system, including higher education. There had been no systematic training of teachers during the ten years of the war. Recruitment of teachers had been difficult because of low incentives: the salary of a starting teacher in 1992 was 32 percent of the 1980 equivalent in constant prices.
- Proliferation of private universities has dramatically reduced the overall quality of higher education. Employers complained that many of the universities were printing degrees. Universities have limited contact with employers, and with the government.

The recommendations in the 640-page report, endorsed by the advisory committee, included: increasing levels of financing of education, particularly for basic education; targeting resources, particularly textbooks for children, to first grade; opening primary schools near the regions where the children not currently enrolled live; training teachers to develop more flexible teaching methodologies; integrating parents in school activities to improve school-community relations; and increasing levels of government finance of education.

Results were delivered, in Spanish, first to presidential candidates, then presented in large meetings of business men and women, labor unions, teacher unions, university professors and students, and the general public, and released to the press, radio and television with interviews and press releases. Eventually the study was printed by UCA, and is available in bookstores throughout El Salvador.

Impact of the Study

The study has a number of impacts, summarized as follows. The top two presidential candidates referred directly to the report in speeches and endorsed the recommendations. The Inter-American Development Bank used the report as the basic document for preparing a US$100 million concessionary loan for basic education.

The Ministry of Education has made expanding access to education in rural areas a policy priority. New sections and new teacher appointments are being made, giving priority to the rural areas. Also, the Ministry of Education has started to experiment with school autonomy. Pilot schools are being given a modest fund that teachers, principals, and parents can allocate to what they perceive as the greatest need to improve teaching effectiveness. The ministry has made teacher training a priority area. Administrative decentralization has continued, transferring responsibilities to the departments as suggested in the assessment.

USAID has allocated US$10 million to create a capacity for policy analysis outside the Ministry of Education, and has funded continuation of a national dialogue on issues in education.

Parent and community participation has been fostered, not only by involving them in decision-making in the management of the school funds, but also by establishing focus groups in communities to consult on education issues. Supporting innovations at the local level, the Ministry is promoting a number of model schools with specially trained teachers to serve as trainers.

Perhaps the most striking consequence of the assessment was that the study unleashed a process of public discussion of education issues. Several organizations in the country produced their own reports on the problems of the education sector and on possible solutions to these problems.

Lessons Learned about Using Research to Support Public Discussion of Education Policy

HIID learned a number of lessons about using research to support public discussion of education policy, as summarized below.

- External consultants can foster and contribute to the design of processes that lead to organizational learning and structural reform. To do this requires recognizing the political nature of planning and identifying the critical stakeholders. The process requires creating spaces for collaboration between ministries of education and other organizations representing civil society, such as NGOs, universities, or advisory committees. HIID has learned that it is possible for ministries to have frank discussions with various stakeholders; these discussions are easier if they refer to the policy implications of technical analysis, but they can also include the conceptualization of problems that need attention.
- Designing a strategy for public debate about education assessments or studies mobilizes stakeholders and creates an impetus for reform that transcends the term of a government in office. This mobilization can generate innovations and additional resources to support change. Some of the innovations observed in these cases include: a minister of education being asked to stay on the job by the next government; a minister of education subscribing to the directions for reform set by the prior government; a minister of education asking an advisory committee, representing different members of the civil society, to become a regular partner in discussing policy; a ministry of education and the national university community learning to cooperate with each other.
- It is possible to improve the quality of education policy choices by the systematic use of analytic techniques in the identification of problems, the exploration of alternatives, the design of the implementation process, careful control of finances, and the evaluation of outcomes. This analysis has several key characteristics: (1) it must address the particular questions being faced by the policymaker; (2) it must be timely in providing appropriate evidence to bear for making the correct decision; (3) it should be written to be understandable to a non-expect on analysis or research; and (4) it should work within the particular political constraints placed upon the policymaker.

- The impact of policy analysis on decision-making is not linear and takes time. Two years after the Paraguay study was completed and an education reform was underway, HIID was asked to support its implementation. Similarly, in El Salvador, some of the most significant impacts of the assessment are expressed in the fact that, more than a year after the assessment was completed, the advisory committee continued to meet and to plan opportunities to influence education policy; after a number of public fora organized by this committee, the committee was recognized by the education minister as a body to be dealt with seriously in the discussion of education reform.

- An important measure of the impact of technical assistance rests not on the studies and reports produced, but on the capacities developed within public and private institutions to approach the search for policy options. A distinguishing feature of the experiences of the HIID education staff is that they all involved collaborative efforts. What counterparts and observers seem to value most are opportunities to do things differently. These opportunities included developing skills in policy analysis, demonstrating to universities how to conduct research with a policy orientation, and demonstrating to ministries of education how to engage in productive dialogue with NGOs, universities, and advisory committees.

- Communication is a crucial element mediating the impact of policy analysis on actual decisions. Attention to communication involves planning opportunities for the dissemination and discussion of results; it also involves listening to stakeholders at the beginning of the analysis or study. As important as talking, making presentations, and using preliminary drafts and computerized presentations, are efforts to ensure that people understand. It is also important for the analysts to listen at the beginning of the project. If HIID staff had anything to offer in terms of problem identification and resolution it was the ability to identify and/or to help resolve conflicts among multiple perspectives of stakeholders. Extended opportunities for communication, in the form of weekly sessions with advisory committees or with ministers, or in the form of continuous exchanges with counterparts in ministries or in NGOs or universities, were essential to establish rapport and to serve as a foundation for trust; these were key to providing credibility for the recommendations of advisors.

- It is possible to innovate in the field of offering education development advice. The role of the advisor is not cast in stone in the terms of reference or in the contract with the funding agency. Finding space for innovation requires negotiating risk-taking with the sponsor. The decisions to write final reports in the local language, to engage organizations that had been in the political opposition, to rely extensively on local consultants, and to invest extensively in dialogue with key stakeholders to conceptualize the problem from multiple perspectives, all involved a certain amount of risk. For HIID, the greatest risk was to become vulnerable to its clients, sponsors, and stakeholders through its use of new approaches, which meant there could be no assurance about outcomes. The good news is that by taking such risks, HIID learned the lessons shared here.

Notes

1 For more information about such studies in the United Kingdom and the United States, see (respectively) the Central Advisory Council for Education (1967) and Coleman et al. (1966).

2 Davis (1980).

3 Snodgrass and Sen (1979).

4 Warwick (1980)

5 McGinn et al. (1979). A similar kind of shift was anticipated in the HIID analysis of the contribution of education to economic growth in Korea. See McGinn et al. (1980).

6 McGinn et al. (1981); McGinn et al. (1982).

7 For example, in 1992 volume 17, number 2 of the *International Journal of Educational Research* was dedicated to BRIDGES research in Thailand. See also, Raudenbush et al. (1991). Other articles on this subject have been published in *International Journal of Educational Development, Review of Educational Research,* and others.

8 McGinn and Borden (1995); Warwick and Reimers (1996).

9 Publication of *FORUM* was continued at HIID under the Advancing Basic Education and Literacy (ABEL) Project.

10 Lockheed and Verspaor (1991).

11 A review of lessons learned about implementation is reported in Warwick et al. (1992).

12 Reimers (1993a).

13 Reimers (1995).

16 Gender Analysis for Economic Development

Martha A. Chen and Pauline E. Peters

Introduction

The field of women in development, or gender and development (as it is sometimes called) was formally established in 1975, with the official declaration of the United Nations Decade for Women. The early phases of work on women in development were concerned to document women's roles in economic and family management and, in particular, to make visible women's contribution in work within and outside the household. By the end of the decade, there were considerable gains in knowledge about women, some signs of improvement in women's access to education, health services, and new technologies, and growing experience in organizations by and for women. There remained—and still remains—a long way to go before women gain parity with men in fair remuneration for work, access to higher education, rights to land and property, and adequate levels of health and nutrition.

Analytical gains were made throughout the 1970s: there was increased understanding that the differential consequences of development for women were more acutely analyzed through the concept of gender (which privileges the notion of relations between women and men) than through that of women. The increased awareness of differences among women emphasized the need for analysis and policy to develop ways of addressing the variations by age, status, class, and so forth; and the important realization that addressing the effects of development on women required not merely an "add-on"—a section on women-in-development in a project document or a women's office in a government ministry—but also radical rethinking of the ways that research, documentation, analysis, and implementation are conducted.

HIID's work on gender and development issues began in the early 1980s, in the middle of the United Nations Decade for Women. The institute's major contributions to the field have been the development of analytical methods for incorporating a gender dimension into policy research, formulation, and implementation, and into training and teaching activities. The analytical methods have been concerned with women's roles in farming, small enterprise, and natural resource management; with women's needs for social security and education; and with household-based socioeconomic research methods.

In 1980, a group of staff and graduate students from Harvard University and the Massachusetts Institute of Technology (MIT) started the joint Harvard-MIT Women in Development Group, a resource center which HIID has helped to support from its inception. The following year HIID received a grant from the Ford Foundation to establish a position for gender research and training; the position was filled in 1982. Subsequently, other appointments were filled by policy researchers with interest in gender issues. The work on gender issues in economic development carried out at HIID may be divided into research, training and teaching, policy-advising, technical assistance, and program evaluation.

Research

HIID's library and field research has produced publications, teaching, and training materials, and has been linked with activities in policy-advising and technical assistance. The main research themes have been the following:

- gender and household in theory and policy;
- gender in agricultural commercialization;
- gender and access to schooling;
- gender and household coping strategies;
- women and enterprises: a sectoral approach; and
- widows in rural India.

Gender and Household in Theory and Policy

HIID personnel have contributed to the growing literature on "gendering" the household in both research methods and policy analysis. There have been several discrete research projects under this rubric. The first project, carried out in the early 1980s, involved literature reviews that highlighted shortcomings in policy approaches to women in development and indicated more fruitful directions for policy research, formulation, and implementation.[1] In the early attempts to incorporate women's issues, donor organizations, governments, and researchers frequently failed to link women and households. Women—as a topic—tended to be sequestered in a specially defined field, often a bureau or office of women in development, whereas households—as a topic—appeared as units of analysis and action within substantive fields such as rural credit, agricultural development, small-scale enterprise, and nutrition. The literature reviews documented the analytical loss entailed in this separation, and argued that the links between women and households could be achieved through gender analysis. This would enable a rethinking of households and women as analytical categories and as targets for policy research, formulation, and implementation.

A second problem highlighted was the over-reliance on household typologies for addressing differential effects on women. By the early 1980s, several researchers and research organizations had shown (through both national data sources and detailed local studies) that women, on average, had fewer assets and less income than men, and had identified female-headed households as disadvantaged in these respects. This, in turn, led to enormous efforts for disaggregating survey data by gender, to enable both documentation and analysis of these gender-based differences in livelihood and welfare. A further result was the distinction in surveys between female-headed households and male-headed households. And, in parallel, some development projects came to be targeted to female-headed households as a means of reaching disadvantaged women.

While these approaches led to increased documentation of gender-based differences in development outcomes and enabled some targeting of women, they also revealed the analytical shortcomings of the approaches themselves. First, the increased knowledge achieved through data disaggregation led to ever more detailed typologies of households. This created two problems: a proliferation of types makes the distinction of categories for analysis and for policy targeting very difficult; and even the most refined typology is a static framework that is unable to distinguish the processes through which the types of household are produced and change. Secondly, and relatedly, the then prevailing household models for research, analysis, and policy implementation did not allow for intrahousehold differences and processes.

These analytical and methodological dilemmas were addressed during the second phase of HIID's work on gender and household. Field and library research were involved in this effort. They included field research in West Africa, which developed a bargaining model to interpret the kinds of negotiated levels of work and remuneration that husbands and wives engaged in with each other, and which showed the project-level implications of ignoring such intrahousehold transfers.[2]

In addition to the intrahousehold processes that were not captured in prevailing models, the relations between households or interhousehold processes required attention by researchers, projects, and policies. The implications of failing to do so were considered in relation to farming system analysis and to agricultural research and policy in Botswana and, more broadly, in the process of agricultural transformation in Africa.[3]

These research themes were also explored at an international conference on Conceptualizing the Household: Issues of Theory, Method, and Application, held at Harvard in late 1984.[4] The conference addressed the issue of household analysis in sub-Saharan Africa, drawing together a body of scholars and practitioners from Africa, Europe, and the United States. In addition to the conference proceedings,[5] a selection of papers was subsequently published as a special issue of the journal Development and Change.[6] Though the authors of these papers were of various disciplines, all were concerned with a dynamic approach to household analysis. In this perspective, "the concept of 'the household' cannot be assigned invariate characteristics over time and across cultural and social geography," but is seen as "a contributor to, and product of, wider… social processes."[7] The implications of this approach for theory, methodology, and policy were explored in the papers.

Gender in Agricultural Commercialization

The need to incorporate gender analysis into conventional models used in policy research, formation, and implementation is particularly acute today. Agrarian populations are involved in accelerating processes of commercialization, are ever more affected by global economic change, and are striving to cope with the economic recessions and political-economic restructuring of the 1980s and 1990s. HIID has responded by developing research that seeks to document changes over time and to analyze the dynamic processes of agricultural commercialization.

A research project has been developed in Malawi, Central Africa, where the same sample of rural families has been the subject of inquiry at several points in time since 1986.[8,9] One dimension of this research is to document gender relations, the ways in which gender plays into processes of commercialization, and the ways in which these processes affect women and men differently. Some of the findings reinforce earlier themes: for example, the identification of different types of households has led to a clear documentation of significant differences (in terms of assets, income, and welfare) among female-headed households, and of changes in a household's "headship" status over time. Not only does this conclusion suggest caution in defining a single category of female heads for research or action, but it also suggests modification in data collection methods.[10]

The research also investigates the influence of agricultural policies and structural reform programs on patterns of production and income; the question of whether child nutrition varies according to gender differences in income control and decision-making as much as to levels of income; and the issue of rights to and use of land and other resources as these vary for women and men.[11]

Gender and Access to Schooling

Patterns of access to schooling is a component of HIID's large-scale project on Basic Research and Implementation of Development Education Systems (BRIDGES), which is discussed in Chapter 15. HIID project staff investigated the differential access to schooling of girls and boys, especially in Pakistan and Sri Lanka.[12] The results of the research on gender differentials in education took the form of discussion papers and a simulation game (EPICS) used to conduct gender training for education personnel.[13]

Gender and Household Coping Strategies

Rural households, particularly in semi-arid areas, routinely plan for and manage the uncertainties associated with regular seasonal fluctuations and periodic drought-induced crises. The uncertainties pose hardships for the poor who are extremely vulnerable in their ability to respond. A study carried out during the third year of a severe drought in western India examines the range of coping strategies adopted by different types of households, focusing on the differences between seasonal and drought-induced strategies, the sequence and timing of these strategies, and the circumstances that influence the choice of strategies. Two critical dimensions of household coping strategies received particular attention: the significance of women's work and of gender as a basic variable in understanding household behavior; and the centrality of nonmarket resources, relationships, and institutions in the struggle for survival. The study findings explore the spatial and temporal dimensions of the drought, the impact of drought on different occupational groups, and both community and official responses to the crisis.[14]

Women and Natural Resources

The research project, Women and Wasteland Development, funded by the International Labour Organisation (ILO), looked at twenty reforestation projects in eight states of India, covering several different agro-ecological regions. The study traced the origins and development of government policies on reforestation and wasteland development, observing that the government's earlier social forestry programs tended to benefit larger farm households rather than smaller farm (or landless) households, and to promote timber production rather than fuelwood and fodder production. It looked at aspects of the relationship between women, natural resources, and reforestation, and suggested a methodology to enhance the participation of women in reforestation efforts. The study sought to integrate women into a wider analytical framework for promoting wasteland development, arguing that women's participation—including women's knowledge, responsibilities, and rights (both legal and political)—should be seen as integral to the process (indeed to the success) of wasteland development.

The study approach and findings were reported in a paper commissioned and presented as the lead background paper to the National Technical Workshop on Women and Wasteland Development, organized by ILO and held in New Delhi, India, in January 1991. The workshop brought together seventy-five grassroots activists, policymakers, researchers, government officials, and representatives of international and donor agencies to discuss and disseminate different approaches to involving women in wasteland development. The paper has been published in the workshop proceedings.[15]

Women and Enterprises: A Sectoral Approach

With funds from the Ford Foundation, HIID project staff reviewed two pilot-projects in India designed to promote women's work in milk and silk production; drawing on this experience, they wrote a paper detailing a sectoral approach to promoting women's work.[16] The paper argues that a sectoral approach in support of women workers can help to close the gap between the often "invisible" work of women and mainstream macroeconomic planning by increasing the visibility of women within specific subsectors of the economy and by identifying appropriate interventions to address the constraints faced by women in specific subsectors. Mainstream economic programs and policies are typically developed along sectoral lines. That is, critical sectors of the economy are assigned, with significant budget appropriations, to specialized ministries or departments for support and development. Yet women are typically left out of sectoral economic planning because government policymakers do not view women as productive workers. The paper was presented at a symposium on Expanding Income Earning Opportunities for Women in Poverty: A Cross-Regional Dialogue, organized by the Ford Foundation in Nairobi, Kenya, in 1988, and was published, along with other papers presented at that symposium, in a special edition of World Development.

Widows in Rural India

The project on Widows in Rural India, funded by the World Institute of Development Economics Research, the MacArthur Foundation, the Royal Netherlands Government, and the Swedish International Development Authority (SIDA), was designed to understand better the vulnerabilities of different types of widows in rural India and to promote appropriate policy responses by both governmental and nongovernmental organizations (NGOs). Intensive field work was carried out in two villages in each of seven states of India.

The findings suggest five basic sources of the vulnerability of widows: patrilocal residence, patrilineal inheritance, remarriage practices, employment restrictions, and social isolation. The findings have been published.[17]

In March 1994, HIID organized both a national workshop and a conference on Widows in India, to promote better understanding of the social and economic conditions of widows in India. Both events took place at the Indian Institute of Management, Bangalore, India. The informal workshop brought together twenty-five widows from different regions of the country, as well as ten women activists with prior experience of working with widows and other single women. The conference participants included sixty-five activists, scholars, and policymakers who have worked on issues relating to widows.

The purpose of the three-day workshop was to provide opportunities for a group of widows (and organizers of grassroots women's activities) to share problems, exchange experiences, voice demands, and initiate a network of widows and activists concerned with the specific problems of widows. The discussion covered a wide range of issues and concerns raised by the participants, including: changes in women's identity and status with widowhood; taboos regarding the behavior of widows; options, constraints, and choices regarding remarriage; living arrangements and sources of support; struggles by widows to secure their property rights; other actions taken by widows to assert their individual or collective rights; and demands of the widows on society and on the government.

During the three-day conference that followed the workshop, recent evidence was presented on the predicament of widows for the purpose of helping to formulate concrete proposals for policies and action in support of widows. After an opening session that provided a general overview of the economic and social conditions of widows in India, the conference focused on the restrictions and deprivations widows face in the following spheres: inheritance and property; employment and economic opportunities: maintenance and social security; and social identity and relationships. The closing session of the conference opened with a set of recommendations for future action, policy, and research from the participants, and concluded with a charter of demands from the widows who had attended the earlier workshop. The proceedings of the workshop-cum-conference have been published.[18] Another outcome of the two events is a newly-established network of widows and of NGOs working with widows. To keep the network alive and active, a quarterly newsletter, entitled *Widows' Lives*, is being published, and a part-time editor-coordinator has been appointed. The first edition of the newsletter included an illustrated workshop report.

As many as twenty of the NGOs in the newly-established network will soon be engaged in a two-year action-research project to secure pensions and property rights for widows. As planned, each NGO would organize low-income widows (in their respective areas of operation) and would help at least fifty low-income widows to secure pensions and/or property rights and to document the problems encountered in so doing and the steps taken to overcome these problems. The expected outcomes of this follow-up project include: pensions and/or property rights for about one thousand widows; a national association of low-income widows; an expanded and strengthened network of NGOs working with widows; and a set of recommendations for future action and policy in support of widows.

To supplement these efforts at a national policy level in India, HIID faculty have been involved in several initiatives to promote better understanding of the social and economic conditions of widows across the developing world. These include drafting a subsection on widows for the 1995 edition of a United Nations Statistical Bureau publication, entitled *The World's Women 1995: Trends and Statistics*, and writing a background paper on how traditional family and kinship structures treat single women (including widows) for the 1995 edition of the *Human Development Report*, which focused on gender.

Training and Teaching

Gender Training

In 1982, members of the Harvard community, under the auspices of HIID and with funding from the Office for Women in Development of the United States Agency for International Development (USAID), undertook a case study and training project to develop gender training materials. This project resulted in a case-book, entitled *Gender Roles in Development Projects: A Case Book*, which included technical papers, case studies, and a series of training workshops.[19]

The activities undertaken under the case study and training project have had considerable influence in the field of development studies and practice. The case-book has a wide readership, and the analytical framework for gender analysis in development projects has provided a model that numerous agencies and groups worldwide have used. In addition to many agencies using the analytical framework and case method for in-house training, other groups seeking to incorporate gender analysis into development practice have developed and published relevant cases. The attraction of the model developed by Overholt and colleagues is that new cases can be prepared for each agency or group wanting a workshop on gender analysis, and the analytical approach can be adapted to a wide set of sectors and issues in development policy and practice.

HIID's role in sponsoring the case study project was that of the initiator of an activity. The subsequent spread of the methods and materials developed in the project is sufficient testimony to their usefulness to a wide range of people and agencies. However, the framework and materials continue to be referred to as the Harvard approach to gender training. Since that time, HIID has continued to include some gender analysis training in its activities. The concept of gender is given greater prominence than that of women-in-development since it has been found more effective in facilitating the types of analysis required to assess whether and how development activities differentially affect women as compared with men, and certain social categories of women as compared with others.

Workshops have been organized for agencies such as the African Development Bank, and HIID personnel have also developed training courses on gender research and on promoting the micro-enterprises of women (as discussed in Chapter 19).[20]

Gender Courses for University

A different form of training is entailed in university teaching. At Harvard, HIID personnel have developed courses that include the analysis of gender differentiation in development. In the early 1980s, at Harvard there was no connection in teaching between the topics of economic development and those of gender and women. One task taken up by HIID personnel, therefore, was to help develop courses or part courses that would make those connections. The courses developed since that time include both introductory and specialized courses for undergraduates and graduates.

In addition to specific courses on gender, modules on international development have been introduced into courses on gender (such as introduction to women's studies, and gender and inequality) and modules on gender (or gender themes) have been introduced into courses that address international development (such as problems in the analysis of social change and development, environment and environmentalism, and poverty and policy in developing countries).

Policy-Advising, Technical Assistance, and Program Evaluation

Policy-Advising and Technical Assistance

HIID personnel have advised governments and donors on a variety of policy issues from a gender perspective including: evaluating the gender component of national agricultural extension programs; reviewing agricultural policies and programs from a gender perspective; analyzing the differential effects of economic reforms (such as structural adjustment) on women as compared with men or on female-headed households as compared with male-headed or joint households; promoting a subsector approach in support of women entrepreneurs; and promoting policies to secure pensions and property rights for widows.

HIID personnel recently wrote two background papers for the 1995 edition of the *Human Development Report*, and one paper for the United Nations Development Fund for Women (UNIFEM) in preparation for the 1995 World Summit for Social Development and the 1995 Fourth World Conference on Women.[21]

In addition to advising governments and donors on gender-related policy issues, HIID personnel have worked closely with research centers and NGOs in developing countries. HIID's technical assistance to research centers has taken the form of developing research frameworks and methods, including assessment of the appropriate unit of analysis. For example, female-headed households prove in many African countries to be so heterogeneous a category as to obscure key differences; hence, particular types of female-headed households often need to be identified when formulating and implementing projects. HIID's technical assistance to NGOs has taken the form of collaborative research on issues relating to women, training in gender research, and assessing alternative approaches to supporting low-income women (see Chapter 19).

Program Evaluation

Over the years, HIID personnel have engaged in several evaluations of innovative nongovernmental programs targeted primarily or exclusively at low-income women. In addition, HIID staff have conducted evaluations of policy research in several centers in the United States, and served on boards for national and international organizations concerned with environmental policy, agricultural policy, and gender analysis.

THE JOINT HARVARD-MIT WOMEN IN DEVELOPMENT GROUP

Since 1980, HIID has provided space, financial support, and advice to the Harvard-MIT Women in Development Group. This group, managed by graduate students from Harvard and MIT, includes members drawn from the large nonuniversity pool of development interests in the Boston area. The group convenes a speaker series during the academic year, organizes a policy workshop each spring, and publishes a newsletter for graduate students (and others) interested in women in development. The spring policy workshop has focused on such issues as women's work and employment, refugee women, women's reproductive health, and women's rights.

LESSONS LEARNED AND THE WAY FORWARD

Many of the lessons emerging from HIID's work on gender are similar to those in the field of gender and development. First, to develop frameworks for research and policy that will address the differential effects of development on women, one must engage in systematic gender analysis. As Dwight H. Perkins (HIID Director from 1980 to 1995), states: "People working in the field of development have long been concerned with how the benefits of development are distributed. Only recently, however, concern with distributional issues has incorporated differences in income and economic power between men and women. Concern with issues of gender, of course, involves more than how gender affects distribution. Understanding the role played by gender in development can also make a substantial difference as to whether growth-oriented projects succeed or fail. Thus, questions of how men and women define their roles, or have them defined for them, influences all aspects of the development process."[22]

Secondly, HIID's work in research and policy-advising has pointed to the differences among women, differences that are conceptually and methodologically captured by considering the intersection of gender with other social differences (such as age, marital status, caste, and class).

Thirdly, HIID personnel, along with other gender analysts, have directly addressed the need to rethink the conventional models of household, which tend to assume complementarity of interests and/or altruism, and to develop paradigms that include different interests and power, bargaining, and "cooperative conflict."

Fourthly, gender analysts have emphasized that addressing differences and crises within households must be part of an analysis of the place of households within broader social, economic, and political processes. In addition to understanding gender relations in household strategies of livelihood, coping, and survival, gender analysts have to recognize that households cope not only with localized conditions of season, drought, or flood, but also with national forces related to political economic restructuring and the "globalization" of economic life.

Finally, gender analysis is necessary not only to assess the differential effects of policy and other conditions on women as compared with men but also to understand some of the key dynamics in processes of agricultural commercialization and social change more generally. Intrahousehold differences between men and women vis-à-vis land rights, labor allocation, income, and expenditure patterns are as crucial to deciphering how different forms of commercialization take place as they are for assessing the determinants of chronic poverty. Gender analysis is not concerned only with disadvantage but with the fundamental processes of socioeconomic life.

HIID, like other institutions in the United States and elsewhere, has found it easier to undertake specific research, training, and policy-advising projects on gender issues than to integrate gender analysis into all work done at the institute. Also, it has proved easier for HIID personnel, as others have found, to integrate gender analysis into policy research at the household and sectoral levels than at the national level. Nevertheless, current work at HIID continues to seek ways of integrating gender analysis at the several levels of institutions and policy. HIID's future work on gender will continue on the thematic interests discussed above as well as newer themes and will continue to attempt to integrate gender analysis at all levels.

Notes

1 Peters (1983a, 1983b).

2 For a more detailed discussion see Jones (1983, 1986).

3 See Peters (1986) for details relative to farming system analysis and agricultural research and policy in Botswana, and Peters (1988) and Jones (1988) on the process of agricultural transformation in Africa.

4 The conference on Conceptualizing the Household: Issues of Theory, Method, and Application, was organized by Jane Guyer, then at the Department of Anthropology at Harvard University and now at Northwestern University; and by Pauline Peters. It was sponsored by the Social Science Research Council, American Council of Learned Societies (SSRC/ACLS) and funded by the Rockefeller Foundation, the Ford Foundation, and the United Nations International Children's Emergency Fund (UNICEF). For conference proceedings, see Guyer and Peters (1986).

5 Guyer and Peters (1986).

6 Guyer and Peters (1987).

7 Guyer and Peters (1987, p. 198).

8 See Peters et al. (1989) and Peters (1992).

9 The research project in Malawi, Central Africa, has been funded by the United States Agency for International Development (USAID) and by the World Bank.

10 See Peters et al. (1989) and Peters (1992).

11 For discussion of these issues see Kennedy and Peters (1992); Peters and Herrera (1994); and Kennedy et al. (1994).

12 Anderson (1988, 1989).

13 Brown et al. (1989).

14 This study in discussed in detail in Chen (1991).

15 Chen (1993).

16 Chen (1989a); see also Chen (1989b, 1989c).

17 Chen and Dreze (1995).

18 A report on the conference appears in Chen (1995b).

19 Chen (1994, 1995a) and Overholt et al. (1985).

20 This activity was funded by the Aga Khan Foundation Canada and the United Nations Development Fund for Women (UNIFEM).

21 Chen (1994, 1995a).

22 See Overholt et al. (1985, Foreword).

Part V

Research, Capacity Building, and New Initiatives

Through collaborative research, HIID has worked to help strengthen research institutes in a number of developing countries. In Singapore, Vietnam, and Bolivia, HIID has also worked with local universities to design and implement new graduate programs in public policy.

17 Policy Research Institutes

Donald R. Snodgrass[1]

Introduction

Research institutes in developing countries can significantly improve development policy. Successful institutes operate with independence and integrity to do high-quality work on important policy issues, thereby informing policymakers and enriching public debate. Their potential can best be realized when the relationship to government is right, the quality of work is high, and a judicious balance is struck between response to short-term requests and conduct of long-term research. Establishing a good research institute, however, is no easy task. Maintaining viability, influence, quality, and intellectual zest over the longer term is harder still.

The potential of research institutes in developing countries can be enhanced by international cooperation. HIID has assisted in the establishment and development of institutes in: Indonesia (Center for Policy and Implementation Studies, or CPIS, 1982–1992); Thailand (Thailand Development Research Institute, or TDRI, 1985–1991); and Bolivia (Unidad de Analisis de Politicas Economicas, or UDAPE, and Unidad de Analisis de Politicas Sociales, or UDAPSO, 1987–present). It has also collaborated with longer-established research institutes to carry out specific studies in: Korea (Korea Development Institute, or KDI, 1987–present, following earlier cooperation); Malaysia (Institute of Strategic and International Studies, or ISIS, 1992–present); and Taiwan (Chung-Hua Institute for Economic Research, CIER, 1992–present). This chapter summarizes and discusses these experiences, then concludes by weighing the lessons that emerge.

INDONESIA: THE CENTER FOR POLICY AND IMPLEMENTATION STUDIES (CPIS)

From 1979 to 1982, HIID cooperated with five Indonesian universities to carry out the Development Policy Implementation Studies (DPIS). This project examined four mass-oriented development programs intended to spread the benefits of the growing prosperity that Indonesia enjoyed in the 1970s among the population: rice intensification, family planning, primary school expansion, and the decentralized village public works program. Work on the rice intensification program, especially its credit component, offered preliminary evidence that multidisciplinary studies based on a combination of national, regional, and local data could yield useful results. In 1982, HIID was asked to help institutionalize the capacity to do multidisciplinary policy research through the establishment of a permanent policy research center. The new project added training and institution building to the research and policy advising work already taking place.

In its early years, CPIS hired Indonesian researchers from various disciplinary backgrounds and provided them with training, both in-house and overseas. The in-house training covered research methodology, computer use, and English. Adequate performance in the in-house courses was a prerequisite to selection for overseas post-graduate training. Staff training was accompanied by institutionalization. In the beginning, HIID provided day-to-day management of CPIS under the guidance of Indonesian officials. A full-time director was appointed in January 1986, and in November of that year the center moved from the Ministry of Finance to its own offices in central Jakarta. In January 1987, CPIS assumed the legal identity of a foundation (*yayasan*). The principal government economists to whom CPIS had been reporting became the board members of the foundation.

By 1991, the research staff had expanded to fifty members. Most of those who studied abroad had returned by this time. As a result of training and on-the-job experience, the center's Indonesian staff now had considerably greater competence in several relevant disciplines. Senior staff members began to take responsible roles in the work of the center. Some also began to participate in regional and international forums focusing on development issues.

From 1983 to 1992, the HIID project in CPIS worked on a diverse set of topics of interest to the Indonesian Government: local banking, rice cultivation, insecticide policy, tree crops, urban informal sector labor, higher education, public health, capital markets, and the implementation of deregulation in trade and industry. All topics except the last two concerned issues in which research and advising necessarily involved several disciplines, since the problems addressed were too complex to be solved by the tools of any one discipline.

The two CPIS projects generally considered most valuable to the Indonesian Government—local banking and insecticide policy—illustrate how the multidisciplinary approach of CPIS worked at its best.

Local Banking

As part of the massive rice intensification program begun in 1970, about 3,600 banking units were set up by the state-owned Bank Rakyat Indonesia (BRI) to provide subsidized credit (known as BIMAS) throughout the country. Despite the relative effectiveness of this rural banking network, the DPIS found that by the early 1980s the credit program was nearing collapse. As in other countries, the low-cost (and therefore desirable) credit had created opportunities for local corruption, with the result that the subsidies often bypassed those for whom they were intended. Participation in the program was declining and cumulative losses and arrears were high. The DPIS report on rice intensification recommended that BIMAS credit be phased out and suggested that the BRI's banking network be used to implement a better-designed credit program.

The work of formulating a general rural credit program (KUPEDES) to be implemented through the village units of BRI was completed during the early months of the CPIS project. Following an anthropological survey of rural credit needs and practices, the features of the new program and its financial implications were worked out. The design involved charging a rate of interest far higher than had been imposed in earlier subsidized rural credit programs, yet far lower than many farmers were paying to moneylenders from whom they were forced to borrow. With a relatively small initial subsidy, it was expected that the volume of lending in existing programs that would be absorbed by KUPEDES could be doubled, bringing the program into the black after just eighteen months of operation. This prospect was sufficiently appealing that the necessary approvals were obtained.

KUPEDES proved a great success, expanding rapidly and maintaining a high repayment rate. CPIS worked with BRI to implement the new program, helping with reform of its accounting system, staff training, and monitoring and supervisory procedures.

Soon after KUPEDES began, CPIS launched a series of studies on rural savings. These concluded that, contrary to widespread belief, there was a large potential to collect savings through the BRI village units, provided that customers were offered a safe, convenient place to deposit their funds, a reasonable rate of return, and access to their money on demand, conditions not previously available at the local level. By 1985, BRI had initiated a pilot rural savings scheme consisting of four savings instruments offering different rates of liquidity and returns, with SIMPEDES, a fully liquid instrument, as the flagship of the new program. Like KUPEDES, the new program grew rapidly and generated large sums for BRI's use. Rural banking, including both KUPEDES and SIMPEDES, emerged as the bank's leading profit center.

In 1987, the management of CPIS decided that it could no longer provide free technical assistance to BRI and wanted to move on to other things. Accordingly, most of HIID's advisory work for BRI was transferred to a new project based in BRI.

The Rice Seed/Insecticide Project

The DPIS rice intensification report reviewed a series of crop failures from the mid-1970s to the early 1980s that were caused by the brown planthopper (*Nilaparvata lugens Stal*). It also called attention to the rapid loss of diversity in Indonesia's rice gene pool that had occurred since 1970, and recommended that the issue be further investigated. A later study by CPIS documented the decline in diversity and noted scientific findings in a number of countries that nonselective use of certain kinds of insecticides results in the rapid emergence of new biotypes of insecticide-resistant brown planthopper, as well as in the death of the natural enemies of the brown planthopper (for example, spiders and frogs).

As each new biotype of the brown planthopper developed, only the few rice varieties that were resistant to that biotype could be planted. The need to protect against crop devastation resulted in massive erosion of Indonesia's rice gene pool. The combination of increasing genetic uniformity and continued use of resurgence-causing insecticides brought Indonesia to a crisis by 1986, when the worst outbreak occurred. This led the government to accept a CPIS recommendation to adopt a new pest control policy. A Presidential Decree banned the use on rice of fifty-seven varieties of insecticides and began a national policy of integrated pest management. (The subject of Integrated Pest Management is discussed in more detail in Chapter 3). Later work consisted largely of training for farmers and extension workers.

Thailand: The Thailand Development Research Institute (TDRI)

TDRI was founded in 1984 as a private foundation, established under a special law passed by the Thai Parliament. It is a large institute with research programs on macroeconomic policy, sectoral economics, international trade, natural resources and the environment, science and technology, and human resources and social development. In 1985, HIID was asked to assist TDRI during its formative years by advising on research designs and institutional planning. The early years of the project were devoted to defining major areas of research, planning research activities, developing institutional capacity, and establishing a research network and linkages with research institutes abroad. In time, a far-reaching program of research collaboration emerged. A large number of studies was undertaken by HIID consultants working with Thai researchers. Substantial analyses completed before the project ended in 1991 include: studies of tax and tariff reform, effective rates of protection, Thailand's competitiveness in the international economy, technological capacity in industry, natural resource management, land reform policy, household savings behavior, options for increasing secondary school enrollment, morbidity and demand for health care, repricing and privatization of family planning services, rural industries and employment, and the prospective economic cost of AIDS in Thailand. HIID also helped TDRI to prepare concept papers, plans, and proposals for an expanded publications program and an integrated database. Meanwhile, TDRI responded to short-turnaround government requests for help on issues as diverse as trade negotiations with the European Community, the introduction of a value added tax, a proposal to offer free health care to all children under five, the design of an earnings survey, the evaluation of government revenue assumptions, and the adequacy of a proposed education reform.

TDRI has senior government technocrats on its board of directors. At the operational level, this involves middle-level government officials on ad hoc research teams for particular projects. These teams set the agenda, plan and participate in the work, and write up and disseminate the results. Participation in TDRI project teams provides technocrats with hands-on training in policy research and gives them a strong sense of ownership of the results. This helps to focus the agenda, improve the research, build networks, and increase the likelihood that policy recommendations will be implemented.

TDRI has also come to be seen by the government as an arbiter of data quality on contentious policy issues. It serves as an "honest broker" and "neutral site" for resolution of policy disagreements on critical issues—for example, whether to construct a new hydroelectric dam or a fertilizer factory—and for building consensus on development policy. This function is recognized as useful by policymakers.

Since its founding, TDRI has survived cabinet and party changes, a military coup, two interim governments, and the restoration of civilian rule. It has remained close to succeeding governments through changes in its board of directors and the continuing involvement of government technocrats on ad hoc project committees. As governments changed, some TDRI researchers, because of their networks, became more influential, while others became less so. The overall influence of the institution has remained high throughout.

Bolivia: Unidad de Analisis de Politicas Economicas (UDAPE) and Unidad de Analisis de Politicas Sociales (UDAPSO)

In the aftermath of economic stabilization in the early 1980s, the Government of Bolivia needed to monitor the country's macroeconomy and required technical advice to do so. UDAPE was created as a government agency in 1984 with USAID funding, and in 1985 HIID won a contract to provide UDAPE with technical assistance on macroeconomic management. UDAPE was ideally placed to oversee the macroeconomic management of the country. During 1985, top officials of UDAPE had taken part in the discussions that brought about stabilization; they knew the background and context of hyperinflation, had macroeconomic information, and understood the rationale of the government's stabilization policy. Top government officials had thus been exposed to UDAPE's analytical strengths. With the achievement of macroeconomic stability, UDAPE became the watchdog of the country's economy.

Starting in 1987, HIID provided UDAPE with technical assistance in macroeconomic management and planning. Much of its early work focused on building economic models that would promote systematic thinking about economy-wide topics. During 1987–1990, UDAPE developed and used social accounting matrixes and computable general equilibrium models to evaluate the effect of large-scale investment projects on the national economy, measure the stabilization program's impact on small holders, gauge the macroeconomic effect of coca eradication, and estimate the respective impacts on tax revenues and trade of uniform and differentiated tariff structures.

Besides carrying out such analyses, UDAPE monitored national macroeconomic indicators, collected and synthesized information on various aspects of the economy, disseminated the information widely to national and international users, evaluated proposals of the International Monetary Fund (IMF), and became a leading player in negotiations with the IMF. UDAPE became a mandatory pit-stop for international delegations visiting Bolivia.

As UDAPE strengthened its expertise in the management of the macroeconomy and information collection, and as other institutions took over its former tasks, it increasingly emphasized educating the public, opposition leaders, and policymakers about the need for economic growth after stabilization. Through large conferences for the public and government officials held in 1989 and 1991, UDAPE brought international scholars to La Paz to discuss the need to invest in human capital and agriculture and to undertake sectoral reforms. Later UDAPE helped the government to strengthen and modernize Bolivia's agricultural research system, labor laws, customs administration, corporate taxes, and banking regulations. It also monitored and evaluated the economy-wide effects of all the reforms the government was trying to bring about.

UDAPE developed the first social strategy for Bolivia, which placed human capital at the center and stressed a focused approach to the alleviation of poverty. But UDAPE lacked the expertise and resources to do in-depth research on policies for reforming education and health. To fill this gap, in 1992 the government created UDAPSO as a parallel think tank to UDAPE, specializing in human capital and the social sectors. HIID provided short-term consultants, and in 1994 it was able to place a resident advisor in UDAPSO.

Like UDAPE, UDAPSO collects, synthesizes, analyzes, and disseminates information to a broad audience. So far, UDAPSO has monitored and evaluated the reform of primary education, planned a strategy for reforming the delivery of health services, analyzed the costs and inefficiencies of university education, collaborated with the World Bank on a study of the socioeconomic determinants of poverty, and evaluated and monitored public investments in early childhood education.

In its short lifespan, UDAPSO has greatly strengthened the government's ability to analyze and formulate public policy in the social sectors. By conducting studies on gender, UDAPSO gave the topic political saliency and legitimacy. Through studies of higher education, it became a broker in a technical dialogue between the government and public universities over public support for institutions of higher learning. UDAPSO's work led to the creation of two new positions: Undersecretary for Gender Affairs, and Undersecretary for Higher Education.

UDAPSO became a technical counterpart for public and private institutions. It trained a small cadre of young economists and retained them by making the analysis of social policy attractive to them. It added a fresh focus to social issues by stressing the demand for social services by households, rather than solely emphasizing supply.

Besides supplying many short-term consultants to assist with these studies, HIID has also provided in-house training through short courses.

Research Collaboration in Korea, Malaysia, and Taiwan

The Korea Development Institute (KDI)

Following its establishment in 1971, KDI became a model for research institutes established in many other developing countries. In 1972–1975, Harvard assisted the development of KDI as an institution by providing consultants on individual research projects and by aiding in the recruitment and training of research staff. Later, KDI and HIID collaborated on a landmark ten-volume series, *Studies in the Modernization of the Republic of Korea: 1945–1975* (Council on East Asian Studies, Harvard University, 1979–1986).

During 1990–1995, a three-volume follow-up study was carried out, organized around three central issues. First, the political economy of Korea's macroeconomic policy was examined by constructing an analytical history of the past two decades. Combining in-depth interviews of key policymakers with more traditional forms of economic and political analysis, the study examined why specific policies were chosen, implemented, or abandoned. Second, Korea's pursuit of industrial policies, especially the targeting of heavy and chemical industries in the 1970s, remains controversial. This topic was studied by combining industry studies with several analytical frameworks for judging the consequences of industry targeting. Third, Korea's economic success is well established; less well understood are the reasons for widespread popular dissatisfaction with economic conditions. This study documents the consequences of rapid economic growth for the Korean people, especially Korean labor, and examines the sources of economic discontent.

The Institute of Strategic and International Studies (ISIS)

More than a decade after the conclusion of a long period of Harvard advisory and training work in Malaysia (1966–1981), HIID agreed in 1992 to collaborate with ISIS, Malaysia, on a three-volume set of studies on Malaysian economic development. The books deal, respectively, with the management of economic development in an ethnically diverse society, with industrialization and structural change, and with natural resources and the environment. These topics were chosen to highlight critical differences between the Malaysian example of rapid economic development and the better-known Northeast Asian cases such as Japan, Taiwan, and Korea, differences that may make Malaysia a better source of lessons for other developing countries. The studies concentrate on development since 1970, and also try to identify emerging problems and opportunities. All the studies are being written jointly with Malaysian collaborators.

The Chung-Hua Institute for Economic Research (CIER)

In 1992 HIID, in collaboration with CIER of Taipei, undertook a research project intended to produce five volumes on Taiwan's economic development experience. These books will review the past five decades of development in Taiwan and will attempt to draw lessons from that historical experience for the future. Research is underway on four topics: (1) the evolution of the labor market; (2) the changing structure of Taiwan's industry, with special emphasis on the role of small- and medium-scale firms; (3) the historical development and future prospects of Taiwan's fiscal system; and (4) the role of the state in the management of Taiwan's economy, with special emphasis on its role in macroeconomic management and industrial policy.

Discussion

What can be learned from HIID's experience regarding the role of policy research institutes in developing countries and the role of international assistance in helping them to realize their potentials?

Although no single case perfectly fits this paradigm, HIID's involvement in policy research institutes can be conceptualized as involving the second and third phases in a three-phase technical assistance sequence. During the first phase, HIID (or in earlier cases, its predecessor, the Harvard Development Advisory Service, or DAS) advises official agencies on economic planning and policy, sometimes working in sectoral ministries or other government bodies as well and usually engaging actively in staff development processes. This activity, if successful, tends to be time-limited, since local officials eventually acquire the ability to do many of the things that could only be performed by foreign advisors in the beginning. Thus, traditional advisory teams tend to "work themselves out of a job." Advisory projects typically come to a natural end after a few years, although some have ended prematurely and others continue to function after their original task has been fulfilled (or linger on because something has prevented the intended buildup of local capacity).

The learning of important analytical techniques and the academic training of a number of local people does not, however, exhaust a developing country's need for technical assistance in development policymaking. Even after key policymakers and their senior staff have attained a high level of sophistication, the ability to generate the information upon which rational strategic and tactical decisions can be based is likely to be lacking or very limited. Key policymakers and technocrats lack the time to do policy research themselves, even if they have the ability. Yet their increased sophistication boosts the demand for applicable research results. Reliable, unbiased, and often highly specific information is typically needed, about relevant local conditions, about comparative experience in other countries, and about the workings of the international system. A logical next step in the technical assistance process, therefore, is the establishment of a policy research institute that can generate and package the kinds of information that the policymakers need, both to inform them about their policy options and to provide them with "ammunition" that can be used in political debate over development policy. In the more open and democratic countries, the desire to inform and mobilize public opinion is often an additional important objective.

During this second phase of technical assistance, the nascent policy research institute must work to achieve two interrelated but distinct goals. The first goal is to provide policymakers with the kinds of information just described in relation to the wide range of development policy decisions that they face presently, as well as those that are likely to arise in the future. The second goal is to create the capacity to supply policymakers and the public with a steady flow of policy-relevant information in the future. During the second phase, HIID typically contributes both to the direct provision of research results and to the creation of policy research capacity.

The projects in Indonesia, Thailand, and Bolivia described above are second-stage technical assistance projects. KDI in Korea passed through this stage during the period of DAS assistance that occurred in the early 1970s. In all cases, Harvard was involved both in planning and in carrying out specific policy studies and in helping in various ways to develop the research institution. The precise nature of HIID's role varied across countries and usually diminished over time in inverse proportion to the growth of local capacity. The formation and early years of CPIS, when HIID consultants drew up plans for the new center, planned and carried out all the major studies undertaken by CPIS, trained the newly-hired Indonesian research staff and even met the payroll and provided CPIS with day-to-day management, represent the deepest extent of HIID involvement. Such a situation did not exist for long. In Korea and in Thailand, where large numbers of trained and experienced local researchers were available (in some cases through recruitment among nationals working or studying abroad), HIID's role was more limited from the start. In all four countries, HIID was heavily involved in providing leadership for the actual conduct of policy studies. Its contributions to capacity building in these countries involved such diverse matters as: critiquing local research designs and completed studies; demonstrating improved research methodologies; advising on staff recruiting; providing on-the-job training; assisting with overseas training; helping with libraries, computer systems and publications; and advising on private fund-raising.

The third stage in the technical assistance process arises because in a successful project local researchers gradually acquire many of the skills that HIID consultants have been providing. In this third stage, management of the research institute passes entirely into local hands and many of the policy studies undertaken are designed and conducted entirely by local researchers. Research institutes that have reached this stage—like KDI in Korea, TDRI in Thailand, and ISIS in Malaysia—may, however, invite HIID to join them in collaborative research on specific studies. Their motives for doing so often involve the acquisition of high-level skills, substantial prior experience, and access to comparative international information. Another common motivation is the desire to associate a relatively new local research institution with a prestigious foreign university, often to lend added legitimacy to studies that document national development achievements (as in both rounds of studies in Korea and HIID's research collaborations in Taiwan and Malaysia). This is a mutually beneficial opportunity, since HIID in turn acquires access to local information and experience that can be combined with expertise from HIID and elsewhere to produce high-quality, well-grounded analyses.

What has been described as HIID's stage-three involvement with a research institute can occur as a follow-on to earlier stage-two involvement (as with KDI in Korea), or it can take place with institutes in whose earlier development HIID took no part (as with ISIS in Malaysia and CIER in Taiwan).

All the HIID involvement with policy research institutes discussed above, with the exception of the two Bolivia projects, took place in Asia, the continent in which HIID was most active in 1980–1995 and also the one that had most of the world's most rapidly developing countries over those years. In Africa, the most severely lagging continent, technical assistance is still mostly in the initial phase. HIID has recently begun to work closely with African researchers, but not yet with African research institutes.

Helping policy research institutes to get started and then to develop a capacity both to support the policymaking process effectively and to sustain themselves through time as political administrations and other important circumstances change is not easy, as noted at the start of this chapter. Some of the larger issues that characteristically arise are discussed below.

Political Support versus the Need for Independence

A successful policy research institute must maintain a delicate balance in its relationship to the government, including both the bureaucrats and the current political leaders. On the one hand, it needs to be close enough to the government to be trusted with sensitive information and to have its research conclusions and policy recommendations accepted in good faith as objective findings. On the other, it must be far enough removed from political control to permit independent judgments to be reached, even when they are critical of current government policies and practices. Insightful political leaders appreciate the need for this kind of independence, but even they may worry about whether research findings produced by the institute will be used against them by their political enemies. In many countries, competing political parties and factions, private industries and labor unions, among others, maintain their own think tanks that turn out research to serve the political needs of the faction. In others, a larger measure of political independence is prized as a means of promoting dialogue across a range of social groups.

HIID has preferred to work with research institutes that are independent of any particular political party, government, or ideological point of view, and are committed to high standards of objectivity with the goal of informing policy choice, rather than of advocating particular choices. Only by establishing its independence from particular parties and ideologies can a research institute hope to survive future political changes, as it must if time is to be gained for the process of capacity development to work itself out.

Leadership and Staffing

Identifying and retaining individuals with the personality, training, and experience required to staff and lead a research institute successfully is usually a challenging task. In countries with relatively low levels of human resource development, the supply of such people is desperately limited. A well-known Indonesian economist who was approached about becoming director of CPIS replied that he already had eight full-time jobs. Often in these circumstances, senior staff members of the institute put in limited hours and effort because of their heavy competing responsibilities that detract significantly from the quality of their work for the institute. On the other hand, countries in which the supply of trained people has been successfully expanded tend to have booming economies with strong demand for these high-level skills. Thus, one of the studies undertaken in Thailand, with HIID collaboration, boasted ten Thai economists with Ph.D. degrees on the staff, but the strongest members of this group were too heavily engaged in other activities to contribute significantly to the study. In countries with a booming private sector, those with Ph.D. degrees, while having excellent potential as researchers, are frequently drawn into business-related activities by the lure of incomes far higher than the research institute can afford to pay (even if the institute salaries are not tied to the government salary and benefit scales, as some are). Labor market competition can generate a high turnover rate in the research institute's staff, and this in turn can have severe consequences for the development of institutional capacity. Technical assistance cannot fully or indefinitely substitute for qualified local research personnel.

Type of Research: Short-Term versus Long-Term; Basic versus Applied

Research institutes are intended to do policy research in considerably greater depth than is involved in the relatively cursory inquiries and rough calculations routinely undertaken by staff members of government agencies. Many individual researchers also seek academic respectability, and for this reason want to do studies of a more high-tech and "basic" nature. Yet political and official support for a research institute generally depends on its immediate usefulness as perceived by government officials. An institute that is seen as unresponsive to the short-term needs of policymakers will not be influential, or perhaps even survive, for long. These conflicting criteria can create ambiguity and tension within the institute. One extreme to be avoided is excessive, or even sole, dedication to short-term "fire-fighting" on behalf of particular politicians or government agencies. This practice can undermine genuine research and provoke some of the most talented researchers on the institute's staff to seek employment elsewhere. At the other extreme, an institute that allows the personal preferences of its staff members or their notions of academic merit to lead it into a research program that bears little relationship to the needs of policymakers risks losing its political support. Faced by the need to avoid both these extremes, directors of research institutes may be uncertain about the appropriate criteria for judging the quality of work done by their staff. In one case, for example, an HIID consultant was asked by the director of the institute for which he was working to provide an independent evaluation of a policy study done by another HIID consultant. The evaluation criterion suggested was how good a professional journal the paper could be published in.

The solution to this type of dilemma is a judiciously balanced portfolio of short- and long-term studies. The best institutes are sometimes able to identify, and initiate work on, important issues with which policymakers will have to grapple in the future, even before the policymakers themselves are aware of the significance of these issues.

Institutional Viability

Maintaining the vitality and viability of a policy research institute in a developing country over the long run is even more difficult than establishing the institute and building up its initial capacity. The potential for loss of political and financial support is usually present. The political administration that created the institute may be replaced by another that holds the institute in lower regard, or may even consider it a threat. If foreign financial assistance was involved in the institute's creation and early-stage development, withdrawal of that aid may provoke a crisis. Some institutes have been able to attract adequate local funding, from either official or private sources, while others have not. Heavy reliance on foreign aid can have the perverse effect of dulling the government's incentives to pay for the institutions or diversify their funding once foreign aid ends. A successful research institute must find ways to demonstrate its social worth repeatedly, in different ways and to different people.

Conclusions

Collaboration with research institutes in developing countries has proven to be a logical follow-on to direct technical assistance to government planners and policymakers, as well as a mutually beneficial activity for HIID and the institutes involved. In several cases, HIID has been able to help research institutes to carry out objective research that is responsive to the near-term concerns of policymakers yet focused on medium- and longer-term issues important for future social and economic development. In a subset of these cases, assistance has also been provided on the complex and challenging matter of building and sustaining an effective research institute. The principal benefit of this activity to HIID has been access to local information and collaborators, resulting in recognized research products like the ten-volume study of Korean modernization and the more recent and forthcoming works on Korea, Taiwan, and Malaysia.

With the decline in demand for direct government advisory services in most Asian and Latin American countries, collaboration with local research institutes appears a logical next step; HIID seems likely to seek more relationships of this type in the future, of either the "second-stage" or "third-stage" variety. Increasing involvement with research institutes in Africa is also likely. In most African cases, a strong effort at capacity building will be required.

NOTES

1 Based in part on conference papers by Manuel Contreras and Ricardo A. Godoy; by Charles N. Myers; and by Marguerite S. Robinson.

18 Teaching, Training, and Public Policy Programs

Mary E. Hilderbrand and John W. Thomas[1]

Introduction

Strengthening public policymaking and public management in developing countries has been one of HIID's primary missions and an essential complement to its work in providing technical and policy advice. Education and training have been central to the Institute's efforts and contributions in this priority area. The first educational initiative of HIID and its predecessor, the Development Advisory Service (DAS), was the Public Service Program in Economic Development, founded in 1957, even before the organization of DAS. Subsequently renamed the Edward S. Mason Program in Public Policy and Management, the Mason Fellows Program has continued to be an essential activity of HIID, training a select group of developing country officials for leadership in development. More recent efforts, including placing foreign officials in other graduate programs in the United States, offering intensive summer workshops in Cambridge, and building educational institutions in other countries, all represent a continuation of this concern to strengthen public policy and management through education and training. These activities were expanded during the 1980s.

Recognizing that building management and policy capacity depends not only on the development of human resources but also on their effective use within public organizations, HIID has also been involved in projects that paired public management training with advice on strengthening organizations and institutions. In addition, by carrying out research on capacity in the public sector, HIID has taken an active part in the recent and continuing discussion within the development assistance community about how to be more effective at supporting capacity-building efforts in developing countries.

Increased linkages with Harvard's John F. Kennedy School of Government have strengthened HIID's involvement in training and public management. Although some ties had existed previously, HIID's move to a building site adjoining the Kennedy School in the early 1980s focused attention on the institute's commitment to training development professionals. Thereafter, HIID faculty became the principal development faculty for the Kennedy School. In the process, some HIID professionals became immersed in helping the Kennedy School build a professional school for public officials. This has provided a solid base at Harvard for developing public policy and other professional development training programs and for working with issues of public management in developing countries.

The activities reviewed in this chapter have had training of public officials and strengthening of public management as a central goal. Some, including the Mason Fellows Program and the establishment of public policy programs, have been independent of specific technical advisory projects. In others, most notably the HIID Training Office and the Indonesia State Bank Training project, the training activities have developed out of (or have been linked to) advisory projects and have made an important contribution to the impact of those projects.

The Mason Fellows Program

The Mason Fellows Program has as its mission to prepare public officials from developing and newly industrialized countries for critical leadership roles in policymaking and management. With many former Mason Fellows working as implementers of reform programs, the program contributes to the sustainability of economic reforms that HIID supports through its advisory projects. In addition, its alumni create important linkages between Harvard and the developing world.

While the Mason Fellows Program is one of HIID's longest-standing programs, it has undergone substantial evolution over the years. The period since 1980 has been one of expansion, both in professional and geographical representation and in numbers. In the early days, Public Service Fellows were recruited out of the DAS/HIID projects overseas or through the international contacts of the Ford Foundation. At the time, HIID staff were economists; most Mason

Fellow nominees therefore emerged from a pool of young economists. Fellows came to Harvard for a year to study economics: some earned degrees; others did not. The first class, in 1957–1958, had eight participants from Burma, India, Indonesia, and Pakistan. By 1971–1972 there were twenty students from Africa, Asia, and Latin America. Class size remained around twenty five during the 1970s.

Beginning in the early 1980s, two major changes occurred. HIID's location near the Kennedy School resulted in greater coordination concerning the Mason Fellows Program. Since then, Mason Fellows have gone through the regular mid-career admission process and the program director has had a joint appointment rather than an exclusive one with HIID. Then, during the 1981–1982 academic year, the decision was made that all students from developing countries participating in the mid-career program were to be Mason Fellows. As a result, the size of the Mason Program doubled to fifty fellows each year. By 1987, the number had increased to sixty.

As HIID became multidisciplinary, recruiting for the Mason Fellows Program broadened from planning commissions to operating ministries, nongovernmental organizations (NGOs), and even the private sector. The program came to represent a wide spectrum of disciplines, including, besides economics, other social sciences, law, engineering, transportation, journalism, public health, foreign affairs, tax policy, agriculture, and business and government. Since 1990, the highest numbers of Mason Fellows have come from the foreign affairs, economic, and financial/budgetary sectors. There is regular participation also from the areas of education, media, military/police, and science and technology.

Mason Fellows come from an average of thirty countries each year. Over the period 1980–1995, the largest proportion of Mason Fellows was from Asia, with Latin America second, and Africa third. Since the 1990s there have also been Fellows from Eastern Europe and South Africa. The current regional target for recruiting is Africa, but inadequate funding limits the number of African candidates able to attend. A special area of concern to the Mason Fellows Program is the participation of women. The percentage of women in each class has ranged from a low of 18 percent to a high of 33 percent over 1980–1995. Increasing African and women participants remains a priority.

HIID professionals work with the Mason Fellows in many ways: through increased recruiting, by teaching many courses the Fellows take at Harvard, and by providing them with academic counseling. The

Mason Fellows Program has targeted the highly talented. Predictably, many former Mason Fellows have become national leaders, including several heads of states, numerous cabinet members, and professionals in many different leadership roles. With more than eleven hundred graduates from ninety countries, the Mason Fellows Program has made an important contribution to leadership world wide.

Summer Workshops

HIID has trained a substantial number of developing country officials through short, intensive nondegree workshops in Cambridge each summer. The origins of these workshops can be traced to the mid-1970s, with the beginning of the Public Enterprise Workshop (now the Program on Global Reform and the Privatization of Public Enterprises). Since the mid-1980s HIID's efforts in the design and implementation of these programs have grown into a major activity. The number of workshops offered in Cambridge has now increased to eleven annually, with many being offered in slightly revised form overseas. The topics range from macroeconomic policy to fiscal decentralization and leadership in development. Current workshops are

BOX 18-1

HIID Summer Workshops in Cambridge, 1997

Environmental Economics and Policy Analysis Workshop

Program on Financial Institutions for Private Enterprise Development

Program on Fiscal Decentralization and Financial Management of Regional and Local Governments

Program on Global Reform and Privatization of Public Enterprises

Program on Investment Appraisal and Management

Program on Macroeconomic Policy and Management

Program on Tax Analysis and Revenue Forecasting

The Global Social Security Crisis Workshop (A Joint EDI-HIID Workshop on Pension Reform)

Workshop on Budgeting in the Public Sector

Workshop on Educational Policy Analysis and Planning

Executive Program for Leaders in Development (HIID-Kennedy School of Government Joint Program)

listed in Box 18-1. In 1996, nearly 350 people attended the Cambridge workshops.

These intensive programs have originated mostly because of the experience of an HIID advisor in the field who recognized a generalized need for a particular kind of skill and took action to address that need. The Public Enterprise/Privatization Program, for example, was begun in the wake of an advisor's work in Pakistan and his identification of managerial and economic policy weaknesses that hindered the effectiveness of public enterprises. Similarly, the formation of the Program on Investment Appraisal and Management (PIAM) can be traced to the strong demand for a course on project appraisal under an HIID project in Malaysia and the recognition of deficiencies in investment appraisal in many governments. The Public Sector Budgeting Workshop and the Agricultural Policy Workshop both developed out of projects in Kenya and were initially held in Kenya as African regional workshops. The workshop on Banking and Monetary Policy was initiated as a forum for the trainees under the Indonesia State Bank Training project (discussed below) and was quickly broadened to include participants from other countries as well.

There have been some valuable spin-offs from the workshops. HIID faculty have been able to fund graduate students to develop workshop materials, thus strengthening both the human resource base in these areas and the availability and quality of teaching materials, such as case studies. Strong linkages have been established between research and writing through the workshops and more general research projects, and many publications have resulted from these linkages.

Indonesia Projects and the HIID Training Office

HIID's involvement in Indonesia's economic and financial reforms through the provision of policy advice is discussed in Chapter 3. Training played a large part in several of the Indonesia projects, as part of an effort to build Indonesian capacity to carry out and sustain the reforms. These capacity-building efforts were not only important to the success of the reforms in Indonesia but also marked a new emphasis on training for HIID in the 1980s and the formation of HIID's Training Office. The projects in Indonesia, begun in 1981, were by far the largest training activity for HIID. The work under these projects was linked to the financial and fiscal reforms and primarily involved collaboration with the Ministry of Finance. Joint work continued under the State Bank Training Project, which had training as its centerpiece.

The State Bank Training Project

In 1983, a consortium of four Indonesian state banks contracted with HIID for a new training project, which ran from February 1983 to December 1991. The project sought to help the four banks, which dominated the financial system, to strengthen their human resources and adjust to the changing demands of a more competitive, market-oriented environment.

HIID's three resident advisors worked with the head of the training department of each bank. The advisors' main functions for overseas training were to: (1) identify candidates from the banks for graduate training in the United States; (2) arrange for preparatory training in English, economics, mathematics, and statistics in Indonesia and use performance in that training as a basis for selecting the candidates to be sent overseas; and (3) oversee placement of the trainees in appropriate graduate-level programs, monitor their performance, and report back to the respective banks.

The project also conducted six annual seminars for the bank presidents and managing directors, eighteen one-to-two week workshops in Indonesia for senior bank officers on topics deemed most relevant by the directors, and eight conferences in the United States for state-bank trainees. All told, thirty-one workshops, seminars and student conferences were held in Indonesia and abroad under the State Bank Training project. All workshops and seminars were planned and led by the project coordinator and the resident advisors with the assistance of consultants from various countries. Many Indonesian experts were involved in the training.

In addition, the HIID coordinator of the State Bank Training project initiated a six-week workshop on banking and monetary policy in 1984, as part of the Harvard University Summer School. This workshop was designed for the Indonesian state bank officials studying in the United States to help keep them informed about recent developments in Indonesia and also to apply the principles being learned in their academic courses to current Indonesian problems. Later this workshop was broadened to include participants from other Indonesian banks and other countries. Six of these workshops were held over this period.

Under the State Bank Training project, 119 out of 123 sent for training overseas received advanced degrees. The various training programs under both the Ministry of Finance project and the State Bank Training project reached more than one thousand people. In addition, teaching materials based on Indonesian conditions have been developed and published locally and are used in banking and management training institutions in Indonesia.

While the training programs addressed the shortage of trained and experienced personnel in financial institutions, they could not change the conditions in which these institutions operated: political manipulation of financial institutions, continuing corruption, and insufficiency of adequate legal and prudential regulatory systems. These constraints, which are particularly severe for the state banks, have limited the ability of the training program to strengthen the performance of the state banks. In contrast, the ministries and other government agencies with which the projects have been associated are now reasonably well staffed with trained personnel to carry out their responsibilities effectively.

HIID Training Office

HIID's Training Office was formed in 1981 as the Indonesia Training Office. A resident training advisor in Jakarta was hired in 1982 and was responsible for assisting the Ministry of Finance in the selection and in-country preparation of new trainees, while the Training Office in Cambridge handled the university placement, academic monitoring and advising, and financial and logistical support of trainees after their departure from Indonesia. The Training Office played the same role under the State Bank Training project. In 1984, under a subcontract with the Midwest Universities Consortium for International Activities (MUCIA), HIID took on responsibility for managing part of the USAID-funded Indonesia General Participant Training II project, which included sending many participants to the United States for training. These projects solidified the role of the Indonesia Training Office in the centralized management of the overseas training activities of HIID's Indonesia training projects. The office also began to handle the relatively small overseas training components of other Indonesia projects, such as the Indonesia Urban Policy Analysis project and Center for Policy Implementation Studies project.

The level of activity of those projects increased throughout the mid- to late-1980s. By the end of the decade, two major follow-on projects, the Indonesia Overseas Training Office Support project and the Indonesia Professional Human Resources project, were also being managed by the Training Office. In addition, during that time of considerable growth and expansion in many areas of HIID, a number of ongoing and new projects in other countries began to use the Indonesia Training Office's services, so that by 1986 it had evolved into the HIID Training Office.

Under the centralized management of HIID's Training Office, from early 1982 through mid-1995, twenty-six HIID projects supported 1,253 graduate, undergraduate, and nondegree participants from Brunei, Cameroon, The Gambia, Indonesia, Kenya, Malawi, Morocco, the Philippines, Russia, Senegal, and Zambia, who attended overseas training programs at 148 institutions and agencies in the United States, the United Kingdom, and several other countries. The primary fields of study were economics, business administration, accountancy, public administration, law, and public health.

By the early 1990s, the large Indonesia projects that had kept the Training Office in operation had ended or were beginning to phase down. Beginning in 1991, the declining levels of activity led to gradual cutbacks in the size of the Training Office staff. By March 1995, only two full-time staff remained, and the Training Office was closed down when the last major training contract expired at the end of 1995.

The overseas training handled by the HIID Training Office, particularly under the various Indonesia projects, was highly successful. The Training Office took a hands-on approach both to placement and to ongoing mentoring and follow-up of students' progress, resulting in appropriate programs of study and a high rate of degree completion. In addition, several innovations contributed to the positive record. First, candidates were chosen not on the basis of their English-language level, as is often done, but for their intellectual ability. Then, programs were developed to give those selected in Jakarta what they needed to gain entrance into and to succeed in graduate programs in the United States: very intensive English preparation and preparatory courses in macro and microeconomics and statistics, along with some cultural orientation. Finally, support was provided for students' families to accompany them for the period of training in the United States. Perhaps most importantly, what allowed these innovations to be carried out was the commitment of Indonesia's Minister of Finance to provide necessary support for effective training and to allow HIID the leeway to make it work.

Establishing Public Policy Degree Programs Abroad

While training of developing country officials in the United States and at Harvard University may be an excellent way to hone particularly talented potential leaders, it is not a solution for widespread capacity building. Thus, HIID has provided support and assistance to other efforts to build educational organizations in the developing world.

Because of broader questions that this type of activity raises for Harvard, certain guidelines for working with institutions of higher learning abroad have been informally established: Harvard would not set up foreign campuses or joint programs, or offer Harvard degrees abroad; it would support the efforts of other institutions. And it would only be involved if the educational institutions had very high standards, were committed to the principle of merit as the basis for admissions, grading, and faculty selection and promotion; and were free of direct political control.

Under these conditions, there have been several important efforts. The Aga Khan University and the Indian Management Development Institute (MDI) are two cases for which HIID's involvement in feasibility studies and program design did not lead to HIID's further involvement in carrying out the proposed programs. More recently, HIID has been involved in a project to help establish and support a Masters' degree program in public policy at the National University of Singapore, and it also launched a similar program at the Catholic University of Bolivia.

The Aga Khan University

In 1982, Harvard was asked by the Aga Khan Foundation to study the best plan for the development of the newly established Aga Khan University, which at that time consisted only of a school of nursing, a medical school, and a hospital. Harvard established a high-level team chaired by its (then) president and including the director of HIID, a dean and the director of the Middle East Study Center, and several other distinguished faculty members. That team conducted a feasibility study that assessed the state of higher education in the Third World and the Aga Khan University's potential for responding effectively to needs and constraints, and made recommendations about the content and structure of the Aga Khan University.

The team concluded that the Aga Khan University should respond to the particular needs of the Third World and the Muslim world. As the next element of the university, it recommended a center of development policy and management, emphasizing policy and management in the areas of rural development, health, and private and public enterprises, to be located in East Africa. It also recommended giving priority to research, with the proposed founding of: (1) an institute of biomedical research in Karachi to support the Aga Khan medical training institutions there; (2) a center for research in the social sciences and humanities, with a focus on analysis of Muslim cultures rather than a traditional liberal arts faculty; and (3) a center or school of education to address the needs of educational administrators. The team also provided recommendations on the governance of such a decentralized university.

Since the issuance of the Harvard report, the Aga Khan University has more solidly established its medical education and hospital elements and has added an institute for educational development. Other elements remain to be implemented.

The Management Development Institute

The history of HIID's involvement with the Government of India to plan the MDI illustrates some of the difficulties that can arise with this type of endeavor. The effort arose in response to a request in 1987 from the Minister of State for Home Affairs to Harvard's President for the university to cooperate in establishing a new mid-career training institute in Delhi. The proposal was to establish a one-year, residential, public policy and management training program. The participants were to be a highly select group of mid-career managers composed of equal numbers of civil servants from the elite Indian administrative service, private sector managers, and public enterprise managers. These three groups traditionally harbored considerable suspicion of one another. It was hoped that by bringing them together to study modern approaches to policy formulation and management they would: (1) improve their skills as managers; (2) come to appreciate that the problems they confronted were fundamentally overlapping and thus develop a sympathy for the challenges the others faced; and (3) develop a network that they would take back to their work environment to improve communication among leaders in various key sectors of the economy.

HIID became deeply involved with the Government of India in planning the MDI. Ultimately, the plans broke down because of leadership issues in India. When it was clear that there would not be a full-time director or independent faculty, issues of quality became paramount, and Harvard felt it necessary to withdraw from involvement before the course got underway.

Master's Program in Public Policy in Singapore

During the late 1980s, various groups within the National University of Singapore (NUS) discussed the possibility of establishing a program for a master's in public policy (MPP). These discussions generally were on the issue of where such a program should be located, whether in the political science department, as an independent school, or as a free-standing program in one of the faculties. In 1990, the director of the university's Center for Advanced Studies of the Faculty of Arts and Social Sciences was able to persuade the NUS and the Government of Singapore to support an internationally focused MPP program located in the center. He was able to get funding to support scholarships for Southeast Asians who were not citizens of Singapore and to set up a collaborative link with Harvard.

In 1990, the center's director approached HIID with a request that it collaborate with NUS on establishing the new public policy program. Singapore proposed to use its own funds to support the program and the contract with Harvard. As suggested by NUS, and with HIID's support, an HIID Fellow with a joint appointment at the Kennedy School agreed to take the lead in working with NUS in setting up the program and then to join the resident faculty in Singapore.

In September 1991, an intense period of preparation began with the goal of initiating instruction at the start of Singapore's next academic year, July 1992. During that period, the program's purpose was defined: to create a center for high quality training for young officials from Southeast Asia or those from elsewhere with career interests in Asia. In preparation, a curriculum was designed, faculty members were recruited from other departments, and a system of making joint appointments was established. The first five faculty members traveled to Harvard to observe the public policy program at the Kennedy School. Talks on pedagogical techniques for teaching public policy were held. A case program was established with a visit to Singapore by the director of the Kennedy School's case program. In Singapore, an international recruiting drive was launched, admissions standards and procedures were established, grading standards were set up, and an administrative system was developed to support the program and its foreign students.

It was agreed that in addition to a senior faculty member, Harvard would provide a junior faculty member to work as an assistant to several of the MPP faculty and several short-term faculty, up to six weeks each, to teach intensive courses. These initial arrangements took considerable accommodation on both sides. NUS is modeled on the British system with year-long courses consisting of lectures and tutorials, with the grade dependent on a final exam. The MPP program was set up on a semester system, and even had some intensive half-semester modules. Permission had to be obtained to allow up to 50 percent of the MPP grades to be based on performance other than exams, if a faculty member so chose. Harvard had to accept the importance given to exams, as well as the use of an external examiner. There were many other issues on which Harvard suggestions and NUS procedures had to be accommodated, from the lack of feedback on exams to the fact that the Registrar's rules often superseded faculty views on appropriate pedagogical techniques.

The speed with which the program had to be set up and the pragmatism at the operating level meant that issues were easily worked out within the program at the outset. During the months that followed, the university administration discovered practices at variance with university rules or traditions. It took many meetings and discussions to resolve these differences. The time pressure in initiating the program, the respect for Harvard, and cordial, pragmatic relations at the operating level meant that many innovations were established despite NUS rules that seemed immutable. Nevertheless, innovation has proven far more difficult since the program has been underway than it was before.

Harvard activities, in addition to teaching a total of nine courses, have included conducting a faculty workshop on teaching public policy, working to define the differences between discipline-based and professional training, and making efforts to persuade NUS that a public policy program must have an outreach component and that there should be a regular series of speakers featuring practitioners in public affairs. Curriculum development, including a comprehensive curriculum review, has continued, with new courses added and others dropped.

The program is designed on the model of the Kennedy School with a core curriculum and electives. Students are also required to do a policy analysis exercise on the Kennedy School model. This has proven more difficult in Singapore than in the United States, as Asian governments and organizations are much more reluctant to give outsiders access to issues and information. The program is also distinctly different in that it has a Southeast Asian focus. There are a number of core and elective courses concentrating specifically on Southeast Asia, and teaching materials, such as cases, are drawn from Asian experiences. Whereas students are primarily Asian, there is a Canadian graduate, and the Mexican Ministry of Foreign Affairs regularly sends one or two foreign service officers from its Pacific Rim Division.

The program has not escaped the problems of institutionalization. A change of director at the beginning of 1993 brought in an individual with a strong disciplinary background but with little experience in professional training or public affairs, whose goal was maintaining, not enlarging, the scope and innovation of the program. Located within the Faculty of Arts and Social Sciences, the program struggles to ensure that decisions affecting its future are based on a professional school model, as opposed to an academic discipline-based department model. NUS faculty members teaching in the program, while based in their departments, have made only limited adaptations in their courses for the MPP student. For this reason plans for case development have languished, and rarely are cases used except by the Harvard instructors.

The creation in early 1995 of two new tenure-track faculty positions exclusively for the MPP program is an encouraging, and long-sought, development. In addition, a young NUS faculty member who is assigned to the MPP program is abroad studying for a Ph.D. in public policy. Thus the program can anticipate a core faculty of its own in the future. This will mean that both course content and pedagogy can be increasingly shaped to the particular requirements of training professionals in public policy.

On balance the MPP program has done well and the relationship between NUS and Harvard has been successful. Three classes of students have graduated with MPP degrees as of the end of 1995. Many of them are now occupying important positions in their own countries. As the initial Harvard contract nears conclusion, discussions are underway as to how to extend it and enter a new phase of cooperation between the two universities. In the fourth year of the MPP program it is not possible to draw any definitive conclusions about its future institutionalization. It is possible to say that a strong base has been established and the program is training highly talented young professionals for careers in public service in Asia.

Two Master's Programs in Bolivia

In 1992, a former Mason Fellow approached HIID about its interest in bidding on an upcoming USAID-funded project to support the establishment of Master's programs in public policy and management and in auditing and financial control at the Catholic University of Bolivia. In mid-1993, an HIID team submitted a bid for the contract to work for five years with the Catholic University in developing the master's programs. The contract was awarded to the HIID group, which included the Latin American Scholarship Program for American Universities (LASPAU) as a Harvard partner, and the Interamerican Management Consulting Corporation (IMCC), as a subcontractor to provide support for the auditing and financial control program. The government, with support from the World Bank, was also involved in the project, providing part of the funds to support the auditing and financial control program.

The Master's programs got underway in April 1995, with an initial class of fifty-five students (thirty-three in public policy and management and twenty-two in auditing). The program is targeted primarily at mid-career public officials, but has also attracted a number of private sector managers.

Program design is built directly on the experience of the Singapore project, particularly the definition of responsibilities of the project team and the content of the curriculum. HIID fielded a team headed by a chief of party who had long experience with case teaching of management and public policy at INCAE in Costa Rica and included an advisor for auditing and financial control who was an accounting professor. In addition, the project created a position for institutional development and outreach and appointed a Bolivian with a Ph.D. degree who had both academic and public sector experience. Whereas the NUS program did not initially have such a position, its creation in the Bolivia project was a direct response to the lessons learned from Singapore about the importance and difficulty of institutionalizing such programs within existing universities and different political and social systems. Along with central involvement in developing the program, the three advisors have been the core teaching faculty for the first years of the project. They also teach short courses that are open to a wider range of Bolivian public and private sector managers.

The public policy and management curriculum is also patterned after the Singapore program. It is a two-year program with a series of courses derived from economics and a number of integrative public policy courses. The curriculum for the auditing program includes not only training in technical skills but also courses in management and leadership, shared with the other master's program. Both programs require students to do the equivalent of a policy analysis exercise. A case-writing program is being instituted from the start, to train a group of students in case writing and to develop Bolivian cases for use in the classroom.

Scheduling has had to be creative to meet the needs of mid-career students who continue to hold down jobs. Each semester begins with a one-week intensive training "retreat" to introduce students to the style and standards of applied and problem-solving course work. After this, students attend classes on Fridays and Saturdays. This schedule is a major innovation in graduate education in Bolivia, where the norm has been to schedule early morning and evening classes that are poorly attended by students and faculty alike.

One of the primary long-term challenges is to develop a full-time faculty for the program. In Bolivia, there is very little experience with full-time academic careers. Project leaders are taking actions to attract potential faculty on a part-time basis and to provide experience, exposure to new teaching methods, and training as one way of building a Bolivian faculty. They are also working to identify the strongest and most committed students for Ph.D. level training overseas in subjects relevant to the future development of the programs. Developing faculty positions and attracting qualified professors also require sustainable funding, and another innovation of the project has been to charge fees for degree and nondegree training as a way of moving toward sustainability and self-sufficiency.

The project has made considerable progress in linking the degree programs to the world of practitioners through its advisory board of high level professionals from the public, private, and NGO sectors. It has engaged in ongoing discussions with public and private sector clients of the degree programs and has established good relationships with both USAID and the Harvard Club of Bolivia. Each of these activities is important to the program and promises to result in support for recruiting, teaching activities, and research. A current effort is underway in Cambridge and in La Paz to strengthen links to the Unidad de Analisis de Politicas Economicas (UDAPE) and Unidad de Analisis de Politicas Sociales (UDAPSO), research institutions for economic policy analysis and social policy analysis, respectively, particularly around research activities and the development of topics for student policy analysis exercises. Both institutes are part of the Bolivian Government and both have been linked to HIID through technical assistance projects.

From the beginning, the Catholic University of Bolivia has been supportive of the aims of the project. In particular, high-level commitment to the standards set for faculty, students, and teaching has been an important factor in the development of the master's programs. The university has worked with the project team to develop the infrastructure of offices, classrooms, and technology that are required to attract faculty, students, and sponsors to innovative efforts in professional graduate training. The university has recently introduced (and asked the project to encompass) a third Master's program focusing on private sector management, to replace a series of existing programs that have experienced declining enrollments and prestige.

In Bolivia, as in Singapore, many of the challenges relate to long-term institutionalization of a program that is innovative and does not always fit easily into the local context. While it is too early to assess results, significant strides were made in that direction during the first year of the project.

PUBLIC MANAGEMENT AND ORGANIZATIONAL STRENGTHENING PROJECTS

Projects in the African Development Bank and in Brunei focused on strengthening organizational performance and public management. These projects demonstrated accomplishments, but also disappointments, and offer lessons on some of the difficulties of and factors critical for the success of such endeavors.

The African Development Bank

In 1977, the African Development Bank (the youngest of the multilateral banks) asked HIID to help strengthen its new Economic Studies and Policy Department (later, the Planning and Research Department). The department was to conduct economic studies of member countries, analyze developments in the world economy and international financial markets, evaluate the impact of bank-financed projects, and conduct research on topics supportive of future bank lending. HIID was to engage directly in the necessary analysis and, through training, to help strengthen the department's capacity to do such work.

The project faced major challenges from the outset. Although the original plan called for five resident advisors and a number of short-term consultants, funds were insufficient to support that level of activity, and the project was scaled down. Work began in 1979 with two HIID advisors and a special studies coordinator under contract to a bilateral donor; financing was not available for any consultants. Frequent changes in organizational structure, staffing, and responsibilities within the department marked the first two years of the project, and there were also changes in advisors.

Perhaps most important, the top management of both the planning/research department and the bank's operations department did not display initial interest in the planning/research department's policy analyses or project appraisals. Furthermore, the bank's vertical organization was an impediment to cross-communication with other departments. It quickly became evident that, for the planning/research department to fulfill its role as a service unit for the rest of the bank, there needed to be both a real demand for the department's output and improved intrabank communications. Interdepartmental collaboration eventually improved after responsibility for the member country economic studies was transferred to the bank's operations department and after staff economists who had previously moved from the planning/research department to the operations department assumed senior positions in the latter. Moreover, top management's interest in some of the planning/research department's analytic output was exhibited only after the department produced a set of documents justifying a Third Replenishment, an annual report, and numerous speeches.

The planning/research department's work program and staffing were also critical and created early difficulties for the project. The number of studies projected for the year imposed a workload far beyond the department's capacity. Each officer was assigned multiple research tasks without any indication of priority. Thus, output was negligible in the project's first year. At the urging of the advisors, a more realistic work program was devised. The number and quality of departmental staff were also inadequate. A substantial transfer of economists out of the department during the second year of the project contributed to the problem, as did the bank's practice of hiring generalists with a first degree or candidates with graduate degrees unrelated to the work of the bank. By the project's third year, more specialized appointees with higher levels of training began to be more common.

Despite these difficulties, the project contributed positively to the fundamental objective of enhancing the role of the planning/research department. At the time the project began, the department had yet to convince other parts of the bank of its utility. When the project ended, the department had an established reputation for high quality work and for making contributions to planning, resource mobilization, policymaking, and thinking about development issues facing the bank. The project was an integral part of the strategy of the department's director for achieving this objective. It contributed, in particular, to the establishment of new units in the department and to the setting of goals and priorities for the work program and high standards for the quality of work.

Although the project originally envisaged formal and informal training of bank staff, very little work was done. The idea of formal training courses was resisted by staff, who wished to be viewed as colleagues, not students of the HIID team members. Training was therefore limited to a few informal sessions on certain topics and on-the-job training through collaboration. No candidates were sent for overseas training, although a number of staff have attended the Mason Fellows Program and HIID's workshops in the years since the project ended.

The lack of clarification of institution-building objectives from the outset was one obstacle to their success, and the project's final report observed that the experience demonstrated the need to incorporate clear institution-building objectives and advisor responsibilities in the project agreement and the terms of reference.

A larger obstacle was the unfriendly environment of vested interests that confronted the planning/research department as a new entity. Its management felt the need for early demonstrations of performance and tended to turn to the advisors for rapid, technically competent responses to their perceived needs, rather than for assistance in building the department's own capacity. Ironically, the advisors' responsiveness to such short-term demands provided the groundwork for building the department: their actions established sufficient credibility with the department's management so that recommendations for the development of orderly work programs found a sympathetic ear, and helped the department to acquire a reputation for reliability and competence that solidified its position within the bank and created the critical demand for its output.

The Public Management Development Project, Negara Brunei Darussalam

Brunei is a small, resource-rich country that offered a challenging environment for HIID activities in 1986, when the Public Management Development project was initiated. Rich in oil and with a high per capita income, Brunei did not suffer from lack of capital, but rather from limited human resources, a lack of leadership and clear objectives for national development, and the absence of incentives for individual and organizational performance.

HIID initiated activities in Brunei through a series of discussions with senior government officials about priority areas for technical assistance. These meetings produced an agreement that HIID would assist in introducing performance appraisal to the civil service for exploring ways to: (1) encourage more effective public sector recruitment, (2) provide short courses in project analysis and appraisal, (3) rationalize the use of computers in government service, (4) introduce management improvements in selected ministries, and (5) arrange in-service overseas training for promising public officials. The initial contract extended from October 1986 to September 1989. A second contract with more focused terms of reference extended the project through December 1993.

In the first three years, activities focused primarily on civil service strengthening and natural resource management. A government task force on performance appraisal asked for HIID assistance in developing the system and training staff in its implementation. Workshops on personnel management and project appraisal, recommendations about recruitment procedures, and training module development followed this activity. The project offered a series of workshops on macroeconomic and human resource planning in the Economic Planning Unit to assist in the development of the sixth five-year national development plan. As for natural resource management, HIID worked with the Ministry of Development on issues related to economic diversification and alternative development strategies. The project focused on improving analytic skills, increasing the technical knowledge of staff, and encouraging senior managers to consider long-range development activities. In particular, project appraisal workshops and studies of alternative development strategies provided ministry officials with skills and ideas to assess investment alternatives.

Under the second contract for the project, activities focused more specifically on civil service reform. The project continued to assist with the government's performance appraisal system and offered a series of leadership training workshops. In addition, HIID assisted the government in a national civil service review process and a performance improvement program modeled on those undertaken by many other governments. Action teams in each ministerial department were formed and trained by HIID consultants to audit departmental objectives and activities and recommend ways to improve efficiency. Directors of departments were also trained in the purpose and implementation of the civil service and performance improvement.

The project provided a series of valuable services and considerable technical expertise through consultant activities. The project introduced Brunei government officials to new ideas and techniques for considering national development strategies and programs. It offered extensive training in development and public management fields in Brunei and encouraged a number of Bruneians to take study leaves for advanced training abroad. It introduced structures and processes to carry out performance appraisals on an annual basis and an ongoing civil service review program to streamline government activities.

These activities did not, however, add up to significant change in the public sector in Brunei. In assessing the civil service reform and performance improvement activities, the project relied heavily on HIID consultants and demonstrated little Brunei ownership of the initiatives. The project was also hampered by the lack of a full-time resident advisor who could facilitate continuous activity on the civil service reform initiative. In the last year of the project, at the government's request, there was no resident advisor. During the second contract period, the project continued to field consultants, but without the direction or coherence of earlier efforts.

A number of lessons can be drawn from this project that are broadly relevant to development assistance efforts. First, public management reform projects are probably destined to make only modest progress. Altering bureaucratic behavior and organizational cultures is a time-consuming and long-term process. While a project that focuses on economic policy advising can make a significant difference to the management of the macroeconomy in a few years, changing bureaucratic behavior and routines requires much longer than the seven years of this project; moreover, the results are less likely to be highly visible outside the affected organizations than is the case with economic policy advising.

Second, the Brunei project confirms conventional wisdom that public management reform requires deep and sustained commitment of high level government officials who must be consistent in sending the message to the public sector that efficiency and responsiveness are important. Public management reforms are also encouraged when the consumers of public sector services are mobilized to insist on efficiency and responsiveness. In Brunei, high level leadership of the reform process was elusive and there was little tradition for citizens to mobilize to insist on good performance from government. There were, in fact, few reasons for leaders, organizations, or individuals to identify themselves with the project objectives. While there was great frustration with the rigidity, inefficiency, and ineffectiveness of the civil service, there were no reform-oriented pressures on the system from citizens, government leaders, or external forces.

The project confirms the critical importance of a strong sense of national ownership. It also indicates how difficult it is for assistance organizations to gauge when that ownership does or does not exist where there is periodic verbal encouragement from government officials, supportive project "friends" in the bureaucracy, widespread consensus that "something needs to be done," and considerable foot-dragging when it comes to real changes.

Research on Capacity Building

Development assistance has long been committed to building national capacity to manage critical development tasks, including formulating sound economic policies, developing social and physical infrastructure, and investing wisely in human resource development. All of the projects and programs discussed above are strong examples of such efforts. Increasingly, however, donor agencies have come to question the productivity of many of their efforts in building sustainable capacity for development. Technical assistance, they have argued, is often supply-driven, overemphasizing the use of expensive expatriate expertise and underemphasizing sustainability.

Guided by such concerns and responding to instructions from the United Nations General Assembly to place capacity development at the center of its programming, the United Nations Development

Programme (UNDP) requested HIID assistance in carrying out a comprehensive study to assist it and other donors in designing more effective capacity building interventions. HIID undertook the research in 1993. The project was under the UNDP's policy division and was sponsored as part of the effort to put its policy and programming on firmer analytic and empirical ground and to provide leadership in capacity development for the donor community generally. The research was expected to generate a conceptual framework for understanding factors that affect the ability to build capacity, to carry out comparative case studies in six countries, and to develop guidelines to assist governments and international aid agencies to build sustainable public sector capacity. The UNDP and the World Bank selected six countries for focused research: Bolivia, Central African Republic, Ghana, Morocco, Sri Lanka, and Tanzania. A national researcher from each country carried out the case study research under the supervision of HIID professional staff.

In October 1993, HIID organized a workshop with the UNDP and World Bank staff and the six national researchers. Participants contributed to the outlines of the analytical framework that would guide the research, and they jointly defined the focus of the research. Research was conducted between October 1993 and June 1994. During this period, HIID professionals visited the researchers in the field to help ensure the application of the framework, the focus of the studies, and the comparability of the findings. In July 1994, a second workshop provided an opportunity for the researchers to present their case study findings to donor officials and HIID staff.

The framework developed in the study and applied in the comparative cases presents five dimensions, or levels of analysis, of capacity: (1) the action environment, or the broad social, economic, and political context of the country; (2) the public sector institutional context; (3) the task network, the various organizations that must work together to accomplish a particular development task; (4) the organization itself; and (5) the human resources within the organization—their training, recruitment, utilization, and retention. Whereas many capacity-building programs have focused narrowly on training and human resource development, in many cases the constraints at other levels prevent such programs from being effective at building sustainable capacity. The framework serves as a tool for strategic capacity-building interventions—for assessing capacity needs and identifying where interventions in support of capacity development can be most effective.

The final report, *Building Sustainable Capacity: Challenges for the Public Sector,* which was completed in November 1994, incorporates a discussion of the framework, comparative analysis of the cases, guidelines for capacity building, and summaries of the six cases. It formed the cornerstone of a document on capacity development produced in the policy division of the UNDP and distributed, along with the final report, to all the resident missions, within the New York office, and to other donors. It has underpinned the UNDP's contribution to discussions with donor partners on technical assistance and capacity building. Shortly after its completion and the distribution of the policy document, however, the UNDP unit that had sponsored the research disbanded, and the extent to which the project will have a lasting impact on UNDP policy or practice is unclear.

The accomplishments of the project include the research process itself. The collaboration between the HIID team and the six national research studies led to a successful research output—comparable case studies based on a common framework. It also resulted in mutually rewarding collegial relationships, some of which may lead to future collaborative efforts. The project demonstrated the viability and the potential fruitfulness of this kind of participatory research.

Conclusions

HIID has carried out its education mission through direct training efforts for developing country officials at Harvard in both degree and nondegree programs, through assisting foreign institutions in establishing training programs to promote development, and through technical assistance and research to increase the capacity of governments or development agencies to effectively promote development. Evaluating the success of education and capacity building is notoriously difficult. Clearly the most difficult and least successful have been the efforts in direct capacity building with governments. Direct programs to provide education give some evidence of being successful, given the success of the graduates. The assistance in establishing degree programs in foreign institutions appears to have been more successful, but it is still too early to make judgments.

Certainly, the educational programs did not receive as high a priority at HIID as technical assistance, and many educational efforts were either an outgrowth of technical assistance or a variation on them. That does not necessarily mean they are of lesser value.

HIID has generated enormous experience in development. It has both access to the immense educational resources of Harvard and a responsibility to contribute to the depth and relevance of Harvard's teaching in the field of development. A broad and effective base of experience has been acquired. HIID now has an opportunity to think more systematically about how it can carry out its educational mission. Its accomplishments and knowledge are unique. How can these best be built upon?

Notes

1 Based in part on conference papers by Lester E. Gordon; by Merilee S. Grindle; by Merilee S. Grindle and Mary E. Hilderbrand; by Carol Grodzins; by Thomas J. Skerry; and by John W. Thomas.

19 New Initiatives

Joseph J. Stern[1]

In response to Harvard University's mandate, HIID has broadened the scope of its overseas activities, becoming more multidisciplinary in the process. Fifteen years ago the institute's projects were still heavily focused on providing economic analysis to government agencies and, to a lesser extent, to research organizations. Economists dominated the institute's staff. Today, HIID has projects in such diverse fields as health, public administration, and education, it is involved with a number of faculties of Harvard other than the Economics Department, and economists no longer form the majority of its staff. These changes reflect a conscious effort by HIID to seek new areas in which the institute might bring its skills to bear and to recruit staff with the appropriate background to undertake new activities. The two activities under discussion here reflect the institute's efforts to broaden its scope and to seek new ways in which it can link the talents of HIID and Harvard to the needs of developing and transition economies.

Nongovernmental Organizations and International Development

The development community increasingly recognizes that nongovernmental organizations (NGOs) can play a vital role in the development process. Such organizations have demonstrated an ability to complement the functions of governments, to mobilize citizenry, and to experiment with new development paradigms. In response to the growing significance of the NGO experience, and the growing interest in NGOs among students, the institute has steadily increased its activities relating to NGO activities and, in 1993, established a program on NGOs.

One of the earliest efforts by HIID to work with NGOs grew out of its involvement in the Assistance to Resource Institutions for Enterprise Support (ARIES) project. The United States Agency for International Development (USAID) has long supported the development of small-scale and micro enterprises in developing countries and believed these efforts could be enhanced by strengthening the capacity of NGOs to support such institutions (see Chapter 11). Under the USAID-funded ARIES project, HIID worked with the NGO community to define its main capacity constraints and to identify means to overcome them.[2] Four related activities were carried out. First, a review and assessment of small enterprise development as carried out by NGOs was undertaken and measures to improve performance were identified. This provided the framework for the rest of the project activities. Second, a computerized framework to categorize, summarize, and present information on the constraints identified was created. Third, HIID and NGO collaborators developed a series of teaching cases focused on key points in the evolution of various models of small enterprise development. And fourth, to allow the NGO community to learn more systematically from its own experience, HIID, together with case-method teachers from the Harvard Business School, developed two case-method workshops for the NGO community. A core of about a dozen case writers and teachers went on to give numerous training sessions for the NGO membership of the Small Enterprise Encouragement and Promotion (SEEP) network.

The first and third activities were developed into a text and cases book with a companion case leader's guide. The database was published as a companion computer software package, the *AskARIES Knowledgebase*.[3] The books have been used extensively in courses relating to NGOs and small enterprise development. In a particularly innovative use of the database, USAID sent HIID staff to twelve Peace Corps national programs to install the program and train project directors and volunteers in its use.

Since the ARIES project, HIID project staff have become increasingly involved in NGO-related activities. Project staff analyzed and documented innovative nongovernmental programs for women in the fields of microcredit and enterprise and of natural resource management. Two of HIID's gender research projects were carried out in collaboration with NGOs, notably a study of household coping strategies in western India and a study of widows in rural India (see Chapter 16).

HIID has also participated in several evaluation missions of innovative nongovernmental programs. These include the Working Women's Forum in south India, which operates a credit cooperative for 100,000 low-income women; the Bangladesh Rural Advance Committee (BRAC) in Bangladesh, which operates an integrated rural development program with nearly one million beneficiaries; and the Grameen Bank in Bangladesh, a rural bank with about 1.5 million borrowers, mainly women. After each evaluation, a set of policy recommendations was made to the NGO and its donors.[4] HIID has also engaged in strategic planning with several NGOs, including a strategic review for the Ford Foundation of its programs for women in Bangladesh and a strategic planning exercise with BRAC to help it establish a gender research program. The latter was undertaken with a senior staff member of the United Nations Development Fund for Women (UNIFEM).

HIID's NGO program has three major components: teaching and training, seminars and conferences, and research and documentation The current focus of the program is on the role of NGOs in conflict resolution, recognizing that a growing number of NGOs work under conditions of conflict, and on the role of NGOs in promoting economic opportunities for low-income women.

Teaching and Training

For the past three years, a member of the HIID faculty has offered a course on the role of nongovernmental organizations in international development, at Harvard's John F. Kennedy School of Government. The NGO program also plans to offer one or more short training programs for the staff of NGOs each year. The themes for the training programs will be determined in consultation with the program's International Advisory Committee and NGOs working in developing countries. The curriculum for each training program will include case studies of relevant NGO experience (to be developed by the program), and the faculty for each training will include NGO staff with relevant experience.

In May 1994, at the request of, and with funding from, the Aga Khan Foundation of Canada, the NGO program developed and ran a training workshop, entitled "Beyond Credit: A Subsector Approach to Promoting Women's Enterprises," which featured the experience of NGOs from Asia, Africa, and Latin America that have adopted a sectoral approach to promoting women's enterprises. The sectoral approach recognizes women's work within sectors of the economy and addresses the constraints they face. The curriculum and case material for the training program was based on an earlier research project. Senior staff from two South Asian NGOs—the Self-Employed Women's Association (SEWA) and BRAC—as well as from UNIFEM, were the training faculty for the workshop. A book describing the subsector approach and eight subsector projects, edited by the NGO program director, has been published.

Seminar and Conferences

In April 1993, HIID inaugurated its new NGO program with a two-day symposium on Shaping the Policy Debate: The Role of NGOs. The symposium included a panel presentation at the Kennedy School, and a series of workshops on the role NGOs have played in shaping the debate on the environment, structural adjustment, the informal labor sector, democratization, and human rights. In December 1993, the NGO program, together with the Common Security Forum at Cambridge University (United Kingdom) and the Center for Population and Development Studies at Harvard University, sponsored a panel discussion entitled From Somalia to Cambodia: the NGOs and the International System. The main speaker, Jan Eliasson, then the United Nation's Undersecretary General for Humanitarian Affairs, together with senior executives from NGOs, explored the complex ethical, political, and logistical dilemmas involved in providing humanitarian assistance in conflict situations. In February 1995, the NGO program hosted a conference on Local Capacities for Peace, which was organized by the Collaborative for Development Action, a Boston-based consulting firm, as part of an ongoing project reviewing a variety of experiences where NGOs have provided international relief or development assistance in conflict situations. In March 1995, the NGO program organized a New England-wide regional conference, Toward Beijing: Priorities '95, in collaboration with the Bunting Institute, Radcliffe College, the Center for Research on Women, Wellesley College, and number of other institutions and individuals. The conference focused on the priority issues that were later discussed at the Fourth World Conference on Women, held in Beijing, China, in September 1995. The keynote speaker at this regional conference was Noeleen Heyser, Director of UNIFEM. Finally, in April 1995 the

NGO program, in collaboration with the World Peace Foundation, organized a conference to analyze the comparative experience and advantages of indigenous and international NGOs in addressing ethnic conflicts.

In January 1995, at the request of BRAC, the NGO program ran a training program on gender research for the staff of BRAC's Research and Evaluation Department. The training syllabus included a brief history of feminist thought, a discussion of gender analysis in various social sciences, the application of relevant gender analysis frameworks in the Bangladesh context, and a gender "audit" of selected BRAC research studies. The resource persons for that training program included two women scholars from Bangladesh and a gender trainer from India. The training course on gender research can be readily adapted for training in other countries.

At the suggestion of various NGO leaders, the program has started to develop curricula and to identify cases for the following two training programs:

- *NGOs and Economic Reforms*: to strengthen the policy analysis capacity of NGOs by reviewing the basic assumptions underlying economic reforms and the alternative roles NGOs have played during the reform process, and to foster a dialogue between NGOs and economic policy analysts; and
- *NGOs and International Negotiation*: to strengthen the capacity of NGOs to participate in international negotiations by reviewing the strategies and methods NGOs have used in recent international policy debates in the fields of environment, human rights, and population.

Research and Documentation

The documentation component of the NGO program will promote the writing of short teaching cases and of longer case histories of relevant NGO experience. To date, fifteen cases of NGO experience in early warning and preventive diplomacy during complex humanitarian crises have been developed. With funds from the Aga Khan Foundation, HIID commissioned eight case studies of sectoral projects for women from Asia, Africa, and Latin America.

For the past several years, HIID has been working with the research department of BRAC to develop its capacity to carry out gender research, as noted above. In 1993, HIID staff and a senior researcher from the Bangladesh Institute of Development Studies (BIDS) codesigned a one-year research project to assess the impact of BRAC's programs on women's lives. The research project was designed to assess different types of change (such as material, cognitive, and relational) in different spheres of women's lives (such as family, community, and the market). That research project has been completed by BRAC researchers, and the findings from it have been used to inform the design of a large collaborative research project between BRAC and an international health research institution in Bangladesh.

The Aga Khan Foundation and UNIFEM recently initiated a collaborative research program with South Asian NGOs to analyze the lessons from NGO experience in several fields, including women in development. HIID's NGO program director was asked to join the research advisory team for the collaborative research on women on development issues. The focus of the research is the lessons from ten South Asian NGOs in organizing low-income women for economic empowerment. A research design workshop was held in Bangladesh in January 1995, to develop a common conceptual framework and a common case study outline. Ten NGOs (from Bangladesh, India, Pakistan, and Sri Lanka) sent two persons each to the workshop: an outside researcher and one of their own staff. Each NGO team is preparing a case study of the grassroots women's organization the NGO has helped to develop, which will describe the form of organization (cooperative, peer lending group, village organization, or trade union), the types of women organized, the strategies adopted to overcome constraints in the women's working environments, and the women's perspectives on economic empowerment. The case studies were published by UNIFEM and distributed at the Fourth World Conference on Women, held in Beijing, China, in September 1995.

In addition to these activities, the NGO program has been called upon to provide advisory services. For example, the NGO program director serves on the boards of three NGOs in the United States and on editorial advisory committees of an NGO in the United States and one United Nations organization. In 1993, the program director was asked by the Commission on Global Governance, established in 1992, to explore the opportunities created by the end of the Cold War to build a more effective system of world security and governance, to make suggestions regarding the role of NGOs in global governance, and to review the sections of its report which dealt with NGOs.

In many current crisis situations, NGOs are seen as the only set of institutions with the "moral authority" to operate across national borders, particularly in areas facing humanitarian crises or human rights violation and, increasingly, in areas torn by civil war. More and more, NGOs are helping to set international policy agendas by identifying and defining critical issues regarding economic and social development. NGOs have also entered the debate about economic reform and have helped to develop and run special debt relief measures for poor countries, in addition to special relief measures for poor communities in countries undergoing economic reforms.

The NGO program has found that standard academic research and training need to be adapted to fit the realities within which NGOs operate. From the NGO perspective, standard social science suffers three types of limitations. First, disciplinary boundaries often limit the capacity of academics to "see" what falls in the gaps between disciplines or to undertake cross-disciplinary research. Most notably, NGOs themselves fall in the gap between economic and political theory. Second, theoretical training often fails to analyze or to anticipate the complexities of real-life situations. For example, there is limited political theory on the complex and changing role of the UN system, much less on the varied and changing relationships between NGOs and the UN system. Third, methodological training often fails to point out the relevance of different methods to different problems and contexts. For example, cost-benefit analysis may need to be adapted to incorporate the complex mix of economic, social, and political objectives pursued by many NGOs. Finally, the NGO program has found that the information exchange between academia and NGOs flows both ways—particularly so in the more applied academic fields. For example, lessons and innovations from the NGO sector have greatly influenced the fields of public health and microcredit and enterprise. More notably, the fields of human rights, environment, and gender and development have been greatly influenced by—indeed might not exist were it not for—the pioneering role of NGOs.

Urban Policy

HIID has worked in the area of finance and urban development since the mid-1970s, when it managed a small urban project in Iran. In 1980, the Urban Development Policy and Finance project began in

Indonesia. This activity (which focused on training and on developing an institute for urban policy analysis that would coordinate urban policymaking) ended in 1994. Currently efforts are underway to reestablish the institute's presence in the field of urban policy and to develop the institute's capacity to staff such activities. This intention took concrete shape with the initiation of an urban project in Chile in 1993 and the recruitment in 1994 of an urban specialist to develop other new urban initiatives.

The inspiration and funding for the Chile project came from Forestal Valparaíso S.A., an international conglomerate with interests in urban development in Chile. Leaders of Forestal Valparaíso S.A. (and its parent banking group, Cruza Blanca) have had a long-term interest in urban economics. In particular, they are concerned with the distortions that may cause overdevelopment of certain areas while other areas remain inefficiently undeveloped or underdeveloped.

Forestal Valparaíso S.A. has a strong commitment to Chile and has displayed that commitment by consistently sponsoring research for better economic policies. The Cruza Blanca group had earlier played a critical role in researching Chile's widely acclaimed, and now much copied, pension reforms. Its research interests were also fostered by the purely academic interests of its senior management, many of whom had previously been affiliated with Harvard University. The atypical academic focus of this privately-funded project owes much to the unusually academic nature of the senior businessmen in the Cruza Blanca group.

The goals of the Chilean study were to provide more insights both on the Chilean case and on urban development internationally. Indeed, much of the particular interest in Santiago came about because it was an example of the striking concentration of a country's population in a single city: in 1985, almost 35 percent of Chile's population was concentrated in Santiago. This concentration is far from unique, though it is at the high end of the scale. Ranked by percentage of a country's population, Santiago is one of the three largest cities in the world, leaving out the city states of Hong Kong and Singapore. This level of concentration is not necessarily inefficient, since there may be many reasons why agents come together in a single city. Still, an interest in urban concentration is stimulated because this level of concentration is surprisingly common (although a relatively new feature of the world's urban landscape); and the roots of this concentration seem often to rely on forces outside of, or beyond, economic efficiency.

While economic forces usually play a sizable role in supporting urban growth, political forces also play an important part in creating the most concentrated levels of urbanization. If urban concentration has political, not economic roots, then it is more likely that this concentration is inefficient. For example, a large proportion of the populace may live in a capital city because political expression is difficult, or even impossible, in the hinterland. If so, then one might conclude that this concentration is suboptimal and merits a strong policy response. By contrast, if urban concentration was the outcome of economic forces creating special returns from such urban concentrations, then it is more dangerous to tamper. Furthermore, cities may have formed for political reasons, but if they remain because of efficiency considerations, then anti-concentration policy may have large social costs.

To initiate the project, HIID project staff prepared a paper laying out the microeconomics of designing more efficient urban policies. In that paper, as in the final report, the focus was more on the tradeoffs between alternative policies than on determining a "right" policy for every occasion. As a starting point, the analysis assumed (consistent with what is often called the "second welfare theorem" of economics) that independent agents who are free to make market-driven decisions will generally arrive at an optimal economic outcome. The bulk of the final report was devoted to understanding why this often does not happen. In many cases, private costs and benefits do not equal social costs and benefits, and spatial distortions exist that distort private decisions so as to produce less than socially optimal location choices by both households and industry.

The initial paper focused on two primary sources of spatial distortions: (1) congestion and pollution externalities that would exist in the absence of any governmental actions, and (2) problematic government policies. Congestion and pollution externalities distort location decisions because when households or industry choose a particular locale, they do not incorporate the social costs of their location choices adding pollution or congestion to an already dense area. Governmental policies can distort the location decision by making more resources available in different locations; by limiting the ability of new locales to provide infrastructure and services; and by mispricing government services, particularly transportation. This phase of the report provided a general, microeconomic framework; the second phase focused on applying microeconomics to the actual Chilean case.

The second phase of the project involved intensive studies of a number of sectors of urban development. The first of these was devoted to determining the actual monetary damages created by different pollution sources in Chile, with particular emphasis on air pollution. The report developed an economic framework for estimating the social costs of air pollution in Santiago and then turned to analyzing the causes and possible solutions to these problems.

A second study analyzed the adequacy of urban infrastructure services in Chile, and in particular whether the provision of water, sewerage, solid waste, and telecommunication services might distort urban development patterns. The analyses suggested that water and sewerage are more likely to cause interregional locational distortions than solid waste or telecommunications. Although charges for solid waste disposal are typically far below social costs in all Chilean cities, the subsidy probably amounts to only about US$12 to US$14 per household per year in most Chilean cities outside Santiago, while in Santiago these services are probably underpriced by about US$70 per household per year. A third study explored the spatial implications of housing policy in Chile. It found extensive intervention in the housing market by the national government. In recent years, for example, 42 percent of residential construction in Chile had direct public subsidy and, if mortgage subsidies and other indirect subsidies are considered, the government is involved in a much larger portion of the housing market. All government programs emphasize, almost exclusively, home ownership, which results in Chilean cities typically having 80 percent or higher home ownership levels, among the highest in the world. Focusing on the spatial implications of these housing policies, the study considered two types of distortions: interregional and intraregional. It found the potential spatial distortions generated by government policies to be much greater on an intraregional than an interregional basis.

Generally, housing policy makers consider only the construction and land costs when siting subsidized housing. Other costs that can be significant include commuting, congestion, and pollution. In many cases, the study found, inclusion of these other costs would make more central locations viable and economically advantageous.

A senior Harvard professor prepared a report, *Efficiency and Locational Consequences of Government Transport Policies and Spend-*

ing in Chile. The report noted that pre-1970 regulations imposed on intercity and urban transportation reduced incomes and growth rates. Although it proved difficult to establish what impact these policies had on the location of economic activity within Chile, the report guardedly suggested that these regulations disadvantaged outlying regions more than the country's urban centers, particularly Santiago. As a result, it was argued, the Chilean Government has underinvested in all roads (relative to rail and bus transport), but particularly in those roads outside the central metropolis. The effect of this has probably been to encourage more growth in the country's large metropolitan areas, especially its largest, Santiago, than would otherwise have been the case.

Since automobile ownership is likely to continue to grow as Chile's per capita income rises, rapid increases in automobile ownership and use are certain. Without the prompt implementation of policies to charge private vehicle owners fees for road and street use that reflect the long-run social costs of providing additional capacity, these certain increases in automobile ownership and use will cause serious problems, including more congestion and pollution. Experience in other parts of the world suggests that serious congestion in the core parts of large cities tends to accentuate the forces of both population and employment decentralization, particularly the latter. A failure to charge transport users for the congestion they create will result in more dispersed and lower density metropolitan regions than would occur if congestion pricing were used to help create and define more nearly optimal levels of streets and roads. Based on an examination of the spatial distortions created by social welfare programs and on ways of structuring political institutions to eliminate these distortions, the report suggested that, while government transfers may have fueled Santiago's growth in the 1960s, subsequent reforms in schooling and health programs have eliminated most of the spatial distortions that once existed because of these activities.

Chile has had a remarkably slow development of small cities for a country with its rate of economic development. A simple comparison with similar economies reveals that Chile seems to have a major problem creating new smaller cities. The study team hypothesized that this failure of urban entrepreneurship may be the result of the centralization of authority within Santiago.

Major cities inevitably will continue to serve as centers of economic and social activity and as a focus of job-seekers who leave the agricultural sector. Hence analyses of urban policies that can best shape the development of the urban centers, so that they can make a contribution to economic development while providing a reasonably safe and comfortable habitat for their residents, will remain an important part of HIID's activities.

Notes

1 Based in part on conference papers by Martha A. Chen and Charles K. Mann; and by Douglas H. Keare and Edward Glaeser.

2 The prime contractor for ARIES was Robert R. Nathan Associates. HIID was subcontracted to carry out the work described here.

3 See Grindle, Mann and Shipton (1989); Mann, Grindle, and Sanders (1990); and Pradhan, Hornsby, and Mann (1989).

4 The Government of the Netherlands has provided funds for the Working Women's Forum in South India, and the funding for BRAC and the Grameen Bank in Bangladesh has been provided by donor consortia.

Selected Bibliography

Adams, Dale and Douglas Graham. 1981. A Critique of Traditional Agricultural Credit Projects and Policies. *Journal of Development Economics* 8 (3): 347–366.

Aleem, Irfan. 1993. The Rural Credit Market in Pakistan: The Cost of Screening. In Karla Hoff et al., eds., *The Economics of Rural Organization: Theory, Practice and Policy*. New York: Oxford University Press for the World Bank.

Amin, Samir. 1974. *Accumulation on a World Scale.* Sussex: Harvester Press.

Anand, Sudhir and Lincoln Chen. 1996. *Health Implications of Economic Policies: A Framework of Analysis.* Discussion Paper Series No. 3. New York: United Nations Development Programme.

Anderson, G. and T. Żylicz. 1996. "The Role of Environmental Funds in Environmental Policies of Central and Eastern European Countries." Environmental Reprint Series No. 3 (April). Cambridge, MA: HIID, Central and Eastern Europe Environmental Economics and Policy Project.

Anderson, Mary B. 1988. *Improving Access to Schooling in the Third World: An Overview.* BRIDGES Research Report Series No. 1. Cambridge, MA: Harvard Institute for International Development and USAID Office of Education, Bureau of Science and Technology.

———. 1989. *The Impact of the Mosque Schools Policy on Girls' Access to Education in Pakistan.* BRIDGES Casual Papers, Papers on Primary Education in Pakistan, Report No. 7, Cambridge, MA: Harvard Institute for International Development.

Bank Rakyat Indonesia. 1990. *Briefing Booklet: KUPEDES Development Impact Survey,* Ann Dunham Sutoro, Principal Investigator. Jakarta: Planning, Research, and Development Department, BRI.

———. 1994. *BRI Village Units.* Jakarta: BRI

Barichello, Richard R. and Frank F. Flatters. 1991. Trade Policy Reform in Indonesia. In Dwight H. Perkins and Michael Roemer, eds., *Reforming Economic Systems in Developing Countries.* Cambridge, MA: Harvard Institute for International Development.

Berg, Elliot J. 1993. *Rethinking Technical Cooperation: Reforms for Capacity Building in Africa.* New York: United Nations Development Programme and Development Alternatives, Inc.

Biggs, Tyler, Peter Brimble, Donald Snodgrass, and Michael Murray. 1990. *Rural Industry and Employment Study: A Synthesis Report.* Bangkok: Thailand Development Research Institute Foundation.

Blitzer, C. R., P. B. Clark, and L. Taylor. 1975. *Economy-Wide Models and Development Planning.* London: Oxford University Press for the World Bank.

Bluffstone, R. and B. Larson, eds. 1997. *Controlling Pollution in Transition Economies.* United Kingdom: Edward Elgar Publishing Company.

Bodart, Claude, and R. Owona. 1995. *Threats to the Financial Viability of Cost-Recovery of Health Services: Lessons Learned from Two Provinces in Cameroon.* Unpublished work.

Bolnick, Bruce R. 1987. Financial Liberalization with Imperfect Markets: Indonesia During the 1970s. *Economic Development and Cultural Change* 35 (3): 581–589.

Bolnick, Bruce R. and Eric R. Nelson. 1990. Evaluating the Economic Impact of a Special Credit Program: KIK/KMKP in Indonesia. *Journal of Development Studies* 26 (2): 299–332.

Boomgard, James J. and Kenneth J. Angell. 1994. Bank Rakyat Indonesia's Unit Desa System: Achievements and Replicability. In Maria Otero and Elisabeth Rhyne, eds., *The New World of Microenterprise Finance: Building Healthy Financial Institutions for the Poor.* Hartford, CT: Kumarian Press, 206–228.

Boscolo, Marco, J. Buongiorno, and T. Panayotou. 1996. *Stimulating Options for Carbon Sequestration in the Management of a Lowland Tropical Rain Forest.* Cambridge, MA: Harvard Institute for International Development.

Bottomley, Anthony. 1983. Interest Rate Determination in Underdeveloped Rural Areas. In John D. Von Pischke et al., eds., *Rural Financial Markets in Developing Countries: Their Use and Abuse.* Baltimore: Johns Hopkins University Press. Extracted from *American Journal of Agricultural Economics,* 1975, 57 (2): 279–291.

Bouman, Frits J. A. 1989. Small, Short and Unsecured: Informal Finance in Rural India. In Karla Hoff et al., eds., *The Economics of Rural Organization: Theory, Practice and Policy*. New York: Oxford University Press for the World Bank.

Boycko, Maxim, Andrei Shleifer, and Robert Vishny. 1995. *Privatizing Russia.* Cambridge, MA: MIT Press.

Bravermann, Avishay and J. Luis Guasch. 1993. The Theory of Rural Credit Markets. In Karla Hoff, Avishay Braverman, and Joseph E. Stiglitz, eds., *The Economics of Rural Organization: Theory, Practice and Policy.* New York: Oxford University Press for the World Bank.

Brent, Robert S. 1990. Aiding Africa. *Foreign Policy* 80 (Fall): 121–140.

Brown, Claire, Haroona Jatoi, and Christina Rawley. 1989. *Education Policy Simulation (EPICS): Investing in Basic Education for Development. A Strategic Decision-Making Model for Increasing Access with Equity.* Cambridge, MA: Schenkman Publishing Company, Inc.

Brugger, Ernst A. and Sarath Rajapatirana, eds. 1995. *New Perspectives on Financing Small Business in Developing Countries.* International Center for Economic Growth and FUNDES (Fundacion para el Desarrollo Sostenible.) San Francisco: ICS Press.

Canada, Royal Commission on Taxation. 1966. *Report of the Royal Commission on Taxation.* Ottawa: Queen's Printer.

Carrin, G., M. Jancloes, and S. Ibi Ajayi. 1993. Overview and Introduction. In *Macroeconomic Environment and Health.* WHO: Geneva, 1–20.

Central Advisory Council for Education. 1967. *Children and Their Primary Schools.* London: HMSO.

Chandavarkar, Anand. 1987. *The Informal Financial Sector in Development Countries.* Occasional Paper No. 2. Kuala Lumpur: The South East Asian Central Banks (SEACEN) Research and Training Center.

Chen, Martha A. 1983. *A Quiet Revolution: Women in Transition in Rural Bangladesh.* Cambridge, MA: Schenkman Publishing Company, Inc.

———. 1989a. A Sectoral Approach to Promoting Women's Work: Lessons from India. *World Development* 17 (7): 1997–2016.

———. 1989b. Women's Work in Indian Agriculture by Agro-Ecological Zones: Meeting the Needs of Landless and Landpoor Women. *Economic and Political Weekly* 24 (43).

———. 1989c. Women and Entrepreneurship: New Approaches from India. In A. Gosses et al., eds., *Small Enterprises, New Approaches.* The Hague, The Netherlands: Operations Review Unit, Ministry of Foreign Affairs.

———. 1989d. Developing Non-Craft Employment for Women in Bangladesh. In Ann Leonard, ed., *SEEDS: Supporting Women's Work in the Third World.* New York: The Feminist Press.

———. 1989e. The Working Women's Forum: Organizing for Credit and Change. In Ann Leonard, ed., *SEEDS: Supporting Women's Work in the Third World.* New York: The Feminist Press.

———. 1990. Poverty, Gender and Work in Bangladesh. In Leela Dube and Rajni Palriwala, eds., *Structures and Strategies: Women, Work and Family, Women and the Household in Asia*, vol. 3. New Delhi: Sage Publications.

———. 1991. *Coping with Seasonality and Drought.* New Delhi: Sage Publications.

———. 1992. *Impact of Grameen Bank's Credit Operations on it Members: Past and Future Research.* Dhaka: Report to the Donor Consortium.

———. 1993. Women and Wasteland Development in India: An Issue Paper. In A.M. Singh and N. Burra, eds., *Women and Wasteland Development in India.* New Delhi and London: Sage Publications.

———. 1994. The Feminization of Poverty. In Noeleen Heyzer with Sushma Kakaar and Joanne Sandler, eds., *A Commitment to the World's Women: Perspective on Development for Beijing and Beyond.* New York: United Nations Development Fund for Women.

———. 1995a. A Matter of Survival: Women's Right to Employment in India and Bangladesh. In M. Nussbaum and J. Gover, eds., *Women and Health in India.* New Delhi: Oxford University Press.

———. 1995b. Recent Research on Widows in India: Workshop and Conference Report. *Economic and Political Weekly* 30 (39).

———. 1995c. *Beyond Credit: Promoting Enterprise of Low-income Women.* New York: United Nations Development Fund for Women; and Ottawa: Aga Khan Foundation of Canada.

Chen, Martha A. and Jean Dreze. 1992. *Widows and Well-Being in Rural North India.* Discussion Paper No. 40. London: International Centre for Economics and Related Disciplines.

———. 1995. Widowhood and Well-Being in Rural North India. In Monica Das Gupta et al., eds., *Women's Health in India: Risk and Vulnerability.* New Delhi: Oxford University Press.

Chenery, Hollis. 1979. *Structural Change and Development Policy.* New York: Oxford University Press for the World Bank.

Chenery, Hollis, Sherman Robinson, and Moshe Syrquin. 1986. *Industrialization and Growth: A Comparative Study.* New York: Oxford University Press for the World Bank.

Chew, David C. 1990. Internal Adjustments to Falling Civil Service Salaries: Insights from Uganda. *World Development* 18 (7): 1103–1114.

Christen, Robert, Elizabeth Rhyne, and Robert Vogel. 1994. *Maximizing the Outreach of Microenterprise Finance: The Emerging Lessons of Successful Programs.* Washington, DC: USAID.

Cohen, John M. 1984. Participatory Planning and Kenya's National Food Policy Paper. *Food Research Institute Studies* 19 (2): 187–213.

———. 1987. *Integrated Rural Development: The Ethiopian Experience and the Debate.* Uppsala: Scandinavian Institute of African Studies.

———. 1992. Foreign Advisors and Capacity Building: The Case of Kenya. *Public Administration and Development* 12 (5): 493–510.

———. 1995. Capacity Building in the Public Sector: A Focused Framework for Analysis and Action. *International Review of Administrative Sciences* 61 (3): 407–422.

Cohen, John M., Merilee S. Grindle, and John W. Thomas. 1983. *Knowledge Building for Rural Development: Social Science and the Cooperative Agreements.* Report prepared for USAID. Cambridge, MA: Harvard Institute for International Development.

Cohen, John M., Merilee S. Grindle, and S. Tjip Walker. 1985. Foreign Aid and Conditions Precedent: Political and Bureaucratic Dimensions. *World Development* 13 (12): 1211–1230.

Cohen, John M. and Richard M. Hook. 1986. Decentralized Development Planning in Kenya. *Public Administration and Development* 7(1): 85–91.

Cohen, John M. and David B. Lewis. 1979a. Capital Surplus Labor Short Economies: Yemen as a Challenge to Rural Development Strategies. *American Journal of Agricultural Economics* 61.

———. 1979b. *Rural Development in the Yemen Arab Republic: Strategy Issues in a Capital Surplus Labor Short Economy.* Development Discussion Paper 52. Cambridge, MA: Harvard Institute for International Development.

———. 1980. *Rural Development and Local Organizations in Hajja and Hodeidah: Yemen Arab Republic.* Ithaca: Cornell University, Rural Development Committee.

———. 1981. Development from Below: Local Development Associations in the Yemen Arab Republic. *World Development* 9 (11/12): 1039–1091.

———. 1983. *Emerging Rural Patterns in the Yemen Arab Republic: Results of a 21 Community Study.* Ithaca: Cornell University, Rural Development Committee, Yemen Research Program.

———. 1987. Role of Government in Combating Food Shortages: Lessons from Kenya 1984–1985. In Michael Glantz, ed., *Drought and Hunger in Africa: Denying Famine a Future.* Cambridge: Cambridge University Press.

Cohen, John M. and John R. Wheeler. 1994. *Improving Public Expenditure Planning: Introducing a Public Investment Program in Kenya.* Development

Discussion Paper 479. Cambridge, MA: Harvard Institute for International Development.

———. 1997. Training and Retention in African Public Sectors: Capacity Building Lessons from Kenya. In Merilee S. Grindle, ed., *Getting Good Government: Capacity Building in the Public Sectors of Developing Countries.* Cambridge, MA: Harvard Institute for International Development.

Cole, David C. and Richard Huntington. 1994. *Participatory Development in Rural Africa: Lessons from Abyei.* Manuscript. Cambridge, MA: Harvard Institute for International Development.

———. 1997. *Between a Swamp and a Hard Place: Developmental Challenges in Remote Rural Africa.* Cambridge, MA: Harvard Institute for International Development.

Cole, David C., Edward S. Mason, Dwight H. Perkins, M. J. Kim, and K. S. Kim. 1980. *The Economic and Social Modernization of the Republic of Korea.* Cambridge, MA: Council on East Asian Studies, Harvard University.

Cole, David C. and Yung Chul Park. 1982. *Korean Financial Development: 1945–1978.* Cambridge, MA: Council on East Asian Studies, Harvard University.

Cole, David C., Hal S. Scott, and Philip Wellons, eds. 1995. *Asian Money Markets.* Oxford: Oxford University Press.

Cole, David C. and Betty F. Slade. 1991. Reform of Financial Systems. In Dwight H. Perkins and Michael Roemer, eds., *Reforming Economic Systems in Developing Countries.* Cambridge, MA: Harvard Institute for International Development.

———. 1992a. Financial Development in Indonesia. In Anne Booth, ed., *The Oil Boom and After: Indonesian Economic Policy and Performance in the Soeharto Years.* Singapore: Oxford University Press.

———. 1992b. Indonesian Financial Development: A Different Sequencing? In Dimitri Vittas, ed., *Financial Regulation: Changing the Rules of the Game.* Washington, DC: World Bank.

Colemen, James S. et al. 1966. *Equality of Educational Opportunity.* Washington, DC: U.S. Department of Health, Education, and Welfare.

Cuadra, Ernesto, M. B. Anderson, S. Moreland, and F. Dall. 1988. *Female Access to Basic Education: Trends, Policies and Strategies.* BRIDGES Research Report Series. Cambridge, MA: Harvard Institute for International Development.

Cummings, William K., G. B. Gunawardena and James H. Williams. 1992. *Management Reforms and the Improvement of Education in Sri Lanka.* BRIDGES Research Report Series No. 11. Cambridge, MA: Harvard Institute for International Development.

Darling, Malcom Lyall. 1978. *The Punjab Peasant in Prosperity and Debt.* Dourthy edition, originally published in 1925. Columbia, NO: South Asia Books.

Davis, Russel G. 1980. *Planning Education for Development.* (4 volumes) Cambridge, MA: Harvard University Center for Studies in Educational Development.

Development Alternatives, Inc. 1981. *An Evaluation of the Abyei Integrated Rural Development Project.* Evaluation Paper prepared for the USAID Sudan Mission, Khartoum.

Development Program Implementation Studies. 1983. *Report on Rice Intensification.* Coordinated by Marguerite S. Robinson. Jakarta: DPIS.

Duesenberry, James S., Clive S. Gray, Jeffrey D. Lewis, Malcolm F. McPherson, and Stephen D. Younger. 1994. *Improving Exchange Rate Management in Sub-Saharan Africa.* CAER Discussion Paper No. 31. Cambridge, MA: Harvard Institute for International Development.

Duesenberry, James S. and Malcolm F. McPherson. 1991. *Monetary Management in Sub-Saharan Africa: A Comparative Analysis.* CAER Discussion Paper No. 7. Cambridge, MA: Harvard Institute for International Development.

———. 1995. Monetary Policy and Financial Reform. In M. F. McPherson and S. C. Radelet, eds., *Economic Recovery in The Gambia: Insights for Adjustment in Sub-Saharan Africa.* Cambridge, MA: Harvard Institute for International Development.

Economist. 1995. A Silent Revolution: A Survey of Russia's Emerging Market. April 8th.

Evans, Hugh. 1992. A Virtuous Cycle Model of Rural-Urban Development: Evidence from a Kenyan Small Town and its Hinterland. *Journal of Development Studies* 28 (4): 640–667.

Fernando, Nimal A. 1988. The Interest Rate Structure and Factors Affecting Interest Rate Determination in the Informal Rural Credit Market in Sri Lanka. *Savings and Development* 12 (3): 249–267.

Floro, Segrario L. and Pan A. Yatopoulos. 1991. *Informal Credit Markets and the New Institutional Economics: The Case of Philippine Agriculture.* Boulder, CO: Westview Press.

Frank, Andre Gunder. 1969. *Capitalism and Underdevelopment in Latin America.* New York: Monthly Review Press.

Gaile, Gary. 1992. Improving Rural Urban Linkages Through Small Town Market-Based Development. *Third World Planning Review* 14 (2): 131–148.

Germidis, Dimitri, Denis Kessler, and Rachel Meghir. 1991. *Financial Systems and Development: What Role for the Formal and Informal Financial Sectors?* Paris: Development Centre of the Organization for Economic Cooperation and Development.

Ghate, Prabhu, Arindam Das Gupta, Mario Lamberte, Nipon Poapongaskorn, Dibyo Prabowo, and Atiq Rahman. 1993. *Informal Finance: Some Findings from Asia.* New York: Oxford University Press for the Asian Development Bank.

Gillis, S. Malcolm. 1978. *Taxation and the Mining Sector: Non-fuel Minerals in Bolivia and Other Countries.* Cambridge, MA: Ballinger Press.

———. 1984. Episodes in Indonesian Economic Growth. In Arnold C. Harberger, ed., *World Economic Growth.* San Francisco, CA: Institute for Contemporary Studies.

———. 1985. Micro- and Macroeconomics of Tax Reform: Indonesia. *Journal of Development Economics* 19: 221–254.

Gillis, S. Malcolm, ed. 1989. *Tax Reform in Developing Countries.* Durham, NC: Duke University Press.

Gillis, S. Malcolm and Ralph E. Beals. 1980. *Tax and Investment Policies for Hard Minerals: Public and Multinational Enterprises in Indonesia.* Cambridge, MA: Ballinger Press.

Gillis, S. Malcolm, Dwight H. Perkins, Michael Roemer, and Donald R. Snodgrass. 1983, 1992. *Economics of Development.* New York: W.W. Norton.

Glenday, Graham. 1991. On Safari in Kenya: From Sales Tax to Value-Added Tax. *International VAT Monitor* (December): 2–6.

Godoy, Ricardo A. 1990a. *Small-Scale Mining and Agriculture in Highland Bolivia: History, Ecology, and Commerce Among the Jukamani Indians of Northern Potosi, Bolivia.* Tucson: University of Arizona Press.

———. 1990b. The Economics of Sustainable Agroforestry Systems: Smallholder Rattan Cultivation. *Agroforestry Systems* 12: 163–172.

———. 1992. Some Organizing Principles in the Valuation of Tropical Forests. *Forest Ecology and Management* 50: 171–180.

Godoy, Ricardo A. and Christopher A. Bennet. 1989. Diversification Among Coffee Smallholders in the Highlands of South Sumatra, Indonesia. *Human Ecology* 16 (4): 397–420.

———. 1990. The Quality of Smallholder Cloves in Maluku: The Local Response to Domestic Demand for High-Quality Products. *Bulletin of Indonesian Economic Studies* 26 (2): 59–78.

———. 1991. Monocropped and Intercropped Coconuts in Indonesia: Project Goals Which Conflict with Smallholder Interests. *Human Ecology* 19 (1): 83–97.

———. 1992a. The Economics of Monocropping and Intercropping by Smallholders: The Case of Coconuts in Indonesia. *Human Ecology* 19 (1): 83–98.

———. 1992b. The Quality of Smallholder Coffee in South Sumatra: The Production of Low Quality Coffee as a Response to World Demand. *Bulletin of Indonesian Economic Studies* 28 (1): 85–100.

Godoy, Ricardo A. and Mario De Franco. 1992a. High Inflation and Bolivian Agriculture. *Journal of Latin American Studies* 24 (3): 617–637.

———. 1992b. The Economic Consequences of the Coca Industry in Bolivia: Historical, Local, and Macroeconomic Perspectives. *Journal of Latin American Studies* 24: 375–406.

———. 1993. Potato-Led Growth, The Role of Agricultural Innovations in Transforming Bolivian Agriculture: A Macroeconomic Perspective. *Journal of Development Studies* 29 (3): 561–587.

Godoy, Ricardo A., Mario de Franco with Ruben Echeverria. 1993. *A Brief History of Agricultural Research in Bolivia: Potatoes, Maize, Soybeans, and Wheat Compared.* Development Discussion Paper 460. Cambridge, MA: Harvard Institute for International Development.

Godoy, Ricardo A., K. O'Neill, D. Wilkie, S. Kostishack, et al. 1997. Household Determinants of Neotropical Deforestation by Amerindians in Honduras. *World Development* 18 (35).

Godoy, Ricardo A. and Tan Ching Feaw. 1989. The Profitability of Smallholder Rattan Cultivation in Central Borneo. *Agroforestry Systems* 17 (3): 347–363.

———. 1991. Agricultural Diversification Among Small Rattan Cultivators in Central Kalimantan Indonesia. *Agroforestry Systems* 13: 27–40.

Goldman, Richard H. 1991. *Economic Analysis of Agricultural Policies: A Basic Training Manual with Special Reference to Price Analysis.* Rome: Food and Agricultural Organization of the United Nations.

Gonzalez-Vega, Claudio, and Rodrigo A. Chaves. 1992. *Indonesia's Rural Financial Markets: A Report for the Financial Institutions Development Project, Indonesia.* Columbus, OH: Ohio State University.

Government of The Gambia. 1985. *Action Programme for Economic Reform Ministry of Finance and Trade.* Banjul: Ministry of Finance and Trade.

———. 1987. Memorandum by the Honourable Minister of Finance and Trade on the Economic Recovery Programme. Banjul: Ministry of Finance and Trade.

———. 1990. The Programme for Sustained Development. Banjul: Ministry of Finance and Economic Affairs.

Gray, Cheryl W. 1986a. State-Sponsored Primary Health Care in Africa: The Recurrent Cost of Performing Miracles. *Social Science and Medicine* 22: 361–368.

———. 1986b. *Indonesian Public Administration: Policy Reform and the Legal Process.* Doctoral dissertation. Cambridge, MA: John F. Kennedy School of Government, Harvard University.

Gray, Clive S. 1989. On Measuring the Shadow Price of Uncommitted Fiscal Resources in Africa. *World Development* 17 (2).

———. 1991. *Competition Policy in Sri Lanka.* Unpublished report prepared for the Industrialization Commission, Government of Sri Lanka, October.

Gray, Clive S., Jacques Baudouy, Kelsey Martin, Molly Bang, and Richard Cash. 1990. *Primary Health Care in Africa: A Study of the Mali Rural Health Project.* Boulder, CO: Westview Press.

Gray, Clive S. and Andre Martens. 1981. Depenses Recurrentes et Developpement au Sahel. *Canadian Journal of Development Studies* 2 (2).

Gray, Clive S., P. Sabur and P. F. L. Maspaitella. 1985. *Pengantar Evaluasi Projek.* Jakarta: P. T. Gramedia.

Grindle, Merilee S. 1985. *State and Countryside: Development Policy and Agrarian Politics in Latin America.* Baltimore, MD: Johns Hopkins University Press.

———. 1988. *Searching for Rural Development: Labor Migration and Employment in Mexico.* Ithaca, NY: Cornell University Press.

———. 1995. *Challenging the State: Crisis and Innovation in Latin America and Africa.* Cambridge, UK: Cambridge University Press.

Grindle, Merilee S., ed. 1997. *Getting Good Government: Capacity Building in the Public Sectors of Developing Countries.* Cambridge, MA: Harvard Institute for International Development.

Grindle, Merilee S., Charles Mann, and Parker Shipton. 1989. *Seeking Solutions: Framework and Cases for Small Enterprise Development Programs.* Hartford, CT: Kumarian Press.

Grindle, Merilee S. and John W. Thomas. 1991. *Public Choices and Policy Change: The Political Economy of Reform in Developing Countries.* Baltimore, MD: Johns Hopkins University Press.

Grossman, G. M. and A. B. Kruegcr. 1995. Economic Growth and the Environment. *The Quarterly Journal of Economics* (May): 353–375.

Government of the Republic of Zambia. 1984. *Restructuring in the Midst of Crisis* (2 volumes). Republic of Zambia for Consultative Group for Zambia. May 22–24.

———. 1989. *New Economic Recovery Programme Economic and Financial Policy Framework 1989–1993.* Lusaka: Lusaka National Commission on Development Planning, August.

Guerard, Yves, and Glenn P. Jenkins. 1993. *Building Private Pension Systems.* San Francisco: ICS Press.

Gulhati, Ravi. 1989. *Impasse in Zambia: The Economics and Politics of Reform.* World Bank, EDI Development Policy Case Studies. Analytical Case Studies, No.2. Washington, DC: World Bank.

Gupta, Monica, T. N. Krishnan, and L. C. Chen, eds. 1995. *Women and Health in India: Risk and Vulnerability.* New Delhi: Oxford University Press.

Guyer, Jane I. and Pauline E. Peters, eds. 1986. *Proceedings of a Conference on Conceptualizing the Household.* Social Science Research Council, American Council of Learned Societies, Joint Committee on African Studies.

———. 1987. Introduction in Conceptualizing the Household: Issues of Theory and Policy in Africa. *Development and Change,* 18(2) special issue.

Haggard, Stephan, Richard N. Cooper, Susan M. Collins, Choongsoo Kim, and Sung-Tae Ro. 1994. *Macroeconomic Policy and Adjustment in Korea, 1970–1990.* Cambridge, MA: Harvard Institute for International Development.

Hambridge, M. 1990. Migrant Labour and its Impact on AIDS/HIV. *AIDS Analysis Africa* 1: 6–7.

Harberger, Arnold and Glenn P. Jenkins. 1991. *Cost-Benefit Analysis of Investment Decisions.* Cambridge: MA: Harvard Institute for International Development.

Harden, Blaine. 1990. The Good, the Bad, and the Greedy. In Blaine Harden, ed., *Africa: Dispatches from a Fragile Continent.* Boston: Houghton Mifflin Company.

Harley, Richard M. 1990. *Breakthroughs on Hunger: A Journalist's Encounter with Global Change.* Washington, DC: Smithsonian Institute Press.

Hart, Thomas O. 1987. *Issues in Tax Reform: Studies in Indonesia.* Doctoral dissertation. Duke University, Department of Economics.

Hartwick, J. M. 1977. Intergenerational Equity and the Investing of Rents from Exhaustible Resources. *American Economic Review.* 67 (5): 972–974.

Henn, Albert E. and Charles Myers. 1988. Potential Impact of AIDS in Africa. In Robert Rotberg, ed., *Africa in the 1990s and Beyond: U.S. Policy Opportunities and Choices.* Algonac, MI: Reference Publications Inc.

Henry, Fitzroy J., ed. 1994. *Journal of Diarrheal Diseases Research,* Special Issue 12(1): 1–69.

Herrera, M. Guillermo, P. Nestel, A. El Amin, W. W. Fawzi, K. A. Mohamed, and L. Weld. 1992. Vitamin A Supplementation and Child Survival. *The Lancet* 340: 267–272.

Hoff, Karla, Avishay Braverman, and Joseph E. Stiglitz, eds. 1993. *The Economics of Rural Organization: Theory, Practice and Policy.* New York: Oxford University Press for the World Bank.

Hook, Richard. 1995. Financing Small Enterprises in Indonesia: The Experience of Bank Rakyat Indonesia. In Ernst A. Brugger and Sarath Rajapatirana, eds. *New Perspectives on Financing Small Business in Developing Countries.* International Center for Economic Growth and Fundacion para el Desarrollo Sostenible (FUNDES). San Francisco: ICS Press, 111–121.

Hossain, Mahabub. 1988. *Credit for Alleviation of Rural Poverty: The Grameen Bank in Bangladesh.* Research Report No. 65. Washington, DC: International Food Policy Research Institute.

Hussey, Ward and Donald Lubick. 1992 and 1996. *Basic World Tax Code.* Arlington, VA: Tax Analysts.

Hyden, Goran 1983. *No Shortcuts to Progress: African Development Managers in Perspective.* Berkeley: University of California Press.

Jakarta Post, Friday, February 10, 1993.

Jenkins, Glenn P. 1991. Tax Reform: Lessons Learned. In Dwight H. Perkins and Michael Roemer, eds., *Reforming Economic Systems in Developing Countries.* Cambridge, MA: Harvard Institute for International Development.

———. 1992. Privatization and Pension Reform in Transition Economies. *Journal of Public Finance* 47: 141–151.

Jenkins, Glenn P. and Mostafa Baher El-Hifnawi. 1994. *Economic Parameters for the Appraisal of Investment Projects: Bangladesh, Indonesia and The Philippines.* Manila: Asian Development.

Jenkins, Glenn P. and Andrew Kwok-Kong Lai. 1989. *Trade, Exchange Rate and Agricultural Pricing Policies in Malaysia.* Comparative Studies Series. Washington, DC: World Bank.

Jenkins, Glenn P. and Ranjit Lamech. 1992. Fiscal Policies to Control Pollution: International Experience. *Bulletin for International Fiscal Documentation* 46 (10): 483–502.

Jones, Barkely G. 1986. Urban Support for Rural Development in Kenya. *Economic Geography,* 62 (3): 201–214.

Jones, Christine W. 1983. *The Mobilization of Women's Labor for Cash Crop Production: a Game-Theoretic Approach.* Doctoral dissertation. Harvard University.

———. 1986. Intra-Household Bargaining in Response to the Introduction of New Crops: A Case Study from North Cameroon. In Joyce L. Moock, ed., *Understanding Africa's Rural Households and Farming Systems.* Boulder, CO: Westview Press.

———. 1988. *Market and Non-Market Resource Mobilization Strategies: Issues of Differentiation and Growth in Sub-Saharan Africa.* New York: Report for the Ford Foundation.

Jones, Christine, and Michael Roemer, eds. 1989. Parallel Markets in Developing Countries. *World Development* 17 (12) special issue.

Jones, Leroy et al., eds. 1982. *Public Enterprise in Less-Developed Countries.* Cambridge, UK: Cambridge University Press.

Jones, Leroy, and Il Sakong. 1980. *Government, Business and Entrepreneurship in Development: The Korean Case.* Cambridge, MA: Harvard University, Council on East Asian Studies.

Kaldor, Nicholas. 1980. *Suggestions for a Comprehensive Reform of Direct Taxation in Ceylon.* Colombo: Government Press.

Kamble, Namdes D. 1979. *Poverty Within Poverty: A Study of the Weaker Sections in a Deccan Village.* Bangalore: Institute for Social and Economic Change.

———. 1982. *Bonded Labour in India.* New Delhi: Uppal Publishing House.

Kaosa-ard, M., A. Desharo, and T. Panayotou. 1995. *Greening Finance: Valuation And Financing of Khao Yai National Park In Thailand.* Bangkok: Thailand Development Research Institute.

Kaunda, Kenneth. 1969. Zambia Towards Complete Independence. In Bastiann de Gaay Fortman, ed., *After Mulungushi—The Economics of Zambian Humanism.* Nairobi: East African Publishing House.

Kelly, Roy B. 1989. Property Taxation in Indonesia. In Nick Devas, ed., *Financing Local Government in Indonesia.* Athens, OH: Ohio University Center for International Studies.

———. 1992. Implementing Tax Reform in Developing Countries: Lessons from the Property Tax in Indonesia. *Review of Urban and Development Studies* 4: 193–208.

———. 1993a. *A Collection-Led Property Tax Reform Strategy: The Case of Indonesia.* Development Discussion Paper 449. International Tax Program Taxation Research Series 12. Cambridge, MA: Harvard Institute for International Development.

———. 1993b. *The Evolution of a Property Tax Information Management System (SISMIOP): The Case of Indonesia.* Development Discussion Paper 458. International Tax Program Taxation Research Series 14. Cambridge, MA: Harvard Institute for International Development.

———. 1993c. Property Tax Reform in Indonesia: Applying a Collection-Led Strategy. *Bulletin of Indonesian Economic Studies* 29 (1): 1–21.

———. 1994. Country: Indonesia. In Joan Youngman and Jane Malme, eds., *An International Survey of Taxes on Land and Buildings.* Amsterdam: Kluwer Law and Taxation Publishers.

———. 1995. Property Tax Reform in Southeast Asia: A Comparative Analysis of Indonesia, the Philippines and Thailand. *Journal of Property Tax Assessment and Administration* 1: 1021–1028.

Kennedy, Eileen and Pauline E. Peters. 1992. Household Food Security and Child Nutrition: The Interaction of Income and Gender of Household Head. *World Development* 20 (8): 1077–1085.

Kennedy, Eileen, Pauline E. Peters, and Lawrence Haddad. 1994. Effects of Gender Head of Household on Nutritional Status. In Margaret Biswas and Mamdouh Gabr, eds., *Nutrition in the Nineties: Policy Issues.* Delhi: Oxford University Press.

Killick, Tony. 1976. The Possibilities of Development Planning. *Oxford Economic Papers* 41 (4): 161–184.

Korten, David. 1980. Community Organization and Rural Development: A Learning Process Approach. *Public Administration Review* 40 (5): 480–511.

Kouri, Yamil H., Donald S. Shepard, Freddie Borras, Jeannette Sotomayor, and George A. Gellert. 1992. Improving the Cost Effectiveness of AIDS Health Care in San Juan, Puerto Rico. *Lancet* 337 (8754): 1397–1399.

Kuznets, Simon. 1971. *Economic Growth of Nations: Total Output and Production Structure.* Cambridge, MA: Harvard University Press.

Ladman, Jerry R. 1971. Some Empirical Evidence in Unorganized Rural Credit Markets. *Canadian Journal of Agricultural Economics* 19 (3): 61–66.

Lamb, David. 1982.*The Africans.* New York: Random House.

Lange, O. 1961. *Economic Development, Planning and International Cooperation* Cairo: Central Bank of Egypt.

Leonard, David K. 1987. The Political Realities of African Management. *World Development* 15 (7): 905.

———. 1991. *African Successes: Four Public Managers of Kenyan Rural Development.* Berkeley: University of California Press.

Leonard, David K., John M. Cohen, and Charles Pinckney. 1987. Kenya's Introduction of Microcomputers to Improve Budgeting and Financial Management in the Ministry of Agriculture. In S. R. Roth and C. K. Mann, eds., *Microcomputers in Development: A Public Policy Perspective.* Boulder, CO: Westview Press.

Lewis, Blane D. 1991. An Enquiry into Kenya Small Town Development Policy. *Economic Geography* 67(2): 147–153.

Lewis, J. D. and M. F. McPherson. 1994. *Improving Exchange Rate Management in Zambia.* Cambridge, MA: Harvard Institute for International Development.

Lewis, William A. 1966. *Development Planning: The Essentials of Economic Policy.* New York: Harper and Row.

Lindauer, David L. and Michael Roemer. 1994. *Asia and Africa: Legacies and Opportunities.* San Francisco: ICS Press (published jointly with the Harvard Institute for International Development).

Lindblom, Charles E. 1959. The Science of Muddling Through. *Public Administration Review* 19 (2): 79–88.

Lippeveld, Theo J., Anne-Marie Foltz, and Yankalbe Matchok Mahouri. 1992. *Transforming Health Facility-Based Reporting Systems into Management Information Systems: Lessons from the Chad Experience.* Development Discussion Paper 430. Cambridge, MA: Harvard Institute for International Development.

Lipton, David and Jeffrey Sachs. 1992. *Prospects for Russia's Economic Reforms.* Brookings Papers on Economic Activity, No. 2. Washington, DC: Brookings Institute.

Little, Ian M. D., Dipak Mazumdar, and John W. Page, Jr. 1987. *Small Manufacturing Enterprises: A Comparative Analysis of India and Other Countries.* New York: Oxford University Press for the World Bank.

Ljunggren, Börge, ed. 1993. *The Challenge of Reform in Indochina.* Cambridge, MA: Harvard Institute for International Development.

Lockheed, Marlaine and Adriain Verspaor. 1991. *Improving Primary Education in Developing Countries: A Review of Policy Options.* Oxford: Oxford University Press.

Loera, Armando, and Noel McGinn. 1992. *La Repitencia de Grado en la Escuela Primaria Colombiana.* Education Development Discussion Paper. Cambridge, MA: Harvard Institute for International Development.

Lucas, R. E. 1976. Econometric Policy Evaluation: A Critique. In Karl Brunner and Allan H. Meltzer, eds., *The Phillips Curve and Labor Markets.* Carnegie-Rochester Conference Series on Public Policy, vol. 1. New York: American Elsevier.

Mahbub ul Huq. 1994. Foreign Aid: The Kindness of Strangers. *The Economist* May 7: 20.

Mallon, Richard D. 1981. Performance Evaluation and Compensation of the Social Burdens of Public Enterprise in LDCs. *Annals of Public and Cooperative Economy* 52 (3).

———. 1982. Public Enterprise vs. Other Methods of State Intervention as Instruments of Redistribution Policy: The Malaysia Experience. In L. P. Jones, ed., *Multidisciplinary Perspectives on Public Enterprise in Mixed-Economy, Less-Developed Countries.* Cambridge, UK: Cambridge University Press.

———. 1984. State-Owned Enterprise Reform Through Performance Contracts: The Bolivian Experiment. *World Development* 22 (6).

Mallon, Richard D. and Joseph J. Stern. 1991. The Political Economic of Trade and Industrial Policy Reform in Bangladesh. In Dwight H. Perkins and Michael Roemer, eds., *Reforming Economic Systems in Developing Countries.* Cambridge, MA: Harvard Institute for International Development.

Mann, Charles K. 1992. *Final Report on the Economic and Financial Policy Analyses Project.* Manuscript. Cambridge, MA: Harvard Institute for International Development.

Mann, Charles K., Merilee S. Grindle, and Amy Sanders, eds. 1990. *Seeking Solutions: Case Leader's Guide.* Hartford, CT: Kumarian.

Mann, Charles K. and Barbara Huddleston, eds. 1984. *Food Policy: Frameworks for Analysis and Action.* Bloomington: Indiana University Press.

Mann, Charles K. and Stephen R. Roth, eds. 1992. *Expert Systems in Developing Countries: Practice and Promise.* Boulder: Westview Press.

Markandya, Anil, 1993. *Policies for Sustainable Development: Four Essays.* Economic and Social Development Papers. Rome: Food and Agricultural Organization of the United Nations.

Marla, Sarma. 1981. *Bonded Labour in India: National Survey on the Incidence of Bonded Labour.* New Delhi: Biblia Impex Private, Ltd.

Martokoesoemo, Soeksmono Besar. 1993. *Beyond the Frontiers of Indonesian Banking and Finance.* Rotterdam: Labyrint Publication.

Mason, Edward S. 1986. *The Harvard Institute for International Development and its Antecedents.* Cambridge, MA: Harvard Institute for International Development.

McGinn, Noel F. and Allison M. Borden. 1995. *Framing Questions, Constructing Answers: Linking Research with Education Policy for Developing Countries.* Cambridge, MA: Harvard Institute for International Development.

McGinn, Noel F., G. Orozco and S. Street. 1982. *La Asignación de Recursos a la Educación Publica en Mexico: Un Proceso Técnico en un Contexto Político,* Mexico: Fundación Javier Barros Sierra.

McGinn, Noel F., Fernando Reimers, and Armando Loera, 1992a. *Why do Children Repeat Grades? A Study of Rural Primary Schools in Honduras.* BRIDGES Research Report Series No. 13. Cambridge, MA: Harvard Institute for International Development.

McGinn, Noel F., E. Rivera, and A. Castellanos. 1981. El Sistema Educativo Mexicano (un Modelo de Simulación de Escenarios). *Revista Latinoamericana de Estudios Educativos* 11 (3): 33–74.

McGinn, Noel F., E. Schiefelbein, and D. P. Warwick. 1979. Educational Planning as Political Process: Two Case Studies from Latin America. *Comparative Educational Review* 23 (2): 218–239.

McGinn, Noel F., Donald R. Snodgrass, Yong Bong Kim, Shin Bok Kim, and Quee Young Kim. 1980. *Education and the Modernization of Korea,* Cambridge, MA: Harvard University Press.

McGinn, Noel F., Donald P. Warwick, and Fernando M. Reimers. 1992b. The Implementation of Educational Innovations: Lessons from Pakistan. *International Journal of Educational Development* 12 (4): 297–307.

McPherson, Malcolm F. and Steven C. Radelet. 1995. Economic Reform in The Gambia: Policies, Politics, Aid, and Luck. In Malcolm F. McPherson and Steven C. Radelet, eds., *Economic Recovery in The Gambia: Insights for Adjustment in Sub-Saharan Africa.* Cambridge, MA: Harvard Institute for International Development.

McPherson, Malcolm F. and Steven C. Radelet, eds. 1995. *Economic Recovery in The Gambia: Insights for Adjustment in Sub-Saharan Africa.* Cambridge, MA: Harvard Institute for International Development.

Meier, Gerald M. 1976. *Leading Issues in Economic Development.* 3rd Edition. New York: Oxford University Press.

Mukiama, T. and R. Mwangi. 1989. Seasonal Population Changes and Malaria Transmission Potential of Anopheles Pharoensis and the Minor Anophelines in Mwea Irrigation Scheme, Kenya. *Acta Tropica* 46: 181–189.

Mundle, Sudipto. 1976. The Bonded of Palamau. *Economic and Political Weekly* 11 (18): 73–90.

Musgrave, Richard and Malcolm Gillis. 1971. *Fiscal Reform for Colombia: Final Report and Staff Papers of the Colombian Commission on Tax Reform.* Cambridge, MA: Harvard University, International Tax Program.

Myers, Charles N. 1988. Thailand's Community Finance Experiments: Experience and Prospects. *Health Care Finance.* Honolulu, HI: East West Center.

———. 1989. *Private Provision of Family Planning Services in Thailand: Trends and Analysis.* Bangkok: Thailand Development Research Institute.

Myers, Charles N., T. Ashakul, and S. Wattanalee. 1991. *Contraceptive Repricing/Experimentation.* Bangkok: Thailand Development Research Institute.

Myers, Charles N. and A. E. Henn. 1988. Potential Impact of AIDS in Africa. In Robert Rotberg, ed., *Africa in the 1990's and Beyond: U.S. Policy Opportunities and Choices.* Algonac, MI: Reference Publications Inc.

Myers, Charles N., Dow Mongkolsmai and Nancyanne Causino. 1985. *Financing Health Services and Medical Care in Thailand.* Development Discussion Paper 208. Cambridge, MA: Harvard Institute for International Development.

Nisbet, Charles. 1967. Interest Rates and Imperfect Competition in the Informal Credit Market of Rural Chile. *Economic Development and Cultural Change* 16 (1): 73–90.

Nkrumah, Kwame. 1965. *Neo-colonialism: The Last Stage of Imperialism.* New York: International Publishers.

Nordhaus, W. 1993. Reflections on the Economics of Climate Change. *Journal of Economic Perspectives* 4: 11–25.

Organisation for African Unity. 1979. *What Kind of Africa by the Year 2000?* Proceedings of the Monrovia Symposium. Addis Ababa: Organisation for African Unity.

———. 1980. *The Lagos Plan of Action for the Implementation of the Monrovia Strategy for the Economic Development of Africa.* Lagos: Organisation of African Unity.

Overseas Development Institute. 1982. *Africa's Economic Crisis.* Briefing Paper No. 2. London: Overseas Development Institute.

O'Rourke, Kevin. 1993. *Reaching the Rural Poor with Banking Services.* Jakarta: Harvard Institute for International Development and Bank Rakyat Indonesia.

Otero, Maria and Elisabeth Rhyne, eds. 1994. *The New World of Microenterprise Finance: Building Healthy Financial Institutions for the Poor*. Hartford, CT: Kumarian Press.

Overholt, Catherine, M. B. Anderson, K. Cloud, and J. Austin, eds. 1985. *Gender Roles in Development Projects: A Case Book.* Hartford, CT: Kumarian Press.

Panayotou, Theodore. 1991. *Natural Resources*. Bangkok: Obor Foundation and Kobfai Publisher.

———. 1992. Structural Adjustment and the Environment: The Case of Thailand. In D. Reed, ed., *Structural Adjustment and the Environment.* Colorado: Westview Press.

———. 1993. *Green Markets: The Economics of Sustainable Development.* San Francisco: ICS Press (published jointly with the Harvard Institute for International Development).

———. 1994. Conservation of Biodiversity and Economic Development: The Concept of Transferable Development Rights. *Environmental and Resource Economics* 4(1): 91–110.

———. 1994. An Econometric Analysis of the Causes of Tropical Deforestation: The Case of Northeast Thailand. In David Pearce and Katrina Brown, eds., *Causes of Tropical Deforestation.* London: UCL Press.

———. 1996. Environmental Degradation at Different Stages of Economic Development. In Iftikhar Ahmed and Jacobus A. Doeleman, eds., *Beyond Rio: The Environmental Crisis and Sustainable Livelihoods in the Third World.* New York: St. Martin's Press, Inc. 13–36.

———. 1996. An Inquiry into Population, Resources, and Environment. In D. A. Ahlburg, A. C. Kelley, and K. Oppenheim, eds, *The Impact of Population Growth on Well-Being in Developing Countries.* Berlin/Heidelberg: Springer-Verlag, 258–335.

Panayotou, Theodore, ed. 1985. *Food Policy in Thailand.* Bangkok: Agricultural Development Council.

Panayotou, Theodore and Peter S. Ashton, 1989. *The Case for Multiple Use Management of the Tropical Forests.* Yokohama: International Tropical Timber Organization.

———. 1992. *Not by Timber Alone: Economics and Ecology for Sustaining Tropical Forests.* Washington, DC: Island Press.

Panayotou, Theodore, with Vladislav Balaban, and Randall Bluffstone. 1994. Lemons and Liabilities: Privatization, Foreign Investment, and Environmental Liability in Central and Eastern Europe. *Environmental Impact Assessment Review* 14 (2/3): 157–168.

Paredes, P., M. de la Pena, E. Flores-Guerra, J. Diaz, and J. Trostle. 1995. Factors Influencing Physicians' Prescribing Behaviour in the Treatment of Childhood Diarrhea: Is Knowledge the Clue? *Social Science and Medicine.*

Parker, M. 1991. South Africa—Undermined by AIDS. *South* 123: 17–18.

Patten, Richard H. 1995. *The Development of a Viable Rural Banking System in Indonesia.* Cambridge, MA: Harvard Institute for International Development.

Patten, Richard H., and Jay K. Rosengard, 1991. *Progress with Profits: The Development of Rural Banking in Indonesia.* San Francisco: ICS Press (published jointly with the Harvard Institute for International Development).

Patten, Richard H. and Donald R. Snodgrass. 1987. *Monitoring and Evaluating KUPEDES (General Rural Credit) in Indonesia.* HIID Development Discussion Paper 249. Cambridge, MA: Harvard Institute for International Development.

———. 1991. Reform of Rural Credit in Indonesia: Inducing Bureaucracies to Behave Competitively. In Dwight H. Perkins and Michael Roemer, eds., *Reforming Economic Systems in Developing Countries.* Cambridge, MA: Harvard Institute for International Development.

Perkins, Dwight H., 1986. *China: Asia's Next Giant?* Seattle: University of Washington Press.

Perkins, Dwight H. and S. Yusuf. 1984. *Rural Development in China.* Baltimore: Johns Hopkins University Press.

Perkins, Dwight H. and Michael Roemer, eds. 1991. *Reforming Economic Systems in Developing Countries.* Cambridge, MA: Harvard Institute for International Development.

Peters, Pauline E. 1983a. Promoting Research Contributions to Knowledge about Households and Women. In John M. Cohen, Merilee S. Grindle, and John W. Thomas, *Knowledge Building for Rural Development: Social Science and the Cooperative Agreements.* Report prepared for USAID. Cambridge, MA: Harvard Institute for International Development.

———. 1983b. Gender, Developmental Cycles, and Historical Process: A Critique of Recent Research on Women in Botswana. *Journal of Southern African Studies* 10 (1): 98–122.

———. 1986. Household Management in Botswana: Cattle, Crops, and Wage Labor. In Joyce L. Moock, ed., *Understanding Africa's Rural Households and Farming Systems.* Boulder, CO: Westview Press.

———. 1988. *Market and Non-Market Resource Mobilization Strategies: Issues of Differentiation and Growth in Sub-Saharan Africa.* Report for the Ford Foundation. New York: The Ford Foundation.

———. 1991. Debate on the Economy of Affection: Is It a Useful Tool for Gender Analysis? In C. Gladwin, ed., *Structural Adjustment and African Women Farmers.* Gainesville, FL: University of Florida Press.

———. 1992. *Monitoring the Effects of Grain Market Liberalization on the Income, Food Security and Nutritional Status of Rural Households in Zomba South.* HIID Final Report to U.S. Agency for International Development and the World Bank, Lilongwe, Malaysia.

———. 1994. *Dividing the Common: Politics, Policy, and Culture in Botswana.* Charlottesville: University of Virginia Press.

———. 1996. *Failed Magic or Social Context: Market Liberalization and the Rural Poor.* Development Discussion Paper 562. Cambridge, MA: Harvard Institute for International Development.

———. 1996. The Uses and Abuses of the Concept of 'Female-headed Households' in Research on Agrarian Transformation and in Policy. In Deborah Bryceson, ed., *Women Wielding the Hoe: Lessons from Rural Africa for Feminist Theory and Development Practice.* Washington, DC: Berg Publishers.

Peters, Pauline E. and M. Guillermo Herrera. 1994. Tobacco Cultivation, Food Production and Nutrition Among Smallholders in Malawi. In J. Von Braun and E. Kennedy, eds, *Agricultural Commercialization, Economic Development and Nutrition.* Baltimore, MD: Johns Hopkins University Press.

Peters, Pauline E., M. Guillermo Herrera, with T. F. Randolph. 1989. *Cash Cropping, Food Security and Nutrition: The Effects of Agricultural Commercialization Among Smallholders in Malawi.* Final Report to USAID; Grant PDC-0082-G-SS-6213-00. Cambridge, MA: Harvard Institute for International Development.

Peters, Pauline and E. Kennedy. 1992. Household Food Security and Child Nutrition: The Interaction of Income and Gender of Household Head. *World Development* 20 (8): 1077–1085.

Peterson, Stephen B. 1990a. Institutionalizing Computers in Development Bureaucracies: Theory and Practice in Kenya. *Information Technology for Development* 5 (3): 277–326.

———. 1990b. Microcomputer Training for the Government of Kenya: The Case of the Kenya Institute of Administration. *Information Technology for Development* 5 (4): 381–412.

———. 1991. From Processing to Analyzing: Intensifying the Use of Microcomputers in Development Bureaucracies. *Public Administration and Development* 11 (1): 491–510.

———. 1994a. Budgeting in Kenya: Practice and Prescription. *Public Budgeting and Finance,* 14 (3): 55–76.

———. 1994b. *Saints, Demons, Wizards and Systems: Why Information Technology Reforms Fail or Underperform in Public Bureaucracies in Africa.* Development Discussion Paper 486. Cambridge, MA: Harvard Institute for International Development.

———. 1996. Making It Work: Implementing Effective Financial Information Systems in Bureaucracies in Development Countries. In Glenn Jenkins, ed., *Information Technology in Tax Administration.* The Hague: Kluwer Law and Taxation Publishers.

———. 1997a. Financial Reform in Kenya: Implementing a Public Investment Program in Line Ministries. In Naomi Caiden, ed., *Public Budgeting and Financial Administration in Developing Countries.* Greenwich: JAI Press.

———. 1997b. The Recurrent Cost Crisis In Development Bureaucracies. In Naomi Caiden, ed., *Public Budgeting and Financial Administration in Developing Countries.* Greenwich: JAI Press.

Peterson, Stephen, Charles Kinyeki, Joseph Mutai, and Charles Ndungu. 1997a. Computerizing Accounting Systems in Development Bureaucracies. Lessons from Kenya. *Public Budgeting and Finance* 16 (4).

———. 1997b. Computerizing Personnel Information Systems in African Bureaucracies: Lessons from Kenya. *International Journal of Public Administration* 20 (10). Also, 1995. Development Discussion Paper 496. Cambridge, MA: Harvard Institute for International Development.

Peterson, Stephen and Kithinji Kiragu. 1990. *Recurrent Cost Issues in the Ministry of Agriculture and the Ministry of Livestock Development.* Report prepared for the Ministry of Agriculture and the Ministry of Livestock Development in preparation for the second Agricultural Structural Adjustment Program.

Pfaff, William 1995. A New Colonialism? Europe Must Go Back into Africa. *Foreign Affairs* 74 (1): 2–6.

Pradhan, Rajesh, Anne Hornsby, and Charles K. Mann. 1989. *The AskARIES Knowledgebase; User's Guide and Notebook II Primer.* Hartford, CT: Kumarian Press.

Prebisch, Raul. 1950. *The Economic Development of Latin America and its Principal Problems.* Lake Success, NY: United Nations.

Ramakrishnan, Subramaniam. 1992. Budgeting in Africa: Focus on Reform. *Economic Reform Today*: 9–13.

Ramaurti, Ravi and Ray Vernon, eds. 1991 *Privatization and Control of State-Owned Enterprises.* Washington, DC: EDI Development Studies, World Bank.

Raudenbush, Stephen W., Somsri Kidchanapanish, and Sang Jin Kang. 1991. The Effects of Preprimary Access and Quality on Educational Achievement in Thailand. *Comparative Education Review* 35 (2): 255–273.

Reimers, Fernando M. 1991. The Impact of Economic Stabilization and Adjustment on Education in Latin America. *Comparative Education Review,* 35 (2): 319–353.

Reimers, Fernando, ed. 1993a. *Análisis del Sistema Educativo en el Paraguay.* Asunción: Centro Paraguayo de Estudios Sociológicos.

Reimers, Fernando M. 1993b. Time and Opportunity to Learn in Pakistan's Schools: Some Lessons on the Links Between Research and Policy. *Comparative Education* 29 (2): 201–212.

Reimers, Fernando (coordinador). 1995. *La Educacion en El Salvador de Cara al Siglo XXI: Desafios y oportunidades.* San Salvador: UCA Editores.

Republic of Kenya. 1981. *Sessional Paper No. 4 of 1981.* Nairobi: Government Printer.

———. 1986. *Economic Management for Renewed Growth.* Nairobi: Government Printer.

Reserve Bank of India. 1954. *All-India Rural Credit Survey: Vol.1, The Survey Report; Vol.2, The General Report; Vol. 3, The Technical Report.* Bombay: Reserve Bank of India.

Rhyne, Elizabeth and Linda Rotblatt. 1994. *What Makes them Tick? Exploring the Anatomy of Major Microenterprise Finance Organizations.* Monograph Series No. 9. Cambridge, MA: ACCION International.

Rimmer, Douglas, ed. 1991. *Africa 30 Years On.* London: James Currey for The Royal Africa Society.

Robinson, Marguerite S. 1988. *Local Politics: The Law of the Fishes.* New Delhi: Oxford University Press.

———. 1992. *Rural Financial Intermediation: Lessons from Indonesia, Part One: The Bank Rakyat Indonesia: Rural Banking 1970–1991.* Development Discussion Paper 434. Cambridge, MA. Harvard Institute for International Development.

———. 1994a. *Financial Intermediation at the Local Level: Lessons from Indonesia, Part Two: The Theoretical Perspective.* HIID Development Discussion Paper 482. Cambridge, MA. Harvard Institute for International Development.

———. 1994b. Savings Mobilization and Microenterprise Finance: the Indonesian Experience. In Maria Otero and Elisabeth Rhyne, eds., *The New World of Microenterprise Finance: Building Healthy Financial Institutions for the Poor.* Hartford, CT: Kumarian Press, 27–54.

———. 1995a. *The Paradigm Shift in Microfinance: A Perspective from HIID.* Development Discussion Paper 510. Cambridge, MA: Harvard Institute for International Development.

———. 1995b. Indonesia: The Role of Savings in Developing Sustainable Commercial Financing of Small and Microenterprises. In E. Brugger and S. Rajapatirana, eds., *New Perspectives on Financing Small Business in Developing Countries.* San Francisco: ICS Press, 147–172.

———. 1995c. *Where the Microfinance Revolution Began: The First 25 Years of the Bank Dagang Bali.* GEMINI Working Paper 53. Bethesda, MD.

———. 1995d. *Leading the World in Sustainable Microfinance: the 25th Anniversary of BRI's Unit Desa System.* Jakarta: Bank Rakyat Indonesia.

———. 1997a. Microfinance: the Paradigm Shift from Credit Delivery to Sustainable Financial Intermediation. Forthcoming in a volume edited by J.D. Von Pischke. Washington, DC: The Brookings Institution.

———. 1997b. Sustainable Finance for the Poor: Some Responses to Lady Chalker's Questions. Forthcoming in a World Bank volume *Finance Against Poverty*. Washington, DC: World Bank.

Robinson, Marguerite S., Christopher P. A. Bennet, David E. Bloom, Lakshmi Reddy, and Michael H. Simpson. 1993b. *Enterprises for the Recycling and Composting of Municipal Solid Waste in Jakarta, Indonesia.* Jakarta: Center for Policy and Implementation Studies.

Robinson, Marguerite S. and Donald R. Snodgrass. 1987. *The Role of Institutional Credit in Indonesia's Rice Intensification Program.* Development Discussion Paper 248. Cambridge, MA: Harvard Institute for International Development.

Robinson, Marguerite S. et al. 1993a. The Bank Rakyat Indonesia, 1970–1990: Strategies for Rural Banking. In Bank Raykat Indonesia, ed., *Rural Finance.* Jakarta: Center for Policy and Implementation Studies.

Roemer, Michael. 1979. Resource-Based Industrialization in Developing Countries: A Survey of the Literature. *Journal of Development Economics* 6 (2): 163–202.

———. 1989. Macroeconomics of Counterpart Funds. *World Development* 17 (6): 795–802.

Roemer, Michael and Joseph J. Stern, 1975. *The Appraisal of Development Projects: A Practical Guide with Case Studies from Ghana.* New York: Praeger.

Roemer, Michael and Christine Jones, eds. 1991. *Markets in Developing Countries: Parallel, Fragmented and Black.* San Francisco: ICS Press (published jointly with the Harvard Institute for International Development).

Roemer, Michael and Steven C. Radelet, eds. 1991. Macroeconomic Reform in Developing Countries. In Dwight H. Perkins and Michael Roemer, eds., *Reforming Economic Systems in Developing Countries.* Cambridge, MA: Harvard Institute for International Development.

Rosen, George. 1985. *Western Economists and Eastern Societies: Agents of Change in South Asia, 1950–1970.* Baltimore, MD: Johns Hopskins University Press.

Rosenberg, Richard. 1994. *Beyond Self-Sufficiency: Licensed Leverage and Microfinance Strategy.* Draft. Washington, DC: USAID.

Rosengard, Jay. 1992. Building on a Land Mine: Property Tax Reform in Developing Countries. Doctoral dissertation. Graduate School of Design, Harvard University.

Roth, Hans-Dieter. 1983. *Indian Moneylenders at Work: Case Studies of the Traditional Rural Credit Markets in Dhanbad District, Bihar*. New Delhi: Manohar.

Roth, Stephen R. and Charles K. Mann, eds. 1987. *Microcomputers in Development: A Public Policy Perspective.* Boulder: Westview Press.

Sachs, Jeffrey D. 1994a. Prospects for Monetary Stabilization in Russia. In Anders Aslund, ed., *Economic Transformation in Russia.* London: Pinter Publishers; New York: St. Martin's Press.

———. 1994b. Russia's Struggle with Stabilization: Conceptual Issues and Evidence. *World Bank Research Observer.* Annual Conference Supplement, 57–80.

Sachs, Jeffrey D. and David Lipton. 1992. Towards a Market-Based Monetary System. *Central Banking* 3 (1).

Sachs, Jeffrey D. and Andrew M. Warner. 1995. *Natural Resource Abundance and Economic Growth.* Development Discussion Paper 517a. Cambridge, MA: Harvard Institute for International Development.

———. 1996. *Achieving Rapid Growth in the Transition Economies of Central Europe.* Development Discussion Paper 544. Cambridge, MA: Harvard Institute for International Development.

———. 1996. *Sources of Slow Growth in African Economies.* Development Discussion Paper 545. Cambridge, MA: Harvard Institute for International Development.

Sandbrook, Richard. 1987. *The Politics of Africa's Economic Stagnation.* Cambridge, UK: Cambridge University Press.

Sauerborn, Rainer., I. Ibrango, A. Nougtara, M. Borchert, M. Hien, J. Benzler, E. Koob, and H. J. Diesfeld. 1995a. The Economic Cost of Illness for Rural

Households in Burkina Faso. *Tropical Medicine and Parasitology,* 46 (1): 54–60.

Sauerborn, Rainer, Claude Bodart, and R. Owona. 1995b. Recovery of Recurrent Health Service Costs through Provincial Health Funds in Cameroon. *Social Science and Medicine* 40.

Schmit, L. Th. 1991. *Rural Credit between Subsidy and Market: Adjustment of the Village Units of Bank Rakyat Indonesia in Sociological Perspective.* Leiden Development Series No. 11. Leiden: Leiden University.

Schwefel, Dettef, et al., eds. *Economic Aspects of AIDS and HIV Infection.* New York: Springer-Verlag.

Shepard, Donald S. 1990. Cost of AIDS in a Developing Drea: Indirect and Direct Cost of AIDS in Puerto Rico. In Dettef Schwefel et al., eds. *Economic Aspects of AIDS and HIV Infection.* New York: Springer-Verlag.

———. 1991. Economic Impact of Malaria in Africa. *Tropical Medicine and Parasitology* 42 (3), Supplement 1: 197–224.

Shepard, Donald S. and S. B. Halstead. 1993. Dengue (With Notes on Yellow Fever and Japanese Encephalitis). In D. T. Jamison, W. H. Mosley, A. R. Measham, and J. L. Bobadilla, eds., *Disease Control Priorities for Developing Countries.* New York: Oxford University Press for the World Bank.

Shepard, Donald S., R. N. Bail, and A. Bucyendore. 1992. *Costs of AIDS Care in Rwanda.* Development Discussion Paper 411. Cambridge, MA: Harvard Institute for International Development.

Shipton, Parker. 1988. The Kenya Land Tenure Reform: Misunderstandings in the Public Creation of Private Property. In R. E. Downs and S. P. Renya, eds., *Land and Society in Contemporary Africa.* Hanover, NH: University Press of New England.

———. 1989. *Bitter Money: Cultural Economy and Some African Meanings of Forbidden Commodities.* Washington, DC: American Anthropological Association.

———. 1990. African Famines and Food Security: Anthropological Perspectives. *Annual Review of Anthropology.* 19: 353–394.

———. 1992a. The Rope and the Box: Group Savings in The Gambia. In Dale W. Adams and Delbert A. Fitchett, eds., *Information and Finance in Low-income Countries.* Boulder, CO: Westview Press.

———. 1992b. Debts and Trespasses: Land, Mortgages, and the Ancestors in Western Kenya. In Miriam Goheen and Parker Shipton, eds. *Rights Over Land: Categories and Controversies. Africa,* LXII (3): 357–388 special issue.

Siamwalla, Ammarm, Chirmsak Pinthong, Mipon Poapongsakorn, Ploenpit Satsanguan, Prayong Nettayarak, Wandrak Mingmaneenakin, and Yuavares Tubpun. 1993. The Thai Rural Credit System and Elements of a theory: Public Subsidies, Private Information, and Segmented Markets. In Karla Hoff et al., eds., *The Economics of Rural Organization: Theory, Practice and Policy*. New York: Oxford University Press for the World Bank.

Simon, Jonathon L. and James Trostle. 1995. *Manual of Group Interview Techniques to Assess the Needs of People with AIDS. Global Program on AIDS.* Geneva: World Health Organization.

Singh, Karam. 1983. Structure of Interest Rates on Consumption Loans in an Indian village. In John D. von Pischke, Dale W. Adams, and Gordon Donald, eds., *Rural Financial Markets in Developing Countries: Their Use and Abuse.* Baltimore: Johns Hopkins University Press, 251–254. Extracted from *Asian Economic Review*, 1968, 10 (4): 471–475.

Slade, M. E. 1982. Trends in Natural-Resource Commodity Prices: An Analysis of the Time Domain. *Journal of Environmental Economics and Management* 9: 122–137.

Smoke, Paul J. 1992a. Rural Local Government Finance in Kenya: the Case of Murang'a County Council. *Public Administration and Development* 12 (1): 86–96.

———. 1992b. Small-Town Local Government Finance in Kenya: The Case of Karatina Town Council. *Public Administration and Development* 12 (1): 71–85.

———. 1994. *Local Government Finance in Developing Countries: The Case of Kenya.* Nairobi: Oxford University Press.

Snodgrass, Donald R. and Tyler Biggs. 1996. *Industrialization and the Small Firm: Patterns and Policies.* San Francisco: ICS Press (published jointly with the Harvard Institute for International Development).

Snodgrass, Donald R. and Richard H. Patten. 1991. Reform of Rural Credit in Indonesia: Inducing Bureaucracies to Behave Competitively. In Dwight H. Perkins and Michael Roemer, eds. *Reforming Economic Systems in Developing Countries.* Cambridge, MA: Harvard Institute for International Development.

Snodgrass, Donald R., and Debrabrata Sen. 1979. *Manpower Planning Analysis in Developing Countries: The State of the Art.* Development Discussion Paper 64. Cambridge, MA: Harvard Institute for International Development.

Staley, Eugene and Richard Morse. 1965. *Modern Small Industry for Developing Countries.* New York: McGraw-Hill.

Stern, Joseph J., Ji-hong Kim, Dwight H. Perkins, and Jung-ho Yoo. 1995. *Industrialization and the State: The Korean Heavy and Chemical Industry Drive.* Cambridge, MA: Harvard Institute for International Development.

Sugianto, Satriyo Purnomo. 1989. KUPEDES and SIMPEDES. *Asia Pacific Rural Finance* (July–September): 12–14.

———. 1990a. *Development of Rural Agricultural Financial Policy and the Progress and Benefits of BRI's KUPEDES Program.* Jakarta: Bank Rakyat Indonesia (Photocopy).

———. 1990b. *Transaction Costs at Small Scale Banks Below the Branch Level.* Jakarta: Bank Rakyat Indonesia (Photocopy).

Sugianto, Satriyo Purnomo, and Robinson, Marguerite S. 1993. *Pembiayaan Pertanian Pedesaan [Rural Finance].* Jakarta: Indonesian Banking Institute.

Swanberg, Kenneth G. 1981a. *The Kenyan Ministry of Agriculture's Monitoring and Evaluation Unit 1976–1980: Objectives, Results and Lessons Learned.* Development Discussion Paper 118. Cambridge, MA: Harvard Institute for International Development.

———. 1981b. *Evaluative Research for Agricultural Development Projects.* Development Discussion Paper 127. Cambridge, MA: Harvard Institute for International Development.

Thomas, John W., S. Javed Burki, David G. Davies, and Richard M. Hook. 1976. *Public Works Programs in Developing Countries: A Comparative Analysis.* Working Paper No. 224. Washington, DC: World Bank.

Timmer, C. Peter .1986a. Rice Price Policy in Indonesia: Keeping Prices Right. In Edward B. Rice and Sakwa Bunyasi, eds., *Agricultural Pricing and Trade Policy Background Readings.* Washington, DC: Economic Development Institute of the World Bank.

———. 1986b. The Role of Price Policy in Increasing Rice Production in Indonesia, 1969–1982. In Ray A. Goldberg, ed., *Research in Domestic and International Agribusiness Management.* Greenwich: JAI Press.

———. 1986c. *Getting Prices Right: The Scope and Limits of Agricultural Price Policy.* Ithaca, NY: Cornell University Press.

Timmer, C. Peter, ed. 1987. *The Corn Market in Indonesia.* Ithaca, NY: Cornell University Press.

Timmer, C. Peter. 1989. Indonesia: Transition from Food Importer to Exporter. In Terry Sinclair, ed., *Food Price Policy in Asia.* Ithaca, NY: Cornell University Press.

———. 1990. Crop Diversification in Rice-Based Agricultural Economies: Conceptual Issues. *Indonesian Food Journal* 1 (3) 13–29.

Timmer, C. Peter, ed. 1991a. *Agriculture and the State: Growth, Employment and Poverty in Development Countries.* Ithaca, NY: Cornell University Press, 1991.

Timmer, C. Peter. 1991b. Markets and Government Policy in Setting Prices for Rice Production in Indonesia, 1968–1982. In Sljahrir, ed., *Economic Analysis and Methodology in Indonesia.* Jakarta: Penebit PT Gramedia.

———. 1991c. Food Price Stabilization: Rationale, Design and Implementation. In Dwight H. Perkins and Michael Roemer, eds., *Reforming Economic Systems in Developing Countries.* Cambridge, MA: Harvard Institute for International Development.

———. 1991d. Institutional Development: Indonesia's Experience in Stabilizing Rice Markets. Indonesian Food Journal 2 (3): 8–20.

———. 1992. Food Price Stability and Welfare of the Poor. *Indonesian Food Journal* 3: 42–57.

———. 1993. Building Institutions for Food Policy Analysis. *Indonesian Food Journal* 4: 6–22.

Timmer, C. Peter, Walter P. Falcon, and Scott R. Pearson. 1983. *Food Policy Analysis.* Baltimore, MD: Johns Hopkins University Press

Timmer, C. Peter with Walter P. Falcon. 1991. Food Security in Indonesia: Defining the Issues. *Indonesian Food Journal* 2 (3): 8–20.

Toksoz, Sadik. 1981. *An Accelerated Irrigation and Land Reclamation Program for Kenya: Dimension and Issues.* Development Discussion Paper 114. Cambridge, MA: Harvard Institute for International Development.

Tomich, Thomas P. 1991. Smallholder Rubber Development in Indonesia. In Dwight H. Perkins and Michael Roemer, eds., *Reforming Economic Systems in Developing Countries.* Cambridge, MA: Harvard Institute for International Development.

———. 1992. Survey of Recent Developments. *Bulletin of Indonesian Economic Studies* 28 (3): 2–39.

Tomich, Thomas P. and Colin Barlow. 1991. Indonesian Agricultural Development: The Awkward Case of Smallholder Tree Crops. *Bulletin of Indonesian Economic Studies* 27 (3): 29–53.

Tomich, Thomas P., Peter Kilby, and Bruce F. Johnston. 1995. *Transforming Agrarian Economies: Opportunities Seized, Opportunities Missed.* Ithaca, NY: Cornell University Press.

Tomich, Thomas P., Pauline E. Peters, and Anil B. Deolalikar. 1994. *Social Impact of Agricultural Policy Reform: Evidence from Rural Households in Southern Malawi.* Development Discussion Paper 515. Cambridge, MA: Harvard Institute for International Development.

Trivedi, Praja. 1990. *Memorandum of Understanding.* New Delhi: International Management Publishers.

Trostle, James A., ed. 1992. Building Research Capacity of Health Social Sciences in Developing Countries. *Social Science and Medicine* 35 (11) special issue.

Tun Wai, U. 1977. A Revisit to Interest Rates Outside the Organized Money Markets of Underdeveloped Countries. *Banca Nazionale del Lavoro Quarterly Review* 30 (122): 291–313.

———. 1980. The Role of Unorganized Financial Markets in Economic Development and in the Formulation of Monetary Policy. *Savings and Development* 4 (4).

Ugalde, A. and T. J. Jackson. 1995. *Symposium on the World Bank: World Development Report 1993.* Washington, DC: The World Bank.

United Nations. 1986. *Report on the Preparatory Committee of the Whole for the Special Session of the General Assembly on the Critical Economic Situation in Africa.* United Nations 13th Special Session Supplement No.1 (A/S-13/4).

United Nations Economic Commission for Africa/Organisation for African Unity. 1989. African Alternative Framework to Structural Adjustment Programmes for Socio-Economic Recovery and Transformation (AAF-SAP). UNECA: E/ECA/CM.15/6/Rev.3 Addis Ababa.

USAID. 1993. *Fresh Start in Africa.* Washington DC: Office of Sustainable Development, Africa Bureau, United States Agency for International Development.

Valadez, Joseph J. 1991. *Assessing Child Survival Programs in Developing Countries: Testing Lab Assurance Sampling.* Boston, MA: Harvard School of Public Health.

Varian, Hal R. 1989. *Monitoring Agents with Other Agents.* Center for Research on Economic and Social Theory Working Paper No. 89-18. Ann Arbor: Department of Economics, University of Michigan.

Vernon, Raymond, ed. 1988. *The Promise of Privatization.* New York: The Council on Foreign Relations.

Vernon, Raymond and Yair Aharoni, eds. 1981 *State-Owned Enterprises in Western Europe.* London: Croom Helm.

Vincent, Jeffrey R. 1992. The Tropical Timber Trade and Sustainable Development. *Science* 256: 1651–1655.

———. 1996. Environmental Funds in Developing and Transition Economies. In *Third Expert Group Meeting on Financial Issues of Agenda 21.* Proceedings of a conference sponsored by the Governments of Japan and the

Philippines, the Asian Development Bank, and the U.N. Department of Policy Coordination and Sustainable Development, held February 6–8 in Manila. New York: United Nations.

Vincent, Jeffrey R., Rozali Mohamed Ali, et al. 1997. Environment and Development in a Resource-Rich Economy: Malaysia under the New Economic Policy. Cambridge, MA: Harvard Institute for International Development.

Vincent, Jeffrey R. and S. Farrow. 1997. A Survey of Pollution Charge Systems and Key Issues in Policy Design. In Randall Bluffstone and Bruce Larson, eds., *Pollution Charges in Transition Economies.* United Kingdom: Edward Elgar Publishing Company.

Vincent, Jeffrey R., et al. 1995a. Impediments to Environmental Investments in CEE and the NIS. In G. Klaasen and M. Smith, eds., *Financing Environmental Quality in Central and Eastern Europe: An Assessment of International Support.* Laxenburg, Austria: International Institute for Applied Systems Analysis.

———. 1995b. *The Economics of Watershed Management: A Case Study of Mae Taeng.* Bangkok: Thailand Development Research Institute.

Viravaidya, M., S. A. Obremskey, and C. N. Myers. 1993. The Economic Impact of AIDS on Thailand. In D. E. Bloom and J. V. Lyons, eds., *Economic Implications of AIDS in Asia.* New Delhi, India: United Nations Development Programme, 7–34.

Von Pischke, John D. 1991. *Finance at the Frontier: Debt Capacity and the Role of Credit in the Private Economy.* EDI Development Series. Washington, DC: The World Bank.

Von Pischke, John D., Dale W. Adams, and Gordon Donald, eds. 1983. *Rural Financial Markets in Developing Countries: Their Use and Abuse.* Baltimore, MD: Johns Hopkins University Press.

Wai, Dunstan M. and Gerald T. Rice. 1991. *The African Capacity Building Initiative: Toward Improved Policy Analysis and Development Management.* Washington, DC: World Bank.

Ward, Haskell G. 1989. *African Development Reconsidered: New Perspectives from the Continent.* New York: Phelps-Stokes Institute.

Warwick, Donald P. 1980. Integrating Planning and Implementation: A Transactional Approach. In Russell Davis, ed., *Planning Education for Development, Vol. I.* Cambridge, MA: Center for Studies in Education and Development, Harvard University.

———. 1982. *Bitter Pills: Population Policies and their Implementation in Eight Developing Countries.* New York: Cambridge University Press.

———. 1986. The Indonesian Family Planning Program: Government Influence and Client Choice. *Population and Development Review* 12 (3): 453–90.

———. 1994. The Politics of Research on Fertility Control. In J. L. Finkle and C. A. McIntosh, eds., *The New Politics of Population.* Supplement to *Population and Development Review* 20: 179–203.

Warwick, Donald P. and Haroona Jatoi. 1994. Teacher Gender and Student Achievement in Pakistan. *Comparative Education Review.*

Warwick, Donald P. and Fernando Reimers. 1996. *Hope or Despair: Learning in Pakistan's Primary Schools.* New York: Praeger Publishers.

Warwick, Donald P., Fernando Reimers, and Noel McGinn. 1992. The Implementation of Educational Innovations: Lessons from Pakistan. *International Journal of Educational Development* 12 (4): 297–307.

Westcott, Clay. 1987. Microcomputers for Improved Government Budgeting: An African Experience. In Stephen R. Roth and Charles K. Mann, eds, *Microcomputers in Development: A Public Policy Perspective.* Boulder, CO: Westview Press.

Westlake, Michael J. 1987. The Measurement of Agricultural Price Distortion in Developing Countries. *Journal of Development Studies* 23 (3): 367–381.

White, Lawrence H. *Overview of ADB Study on Financial Sector Policies of Selected Developing Member Countries* (forthcoming).

WHO/USAID/NEI. 1993. *Vitamin A Mortality and Morbidity Studies.* Geneva: World Health Organisation.

Wolf, C. R., Jr. 1979. A Theory of Nonmarket Failure. *Journal of Law and Economics* 22 (1): 107–139.

———. 1988. *Markets or Governments: Choosing between Imperfect Alternatives.* Cambridge, MA: The MIT Press.

World Bank. 1981. *Accelerating Development in Sub-Saharan Africa: An Agenda for ACTION.* Washington DC: World Bank.

———. 1984. *Towards Sustained Development in Sub-Saharan Africa.* Washington DC: World Bank.

———. 1985. *The Gambia: Development Issues and Prospects.* Washington DC: World Bank/West Africa Region No. 5693-GM.

———. 1986. *Financing Adjustment with Growth in Sub-Saharan Africa, 1986–90.* Washington DC: World Bank.

———. 1989. *Sub-Saharan Africa From Crisis to Sustainable Growth A Long-Term Perspective Study.* Washington DC: World Bank.

———. 1992. *Development Report 1992: Development and the Environment.* New York: Oxford University Press, Inc. for the World Bank.

———. 1993a. *Zambia: Prospects for Sustainable and Equitable Growth.* Report No. 11570-ZA. Washington DC: Country Operations Division, Southern Africa Department.

———. 1993b. *World Development Report 1993: Investing in Health.* New York: Oxford University Press.

———. 1994a. *Adjustment in Africa: Reforms, Results and the Road Ahead.* New York: Oxford University Press.

———. 1994b. *Averting the Old Age Crisis.* New York: Oxford University Press for the World Bank.

———. 1995. *Reducing Poverty in Zambia: Getting from Ideas to Action.* Washington DC: World Bank.

Yaron, Jacob. 1992a. *Successful Rural Financial Institutions.* World Bank Discussion Papers 150. Washington, DC: World Bank.

———. 1992b. *Assessing Successful Rural Financial Institutions: A Public Policy Analysis.* World Bank Discussion Papers 174. Washington, DC: World Bank.

Young, C. 1982. *Ideology and Development in Africa.* New Haven, CT: Yale University Press.

Appendices

APPENDIX 1-A

HIID Overseas Projects, 1980–1995

(Assigned number cross-referenced with staff and consultant lists; no end date indicates project end after 1995)

#	Country	Project Name	Begin	End
1	Bangladesh	Trade and Industrial Policy Reform Programme	1983	1989
2	Bolivia	Credit for Micro-Enterprises	1992	1993
3	Bolivia	Human Resources for Development	1994	–
4	Bolivia	Reordering State-Owned Enterprise	1990	1993
5	Bolivia	Rural Finance	1993	1994
6	Bolivia	Technical Support for Policy Reform	1993	–
7	Bolivia	Technological Improvement in Agriculture	1990	1990
8	Bolivia	Tropical Deforestation	1995	1995
9	Bolivia	Unidad de Analisis de Politicas Economicas (UDAPE)	1987	1992
10	Bolivia	Unidad de Analisis de Politicas Sociales (UDAPSO)	1993	–
11	Brunei	Public Management Development Project	1986	1993
12	Cameroon	Child Survival/Maternal and Child Health Care	1987	1994
13	C. & E. Europe	Environmental Action Program Support	1995	–
14	C. & E. Europe	Environmental Reform and Economic Policy	1992	–
15	Chad	Health Planning Restoration and Rehabilitation	1985	1989
16	Chad	Population Advisory Project	1987	1988
17	Chile	Urban Development	1993	1994
18	China	Institute for International Economic Management, PRC	1981	1982
19	Colombia	Education Policy	1991	1992
20	Colombia	Evaluation of the Health and Population Program	1991	1992
21	Costa Rica	Peripheral Health Care Research	1986	1990
22	Djibouti	Health Management Training Workshops	1987	1987
23	Dominican Rep.	Public Enterprise Seminar	1986	1987
24	Dominican Rep.	Tax Reform	1990	1994
25	Ecuador	State Petroleum Corporation	1981	1982
26	Egypt	Educational Planning Unit	1989	1994
27	Egypt	Public Enterprise Workshop	1992	1992
28	Egypt	Public Enterprise Workshop	1995	1995
29	El Salvador	Educational Sector Assessment	1993	1994
30	The Gambia	Economic and Financial Policy Analyses (EFPA)	1985	1992
31	The Gambia	Tax Administration Modernization Project	1993	1995
32	Ghana	Collection of Sales Tax	1989	1989
33	Guatemala	Education Policy	1993	1993
34	Honduras	Effect of Markets on Indigenous People	1993	–
35	Honduras	Zoological Research in the Rain Forest	1994	–

36	India	Widows in Rural Areas	1990	1994
37	India	Women and Household Livelihoods in Rural India	1988	1989
38	Indonesia	Analysis of Manufactured Export Growth	1995	1995
39	Indonesia	Bank Dagang Bali	1994	1995
40	Indonesia	Bank Danamon	1995	–
41	Indonesia	Bank Rakyat Indonesia (BRI)	1987	–
42	Indonesia	Center for Financial Policy Studies & Training (CFPST)	1983	1987
43	Indonesia	Center for Policy and Implementation Studies (CPIS)	1982	1992
44	Indonesia	Customs and Economic Mgt., Economic Analysis	1986	–
45	Indonesia	Development Program Implementation Study (DPIS)	1979	1982
46	Indonesia	Fiscal Reform	1980	1983
47	Indonesia	General Participant Training II	1984	1989
48	Indonesia	Ministry of Finance Training (MOFT)	1981	–
49	Indonesia	OTO Support Office Contract (OTOSOC)	1989	1992
50	Indonesia	Professional Human Resource Development (PHRD)	1990	1995
51	Indonesia	Program for Financial Policy Studies & Training	1983	1994
52	Indonesia	Property Tax Administration	1988	1994
53	Indonesia	Rural Electrification	1980	1985
54	Indonesia	Small Enterprise Program/Bank Indonesia	1980	1985
55	Indonesia	State Bank Training	1983	1991
56	Indonesia	Study of Bank Dagang Bali	1992	1993
57	Indonesia	Training and Technical Assistance	1979	1982
58	Indonesia	Urban Development Policy and Finance	1980	1994
59	Ivory Coast	African Development Bank	1979	1983
60	Jamaica	Policy Analysis, Planning, and Management	1993	–
61	Jordan	Educational Reform	1992	1995
62	Kenya	Agricultural Planning, Policy and Management (TAP)	1976	1992
63	Kenya	Agricultural Sector Adjustment II (ASAO)	1993	1994
64	Kenya	Budget and Economic Management (BEMP)	1990	–
65	Kenya	Customs Computerization Review	1990	1991
66	Kenya	Pop. Growth and Renewable Resources Research	1986	1987
67	Kenya	Rural Planning (RP)/ Rural Development (RMRD)	1976	1992
68	Kenya	Tax Modernization-Customs Systems Reform	1991	–
69	Kenya	Tax Policy Development	1992	1994
70	Kenya	Tax Policy Reform	1990	1992
71	Kenya	Tax Reform Studies	1986	1987
72	Korea	Korea Development Institute Studies (KDI)	1987	–
73	Lesotho	Customs, Value-Added Tax & Trade Policy	1993	1995
74	Malawi	Agricultural Commercialization and Nutrition Project	1986	1988
75	Malawi	Food Security and Nutrition Policy	1987	1991
76	Malawi	Food Security Monitoring & Policy Development	1992	–

77	Malawi	Grain Liberalization among Smallholders	1990	1992
78	Malawi	Strategy for Economic Growth with Equity	1994	–
79	Malawi	Tax Reform	1994	1994
80	Malawi	Tax Reform Implementation	1987	1995
81	Malaysia	Development Studies	1992	–
82	Malaysia	International Inflation and Price Formation	1980	1981
83	Mali	Rural Health Delivery	1978	1982
84	Mexico	Fiscal Reform and Urban Planning	1992	1994
85	Mexico	International Tax Course	1994	1995
86	Mexico	Research on Education	1979	1981
87	Mexico	Tax Course (ITAM)	1993	1994
88	Mongolia	Economic Reform	1993	1994
89	Morocco	Pricing Policy (Economic Policy Analysis)	1986	1991
90	N.I.S.	Policy Reform in Environmental Economics & Mgt.	1993	–
91	Nepal	Value-Added Tax	1994	1994
92	Nicaragua	Sumu Indians/Non-Timber Tropical Forest Products	1992	1994
93	Oman	Budgeting Workshop	1994	1994
94	Pakistan	Child Survival and Health	1990	1994
95	Pakistan	Primary Education Development (PED)	1990	1994
96	Paraguay	Education Reform	1995	–
97	Philippines	Health Finance Development Project	1992	1994
98	Puerto Rico	AIDS Strategic Planning for the City of San Juan	1987	1993
99	Puerto Rico	Community-based Primary Care	1989	1992
100	Puerto Rico	San Juan AIDS Institute	1987	1993
101	Romania	Social Security	1993	1994
102	Russia	Center for Economic Reform, Macro & Finance Unit	1993	1994
103	Russia	Establishment of Institute for Economic Analysis	1994	1995
104 –106	Russia	Management of State Property (GKI); Privatzation; Legal Reform; and Establishment of Securities Market	1992	–
107	Russia	Transport Challenge in the Former Soviet Union	1993	1994
108	Rwanda	Cost of AIDS	1991	1991
109	Sahel	Recurrent Costs of Development Programs	1978	1985
110	Senegal	Rural Health Care II	1985	1989
111	Singapore	Masters in Public Policy Program Development	1991	–
112	South Africa	South Africa Education Workshop	1992	1993
113	Sri Lanka	Biological Resources in the Sinharaja Forest	1994	–
114	Sri Lanka	Economic Policy Studies	1980	1982
115	Sri Lanka	Sustainable Use of Non Timber Forest Products	1993	1994
116	Sri Lanka	Tax Analysis	1993	1994
117	Sudan	Rural Development: Abyei	1976	1981
118	Sudan	Vitamin A Supplementation and Child Health	1986	1992

119	Taiwan	Economic Research	1992	–
120	Thailand	Management of Natural Resources & the Environment	1990	1995
121	Thailand	Rural Industries and Employment	1988	1990
122	Thailand	Thailand Development Research Institute (TDRI)	1985	1991
123	Togo	Togo Health Sector Support For Child Survival	1990	1991
124	Venezuela	Agriculture and Rural Development Policy Studies	1981	1982
125	Vietnam	Fulbright Teaching Program	1994	–
126	Vietnam	Public Enterprise Workshop	1992	1992
127	Vietnam	Research & Scholarly Exchange in the Health Field	1993	1994
128	Zaire	Zaire School Of Public Health Project	1986	1991
129	Zambia	Macroeconomic Technical Assistance	1991	–
130	Zambia	Tax Administration and Computerization	1992	–
131	Zimbabwe	Competition Policy	1992	1992

APPENDIX 1-B

Cambridge–based Projects, 1980–1995

Global projects with no overseas base of operations

(Assigned number cross-referenced with staff and consultant lists; no end date indicates project end after 1995)

#	Project Name	Begin	End
132	Advancing Basic Education & Literacy (ABEL)	1989	–
133	Aga Khan University Feasibility Study	1982	1985
134	Agricultural Policy Analysis Project (APAP)	1988	–
135	Applied Diarrheal Disease Research (ADDR)	1985	1995
136	Asia Environmental Training	1992	–
137	Assistance to Resource Institutions for Enterprise Support (ARIES)	1985	1990
138	Basic Research in Developing Educational Systems (BRIDGES)	1985	1992
139	Book on Achieving Change in Higher Education	1994	–
140	Case Studies on Strategic Management of Policy Reforms	1989	1990
141	Case Study and Training Project for AID/WID	1982	1985
142	Conference on Trade in the Far East	1994	1994
143	Consulting Assistance on Economic Reform (CAER)	1989	–
144	Curriculum to Train Leaders of Social Policy in Latin America	1994	1995
145	Dengue Fever Control Strategies Study	1989	1990
146	Economic Analysis of International Forestry Issues	1992	–
147	Education Policy Papers for Latin America	1992	1992
148	Employment & Enterprise Policy Analysis (EEPA)	1984	1991
149	Food Systems	1990	1991
150	Gender and Development	1982	1987
151	Global AIDS Research	1989	1992
152	Indochina Program	1989	–
153	Information Technology and Fiscal Compliance	1992	1993
154	International Tropical Timber Organization (ITTO)	1987	1988
155	Latin America & Caribbean Management Training for Mayors	1991	1993
156	Lessons of Foreign Assistance	1986	1987
157	Long–Term Social Science Research in Rain Forests	1994	–
158	Microenterprise Development Course	1993	1993
159	Middle East Water Technical Assistance	1994	–
160	Non–Governmental Organizations	1993	–
161	ODA Economic and Social Committee Evaluation	1990	1991
162	Palestinian National Authority	1994	–
163	Pilot Study in Capacity Building	1993	–
164	Policy Analysis & Training in Environmental Economics in Asia	1993	1995
165	Political Economy of Urban Development with Chilean emphasis	1994	–

166	Priorities for Rural Development Research	1983	1984
167	Regional Program for Enterprise Development in Africa	1991	1991
168	Resource Mobilization Strategies in Sub–Saharan Africa	1986	1988
169	Resources for Child Health and Health Finance (REACH)	1986	1987
170	Role of Savings in Local Financial Markets	1992	1992
171	San Pablo Health Care Facilities Evaluation	1987	1987
172	Social Sector Policy Analysis Project	1989	1992
173	Structural Adjustment and the Environment	1993	1995
174	Training Materials for Agricultural Policy Analysis	1990	1991
175	Tropical Forest Management	1990	–
176	Workshop in Educational Policy	1993	1993
177	Workshop on Chinese Economic Reforms	1993	1993
178	Workshops on Gender Training	1990	1991
179	World Hunger Media Project	1984	1990

APPENDIX 2

Sources of Funding, 1980–1995

Sources of funding throughout the fifteen-year period have included private foundations, multilateral and bilateral aid agencies, regional and national development banks, United Nations organizations, and host governments. Some of the funds were provided directly to HIID, while others were provided to governments and firms, which in turn contracted for HIID Services.

Abt Associates
Academy for Educational Development
African Development Bank
Aga Khan Founation
Aga Khan Foundation of Canada
American Council of Learned Societies
Asia Foundation
Asian Development Bank
Bank Danamon (Indonesia)
Bank Rakyat (Indonesia)
Beinecke Foundation
Binational Fulbright Commission (Egypt)
Canadian International Development Agency
Carnegie Foundation
Center for Human Services
Christopher Reynolds Foundation
Chung-Hua Institution for Economic Research (Taiwan)
City of San Juan (Puerto Rico)
Conservation, Food, and Health Foundation
Cornell University
Corporation Estatal Petrolera Ecuatoriana
Creative Associates, Inc.
Department of Technical and Economic Cooperation (Thailand)
Deutsche Gesellschaft für Technische Zusammenarbeit
Development Alternatives, Inc.
Development Assistance Corporation
Eurasia Foundation
European Bank for Reconstruction and Development
Exxon
Ford Foundation
Forestal Valparaíso S. A.
Fulbright Commission
Fundacion Javier Barros Sierra
Government of Bangladesh
Government of Bolivia
Government of Colombia
Government of Germany
Government of Ghana
Government of Indonesia
Government of Kenya
Government of Lesotho
Government of Malawi
Government of Malaysia
Government of Mali
Government of Negara Brunei Darussalam
Government of Netherlands
Government of Norway
Government of Paraguay
Government of Senegal
Government of Sri Lanka
Government of Sweden
Government of Thailand
Government of Venezuela
Government of Zambia
Greeley Foundation
Harvard University Departments (teaching)
Henry Luce Foundation
Hospital Management Corporation of America-PR
ICDDR (Bangladesh)
Institute of Strategic and International Studies (Malaysia)

Instituto Tecnológico Autónomo de México
Instituto de Credito Agricola y Pecuario (Venezuela)
Instituto de Estudio Fiscales (Spain)
Inter-American Development Bank
Inter-American Foundation
Interamerican Foundation of Cities (Puerto Rico)
International Consortium
International Development Association (World Bank affiliate)
International Fund for Agricultural Development
International Human Assistance Program, Inc.
International Tropical Timber Organization
Japan Economic Research Institute
John Merck Fund
John Snow Public Health Group, Inc.
Johns Hopkins University
KPMG Peat Marwick
Korea Development Institute
Lincoln Institute for Land Policy
MacArthur Foundation
Management Sciences for Health
Maxon Foundation
Mellon Foundation
Midwest Universities Consortium for International Activities
National Center for Education Research and Development (Jordan)
National Science Foundation
National University of Singapore
Organization for Economic Cooperation and Development (OECD)
Overseas Development Administration (United Kingdom)
P.T. Krakatau Steel
Pacific Management Resources, Inc.
Partners for International Education and Training
Research Triangle Institute
Resources for the Future
Robert R. Nathan Associates
Robert Wood Johnson Foundation
Rockefeller Foundation
San Juan Aids Institute
Scaife Family Charitable Trust
Sir Run Run Shaw Foundation (Hong Kong)
Smithsonian Tropical Research Institute
Social Science Research Council
Swedish International Development Authority
Tinker Foundation
Tulane University
U.S. Agency for International Development (USAID)
U.S. Department of Agriculture
U.S. Environmental Protection Agency
United National Educational, Scientific and Cultural Organization
United Nations Department of Technical Cooperation for Development
United Nations Development Programme (UNDP)
United Nations International Children's Emergency Fund (UNICEF)
United Nations University
Universidad Catolica Madre Y Maestra (Dom. Republic)
University of Michigan
University of Nuevo León (Mexico)
W. Alton Jones Foundation, Inc.
World Bank
World Bank Group
World Environment Center
World Health Organization
World Wildlife Fund

APENDIX 3

Financial Overview

Chart 1: HIID Expenditures by Federal and Non-Federal Funding

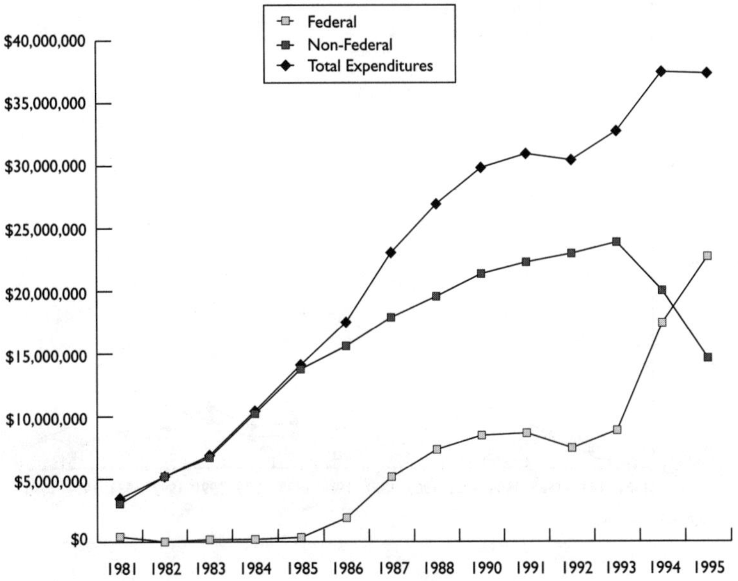

see page 518 for notes

Chart 2: HIID Endowment and Total Capital Assets

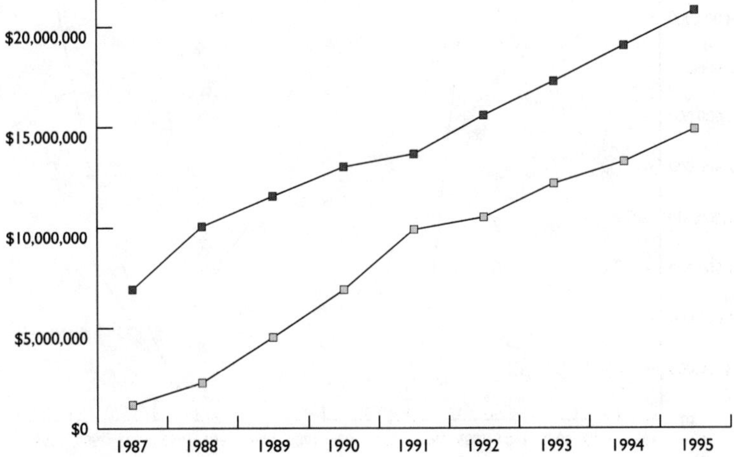

see page 518 for notes

HIID Income by Activity

Chart 3: Economic Policy, Fiscal Policy, and Management Reform

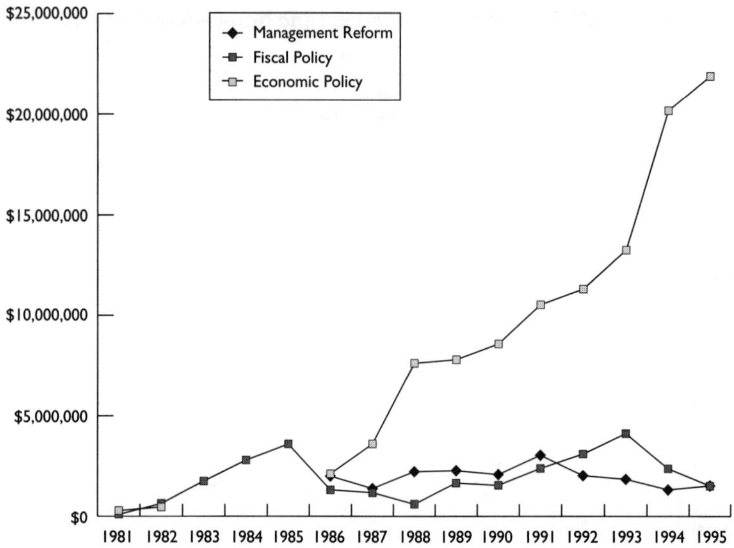

see page 518 for notes

Chart 4: Agriculture and Rural Development and Environmental Reform

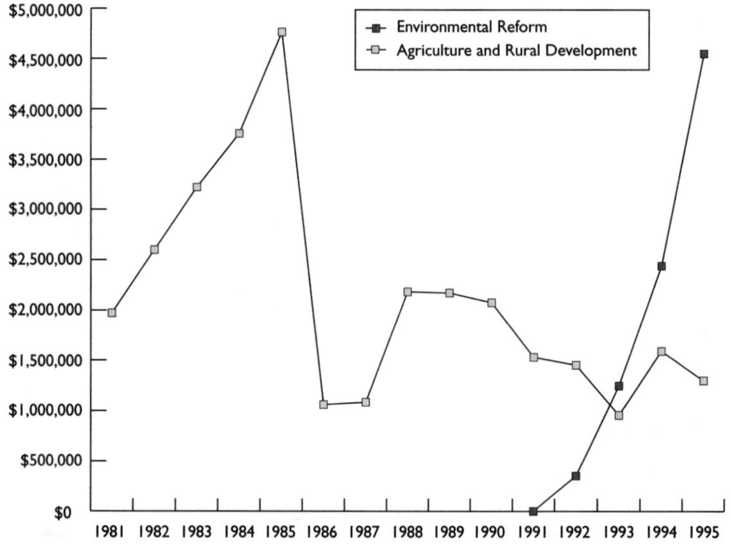

see page 518 for notes

Chart 5: Education and Public Health

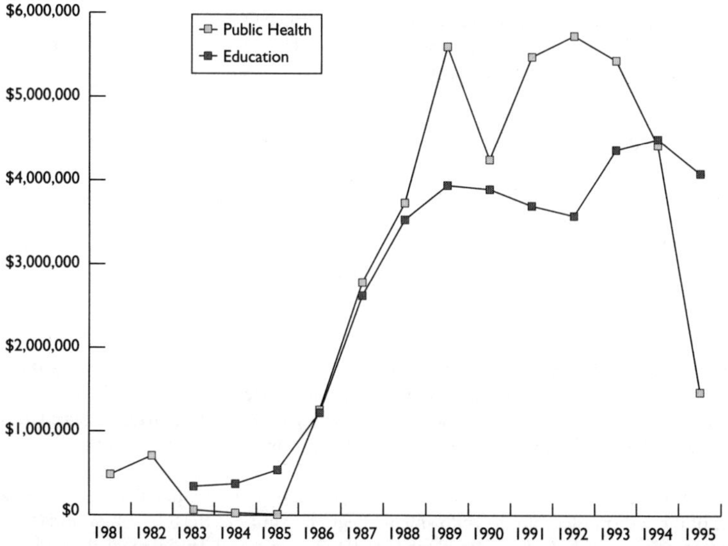

see page 518 for notes

Chart 6: Teaching and Training, Collaborative Research, and Research and Other Activities

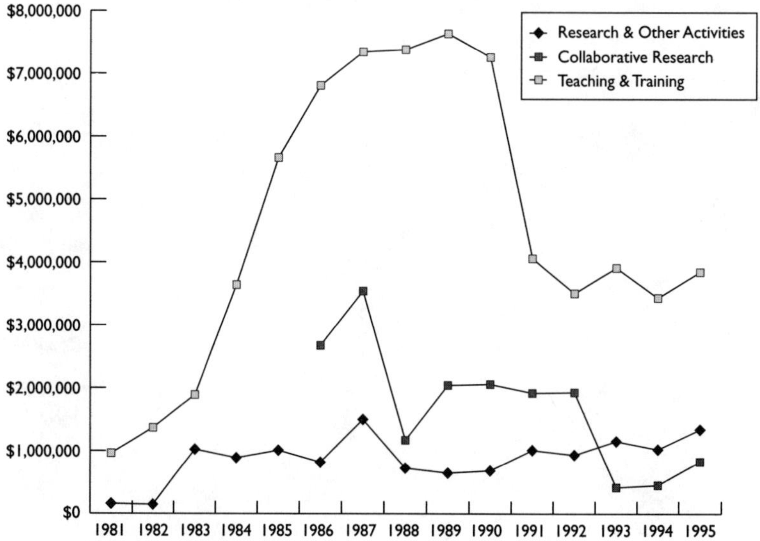

see page 518 for notes

Notes to Financial Appendices, Charts

Sources: The data for these charts were compiled by Gretchen O'Connor from HIID biennial reports, from HIID capital asset tables originally prepared by the Institute's financial office, and from the financial reports of the central administration of Harvard University.

Chart 1: The Federal and Non-Federal breakdown follows Harvard University's definition of these categories. Non-Federal thus includes contracts with host countries where the original source of money was USAID. If these host country contracts funded by USAID were included within the Federal category, the Federal share in 1981 and 1982 would account for a substantial share of HIID activity at the time. Host country contracts funded by USAID continued to exist throughout the 1980's and into the 1990's, but they were a small and declining share of the Non-Federal total.

Chart 2: HIID's reserve funds were first shifted into the Harvard endowment in 1987, thus there are no endowment figures prior to that date. In 1980, HIID had a capital fund of $500,000 provided by the Ford Foundation to help cover the costs involved if the university should decide to close down HIID. There was also an HIID debt to the central administration of the university in that year of $200,000. In the early 1980s, HIID built up a reserve fund to protect it against unforseen downturns in activity and it was part of that reserve fund that was the initial source of the first transfer into the endowment. Beginning in 1991, the total capital and endowment figures include the endowment of HIID's international development chair and HIID's share of the Edward S. Mason Chair in the Kennedy School of Government.

Charts 3–6: The data in these charts are taken from HIID's biennial reports between 1980 and 1995. For projects that contained components that fell under more than one subheading, the entire project was put under the subheading that best described the largest component of the project's activity.

APPENDIX 4-A

Cambridge-based Development Professionals and Senior Management between 1980 and 1995

(*HIID staff member for at least 10 years; **for at least 15 years)

Anderson, Mary, *Research Associate, Economics*
Ashton, Peter, *Faculty Fellow, Plant Science*
Bates, Robert, *Faculty Fellow, Political Science*
Baxter, Susan, *Assistant Director for Human Resources*
Berg, Andrew, *Research Associate, Economics*
Berry, Brian, *Faculty Fellow, Geography*
Biggs, Tyler, *Research Associate, Economics*
Bolnick, Bruce, *Faculty Associate, Economics*
Boone, Peter, *Research Associate, Economics*
Bowen, John, *Research Associate, Social Anthropology*
Bryant, Malcolm, *Research Associate, Public Health*
Burchfield, Shirley, *Research Associate, Education*
Byrne, Peter, *Research Associate, Law*
Cash, Richard, *Institute Fellow, Public Health***
Cassidy, Thomas, *Research Associate, Education Administration & Planning*
Chen, Lincoln, *Faculty Fellow, Public Health*
Chen, Martha, *Research Associate, South Asia Regional Studies & Women in Development*
Chenery, Hollis, *Faculty Fellow, Economics**
Cohen, John, *Institute Fellow, Political Science, Sociology & Law***
Cole, David, *Coordinator of Financial and Banking Studies, Economics**
Conrad, Robert, *Research Associate, Economics*
Cuadra, Ernesto, *Research Associate, Education Administration & Planning*
Cummings, William, *Research Associate, Education*
D'Anastasio, Mark, *Research Associate, Soviet & East European Studies*
Dall, Frank, *Research Associate, International Development Education*
Dapice, David, *Faculty Associate, Economics*
Davis, Russell, *Faculty Fellow, Education*
DeMarinis, Vicki, *Assistant Director for Finance*
Delp, Peter, *Research Associate, Industrial Engineering*
Djelic, Bozidar, *Research Associate, Business Administration*
Fernholz, Fernando, *Research Associate, Economic Development*
French, Louisa, *Assistant Director for Human Resources*
Gao, Xiao Meng, *Research Associate, National Planning & Statistics*
Gillis, Malcolm, *Institute Fellow, Economics*
Giometti, Patricia, *Assistant Director for Finance*

Glenday, Graham, *Fellow of the Institute (Institute Associate), Public Policy**
Go, Delfin, *Research Associate, Political Economy & Government*
Godoy, Ricardo, *Research Associate, Anthropology**
Goldman, Richard, *Fellow of the Institute, Agricultural Economics***
Good, Mary-Jo, *Research Associate, Sociology*
Gordon, Lester, *Fellow of the Institute, Business Administration***
Gordon, Richard, *Research Associate, Law*
Grant, Marcia, *Assistant Director for Student Programs*
Gray, Cheryl Williamson, *Research Associate, Public Policy*
Gray, Clive, *Institute Fellow, Economics***
Grindle, Merilee, *Faculty Fellow (Research Associate), Political Science**
Grodzins, Carol, *Assistant Director for Student Programs*
Hale, Christopher, *Associate Director for Finance & Management*
Hall, Malcolm, *Research Associate, Agricultural Economics*
Hall, Pamela, *Research Associate, Biology*
Harley, Richard, *Research Associate, World Religions*
Harwood, Alison, *Research Associate, Finance and Economics*
Haughton, Jonathan, *Research Associate, Economics*
Henn, Albert, *Associate Director Health Programs, Public Health*
Henry, Fitzroy, *Research Associate, Epidemiology*
Herrera Acena, Guillermo, *Research Associate, Medicine**
Hilderbrand, Mary, *Research Associate, Government*
Hook, Richard, *Research Associate, Microfinance**
Jenkins, Glenn, *Institute Fellow, Economics**
Jones, Christine, *Institute Associate, Economics*
Kakar, Narinder, *Research Associate, Economics & Management*
Kamarck, Andrew, *Associate Fellow, Political Economy & Government*
Keare, Douglas, *Research Associate, Urban Planning*
Kelly, Joseph, *Assistant Director for Finance*
Kelly, Roy, *Research Associate, Urban Planning**
Koch-Weser, Dieter, *Faculty Fellow, Internal Medicine*
Kocher, James, *Institute Associate, Agricultural Economics*
Kouri, Yamil, *Research Associate, Public Health*
Kresge, Janet, *Assistant Director for Finance*
Kumar, A.K. Shiva, *Research Associate, Political Economy of Government*
Kumins, Rosanne, *Assistant Director for Contract Administration*
Lazonick, William, *Research Associate, Economics*
Levy, Brian, *Research Associate, Economics*
Lewis, Jeffrey, *Institute Associate, Economics**
Lindauer, David, *Faculty Associate (Research Associate), Economics*
Lippeveld, Theo, *Research Associate, Public Health*

Liu, Jianguo, *Research Associate, Ecology*
Lu, Mai, *Research Associate, Public Administration*
Mallon, Richard, *Institute Fellow, Economics***
Mann, Charles, *Research Associate, Economics*
Markandya, Anil, *Research Associate, Natural Resource Economics*
Mason, Edward, *Faculty Fellow (Professor Emeritus), Economics**
McGinn, Noel, *Institute Fellow, Social Psychology***
McPherson, Malcolm, *Fellow of the Institute (Research Associate), Economics**
Montes, Marco, *Research Associate, Mechanical Engineering*
Morduch, Jonathan, *Research Associate, Economics*
Morrison, Donald, *Research Associate, Political Science & Economics*
Myers, Charles, *Research Associate, Economics**
Nelson, Courtney, *Research Associate, Economics & Public Policy*
Nelson, Eric, *Project Associate, Economics*
Olivola, Danielle, *Research Associate, Public Health*
Oteh, Arunma, *Research Associate, General Management*
Pagett, Richard, *Executive Director (Associate Director, Special Programs/F&M)***
Panayotou, Theodore, *Institute Fellow (Research Associate), Natural Resource Economics**
Park, Yung Chul, *Research Associate, Economics*
Perkins, Dwight, *Director of HIID & Faculty Fellow, Economics***
Peters, Pauline, *Research Associate (Institute Associate), Anthropology**
Peterson, Karen, *Research Associate, Public Health*
Peterson, Stephen, *Research Associate, Public Administration*
Power, Thomas, *Research Associate, Political Science*
Pujari, Anup, *Research Associate, Economics*
Pyle, Nancy, *Associate Director for External Relations (Student Programs)*
Qazi, Shamim, *Research Associate, Medicine*
Radelet, Steven, *Institute Associate, Public Policy & Economics*
Rasmussen, Zeba, *Research Associate, Public Health*
Reifenberg, Stephen, *Assistant Director for Student Programs*
Reimers, Fernando, *Institute Associate, Administration, Planning and Social Policy*
Riddell, Abby, *Institute Associate, Education*
Robbins, Donald, *Institute Associate, Economics*
Robinson, Marguerite, *Institute Fellow (Fellow of the Institute), Anthropology**
Roemer, Michael, *Institute Fellow & Research Coordinator (Executive Director), Economics***
Rotberg, Robert, *Research Associate, Political Science*
Rugh, Andrea, *Research Associate, Social Anthropology*
Sachs, Jeffrey, *Faculty Fellow, Economics*
Sauerborn, Rainer, *Institute Associate, Maternal & Child Health Care*
Seidensticker, Ellen, *Assistant Director for Professional Recruitment*
Shaikh, Abdul Hafeez, *Research Associate, Economics*

Shepard, Donald, *Research Associate, Public Health*
Shipton, Parker, *Institute Associate, Anthropology*
Shleifer, Andrei, *Professor of Economics, Harvard University, Economics*
Shukla, Gangadhar, *Research Associate, Political Economy & Government*
Simon, Jonathon, *Research Associate, Public Health*
Skerry, Thomas, *Assistant Director for Training**
Snodgrass, Donald, *Institute Fellow (Chairman Transition Committee), Economics***
Sommerfeld, Johannes, *Research Associate, Cultural Anthropology*
Srivastava, Pradeep, *Institute Associate, Economics*
Stern, Joseph, *Institute Fellow (Executive Director), Economics***
Strong, John, *Research Associate, Business Economics*
Summers, Victoria, *Research Associate, Law*
Supit, Frank, *Research Associate, Law*
Swanberg, Kenneth, *Research Associate, Agricultural Economics*
Syrquin, Moshe, *Research Associate, Economics*
Thomas, John, *Institute Fellow, Political Economy & Government***
Timmer, C. Peter, *Faculty Fellow, Economics***
Toledo, Alejandro, *Research Associate, Economics*
Tomich, Thomas, *Institute Associate, Agricultural Economics**
Trostle, James, *Research Associate, Medical Anthropology*
Valadez, Joseph, *Research Associate, Public Health*
Vallely, Thomas, *Research Associate, Public Administration*
Vincent, Jeffrey, *Institute Associate, Natural Resource Economics*
Warner, Andrew, *Research Associate, Economics*
Warwick, Donald, *Institute Fellow, Social Psychology***
Weiss, Carol, *Research Associate, Sociology*
Wellons, Philip, *Research Associate, Economics*
Wick, Lisa, *Assistant Director for Human Resources*
Zinnes, Clifford, *Institute Associate, Economics*

APPENDIX 4-B

Overseas Resident Professionals between 1980 and 1995

(numbers denote resident project number as found in project lists, appendix 1.A; *denotes project resident coordinator)

Abraham, William, *industrial statistics, Bangladesh (1)*

Ackroyd, Jay, *economic research, Sudan (117)*

Adam, Andrew, *public policy & managment, The Gambia (30)*

Adjou-Moumouni, B.S.F., *health policy & management, Zaire (128*)*

Aliber, Robert, *exchange-rate policy, Indonesia (51)*

Anderson, Glen, *environmental economics & finance, Poland (14*)*

Andersson, Martin, *voucher auction & privatization, Russia (104)*

Aquino, Rosemary, *natural resource management, Brunei (11)*

Baker, Susan, *trade policy, Indonesia (44)*

Banwell, John, *capital markets, Indonesia (51)*

Barichello, Richard, *economic policy, Indonesia (44*, 46*)*

Barry, Frank, *trade & industrial policy, Indonesia (44)*

Barton, John, *management information systems, Chad (15)*

Bastin, Johan, *urban & regional policy, Indonesia (58*)*

Baudouy, Jacques, *rural health services, Mali (83)*

Bergstrom, Lars, *bankruptcy, Russia (104)*

Berkley, Forrest, *insurance & pension reform, Indonesia (46)*

Bernard, Richard, *capital markets, Russia (104)*

Bethke, Klaus, *rural project development, Kenya (67)*

Betts, Claude, *health, Puerto Rico (98)*

Bikales, William, *macroeconomic policy, Mongolia (88*)*

Black, Bernard, *law, Russia (104)*

Block, John, *programming & information management, Zambia (130)*

Bluffstone, Randall, *environmental economics, Lithuania (14*)*

Bodart, Claude, *public health, Cameroon (12*)*

Bolnick, Bruce, *macroeconomic policy, Zambia (129)*

Bond, Timothy, *macroeconomic policy, Indonesia (44)*

Boulch, Gerard, *macroenomic policy, Ivory Coast (59)*

Boyd, Michael, *environmental economics, Central Asia (90*)*

Brandon, Leslie, *population/demography, Chad (15, 16)*

Breinholt, Mary Jane, *project evaluation & training, Indonesia (58)*

Brenneman, Lyle, *cooperatives study, The Gambia (30)*

Brett, Joseph, *regional financial analysis, Indonesia (58)*

Brimble, Peter, *industrialization, Thailand (121)*

Buehrer, Timothy, *macroeconomic policy, Indonesia (44)*

Byerly, Ann, *public health, Sudan (117)*

Callahan, Loel, *management, Mali (83*)*
Castonguay, Vincent, *customs administration, Kenya (68, 71)*
Cervero, Robert, *local taxation, Indonesia (58)*
Chaine, Jean-Paul, *diarrheal disease control, Senegal (110)*
Chakrabarti, Santi, *macroeconomic policy, Kenya (64)*
Chakwin, Naomi, *trade development, Mongolia (88)*
Chen, Martha, *poverty & gender , India (36*)*
Chesteen, Robert, *computerization, Malawi (80*)*
Clark, David, *education, Indonesia (43)*
Cohen, John, *rural planning, Kenya (62*, 64, 67*)*
Cole, David, *capital markets, Indonesia (51*, 55*), Sri Lanka (114)*
Combs, Sarah, *training, Chad (15)*
Cowell, Richard, *teacher training, curriculum development (Pakistan, 95*)*
Cox, Gordon, *customs administration, Indonesia (44)*
Crawford, David, *tax policy & information management, Zambia (130)*
Cruz, Jose, *computer systems, Zambia (130)*
Cunningham, Bert, *customs reform, Indonesia (44)*
Dalal, Ragini, *social assets, Russia (104)*
Danière, Andre, *education policy, Egypt (26*)*
Davenport, Robert, *training, Indonesia (55)*
Dawe, David, *food policy, Indonesia (44, 134)*
Dax, Paul, *environmental economics & finance, Bulgaria (14*)*
De Franco, Mario, *economics, Bolivia (9, 10*)*
Deal, Bruce, *trade & industrial policy, Indonesia (44)*
Demmer, Josefien, *socioeconomic data, Honduras (34)*
Dennis, Benjamin, *macroeconomic policy, Indonesia (44)*
Diallo, Alpha, *health management, Senegal (110)*
Doe, Albert, *customs administration, Kenya (68, 71)*
Donovan, William, *mechanical arts, Sudan (117)*
Dooley, Christine, *public policy, Singapore (111)*
Dow, J. Kamal, *project development, Kenya (62)*
Eltezam, Zabioullah, *tariff administration, Bangladesh (1)*
Evans, Hugh, *regional planning, Kenya (67)*
Fankhauser, Jana, *project management, Russia (104)*
Farrag, Shireen, *investment promotion, Bangladesh (1)*
Fernholz, Fernando, *economic planning & debt, Brunei (11), Indonesia (46), Zambia (129)*
FitzGerald Ford, James, *intergovernmental transfer, Indonesia (58*)*
Fitzgibbons, John, *foreign investment, Russia (104)*
Flanagan, Donna, *training, Brunei (11)*
Flatters, Frank, *trade reform, Indonesia (46)*
Foley, Ben, *tax administration, Zambia (130*)*

Foltz, Anne-Marie, *epidemiology / biostatsatistics, Chad (15)*
Fuller, Richard, *rural development, Sudan (117*)*
Gaile, Gary L., *regional planning, Kenya (67)*
Gardner, Bruce, *financial management, Russia (104)*
Garza, Octavio, *tax administration, Dominican Republic (24*)*
Geist, Judith, *district planning, Kenya (67)*
Gilligan, Daniel, *trade policy, Indonesia (44)*
Gillis, S. Malcolm, *economic policy, Indonesia (46*)*
Glenday, Graham, *tax policy, Kenya (68*, 71*)*
Goldman, Abram, *tax administration, Indonesia (52)*
Goldman, Richard, *agricultural economic policy, Kenya (62*)*
Gonyea, Lloyd, *engineering studies, Bangladesh (1)*
Goodrich, Gerry, *rural health, Mali (83*)*
Gordon, Lester, *parastatals/ management & economics, Kenya (62), Zambia (129*)*
Gray, Cheryl, *tax reform, Indonesia (46)*
Gray, Clive, *economic policy, Morocco (89*)*
Gray-Molina, George, *social policy, Bolivia (6)*
Greer, Samuel, *tax administration, Malawi (80*)*
Gregory, Wade, *agricultural planning, Kenya (62)*
Greindl, Isaline, *public health, Chad (15*)*
Grenier, Randell, *computer systems, Zambia (130)*
Haddow, Paul, *strategy development, Kenya (62)*
Hall, Malcolm, *project analysis, IvoryCoast (59*), Kenya (62)*
Harriague, Ignacio, *tax administration, Dominican Republic (24*)*
Harris, Karen, *pension reform, Indonesia (51*)*
Hart, Thomas, *tax policy, Malawi (80*)*
Harwood, Alison, *financial markets, Indonesia (51)*
Hay, Jonathan, *law reform, Russia (104–106*)*
Henry, FitzRoy, *epidimiology, Nigeria (135)*
Higgins, Robert, *customs computerization, Indonesia (44)*
Hill, Catharine, *macroeconomics, Zambia (129)*
Hillinger, Jacques, *programming & information management, Zambia (130)*
Hook, Richard, *bank reforms/district planning, Indonesia (41), Kenya (67*)*
Hubbard, Donald, *intergovernmental loan administration, Indonesia (58)*
Hughes, Rodger, *external aid management, Kenya (64)*
Hunt, Joseph, *health systems, Indonesia (43)*
Huntington, Richard, *research direction, Sudan (117)*
Hutcheson, Thomas, *project appraisal, Bangladesh (1)*
Isaakson, Nils, *management, Kenya (62)*
Jabara, Cathy, *agricultural economics, Kenya (62)*
Jenkins, Glenn, *tax policy, Indonesia (46*)*

Johnston, Alan, *training/district focus, Kenya (67)*
Johnston, Donald, *savings policy, Indonesia (41*)*
Jones, Barclay, *rural-urban planning, Kenya (67)*
Junius, David, *project management, Russia (104)*
Kambou, Gerard, *macroeconomics, Zambia (129)*
Kelly, Roy, *training, urban planning, Indonesia (48, 58)*
Kennedy, Thomas, *village bank administration, Indonesia (41)*
Kern, James, *micro finance training, Indonesia (41, 43)*
Kerr, Thomas, *development strategy, Kenya (62)*
Kjallgren, Georg, *auction systems, Russia (104)*
Kobb, Daniel, *macroeconomic policy, Indonesia (44)*
Kroll, Heidi, *competition policy, Russia (104)*
Kudrin, Sergey, *enterprise restructuring, Russia (104)*
Larsen, Henning, *programming, Zambia (130)*
Larson, Bruce, *environmental & agricultural economics, Estonia (14*)*
LeBlanc, Thomas, *management information systems, Pakistan (95, 138)*
Leland, Scott, *public policy, Singapore (111)*
Leonard, David, *budget & management, Kenya (62)*
Letarte, Claude, *rural health services, Mali (83)*
Lewis, Blane, *urban development policy, Indonesia (58)*
Lewis, David, *rural planning, Kenya (67)*
Lewis, Jeffrey, *economic policy, Indonesia (44*, 48*, 50*)*
Lim, Henry, *tax policy, Malawi (80*)*
Linetsky, Eugene, *executive training programs, Russia (104)*
Linser, Wolfgang, *integrated pest management, Indonesia (43, 44)*
Linvill, Margaret, *enterprise restructuring, Russia (104)*
Lippeveld, Theo, *health planning & administration, Chad (15*), Pakistan (94*)*
Litvack, Jennie, *economic analysis/ health services, Cameroon (12)*
Lofti, Sherif, *macroeconomic analysis, Indonesia (44)*
Lourie, Thomas, *enterprise restructuring, Russia (104)*
Luhowy, George, *financial comptrolling, Russia (104)*
Magiera, Steven, *trade policy, Indonesia (44)*
Mallon, Richard, *public enterprise/economic policy, Bangladesh (1*), Venezuela (124*)*
Mann, Arthur, *economic policy, Bolivia (10)*
Mann, Charles, *economic poilcy/food security, The Gambia (30*), Malawi (76*)*
Markandya, Anil, *environmental economics, Russia (90*)*
Marshall, Kathryn, *financial policy, Indonesia (42, 51)*
Mas, Ignacio, *macroeconomics, Indonesia (44)*
Mason, Andrew, *trade analysis & rural poverty, Indonesia (44)*
Mayo-Smith, Ian, *management reform, Brunei (11*)*
McCauley, David, *training, Indonesia (48)*

McCloud, David, *arid lands management, Kenya (67)*
McDonald, Iain, *commodity analysis, Kenya (62)*
McGinn, Noel, *education policy, Colombia (19*)*
McGovern, Joseph, *management systems, Kenya (62)*
McKay, Lloyd, *tariff policy, Bangladesh (1)*
McNamara, Paul, *debt management, tax reform, The Gambia (30)*
McPherson, Malcolm, *macroeconomics, The Gambia (30*), Zambia (129*, 130*)*
McRae, William, *share issues, Russia (104)*
McSweeney, Kendra, *socioeconomic data, Honduras (34)*
Montes, Marco, *property tax, Indonesia (52*)*
Monteverde, Richard, *economics, Indonesia (43)*
Morris, Glenn, *environmental economics, Hungary (14*)*
Morrison, Donald, *tax administration, The Gambia (31*)*
Murdock, Lawrence, *agricultural economics, Indonesia (41)*
Myers, Charles, *social sector economics, Bolivia (6*), Thailand (122*)*
Nelson, Courtney, *management reform, Indonesia (47)*
Nelson, Eric, *economic policy, Indonesia (54)*
Neri, Alberto, *financial management, Russia (104)*
Nestel, Penelope, *public health, Sudan (118*)*
Newfield, Faye, *health management, Senegal (110)*
Niamir, Maryam, *livestock research, Sudan (117)*
Nielsen, Holly, *securities markets, Russia (104)*
Nolan, Sean, *trade & industrial policy, Indonesia (44)*
Norbye, Ole David, *economic policy, Bangladesh (1)*
Ofosu-Barko, Kenneth, *epidemiology, PuertoRico (98)*
Oteh, Arunna, *business, West Africa (148)*
Overman, Johannes, *socioeconomic data, Honduras (34)*
Owen, Thomas, *environmental policy, Slovakia (14*)*
Pagett, Richard, *training, Indonesia (47)*
Panayotou, Theodore, *environmental economics, Thailand (120*, 122*)*
Paredes, Ricardo, *labor markets & legislation, Bolivia (10)*
Parker, Stephen, *trade reform, Indonesia (46)*
Partenheimer, Earl, *strategy & research, Kenya (62)*
Patten, Richard, *microfinance, Indonesia (41*, 43, 58)*
Peters, Pauline, *ethnographic studies/field research, Malawi (74*, 76 *, 77*)*
Peterson, Stephen, *management systems, Kenya (62*, 63*, 67)*
Pickney III, Thomas, *computer applications, Kenya (62)*
Porter, Richard, *trade reform, Indonesia (46)*
Power, Thomas, *insurance & pension reform, Indonesia (51)*
Quinn, Brian, *management, Vietnam (125*)*
Quizon, Jaime, *agricultural policy, Indonesia (43*, 44)*

Radelet, Steve, *macroeconomic policy, Indonesia (30, 44)*
Rajagopalan, P. B., *macroeconomics, Kenya (62)*
Ramakrishnan, Subramania, *budget & finance, Kenya (62*, 64*), Oman (93*)*
Ramirez, Julio, *policy analysis & management, Bolivia (3*)*
Randolph, Thomas, *economics, Malawi (74)*
Read, Colin, *economic policy, Indonesia (46)*
Reimers, Fernando, *educational reform, Paraguay (96)*
Risden, St. Clair, *property tax administration, Indonesia (52)*
Rishkofski, Melinda, *legal management, Russia (104)*
Ritchie, Lyell, *business management, Bangladesh (1*)*
Robinson, Allan, *info management & tax admin, Zambia (130)*
Robinson, Marguerite, *micro finance, Bolivia (2*, 5*), Indonesia (39*, 40*, 43)*
Roe, Emery, *rural planning, Kenya (67)*
Roemer, Michael, *economic policy, Indonesia (44*, 48*, 50*, 58*), Kenya (62)*
Rogers, Halsey, *trade analysis, Indonesia (44)*
Rosengard, Jay, *property tax administration, Indonesia (52)*
Ross, David, *anti-monopoly, Russia (104)*
Rossi, Andria, *computer programming, The Gambia (31*)*
Rutherford, Andrea, *public relations, Russia (104)*
Sahota, Gian, *small industry development, Bangladesh (148)*
Saltzman, Sidney, *rural infrastructure, Kenya (67)*
Saulniers, Alfred, *economic reform, Morocco (89)*
Sen, Lalit, *rural electrification, Indonesia (53*)*
Shaikh, A. Hafeez, *public enterprise reform, Indonesia (44)*
Shalneva, Elena, *press relations, Russia (104)*
Shargorodska, Olga, *library resources, Russia (104)*
Sharp, Joseph, *construction, Sudan (117)*
Shaw, Bruce, *training, Kenya (62)*
Shepard, Donald, *public health economics, Colombia (20*)*
Shipton, Parker, *field research, Kenya (66*)*
Shugart, Christopher, *local government finance, Indonesia (58)*
Simon, Johnathon, *public health, Pakistan (135)*
Simon, Stephen, *epidemiology, Senegal (110*)*
Sinder, Matthew, *project evaluation & training, Indonesia (58)*
Slade, Betty, *financial markets, Indonesia (51*)*
Smart, Christopher, *social assets restructuring, Russia (104)*
Smith, Mary, *privatization, Mongolia (88)*
Smith, Theodore, *environmental finance, Slovakia (14*)*
Smoke, Paul, *urban/regional reform, Kenya (67)*
Snodgrass, Donald, *economic policy, Indonesia (43*, 45*), Malaysia (81*)*
Snyder, Wayne, *research advice, Indonesia (42)*

Sonnermann, James, *public health, Cameroon (12)*
Splettstoesser, Dietrich, *computerization, Kenya (62)*
Steel, William, *economic research, IvoryCoast (59)*
Stegall, Ronald, *management reform, Brunei (11*)*
Stern, Joseph, *economic policy, Indonesia (38*, 44*, 48*, 50*, 58*), Sri Lanka (114*)*
Stuparich, Nicolo, *pension funds, Indonesia (51)*
Sullivan, Gavin, *public education, Russia (104)*
Sullivan, Joan, *nutrition, Malawi (74)*
Sundberg, Mark, *macroeconomics, Indonesia (44)*
Swanberg, Kenneth, *agricultural economic policy, Venezuela (124*)*
Tench, Andrew, *development strategy, Kenya (62)*
Teter, Darius, *trade & tariff policy, Indonesia (44)*
Thomas, John, *management reform, Singapore (111*)*
Toksoz, Sadik, *irrigation economics, Kenya (62)*
Tomich, Thomas, *agricultural policy, Indonesia (43*)*
Toronto, James, *educational policy, Egypt (138)*
Unda, Roberto, *health education, PuertoRico (98)*
Upreti, Tara, *training, Pakistan (94)*
Valdes, Jorge, *management information systems, Pakistan (95, 138)*
Valentine, James, *income tax, Malawi (80)*
Van Buer, Franklin, *financial systems, Kenya (67)*
Van Zorge, James, *economic policy, Indonesia (44)*
Van der Meulen, Yana, *economic policy, Indonesia (44)*
Varley, Robert, *management systems & rural savings, Indonesia (41, 43)*
Venkatesan, Kandaswam, *budget & finance, Kenya (62)*
Villaume, John, *education policy, Egypt (26)*
Vincent, Jeffrey, *natural resources & environment, Malaysia (81*)*
Wakeman-Linn, John, *data management & macroeconomics, Zambia (129)*
Walker, Peter, *agro-economics, Malawi (77)*
Wallace, Michael, *natural resource economics, Newly Independent States (90)*
Walsh, Brendan, *macro policy & management, The Gambia (30*)*
Walsh, James, *customs reform, Indonesia (44)*
Warner, Robert, *tariff policy, Bangladesh (1)*
Wasow, Bernard, *industrial policy, Bangladesh (1)*
Webber, Christopher, *economic policy , Indonesia (46)*
Wells, Louis, *international finance, Indonesia (44*, 48*, 50*, 58*)*
Welsh, Thomas, *education policy, Jamaica (60*)*
West, Karen, *banking reform, Russia (104)*
Westcott, Clay, *management systems, Kenya (67)*
Westlake, Michael, *commodity analysis, Kenya (62)*
Westman, Harald, *enterprise restructuring, Russia (104)*

Wheeler, John, *budget implementation, Kenya (64, 67*)*
Wight, Albert, *procurement, Russia (104)*
Witzel, David, *management information systems, Indonesia (51)*
Wyckoff, Jean, *livestock development strategy, Kenya (62)*
Zagachin, Julia, *deposits & clearing, Russia (104)*
Zezulin, Lena, *nonprofit organizations, Russia (104)*
Zinnes, Clifford, *environmental economics, Romania (14*)*
Zulberti, Carlos, *agricultural economics, Kenya (62)*

APPENDIX 5

HIID Consultants, 1980–1995

This list includes individuals who worked on a short-term contract basis on HIID projects or worked as overseas counterparts on collaborative projects between HIID and other research institutes. (Numbers denote project numbers as found in project lists, appendix 1.A.)

HIID staff, many of whom worked on multiple projects as consultants, are not included in this list. Their names can be found in the Cambridge-based and Overseas Professional Staff appendices 4-B and 4-A.

Abonyi, George, 107
Abraham, Simon, 31
Abramson, Robert, 11
Acciaioli, Gregory, 43
Acevedo, Salvador, 98
Ackerman, Richard, 176
Adjou-Moumouni, Basile, 22, 123, 128
Adler, Barry, 104
Adoni, Hernan, 34
Aguilar Milanes, Xavier, 3
Aguirre, Alejandro, 6
Ahmad, A.M.S., 43
Ahmad, Junaid Kam, 1
Ahmed, Alam Narul, 135
Aikens, Alan, 68, 69, 70
Aime, Eduardo, 9
Airasian, Peter, 176
Akhmedov, Dourbek, 142
Alexander, Jennifer, 42
Ali, Jamee, 69
Ali, Rozali, 81
Allen, Nancy, 38, 44
Allred, Elizabeth, 118
Alvord, Elias, 104
Amann, Eberhard, 44
Amaro, Hortensia, 98
Amsden, Alice, 1
Anderson, Kathryn, 148
Anderson, Lori, 176
Anderson, Robert, 14
Appleton, P. Bryce, 44
Arak, Marcelle, 51
Arboleda, Jairo, 96
Arroyo, Alonso, 85
Arthur, Lesley, 162
Arthur, Paul, 135
Ascherio, Alberto, 135
Ashe, Jeffrey, 137
Ashford, Nicholas, 43
Atkinson, David, 135
Augliere, Reed, 138
Austin, James, 11
Avi-Yonah, Reuven, 85, 162
Axtell, John, 6
Ayer, John, 104
Ayoade, Ruth, 76
Ayres, Ian, 104
Bacon, Hilary, 44
Badruddin, Salma, 135
Bahl, Roy, 143
Bail, Richard, 108
Baird, Douglas, 104
Baker, Michael, 98
Baker, Patrick, 175
Baker, Robert, 137
Balderston, Fred, 42, 43, 44, 51
Balderston, Judith, 43, 44, 51, 55
Baldwin, Robert, 46
Ball, Benjamin, 4
Ballard, Brigid, 44
Bang-Campbell, Molly, 83
Barker, Glenn, 129
Barlow, Colin, 43
Barness, Lewis, 135
Barnett, Vincent M., 11
Barr, Alan, 44
Barrett, Diana, 155
Barrett, Kerrin, 60
Barriex, Alberto, 24, 143
Barroux, Jean, 9
Barth, Roland, 176
Barton, John D., 15

Weiss, Mitchell, 135
Weisskopf, Richard, 148
Weld, Leisa, 21, 118
Welks, Keith, 14
Wells, Jr., Louis, 44, 46, 114, 143
West, Robert, 30, 148
Westphal, Larry, 44, 72, 122
Wetselaar, Robert, 43
White, Geoffrey, 51
Whitehall, Peter, 140
Wickberg, Eric, 31, 80, 129, 130
Widner, Jennifer, 134, 143
Wiebe, Franck, 44
Wilcox, John, 104
Wilkie, David, 34
Williams, Charles, 55
Williams, Dean, 11
Williams, James, 132
Williams, Mark, 58, 135
Willms, Douglas, 61
Wilson, Thomas, 44
Wilson, Thomas, 9, 44
Wiryanto, Kadar, 136
Wong, Christopher, 24, 31
Woo, Wing, 148
Woodward, David, 26, 30
Wornham, Wendy, 135
Wortzel, Lawrence, 148
Xie, Jian, 146
Yang, Dean, 11
Yenton, Philip, 55
Yeow, David, 51
Yiannopoulos, Athanassios, 104
Yong Ahn, Choong, 81
Yoo, Jong-goo, 72
Yoo, Jung-ho, 72
Yoon, Chang-Ho, 148
Yotopoulos, Pan, 143
Youngman, Joan, 24, 46
Yusof, Zainal, 81
Zacarias, Fernando, 100
Zaidi, Sarah, 94
Zalesne, Deborah, 104
Zamora, Ruth, 100
Zimicki, Susan, 135
Zouaoui, Mekki, 140, 143, 148
Zuman, John, 19
Zuniga, Sergio, 6
Zveglich, Joseph, 129

[1]Sources: This list of names was compiled by Gretchen O'Connor from HIID biennial reports, which provide the most complete public record of HIID project personnel. Given the number of people involved, there are bound to be some inaccuracies and omissions. We apologize for any such errors, which we hope to have kept to a minimum.

Index

C

F

K

L

M